THE
NEW
COMPARATIVE
ATLAS

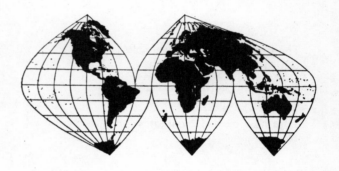

48th Edition

Prepared by the
Cartographic Department
of John Bartholomew & Son Ltd

OLIVER & BOYD

The original Comparative Atlas
was first published in 1898

The present edition, entirely redrawn,
was first published in 1964

Sales now exceed 2 million copies

© 1965 John Bartholomew & Son Ltd

Published by Oliver and Boyd Limited
Tweeddale Court, Edinburgh
39a Welbeck Steet, London W1

Printed in Great Britain by
John Bartholomew & Son Ltd, Edinburgh

CONTENTS

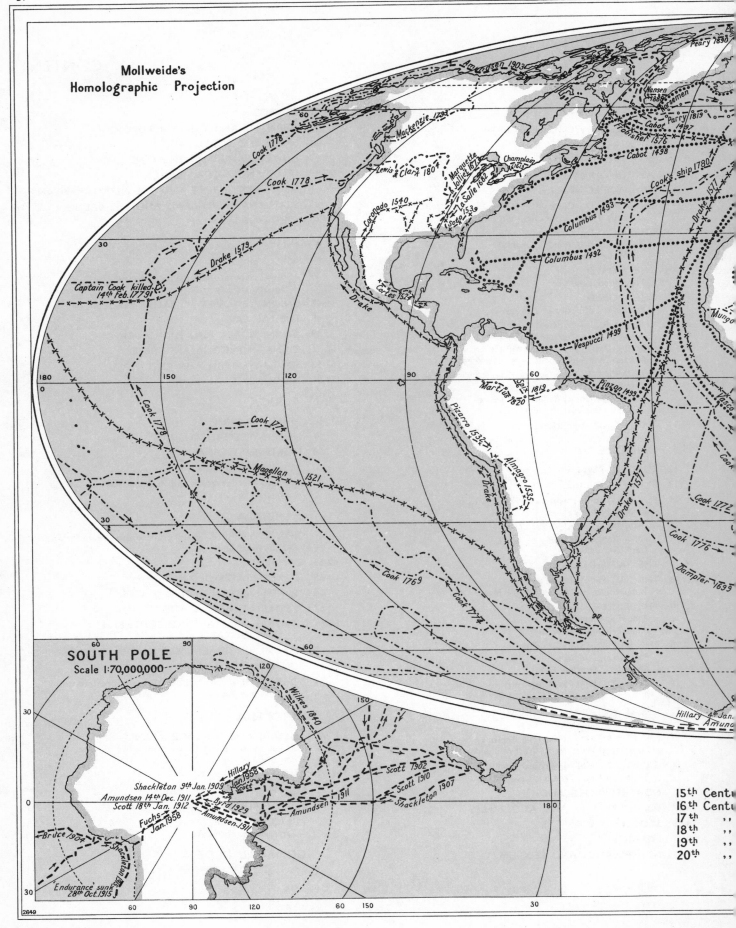

Mollweide's
Homolographic Projection

Captain Cook killed
14th Feb. 1779

Cook 1778
Cook 1778
Mackenzie 1793
Lewis & Clark 1804
Marquette & Jolliet 1673
Champlain 1613
La Salle 1682
Soto 1539
Coronado 1540
Drake 1579
Cortes 1524
Drake
Columbus 1493
Columbus 1492
Vespucci 1499
Pinzon 1499
Martius 1820
Spix 1819
Pizarro 1532
Almagro 1535
Drake
Drake 1577
Cook 1778
Cook 1774
Magellan 1521
Cook 1769
Cook 1774
Cook 1772
Cook 1776
Dampier 1695
Peary 1890
Nansen 1888
Norsemen
Parry 1819
Cabot 1497
Frobisher 1576
Cabot 1498
Cook's ship 1780
Drake 1577
Mungo
Vasco
Cook
Amundsen 1903
Hillary 4th Jan
Amun

SOUTH POLE
Scale 1:70,000,000

Wilkes 1840
Shackleton 9th Jan. 1909
Amundsen 14th Dec. 1911
Scott 18th Jan. 1912
Fuchs Jan. 1958
Hillary Jan. 1958
Scott
Byrd 1929
Amundsen 1911
Amundsen 1911
Scott 1902
Scott 1910
Shackleton 1907
Shackleton 1907
Bruce 1904
Shackleton 1915
Endurance sunk
28th Oct. 1915

15th Cent
16th Cent
17th ,,
18th ,,
19th ,,
20th ,,

2649

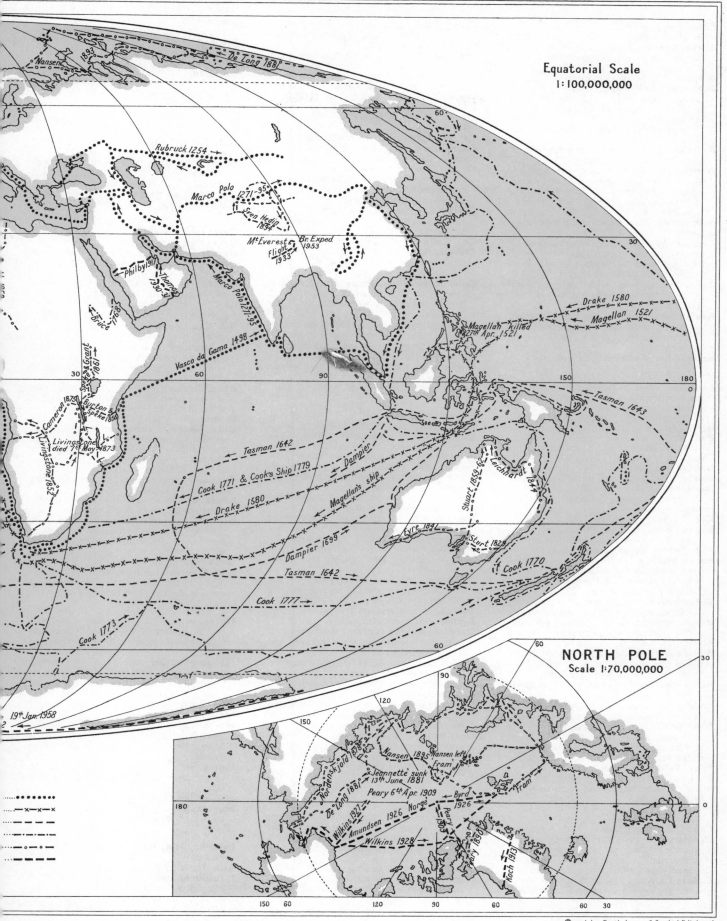

Equatorial Scale
1:100,000,000

Nansen 1893

De Long 1881

Rubruck 1254

Marco Polo 1271-95

Sven Hedin 1894

Mt Everest Flight 1933   Br. Exped. 1953

Philby 1917   Thomas 1930-31

Bruce 1768

Marco Polo 1271-95

Speke & Grant 1861

Cameron 1873   Burton & Speke 1858

Vasco da Gama 1498

Magellan killed 27th Apr. 1521

Drake 1580

Magellan 1521

Livingstone died 1st May 1873

Livingstone 1852

Tasman 1643

Tasman 1642

Dampier

Cook 1771 & Cook's Ship 1779

Magellan's ship

Drake 1580

Stuart 1859-62   Leichhardt 1844

Dampier 1699

Eyre 1841

Sturt 1828

Tasman 1642

Cook 1770

Cook 1777

Cook 1773

19th Jan. 1958

NORTH POLE
Scale 1:70,000,000

Nordenskjold 1878

Nansen 1893   Nansen left Fram

Jeannette sunk 13th June 1881

Peary 6th Apr. 1909   Byrd 1926

De Long 1881   Norge   Fram

Wilkins 1927   Amundsen 1926

Wilkins 1928   Peary 1890   Koch 1913

150   60   120   90   60   60   30

© -- John Bartholomew & Son.Ltd. Edinburgh.

GEOGRAPHICAL TERMS

Abad (*Pers.*), town.
Aber (*Gael.*), mouth or confluence of river.
Adret, Adretto (*Fr., Ital.*), sun-facing (or, in Northern Hemisphere, south-facing) side of valley.
Aiguille (*Fr.*), needle, sharp-pointed peak.
Ain (*Arab.*), well or spring.
Alluvium, fine sand or silt brought down by rivers and deposited in their flood plains and deltas.
Alp, high mountain, also upland summer pasture.
Anticline, arch of strata on both sides of which the rocks dip downwards.
Antipodes, places on the surface of the earth diametrically opposite to each other, especially the region diametrically opposed to our own, in the case of the British Isles, New Zealand.
Ard, Aird (*Gael.*), high point, promontory, headland.
Artesian Well, a water supply obtained by tapping porous rock strata from which the water rises by natural pressure; from occurrence at Artois, France.
Atoll, circular coral reef enclosing a central lagoon connected to the outside sea by an opening.
Avalanche (*Fr.*), mass of loosened snow and ice mixed with earth and rocks which slides with destructive force down the side of a mountain.
Avon, Afon, Abhainn (*Celt.*), river.

Badlands, areas of soft almost horizontal sedimentary rocks severely dissected into a maze of small ravines and ridges devoid of vegetation.
Bahia (*Port. & Sp.*), bay.
Bahr (*Arab.*), sea, lake, river.
Bal, Bally, Baile (*Celt.*), town, village.
Ban (*Siam.*), village.
Bandar (*Ind.*), town.
Bandar (*Pers.*), harbour, landing-place.
Barrier Reef, off-shore reef, usually of coral, separated from the land by a wide and deep channel.
Bas (*Fr.*), low, low-lying.
Bayou (*Amer. Fr.*), sluggish tributary creek, especially in lower Mississippi river system.
Ben, Beann, Beinn (*Gael.*), mountain.
Bench Mark, a height accurately obtained from ordnance datum, shown on the sides of buildings, etc. in Britain by a horizontal line over an arrow-head.
Bergschrund (*Ger.*), crevasse separating glacier ice from the rock of the valley wall.
Billabong (*Austral. Abo.*), elongated water pool in bed of dried up river.
Bir (*Arab.*), see Ain.
Black Earth, fertile black soil developed in temperate grassland climates particularly suited to the growing of grain crops.
Boma (*Swahili*), village protected by earth-work or stockade.
Bore, tidal wave occurring in the estuaries of certain rivers, e.g. Severn.
Boulder Clay, glacial deposit composed of clay, sand, gravel, rocks, etc., often found to considerable extent and depth in gla-ciated valleys and lowlands.
Bugt, Bukt (*Dan., Swed.*), bay.
Burun (*Turk.*), headland, promontory.
Butte, isolated steep-sided and usually flat-topped hill.

Cabo (*Port. & Sp.*), cape.
Cadastral, of maps, surveys, etc., showing accurate details of land and property boundaries.
Campos (*Port.*), grasslands of S.E. Brazil.
Cañon, Canyon (*Sp.*), deep gorge or ravine with lofty sides usually in semi-arid regions.

Carse (*Scot.*), agriculturally rich lands con-stituting wide plains adjacent to slow-flowing rivers.
Catingas (*Port.*), open forest lands on the plateaux of eastern Brazil, north of 15° S. Drier and warmer than the adjoining Cerrados; they contain cactus, mimosa and other types of dry vegetation.
Causse (*Fr.*), limestone plateau area, especi-ally in southern France; a local form of karst landscape.
Cerrados (*Port.*), see under Catingas.
Chernozem (*Russ.*), see Black Earth.
Cidade, Ciudad (*Port., & Sp.*). town, city
Cirque, Corrie, Coire, Cwm (*Fr., Celt.*), steep-sided natural amphitheatre or semi-circular hollow high up on a mountainside; a product of glacial erosion.
Clach, Clachan (*Gael.*), stone(s), small village or group of houses, especially in Scotland and Ireland.
Col, Colle (*Fr., Ital.*), pass or saddle.
Combe, Coomb, short, steep-sided en-closed valley or hollow, especially in S.W. England.
Continental Shelf, gently sloping shallow sea-bed of variable width fringing most continents; of considerable economic im-portance.
Contour, line on a map joining all points situated at the same height above the defined datum, usually mean sea level.
Cordillera (*Sp.*), mountain range.
Crevasse (*Fr.*), crack or fissure in a glacier or ice sheet.
Cut-Off, see Oxbow Lake.

Dagh (*Turk.*), mountain.
Darya (*Pers.*), sea, stream, river.
Date Line, approximately the 180° meridian from Greenwich, marking the position where, by international convention, the day begins. Crossing this line eastward, one goes back a day, while westward, one goes forward a day.
Delta, triangular area of mud and detritus laid down by a river at its mouth.
Desert, barren area of land practically devoid of vegetation, usually in very hot or very cold climates or at very high altitudes.
Detritus, matter worn away from its original source, usually sand, gravel, stones and rock rubbish.
Dip Slope, the slope of the ground in the same direction as the dip or incline of the underlying strata.
Divide, see Watershed.
Djebel (*Arab.*), rock, mountain.
Doldrums, region of calms and baffling winds near the equator, between the N.E. and S.E. Trade Winds.
Dolina (*Slav.*), round, flat-bottomed enclosed hollow in limestone country.
Dune, elongated or crescentic mound formed by wind-blown sand, capable of gradual advance over level surface unless stabilised by planting of suitable grasses (marram) or trees.
Dust Bowl, area in semi-arid plains country previously stabilised under natural grass-cover, which, when over-cultivated loses top-soil by wind erosion.

Eagre, see Bore.
Eilean (*Gael.*), island.
Equator, imaginary line circumscribing the globe midway between the poles and at its greatest circumference (24,901.96 miles). It forms the zero from which latitudes N. and S. are calculated.
Erosion, the slow wearing down of relief by natural forces, physical and chemical, e.g. running water, to a theoretical plane.

Esker (*Irish*), long flat-topped sinuous ridge of post-glacial sands and gravels.
Estuary, open lower portion of a river course affected by the tides where it flows into the sea.
Everglade, swampy area of water channels and low marshy islands covered by tall grass and cane, especially in Florida.

Fault, break, crack or system of cracks in the rocks of the earth's surface.
Fell, Fjeld, Fjäll (*Scand.*), mountain-side, mountain.
Firth (*Scot.*), strait, outer part of estuary or sea loch.
Fjord (*Scand.*), long narrow inlet of the sea, usually steep-sided and very deep but also, as in Denmark, shallow and low-shored.

Gawa (*Jap.*), river.
Gebel (*Arab.*), see Djebel.
Geyser (*Icelandic*), intermittent spouting hot spring associated with volcanic activity, as in Iceland.
Gezira (*Arab.*), area of land partly or wholly enclosed by rivers or the sea.
Gill, mountain stream, especially in North England.
Gja, Gia, Gio, Geo (*Celt.*), narrow cleft in sea cliff, especially in N. and N.W. Scotland.
Glacier, river of ice originating in snowfield and moving slowly down valley carrying down large quantities of rock, stones, gravel, etc.
Glen, Gleann (*Gael.*), mountain valley, often narrow, steep-sided and showing effects of valley glaciation, especially in Scotland.
Graben (*Ger.*), see Rift Valley.
Gran Chaco, "great hunting place," an extensive area between Argentine, Bolivia and Paraguay consisting mostly of swampy plains with varied vegetation rich in bird and animal life.
Graticule, the network of meridians and parallels on a map.
Great Circle, circle whose plane passes through the centre of the earth.
Great Circle Route, shortest distance between two points on the earth's surface, hence used for preference by shipping and air services.
Guba (*Russ.*), bay.
Gulf Stream, warm water current origi-nating in the Gulf of Mexico and flowing across the Atlantic to N.W. Europe.

Hachures, closely drawn lines sometimes used on maps to denote relief. They should follow the direction of slope and vary in thickness with the gradient.
Hanging Valley, tributary valley whose floor is separated from that of the major valley by a steep break of slope, usually the result of the major valley being over-deepened by the former passage of ice.
Havn (*Dan.*), harbour.
Horse Latitudes, regions of calms and variable winds between 25° and 40° N. and S., on the polar margins of the Trade Winds.
Horst (*Ger.*), block mountain left upstanding by the down-faulting of the rocks on either side.
Hsien (*Chin.*), county town.
Huerta (*Sp.*), garden, irrigated intensely-cultivated plots of land.

Ile, Ilha, Isla, Isola (*Fr., Port., Sp., Ital.*), island.
Inch, Innis (*Celt.*), island.
Interfluve, area of land lying between two roughly parallel rivers or streams.

Inver, Inbhir (*Gael.*), see Aber.
Isobar, line joining points of the same mean barometric pressure at a given time.
Isobath, line connecting parts of the ocean of equal depth.
Isohyet, line connecting points with equal rainfall over a given period.
Isotherm, line connecting points of equal temperature at a given time.
Isthmus, narrow strip of land, bordered on both sides by water, connecting two larger land masses.

Jabal, Jebel (*Arab.*), see Djebel.
Jökull (*Icelandic*), mountain area with permanent ice and snow cover, especially in Iceland.

Kame (*Scot.*), ridge or elongated mound of gravel, etc. associated with glacial and post-glacial activity.
Kampong (*Malay*), village.
Karst (*Serbo-Croat*), area of limestone characterised by underground streams, sink holes and xerophytic lime-loving vegetation, especially in warm temperate areas.
Kawa (*Jap.*), see Gawa.
Khrebet (*Russ.*), chain, mountain range.
Kum (*Turk.*), sand.
Kyle (*Scot.*), narrow sound or strait.

Lac, Lago (*Fr., Ital. & Sp.*), lake.
Lande (*Fr.*), sandy heath or waste land sometimes carrying coniferous forest plantings.
Latitude, the angular distance of a place N. or S. of the equator measured on its meridian. Each degree represents sixty geographical or nautical miles, that is, 69.172 statute miles (approximately 111 kilometres).
Levee (*Fr.*), embankment erected along river bank to prevent flooding.
Littoral, of the shore, part of a country lying along the shore.
Littoral Zone, the area of shore between high and low spring tides, also, in lakes, the area where light penetrates sufficiently to allow green plants to grow.
Llan (*Welsh*), church ground.
Llano (*Sp.*), level treeless plain of considerable area sometimes grass covered, especially in South America.
Llyn (*Welsh*), lake.
Loch, Lough (*Celt.*), lake, sometimes open to the sea.
Long Forties, area of the North Sea so called by fishermen because the depth of water approximates 40 fathoms.
Longitude, the angular distance of any place on the globe eastward or westward from a standard meridian; in Great Britain, the meridian of Greenwich. Each degree of longitude represents four minutes of time so that 15° of longitude represent one hour.
Löss, Loess (*Ger.*), post-glacial wind-blown soil of great fertility; found in N. European Plain, Hwang Ho valley of China, and North America.

Machair (*Scot.*), low level fertile land composed of shell sand, especially in the Western Isles of Scotland.
Meander, the winding about of a river in its valley, most conspicuously when it has reached its base line of erosion but still has energy for further lateral corrasion.
Medine (*Arab.*), town.
Mer, Meer (*Fr., Ger.*), sea, large lake.
Meridian, an imaginary line represented by a portion of a circle passing through the earth's poles and on which all places have noon at the same time.

Mesa (*Sp.*), isolated table land formed by a hard horizontal cap rock protecting lower, softer rocks from erosion. The sides fall away in steep escarpments.
Monadnock, residual mountain standing above the general peneplain of its surroundings, from Mt Monadnock, U.S.A.
Moraine (*Fr.*), pile or sheet of rock debris deposited by a glacier on its retreat to higher ground.
Mortlake, see Oxbow Lake.
Muskeg, area of boggy land characterised by sphagnum moss and scattered coniferous trees, especially in North America.

Nagar (*Ind.*), town.
Nant (*Welsh*), small stream.
Neap Tide, period of lowest tide range, when sun and moon are at right angles as seen from the earth.
Ness, Näs, Nos (*Scot., Swed., Russ.*), point, headland.
Nunatak (*Eskimo*), hill projecting above ice-sheet surface.

Oasis, fertile place in a desert owing to the presence of a spring or well.
Ordnance Datum, see Sea Level.
Oxbow Lake, remains of a meander loop which has been short-circuited by the river cutting through its neck, also called mortlake and cut-off.
Ozero (*Russ.*), lake.

Pampa (*Sp.*), temperate grassland of South America.
Pass, gap or depression in mountain range which serves as a way for communication between the lands on either side.
Pen, Pin (*Celt.*), see Ben.
Piedmont (*Fr.*), the mountain-foot or hill-foot zone.
Planina (*Bulg., Serb.*), mountain range.
Plateau, area of relatively flat ground at considerable altitude.
Polder (*Dutch*), land recovered from the sea in Holland and protected by dykes from being flooded again.
Polje (*Serbo-Croat*), enclosed depression, often fertile, with steep sides and little surface water, in karst areas.
Portage, the carrying of goods and boats across a narrow piece of land from one water course to another.
Prairie (*Fr.*), series of grassy plains stretching eastward from the Rocky Mountains in North America, a steppe or savanna.
Pueblo (*Sp.*), village.
Puerto (*Sp.*), port, harbour.
Puy (*Fr.*), small sugar loaf hill formed by weathering of volcanic cone or plug, especially in central France.

Qum (*Turk.*), see Kum.

Ria (*Sp.*), long narrow inlet of the sea formed by the drowning of a river mouth due to change in sea/land level.
Rift Valley, steep-sided valley formed by the sinking of land between two parallel geological fault lines, on a smaller scale, Graben.
Rimaye (*Fr.*), see Bergschrund.
Rio (*Port. & Sp.*), river.
River Capture, process by which one river, having more rapid powers of erosion than another, cuts back into the headwaters of the latter and draws off the water from certain of its tributaries.
Riviera (*Ital.*), narrow strip of sea coast between Toulon and Genoa, noted for mild climate in winter.
Roaring Forties, steady N.W. anti-trade winds between latitude 40° and 60° S. Equivalent to Westerlies of N. Hemisphere.

Rubha, Rhu, Row (*Gael.*), point, promontory.

Sæter (*Nor.*), shieling, summer steading in high mountain pastures.
Savanna, grassland plains with scattered trees in sub-tropical lands.
Scarp, abrupt cliff-like face of a hill.
Schattenseite (*Ger.*), see Ubac.
Sea Level, mean sea level is the mean level of the sea throughout a large number of complete tidal oscillations. Mean sea level at Newlyn, Cornwall, is ordnance datum, that is, the zero from which heights are measured throughout the country.
Selva (*Port. & Sp.*), forest. The name of Selvas is given to the vast equatorial rain forests of the Amazon basin.
Shieling (*Scot.*), summer steading and associated pasture land.
Skerries, Skärgård, Skjergaard, Skjærgaard (*Scot. & Scand.*), rocky islets which, together with the maze of intervening water channels, often form the off-shore barrier to a fjord-type coast.
Sonnenseite (*Ger.*), see Adret.
Spot Height, an accurate height measured, in Britain, from ordnance datum and marked on a map by a small dot and the figure of height. It is not indicated on the ground.
Spring Tide, period of highest tide range at new and full moon when sun and moon are in line with the earth and exert maximum pull.
Stack, Stac (*Gael. & Faeroese*), isolated rock mass or pillar separated from the surroundings by erosion, usually on the sea coast.
Stad, Stadt (*Dutch, Swed., Ger.*), town.
Steppe, mid-latitude grasslands too dry to support tree growth, especially those in European Russia and S.W. Siberia.
Strath (*Scot.*), broad open flat-floored river valley.
Sudd (*Arab.*), large floating islands of vegetable matter on the Upper White Nile impeding navigation.

Tarbert, Tairbeart, Tarbet (*Gael.*), isthmus.
Till (*Scot.*), see Boulder Clay.
Tor, pile of rocks, cairn, or isolated mass of rock on summit or ridge of mountains, especially in S.W. England.
Tundra (*Russ.*), plains lying beyond the polar limit of tree growth supporting scanty natural vegetation of lichens and mosses, hard frozen during the winter and only partially thawed on the surface in summer.

Ubac (*Fr.*), shaded (or, in Northern Hemisphere, north-facing) side of valley.
Ula (*Mongol.*), mountain.

Vatn (*Nor.*), lake.
Veld (*Afrik.*), open plains in South Africa providing rough natural pasture land.
Volcano, vent or fissure in the earth's crust through which molten and shattered rock, ash and steam rise, sometimes under great pressure, from the hot interior to the surface of the earth.

Wallace's Line, line following the deep water channel separating Bali and Lombok and which divides two great zoogeographical regions—the Oriental and the Australian. First described by the naturalist A. R. Wallace.
Watershed, Water-parting, the land-form separating the headstreams of two or more river systems, often Divide in North America.

Zee (*Dutch*), sea.

MAP PROJECTIONS

CONIC PROJECTION WITH TWO STANDARD PARALLELS

In this case the cone is supposed to cut the sphere along two parallels PP and P'P' which, however, are plotted their true distance apart (i.e. the distance along the arc PP', not the chord.) The map has therefore the advantage of coinciding with the globe along two parallels instead of one as in the Simple Conic.

Diagram showing the Principle of the Projection - cone A B C imposed upon sphere and touching it at PP, P'P'

Portion of Surface of Cone spread out representing map. PP, P'P' the parallels where the cone coincides with the sphere.

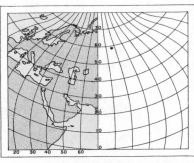

PARALLELS OF LATITUDE

LENGTH OF DEGREES

IN BRITISH MILES

	Pole
90°	0
85°	6·05 Miles
80°	12·05 ,,
75°	17·96 ,,
70°	23·73 ,,
65°	29·31 ,,
60°	34·67 ,,
55°	39·77 ,,
50°	44·55 ,,
45°	48·99 ,,
40°	53·06 ,,
35°	56·72 ,,
30°	59·96 ,,
25°	62·73 ,,
20°	65·03 ,,
15°	66·83 ,,
10°	68·13 ,,
5°	68·91 ,,
0°	69·17 ,,
	Equator

POLAR PROJECTIONS

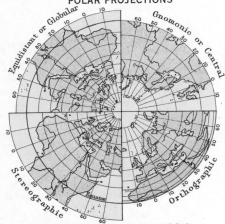

Equidistant or Globular

Gnomonic or Central

Stereographic

Orthographic

The Gnomonic Projection cannot be made to include the whole hemisphere. The Stereographic and Globular Projections can be extended to include more than the hemisphere

BONNE'S PROJECTION

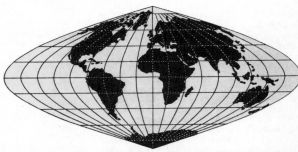

This is a development of the Conic Projection and differs from the pure Conic in that instead of distances being correctly measured along one parallel, true distances are measured along each parallel.

MERCATOR

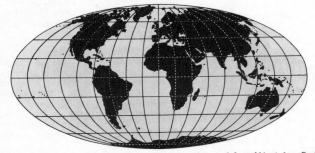

The Plane of Projection is the surface of an imaginary cylinder surrounding the globe and touching its surface at the equator. At the equator its scale agrees with the globe but as each parallel of latitude becomes a great circle equal to the equator the scale increases as we go north and south. The latitude is however increased in same proportion as the longitude. Mercator's projection is the only one which gives the true direction of one point in relation to another and is therefore most used for the purposes of Navigation.

SINUSOIDAL (SANSON)

The parallels are drawn at their true distances from the equator and along each of these correct distances are measured through which the meridians are drawn. The projection is obviously equal-area.

HOMOLOGRAPHIC (MOLLWEIDE)

This is an equal-area projection. The complete circle on the map is made to equal the world hemisphere. Parallels are so drawn that the zone enclosed by them bears the same relation to the area of the circle as the similar zone on the earth bears to the hemisphere. The meridians are ellipses cutting the parallels at equal distances.

RE-CENTRED SINUSOIDAL

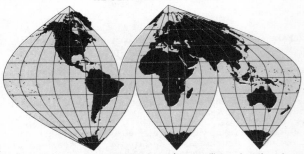

This projection is adapted from Sanson's, but 're-centred' on each continental area to minimise distortion. Distances are true on each centre meridian and along all parallels of latitude.

THE SOLAR SYSTEM

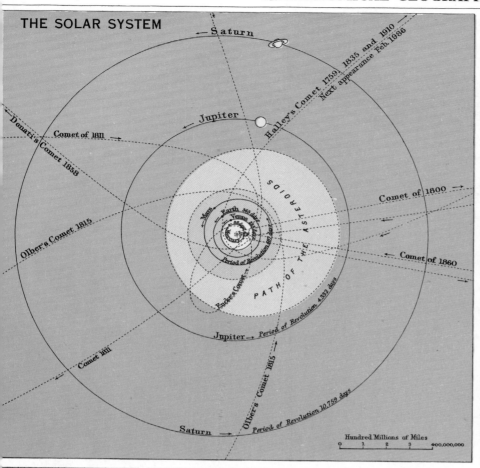

Saturn

Jupiter

Halley's Comet 1759, 1835, and 1910
Next appearance Feb. 1986

Donati's Comet 1858

Comet of 1811

Olber's Comet 1815

Comet of 1800

Comet of 1860

Mars
Earth 365 days
Venus 224 days
Sun

Period of Revolution 87 hours

Comet 1811

Encke's Comet

PATH OF THE ASTEROIDS

Olber's Comet 1815

Jupiter → Period of Revolution 4,332 days

Saturn → Period of Revolution 10,759 days

Hundred Millions of Miles
0 1 2 3 400,000,000

SOLAR ECLIPSE   LUNAR ECLIPSE

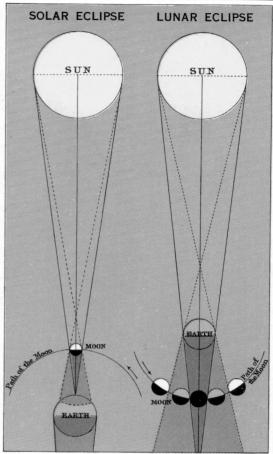

SUN

SUN

Path of the Moon

MOON

EARTH

EARTH

MOON

Path of the Moon

PHASES OF THE MOON

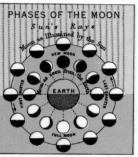

Sun's Rays
Moon as illuminated by the Sun
Moon as seen from the Earth
NEW MOON
FIRST QUARTER
LAST QUARTER
EARTH
FULL MOON

OCEAN TIDES

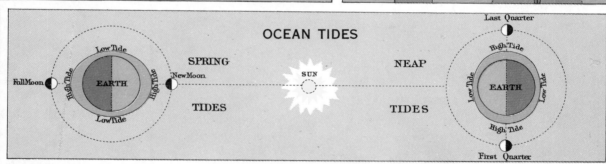

SPRING

NEAP

TIDES

TIDES

Low Tide
High Tide
Full Moon
EARTH
High Tide
New Moon
Low Tide

SUN

Last Quarter
High Tide
Low Tide
EARTH
Low Tide
High Tide
First Quarter

THE SEASONS

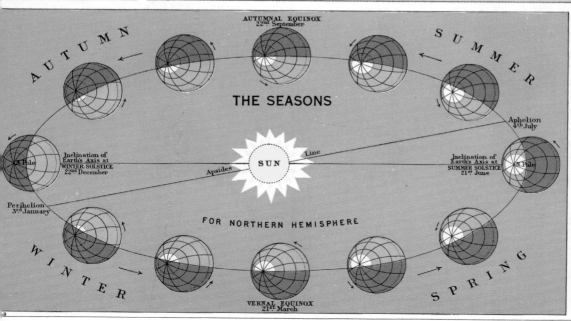

AUTUMN

SUMMER

AUTUMNAL EQUINOX
22nd September

Aphelion
4th July

Inclination of
Earth's Axis at
WINTER SOLSTICE
22nd December

Inclination of
Earth's Axis at
SUMMER SOLSTICE
21st June

N. Pole

Apsides

Line

SUN

N. Pole

Perihelion
3rd January

FOR NORTHERN HEMISPHERE

WINTER

SPRING

VERNAL EQUINOX
21st March

COMPARATIVE SIZES OF THE SUN AND PLANETS

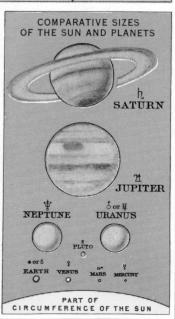

♄ SATURN

♃ JUPITER

♆ NEPTUNE

♂ or ♅ URANUS

♇ PLUTO

♁ or ♁ EARTH   ♀ VENUS   ♂ MARS   ☿ MERCURY

PART OF
CIRCUMFERENCE OF THE SUN

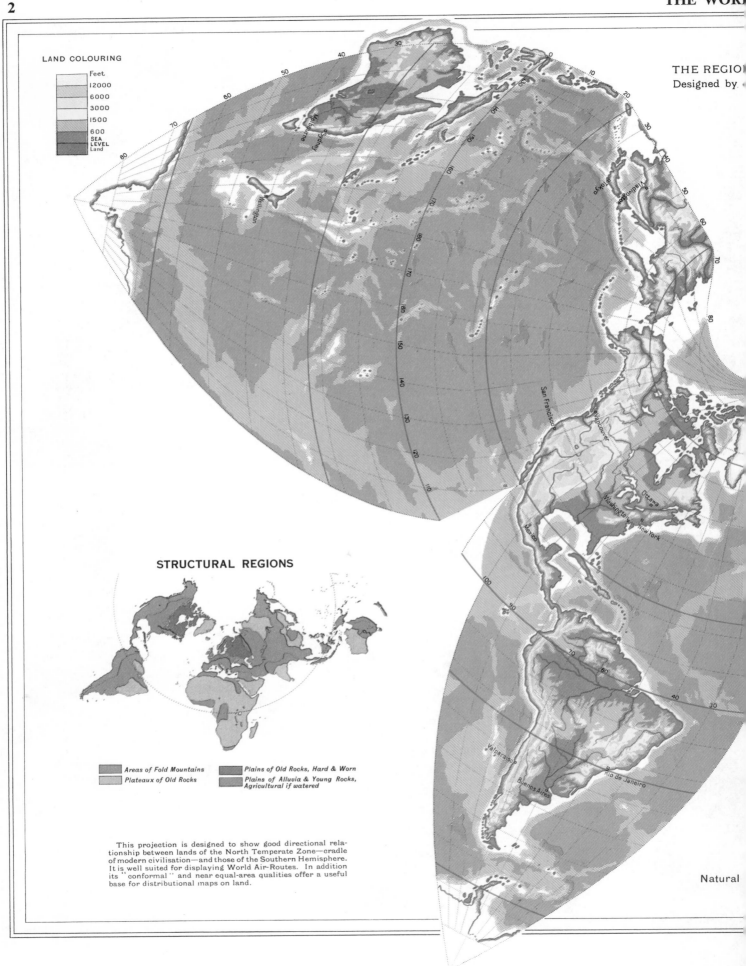

LAND COLOURING

Feet
12000
6000
3000
1500
600
SEA
LEVEL
Land

THE REGIO

Designed by

STRUCTURAL REGIONS

Areas of Fold Mountains

Plateaux of Old Rocks

Plains of Old Rocks, Hard & Worn

Plains of Alluvia & Young Rocks,
Agricultural if watered

This projection is designed to show good directional rela-
tionship between lands of the North Temperate Zone—cradle
of modern civilisation—and those of the Southern Hemisphere.
It is well suited for displaying World Air-Routes. In addition
its "conformal" and near equal-area qualities offer a useful
base for distributional maps on land.

Natural

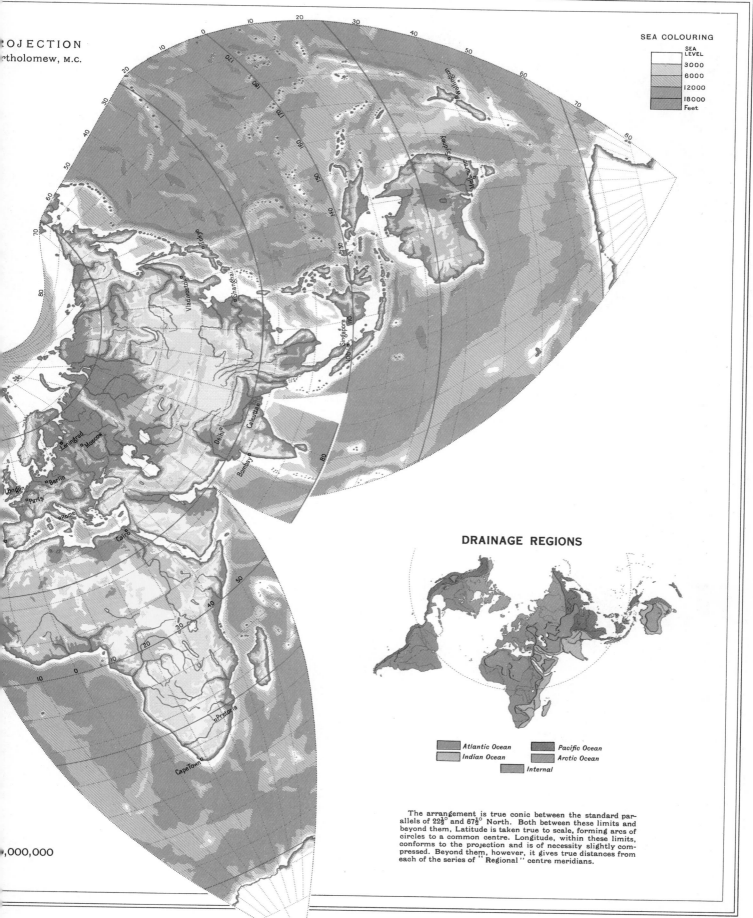

ROJECTION

rtholomew, M.C.

SEA COLOURING

	SEA LEVEL
	3000
	6000
	12000
	18000
	Feet

DRAINAGE REGIONS

	Atlantic Ocean		*Pacific Ocean*
	Indian Ocean		*Arctic Ocean*
	Internal		

The arrangement is true conic between the standard parallels of 22½° and 67½° North. Both between these limits and beyond them, Latitude is taken true to scale, forming arcs of circles to a common centre. Longitude, within these limits, conforms to the projection and is of necessity slightly compressed. Beyond them, however, it gives true distances from each of the series of " Regional " centre meridians.

,000,000

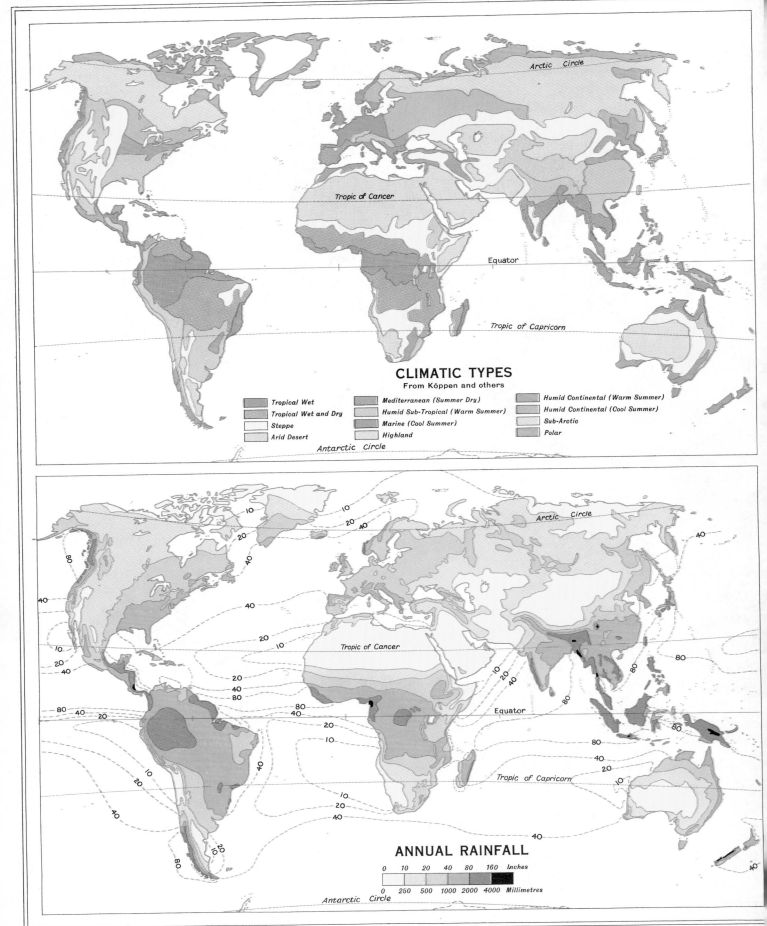

CLIMATIC TYPES
From Köppen and others

- Tropical Wet
- Tropical Wet and Dry
- Steppe
- Arid Desert
- Mediterranean (Summer Dry)
- Humid Sub-Tropical (Warm Summer)
- Marine (Cool Summer)
- Highland
- Humid Continental (Warm Summer)
- Humid Continental (Cool Summer)
- Sub-Arctic
- Polar

Arctic Circle
Tropic of Cancer
Equator
Tropic of Capricorn
Antarctic Circle

ANNUAL RAINFALL

0	10	20	40	80	160	Inches
0	250	500	1000	2000	4000	Millimetres

Arctic Circle
Tropic of Cancer
Equator
Tropic of Capricorn
Antarctic Circle

Winkel's Projection

1:160,000,000

© – John Bartholomew & Son Ltd. Edinbₙ

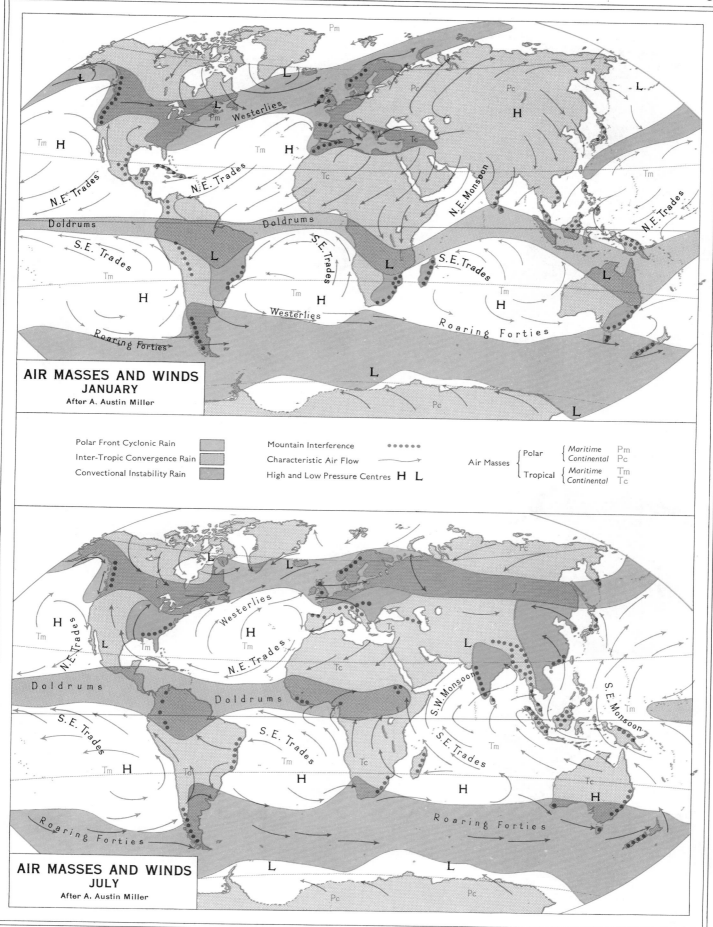

AIR MASSES AND WINDS
JANUARY
After A. Austin Miller

Polar Front Cyclonic Rain	Mountain Interference	Air Masses	Polar	Maritime	Pm
Inter-Tropic Convergence Rain	Characteristic Air Flow			Continental	Pc
Convectional Instability Rain	High and Low Pressure Centres H L		Tropical	Maritime	Tm
				Continental	Tc

AIR MASSES AND WINDS
JULY
After A. Austin Miller

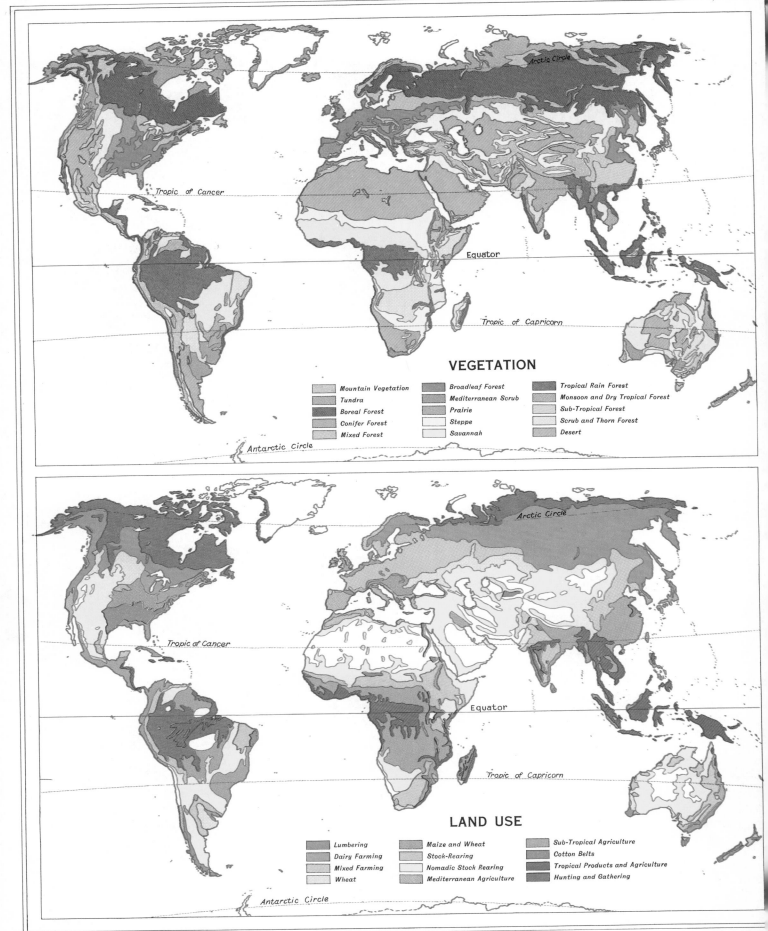

VEGETATION

- Mountain Vegetation
- Tundra
- Boreal Forest
- Conifer Forest
- Mixed Forest
- Broadleaf Forest
- Mediterranean Scrub
- Prairie
- Steppe
- Savannah
- Tropical Rain Forest
- Monsoon and Dry Tropical Forest
- Sub-Tropical Forest
- Scrub and Thorn Forest
- Desert

LAND USE

- Lumbering
- Dairy Farming
- Mixed Farming
- Wheat
- Maize and Wheat
- Stock-Rearing
- Nomadic Stock Rearing
- Mediterranean Agriculture
- Sub-Tropical Agriculture
- Cotton Belts
- Tropical Products and Agriculture
- Hunting and Gathering

Winkel's Projection

1:160,000,000

© — John Bartholomew & Son.Ltd.Edinb

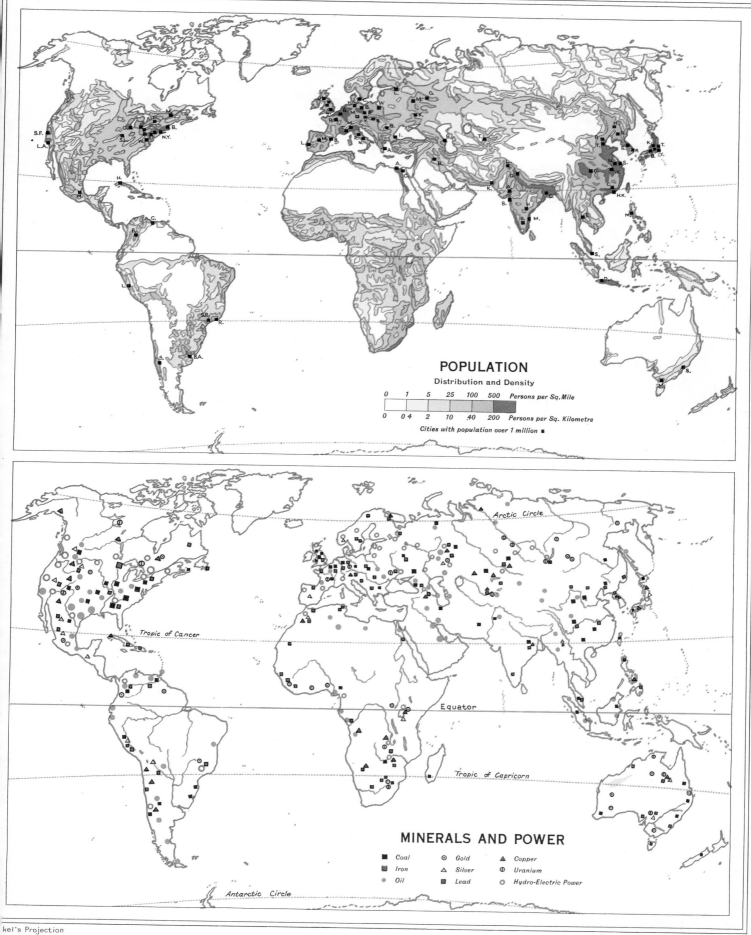

POPULATION

Distribution and Density

| 0 | 1 | 5 | 25 | 100 | 500 | Persons per Sq. Mile |

| 0 | 0 4 | 2 | 10 | 40 | 200 | Persons per Sq. Kilometre |

Cities with population over 1 million ■

MINERALS AND POWER

■ Coal	◉ Gold	▲ Copper
▣ Iron	△ Silver	⊕ Uranium
● Oil	▣ Lead	◎ Hydro-Electric Power

Arctic Circle

Tropic of Cancer

Equator

Tropic of Capricorn

Antarctic Circle

kel's Projection

© – John Bartholomew & Son.Ltd.,Edinburgh

THE WORLD—PRINCIPAL FOOD CROPS

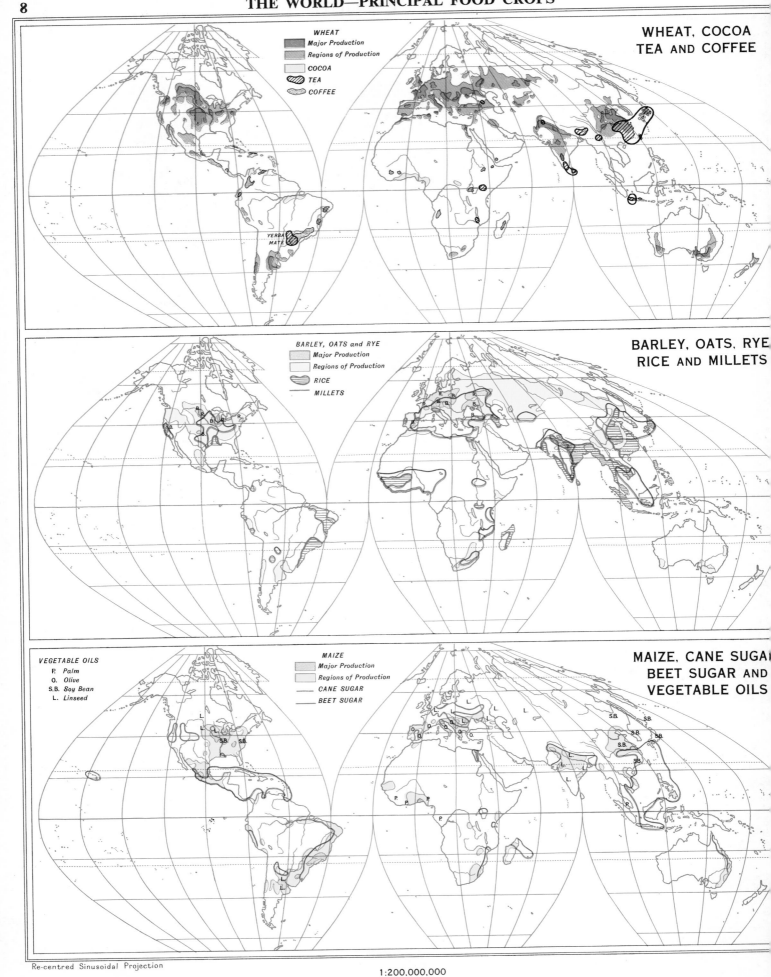

WHEAT, COCOA TEA AND COFFEE

WHEAT
Major Production
Regions of Production
COCOA
TEA
COFFEE

YERBA MATE

BARLEY, OATS, RYE RICE AND MILLETS

BARLEY, OATS and RYE
Major Production
Regions of Production
RICE
MILLETS

MAIZE, CANE SUGAR BEET SUGAR AND VEGETABLE OILS

VEGETABLE OILS
P. Palm
O. Olive
S.B. Soy Bean
L. Linseed

MAIZE
Major Production
Regions of Production
CANE SUGAR
BEET SUGAR

Re-centred Sinusoidal Projection

1:200,000,000

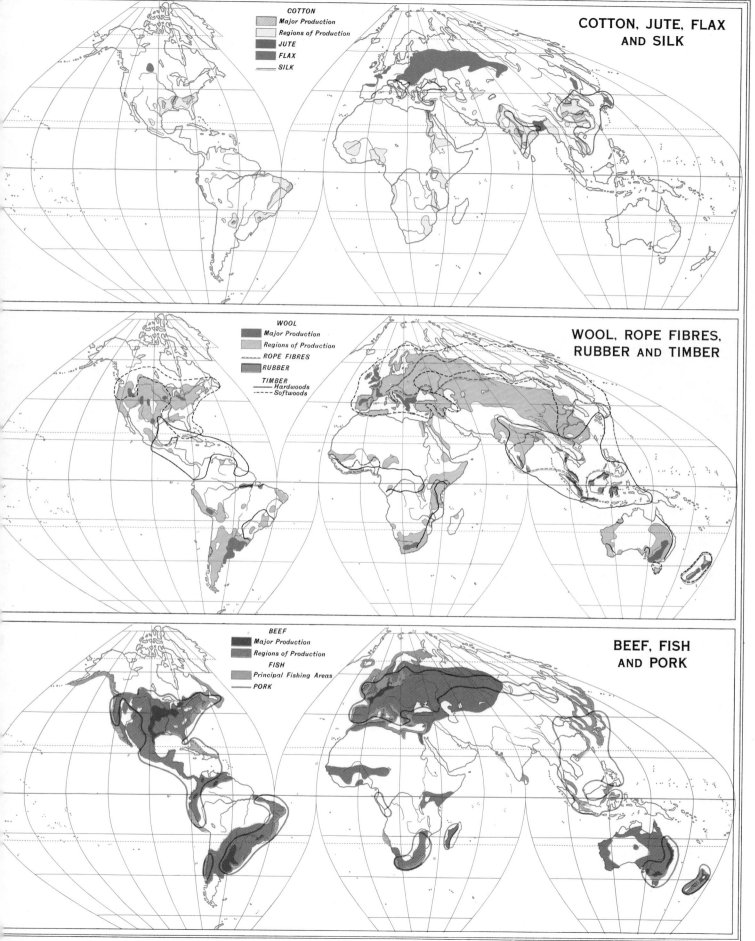

COTTON, JUTE, FLAX
AND SILK

COTTON
Major Production
Regions of Production
JUTE
FLAX
SILK

WOOL, ROPE FIBRES,
RUBBER AND TIMBER

WOOL
Major Production
Regions of Production
ROPE FIBRES
RUBBER
TIMBER
Hardwoods
Softwoods

BEEF, FISH
AND PORK

BEEF
Major Production
Regions of Production
FISH
Principal Fishing Areas
PORK

1:200,000,000

© — John Bartholomew & Son.Ltd.,Edinburgh

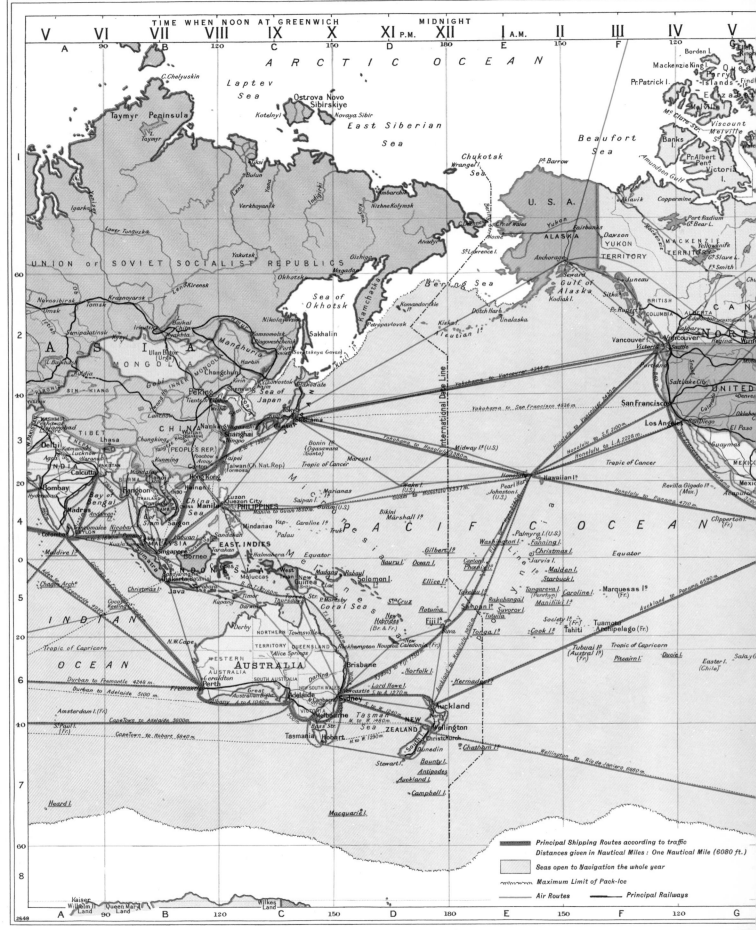

ARCTIC OCEAN

Principal Shipping Routes according to traffic
Distances given in Nautical Miles : One Nautical Mile (6080 ft.)

Seas open to Navigation the whole year

Maximum Limit of Pack-Ice

Air Routes   Principal Railways

EQUATORIAL SCALE 1: 110,000,000

MILES   500   0   500   1000   1500

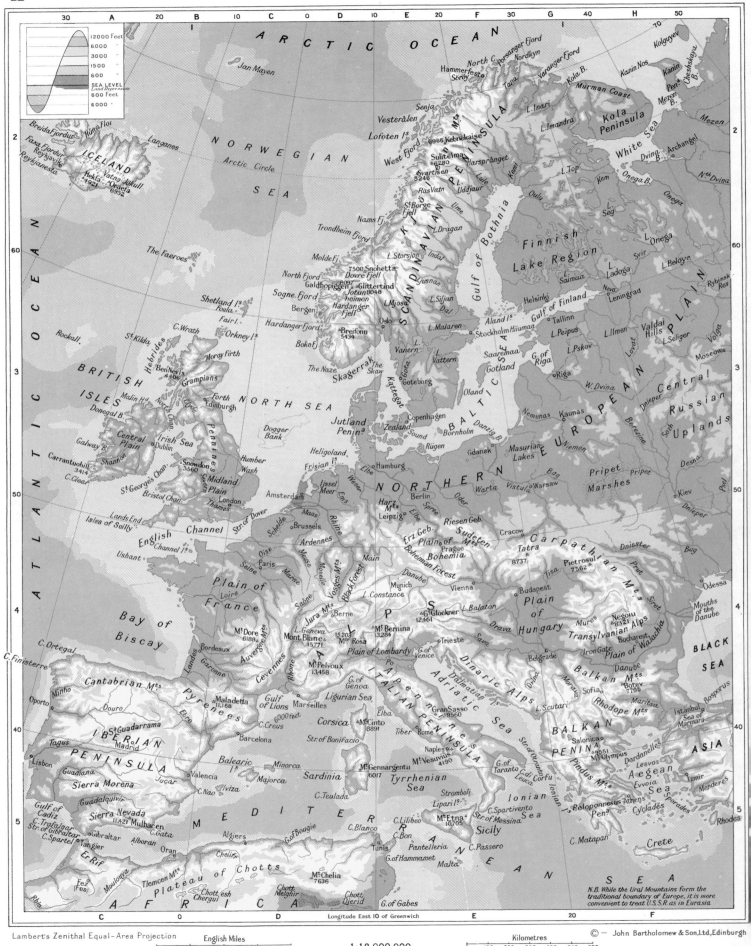

Lambert's Zenithal Equal-Area Projection

Longitude East 10 of Greenwich

English Miles

1:18,000,000

Kilometres

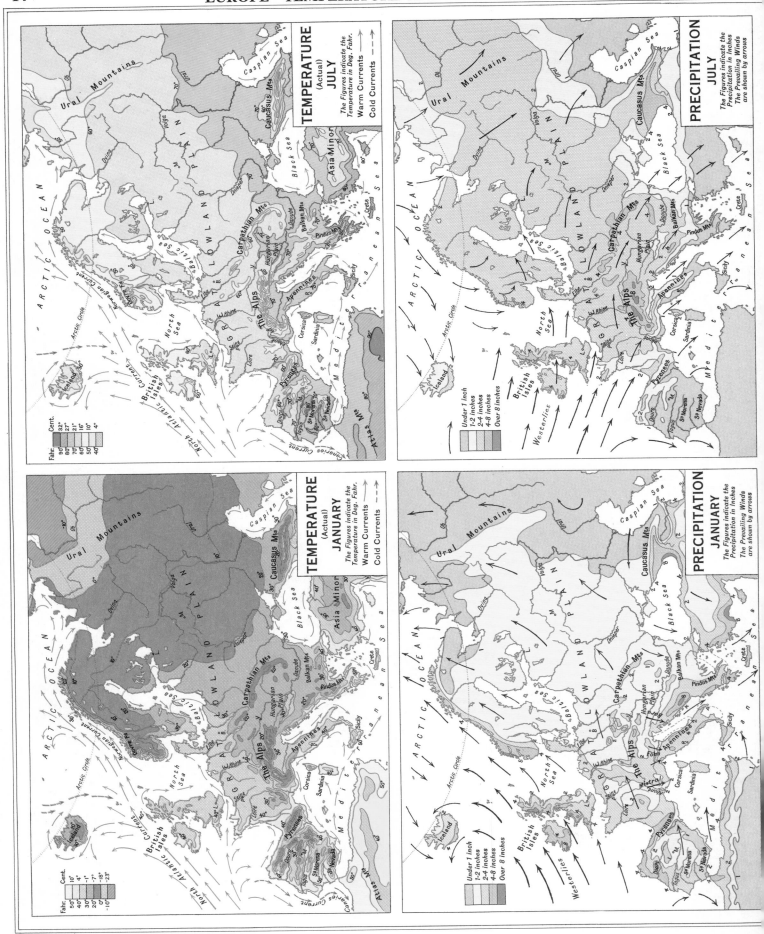

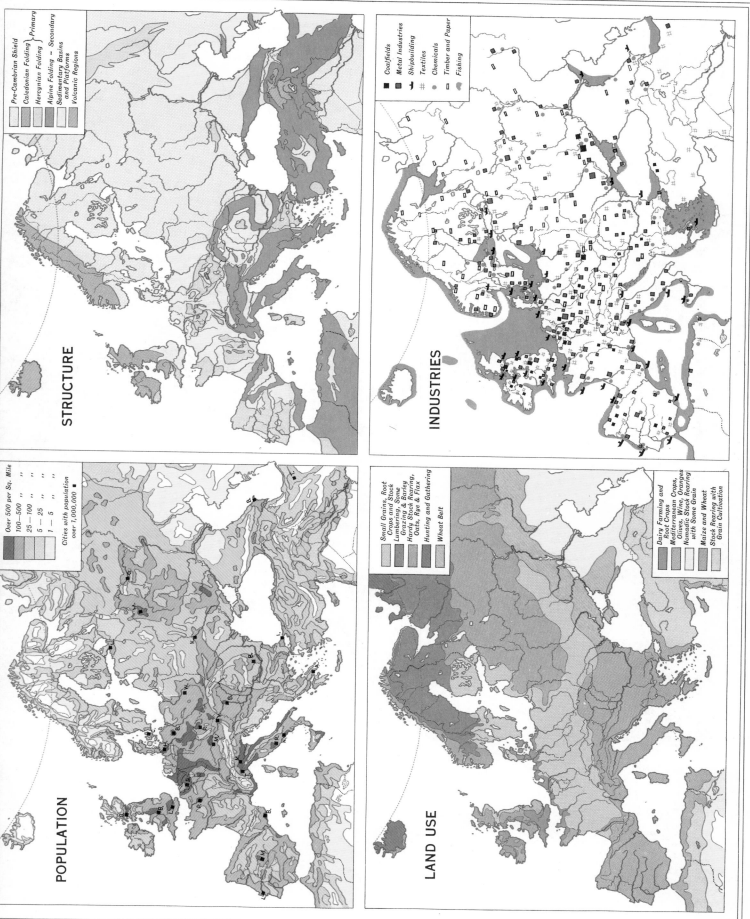

STRUCTURE

Pre-Cambrian Shield
Caledonian Folding — Primary
Hercynian Folding — Secondary
Alpine Folding — Secondary
Sedimentary Basins and Platforms
Volcanic Regions

INDUSTRIES

Coalfields
Metal Industries
Shipbuilding
Textiles
Chemicals
Timber and Paper
Fishing

POPULATION

Over 500 per Sq. Mile
100—500 ,, ,, ,,
25—100 ,, ,, ,,
5 — 25 ,, ,, ,,
1 — 5 ,, ,, ,,
Cities with population over 1,000,000 ■

LAND USE

Small Grains, Root Crops and Stock
Lumbering, Some Grazing & Barley
Hardy Stock Rearing, Oats, Rye & Flax
Hunting and Gathering
Wheat Belt
Dairy Farming and Root Crops
Mediterranean Crops, Olives, Wine, Oranges
Nomadic Stock Rearing with Some Grain
Maize and Wheat
Stock Rearing with Grain Cultivation

English Miles

1 : 45,000,000

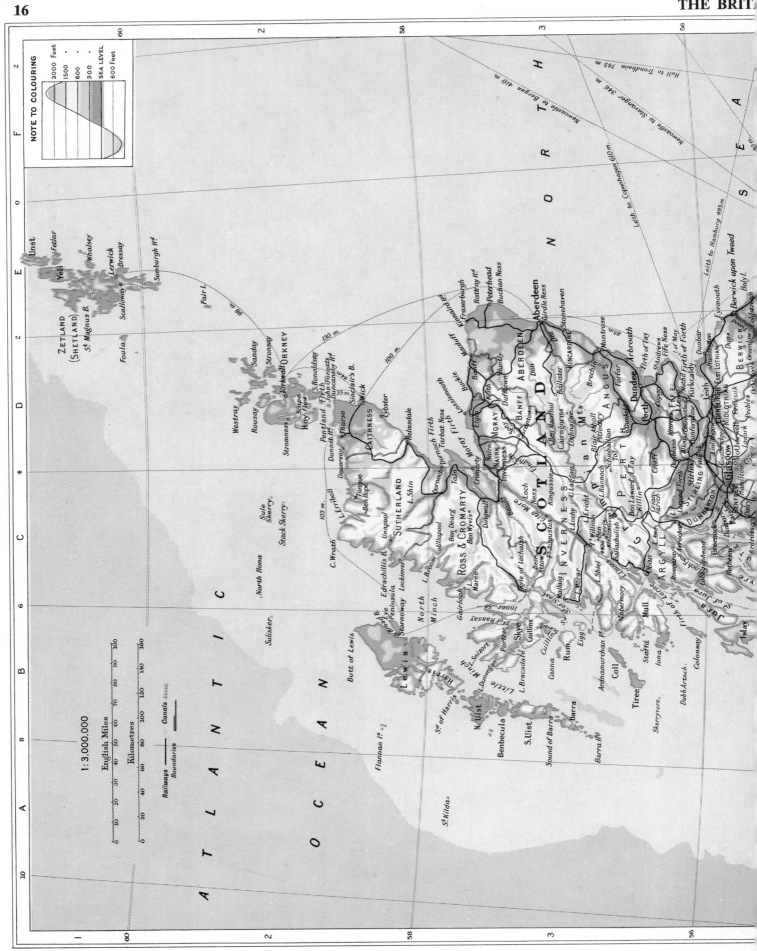

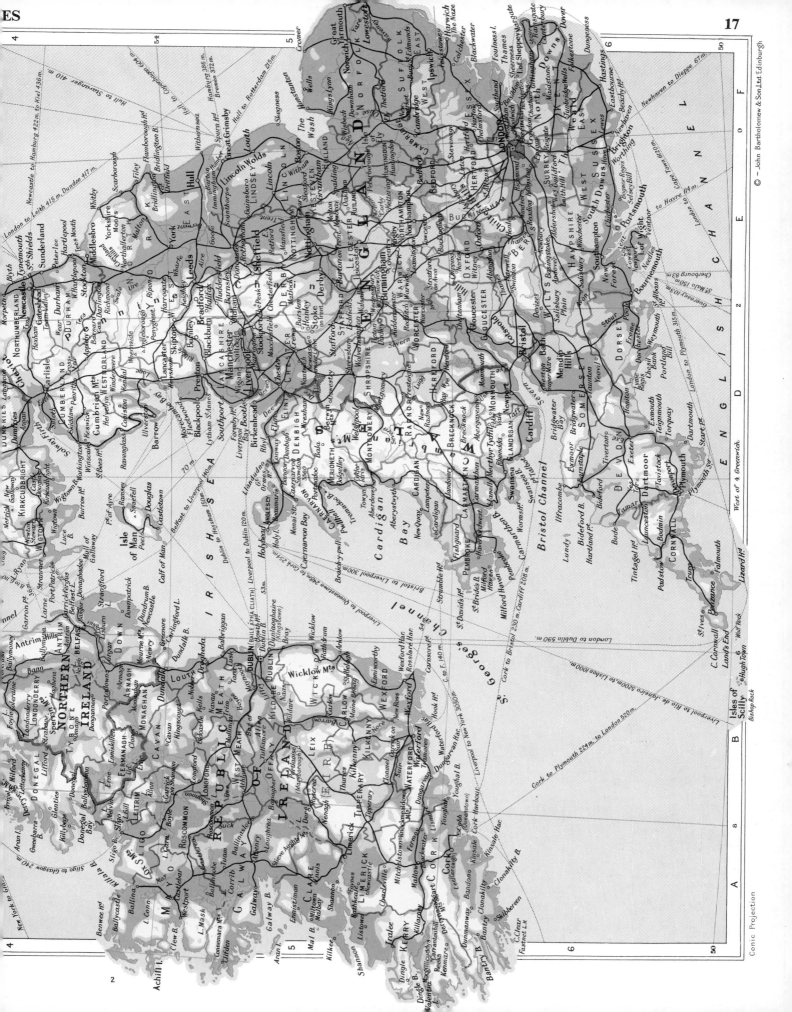

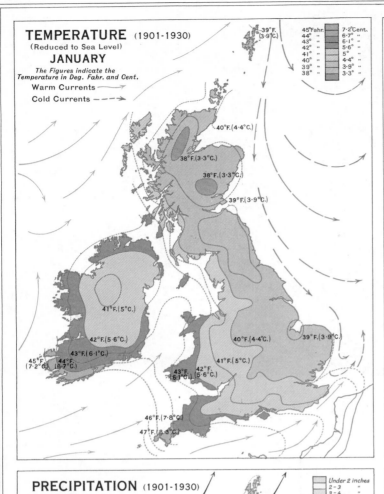

TEMPERATURE (1901-1930)
(Reduced to Sea Level)
JANUARY
The Figures indicate the
Temperature in Deg. Fahr. and Cent.

Warm Currents →
Cold Currents ⇢

°Fahr.	°Cent.
45°	7·2°
44°	6·7°
43°	6·1°
42°	5·6°
41°	5°
40°	4·4°
39°	3·9°
38°	3·3°

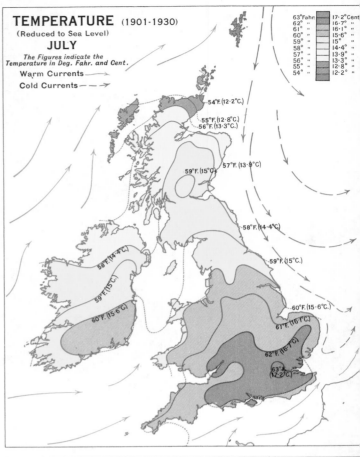

TEMPERATURE (1901-1930)
(Reduced to Sea Level)
JULY
The Figures indicate the
Temperature in Deg. Fahr. and Cent.

Warm Currents →
Cold Currents ⇢

°Fahr.	°Cent.
63°	17·2°
62°	16·7°
61°	16·1°
60°	15·6°
59°	15°
58°	14·4°
57°	13·9°
56°	13·3°
55°	12·8°
54°	12·2°

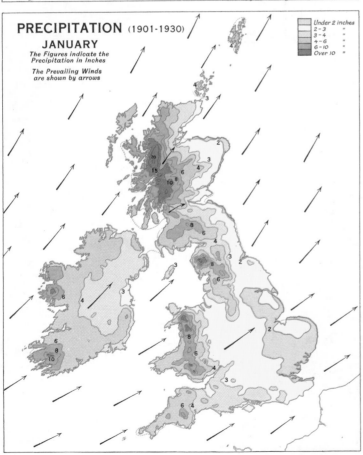

PRECIPITATION (1901-1930)
JANUARY
The Figures indicate the
Precipitation in Inches

The Prevailing Winds
are shown by arrows

	Under 2 inches
	2 – 3 "
	3 – 4 "
	4 – 6 "
	6 –10 "
	Over 10 "

PRECIPITATION (1901-1930)
JULY
The Figures indicate the
Precipitation in Inches

The Prevailing Winds
are shown by arrows

	Under 2 inches
	2 – 3 "
	3 – 4 "
	4 – 6 "
	Over 6 "

English Miles

0 20 40 60 80 100   200

1:10,800,000

© – John Bartholomew & Son Ltd., Edinb

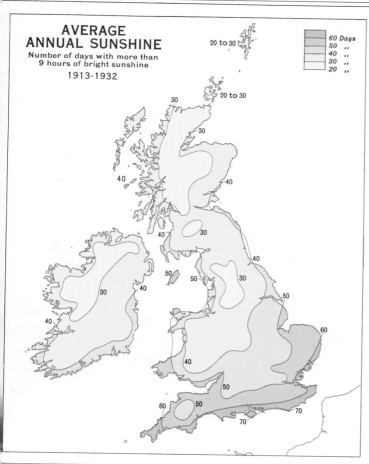

AVERAGE ANNUAL SUNSHINE
Number of days with more than 9 hours of bright sunshine
1913-1932

60 Days
50 „
40 „
30 „
20 „

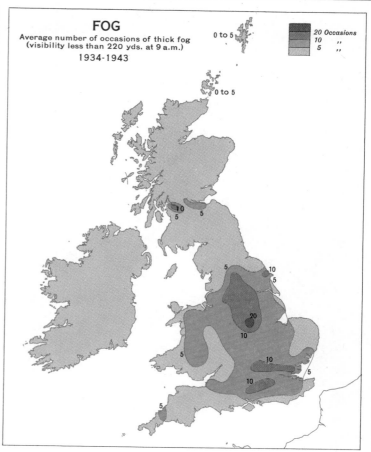

FOG
Average number of occasions of thick fog (visibility less than 220 yds. at 9 a.m.)
1934-1943

20 Occasions
10 „
5 „

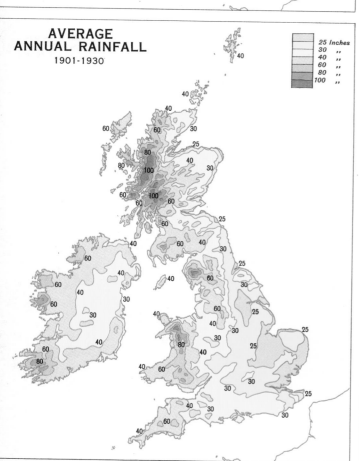

AVERAGE ANNUAL RAINFALL
1901-1930

25 Inches
30 „
40 „
60 „
80 „
100 „

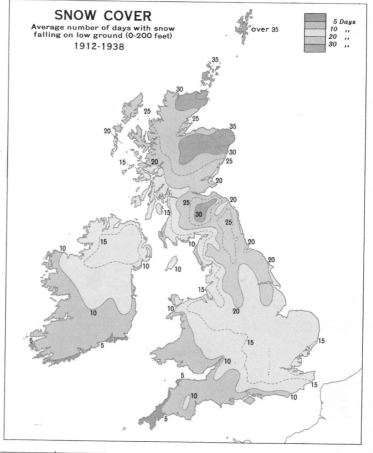

SNOW COVER
Average number of days with snow falling on low ground (0-200 feet)
1912-1938

5 Days
10 „
20 „
30 „

English Miles
0 20 40 60 80 100   200

1:10,800,000

© – John Bartholomew & Son Ltd.-Edinburgh

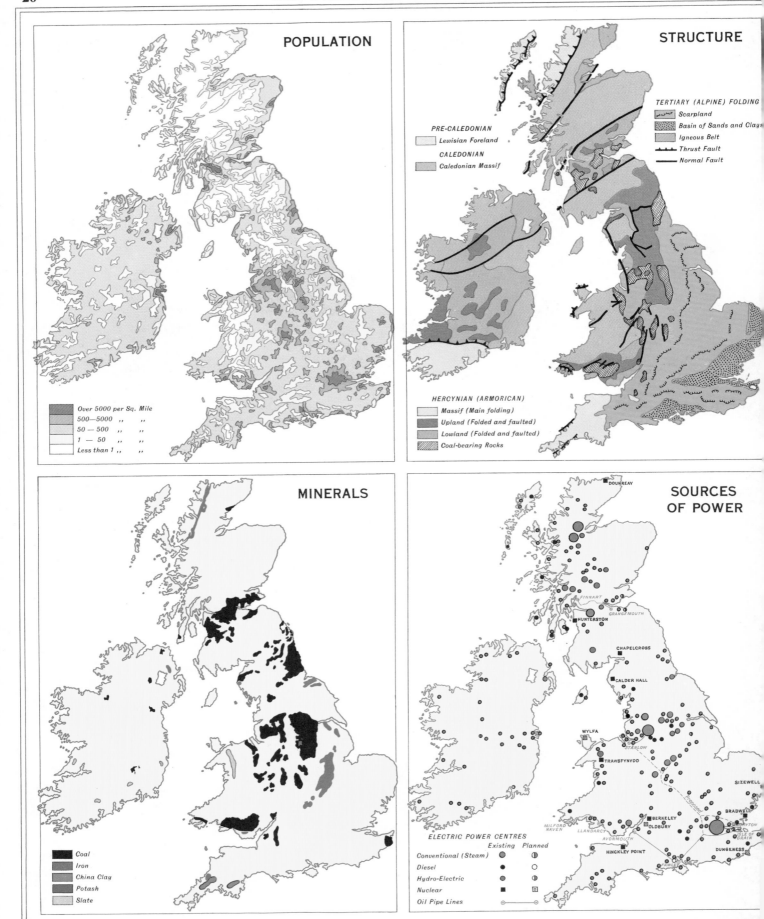

POPULATION

Over 5000 per Sq. Mile
500—5000 ,, ,,
50 — 500 ,, ,,
1 — 50 ,, ,,
Less than 1 ,, ,,

STRUCTURE

PRE-CALEDONIAN
Lewisian Foreland
CALEDONIAN
Caledonian Massif

TERTIARY (ALPINE) FOLDING
Scarpland
Basin of Sands and Clays
Igneous Belt
Thrust Fault
Normal Fault

HERCYNIAN (ARMORICAN)
Massif (Main folding)
Upland (Folded and faulted)
Lowland (Folded and faulted)
Coal-bearing Rocks

MINERALS

Coal
Iron
China Clay
Potash
Slate

SOURCES OF POWER

DOUNREAY

FINNART

GRANGEMOUTH

HUNTERSTON

CHAPELCROSS

CALDER HALL

WYLFA

STANLOW

TRAWSFYNYDD

SIZEWELL

BRADWELL

MILFORD HAVEN

LLANDARCY

BERKELEY
OLDBURY

AVONMOUTH

ISLE OF GRAIN

HINCKLEY POINT

DUNGENESS

FAWLEY

ELECTRIC POWER CENTRES

	Existing	Planned
Conventional (Steam)		
Diesel		
Hydro-Electric		
Nuclear		
Oil Pipe Lines		

English Miles
0 20 40 60 80 100   200

1:10,800,000

© – John Bartholomew & Son.Ltd.Edi

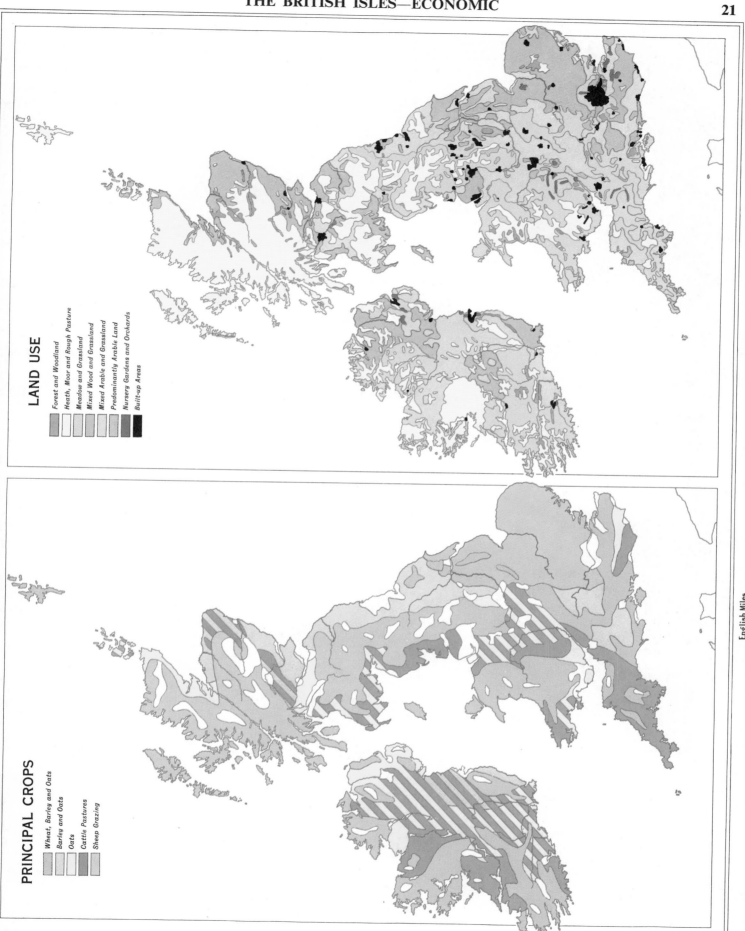

LAND USE

- Forest and Woodland
- Heath, Moor and Rough Pasture
- Meadow and Grassland
- Mixed Wood and Grassland
- Mixed Arable and Grassland
- Predominantly Arable Land
- Nursery Gardens and Orchards
- Built-up Areas

PRINCIPAL CROPS

- Wheat, Barley and Oats
- Barley and Oats
- Oats
- Cattle Pastures
- Sheep Grazing

1:6,800,000

Kilometres
0 20 40 60 80 100 120 140 160

English Miles
0 20 40 60 80 100

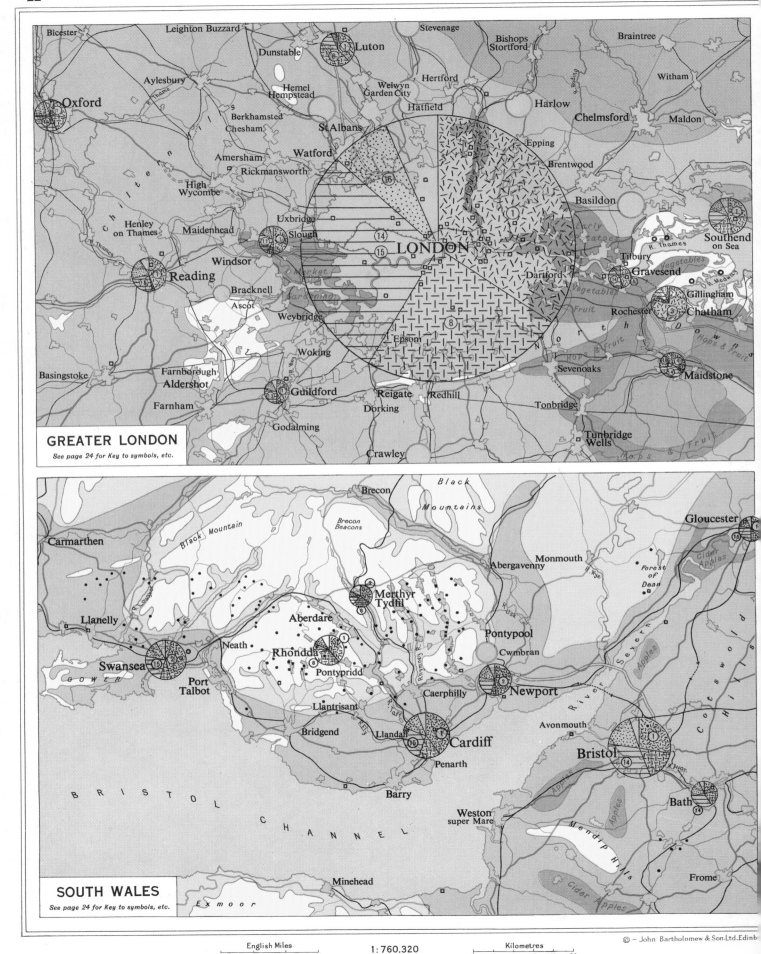

GREATER LONDON

See page 24 for Key to symbols, etc.

SOUTH WALES

See page 24 for Key to symbols, etc.

English Miles

1 : 760,320

Kilometres

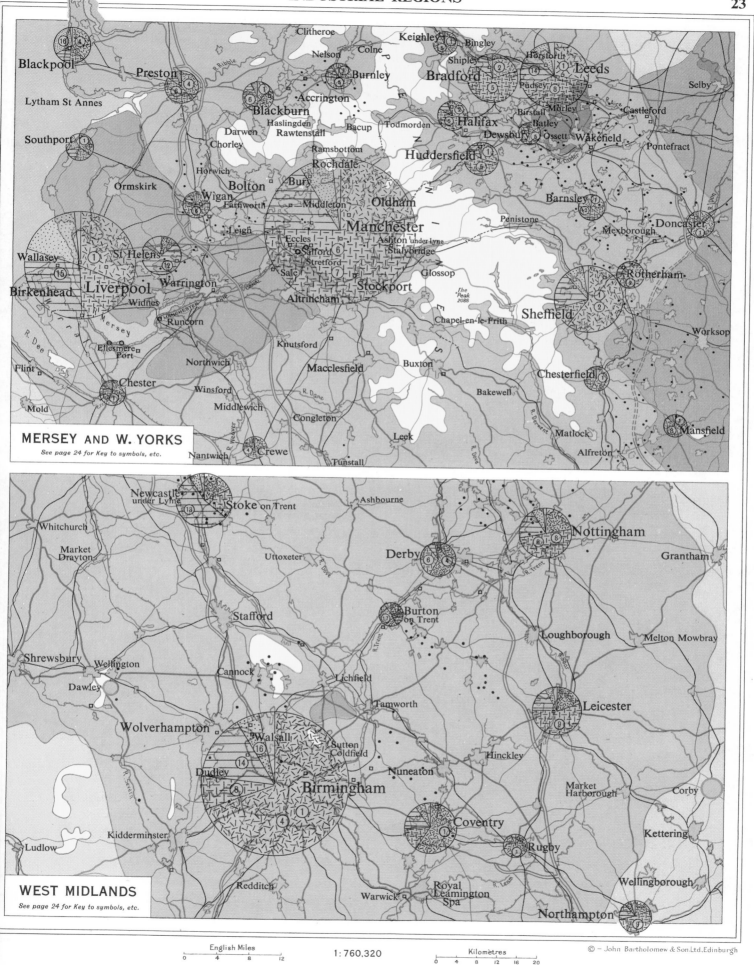

MERSEY AND W. YORKS
See page 24 for Key to symbols, etc.

WEST MIDLANDS
See page 24 for Key to symbols, etc.

English Miles

1 : 760,320

Kilomètres

© – John Bartholomew & Son.Ltd.Edinburgh

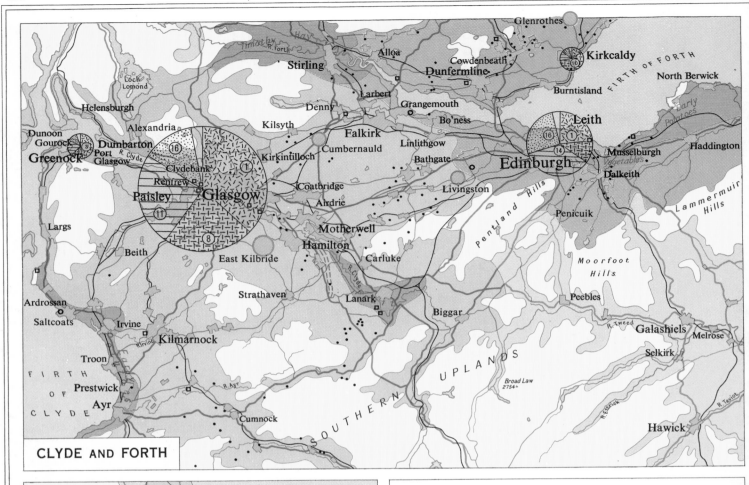

CLYDE AND FORTH

Towns and features on map:

Glenrothes, Kirkcaldy, North Berwick, Alloa, Cowdenbeath, Dunfermline, Burntisland, FIRTH OF FORTH, Stirling, Larbert, Grangemouth, Bo'ness, Leith, Haddington, Denny, Falkirk, Linlithgow, Edinburgh, Musselburgh, Helensburgh, Kilsyth, Cumbernauld, Bathgate, Dalkeith, Alexandria, Kirkintilloch, Livingston, Dunoon, Gourock, Dumbarton, Port Glasgow, Clydebank, Coatbridge, Airdrie, Penicuik, Greenock, Renfrew, Glasgow, Pentland Hills, Lammermuir Hills, Paisley, Motherwell, Hamilton, Carluke, Moorfoot Hills, Largs, Beith, East Kilbride, Carluke, Strathaven, Lanark, Peebles, Ardrossan, Biggar, Saltcoats, Irvine, Kilmarnock, Galashiels, Melrose, Troon, Selkirk, Prestwick, Ayr, FIRTH OF CLYDE, Broad Law 2754, SOUTHERN UPLANDS, Hawick, Cumnock, Loch Lomond, R. Clyde, R. Ayr, R. Tweed, R. Teviot, R. Ettrick

TYNE AND TEES

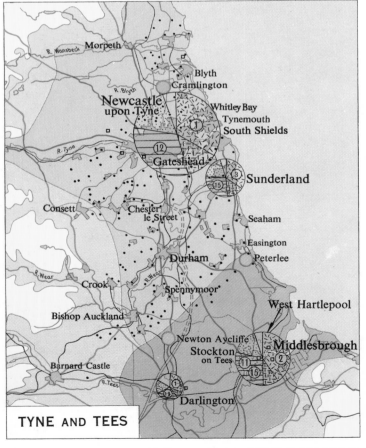

Morpeth, R. Wansbeck, Blyth, Cramlington, Newcastle upon Tyne, Whitley Bay, Tynemouth, South Shields, R. Blyth, Gateshead, Sunderland, Consett, Chester le Street, Seaham, R. Tyne, Durham, Easington, Peterlee, R. Wear, Crook, Spennymoor, West Hartlepool, Bishop Auckland, Newton Aycliffe, Stockton on Tees, Middlesbrough, Barnard Castle, Darlington, R. Tees

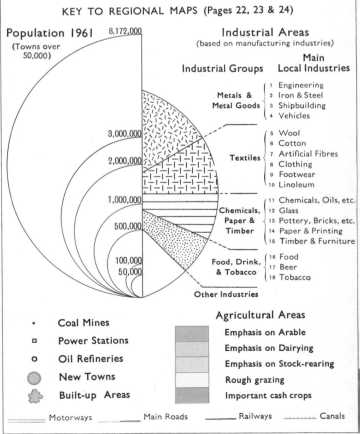

KEY TO REGIONAL MAPS (Pages 22, 23 & 24)

Population 1961 (Towns over 50,000)
8,172,000
3,000,000
2,000,000
1,000,000
500,000
100,000
50,000

Industrial Areas (based on manufacturing industries)

Industrial Groups — **Main Local Industries**

Metals & Metal Goods
  1 Engineering
  2 Iron & Steel
  3 Shipbuilding
  4 Vehicles

Textiles
  5 Wool
  6 Cotton
  7 Artificial Fibres
  8 Clothing
  9 Footwear
  10 Linoleum

Chemicals, Paper & Timber
  11 Chemicals, Oils, etc.
  12 Glass
  13 Pottery, Bricks, etc.
  14 Paper & Printing
  15 Timber & Furniture

Food, Drink, & Tobacco
  16 Food
  17 Beer
  18 Tobacco

Other Industries

• Coal Mines
□ Power Stations
○ Oil Refineries
● New Towns
✿ Built-up Areas

Agricultural Areas
Emphasis on Arable
Emphasis on Dairying
Emphasis on Stock-rearing
Rough grazing
Important cash crops

Motorways   Main Roads   Railways   Canals

English Miles   0 4 8 12
1 : 760,320
Kilometres   0 4 8 12 16 20

© – John Bartholomew & Son Ltd., Edinb

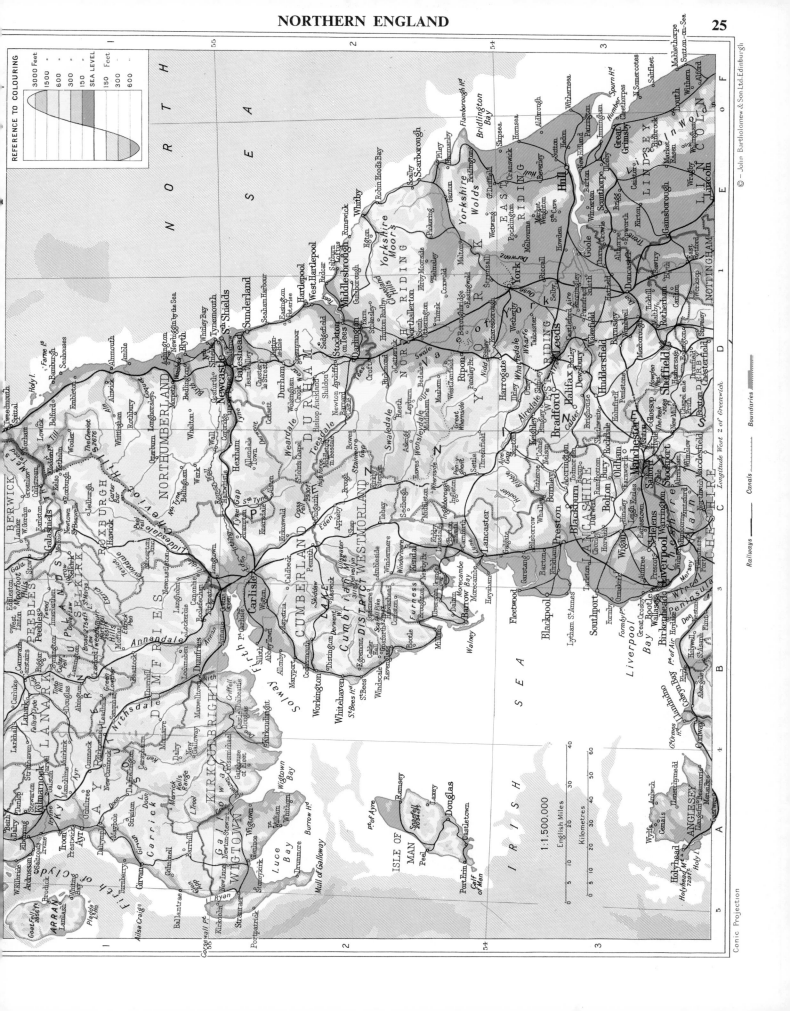

REFERENCE TO COLOURING

3000 Feet
1500 "
600 "
300 "
150 "
SEA LEVEL
Land Depression
150 Feet
300 "

1:1,500,000

English Miles
0 5 10   20   30   40   50

Kilometres
0 5 10   20   30   40   50   60   70   80

St. GEORGE'S CHANNEL

WICKLOW

WEXFORD

Wexford Harb.
Wexford B.

BRISTOL CHANNEL

ANGLESEY
CAERNARVON
Caernarvon Bay
Lleyn Peninsula
Cardigan Bay

DENBIGH
FLINT
CHES

WALES
MERIONETH
MONTGOMERY
SHROPSHIRE
CARDIGAN
RADNOR
HEREFORD
CARMARTHEN
BRECKNOCK
PEMBROKE
GLAMORGAN
MONMOUTH

Swansea
Cardiff
Newport
Bris

SOMERSET
Exmoor
DEVON
Dartmoor
CORNWALL
Bodmin Moors

Plymouth
Exeter
Torquay

Land's End
Lizard Pt.
Isles of Scilly

Longitude West 4 of Greenwich

Conic Projection

Railways ——— Canals........
Boundaries ≡≡≡≡≡≡≡

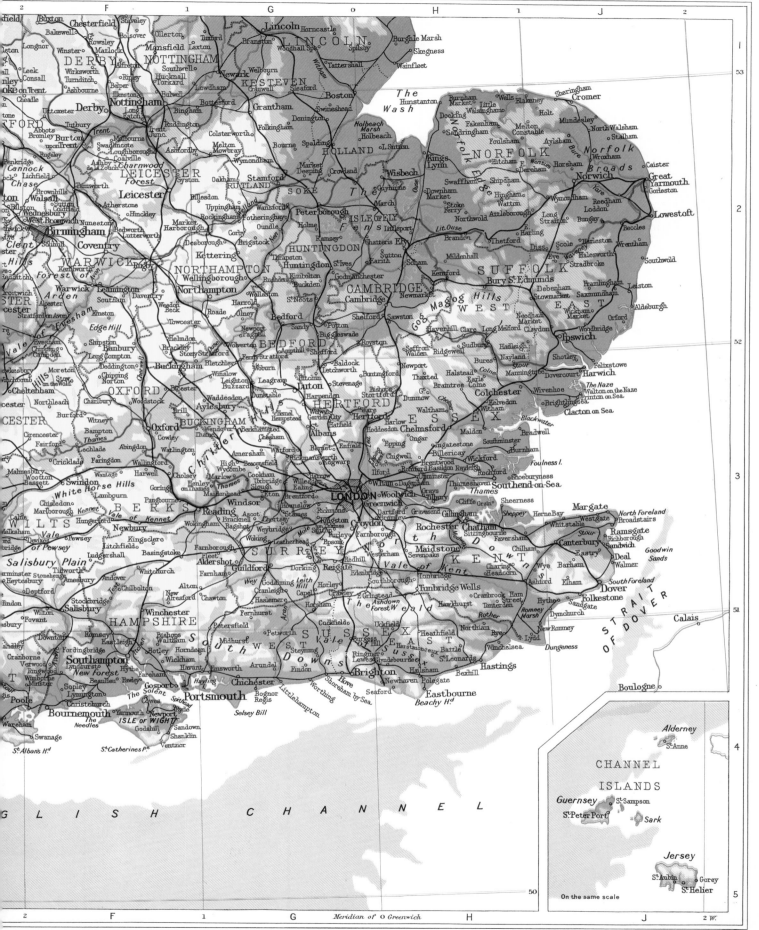

CHANNEL ISLANDS

Alderney
St Anne

Guernsey • St Sampson
St Peter Port • Sark

Jersey
St Aubin • • Gorey
St Helier

On the same scale

ENGLISH CHANNEL

Meridian of 0 Greenwich

© – John Bartholomew & Son Ltd. Edinburgh

ATLANTIC OCEAN

ORKNEY

Fair Isle

North Ronaldsay
Start Pt.
Sanday
North Ronaldsay Firth
Lower Whitehall
Stronsay
Sanday Sound
Eday
Westray
Papa Westray
Egilsay
Rousay
Scrosay
Shapinsay
Auskerry
Copinsay
Mull Hd.
Brough Hd.
Birsay
Marwick Hd.
Skara Brae
Stromness
L. of Stenness
Hoy Sd.
Rora Hd.
HOY
Kirkwall
Mainland or Pomona
St. Mary's
Burray
Hope
South Ronaldsay
Brough Ness
Scapa Flow
Flotta
Swona
Pentland Skerries
Pentland Firth
Stroma
Dunnet Hd.
Duncansby Hd.
Jn. O'Groats

Scrabster
Thurso
Dunnet B.
Dunnet
Halkirk
Watten
Sinclair's B.
Wick
Castletown
Strath Halladale
Latheron
Lybster
Berriedale
CAITHNESS

C. Wrath
Loch Inchard
Scourie
Edrachillis Bay
Handa
P. of Stoer
Enard Bay
Rhu Coigach
Summer Is.
Greenstone Pt.
Gruinart Bay
Loch Broom
Ullapool

Faraid Hd.
Kyle of Durness
L. Eriboll
Loch Laxford
Tongue
Strath Naver
Strathy Pt.
Strathy
Ben Hope 3040 ft.
Ben Loyal
Ben Klibreck
Bettyhill
Kinbrace
SUTHERLAND
Helmsdale
Morven
Ben More Assynt 3273 ft.
L. Assynt
Loch Shin
Altnaharra
Lairg
Oykell
Brora
Golspie
Bonar Bridge
Dornoch
Dornoch Firth
Tain
Inver
Tarbat Ness
Loch Maree
Poolewe
Gairloch
Loch Ewe
An Teallach 3483 ft.
Fionn Loch
Slioch 3217 ft.
Achnasheen
Strathcarron
Lochcarron
Loch Torridon
Applecross
Kinlochewe
ROSS AND CROMARTY
Ben Wyvis 3429 ft.
Sgurr Mor 3637 ft.
Garve
Dingwall
Conon
Beauly
Strathpeffer
Fortrose
Cromarty
Cromarty Firth
Black Isle
Rosemarkie
INVERNESS
Inverness
Beauly Firth
Loch Ness
Glen Affric
Glen Moriston
Glen Cannich
Glen Urquhart
Drumnadrochit
Fort Augustus
L. Lochy
L. Oich
Invermoriston
Falls of Foyers

Buckie
Lossiemouth
Burghead
Findhorn
Forres
Nairn
NAIRN
Cawdor
Grantown
Carrbridge
Boat of Garten
Cairn Gorm 4084 ft.
Aviemore
Kingussie
MORAY
Elgin
Fochabers
Rothes
Keith
Dufftown
Craigellachie
Aberlour
Tomintoul
Grantown-on-Spey

ABERDEEN
Aberdeen
Peterhead
Buchan Ness
Boddam
Cruden B.
Ellon
Newburgh
Dyce
Inverurie
Oldmeldrum
Echt
Kintore
Alford
Tarland
Torphins
Kemnay
Huntly
Insch
Rhynie
Old Deer
Mintlaw
New Deer
New Pitsligo
Strichen
Fraserburgh
Kinnaird's Hd.
Rattray Hd.
Rosehearty
BUCHAN
Turriff
Macduff
Banff
Cullen
Portsoy
Aberchirder
BANFF
DEVERON
Ythan
Don
Dee

Butt of Lewis
Port of Ness
Toista Hd.
Eye Peninsula
Broad B.
Stornoway
Tiumpan Hd.
Barvas
Carloway
Gt. Bernera
L. Erisort
L. Seaforth
LEWIS
NORTH MINCH
Shant Is.
Rubha Reidh
Loch Snizort
Dunvegan
Quiraing
The Storr 2360 ft.
Portree
Bracadale
SKYE
Cuillin Hills
Scalpay
Raasay
Sound of Raasay
Broadford
Kyleakin
Kyle of Lochalsh
Little Minch
Cisham 2622 ft.
Tarbert
W. L. Tarbert
Scarp
Taransay
HARRIS
Leverburgh
Rodel
Sound of Harris
Pabbay
Berneray
NORTH UIST
Lochmaddy
Benbecula
Monach Is.
Sound of Monach
SOUTH UIST

On the same scale

ZETLAND (SHETLAND)
Herma Ness
Muckle Flugga
Unst
Norwick
Baltasound
Haroldswick
Balta
Fetlar
Uyeasound
Gruney
Yell
Mid Yell
Whalsay
Out Skerries
Fedra
Hascosay
Mainland
Hillswick
Ollaberry
Sullom Voe
Brae
Voe
Nesting
L. of Noss
Bressay
Lerwick
Scalloway
Burra
Sandwick
Mousa
Cunningsburgh
Sumburgh Hd.
Fitful Hd.
Sumburgh
Grutness
The Faither
Esha Ness
Hillswick
Papa Stour
Sandness
Walls
Foula
West Burra
St. Magnus Bay

Sule Skerry
Stack Skerry
Sule Stack
North Rona
Sula Sgeir
ST. KILDA
Boreray
Soay
Hirta
Fair Isle

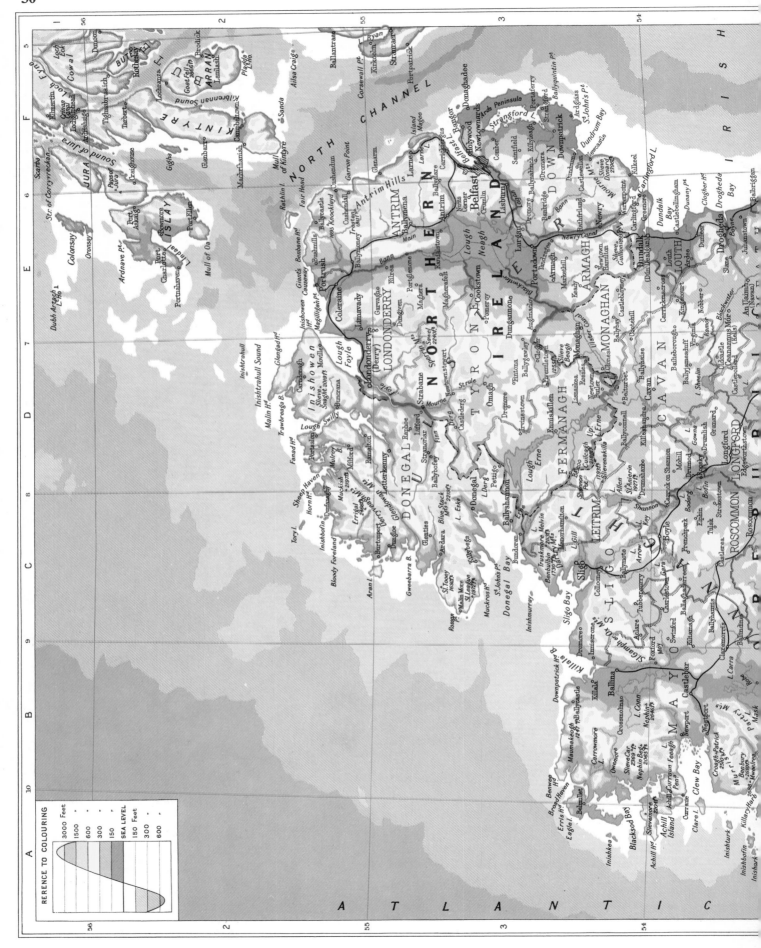

REFERENCE TO COLOURING

3000 Feet
1500 "
600 "
300 "
150 "
SEA LEVEL
150 Feet
300 "
600 "

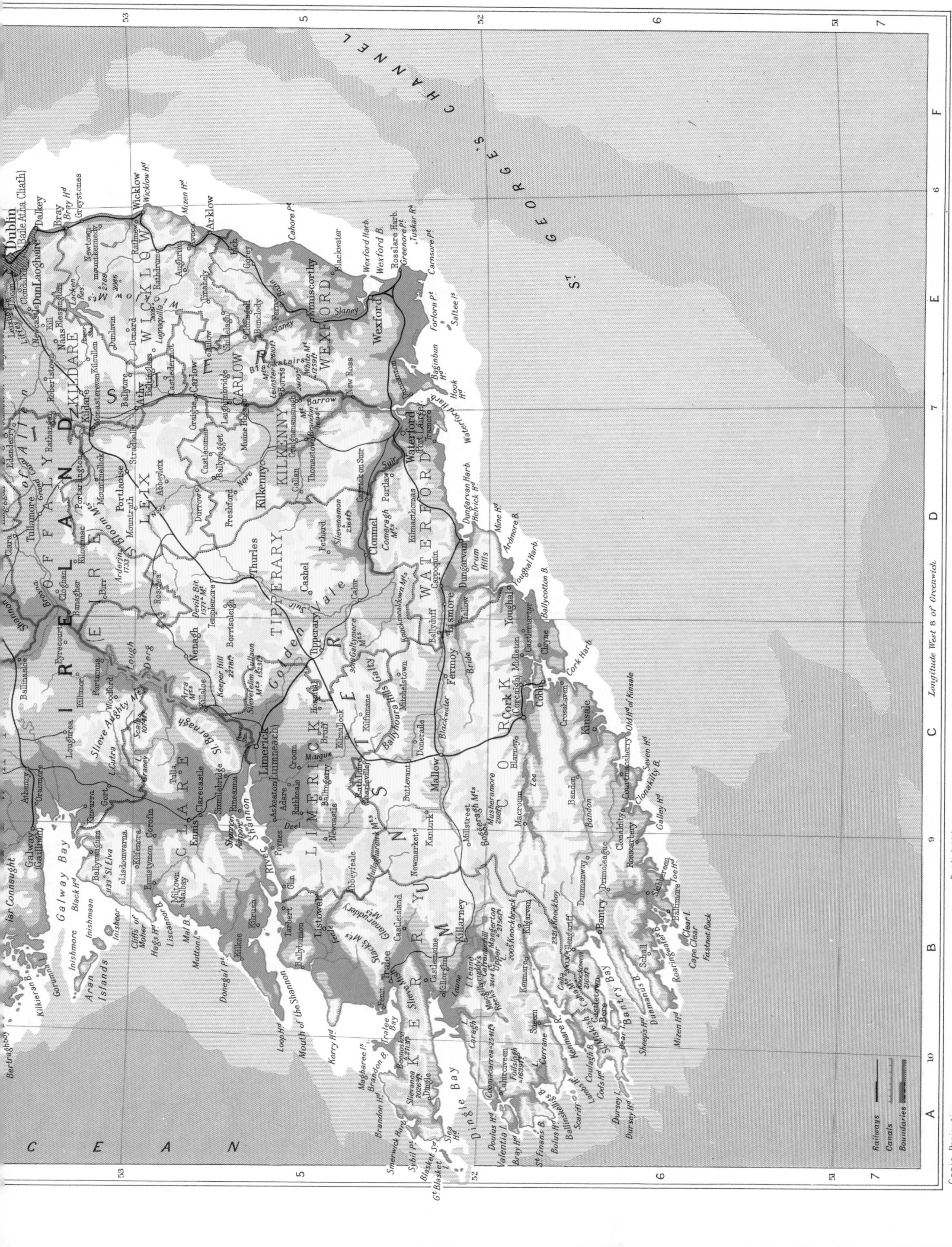

ST. GEORGE'S CHANNEL

OCEAN

Dublin (Baile Átha Cliath)
Dun Laoghaire
Bray Hd
Greystones
Wicklow
Wicklow Hd
Arklow

KILDARE
Naas
Blessington
Newbridge
Kilcullen
Athy
Carlow
CARLOW
New Ross
WEXFORD
Wexford
Wexford Harb.
Rosslare Harb.
Greenore Pt.
Carnsore Pt.
Enniscorthy
Slaney

LEIX
Portlaoise
Mountmellick
Abbeyleix
Durrow
KILKENNY
Kilkenny
Thomastown
Callan

TIPPERARY
Thurles
Templemore
Roscrea
Nenagh
Cashel
Clonmel
Carrick on Suir
Golden Vale
Tipperary

WATERFORD
Waterford
Dungarvan
Dungarvan Harb.
Helvick Hd
Lismore
Cappoquin
Youghal
Youghal Harb.

CLARE
Ennis
Clarecastle
Shannon Airport
Kilrush
Kilkee
Loop Hd.
Ennistymon
Corofin
Cliffs of Moher

LIMERICK
Limerick (Luimneach)
Askeaton
Rathkeale
Newcastle
Abbeyfeale
Croom
Bruff
Kilmallock
Mitchelstown

CORK
Cork (Corcaigh)
COBH
Kinsale
Blarney
Bandon
Mallow
Fermoy
Macroom
Bantry
Bantry Bay
Skibbereen
Cape Clear
Fastnet Rock
Clonakilty
Courtmacsherry
Old Hd. of Kinsale
Galley Hd.
Dunmanway

KERRY
Tralee
Killarney
Dingle
Dingle Bay
Killorglin
Cahirciveen
Kenmare
Valentia I.
Brandon Hd.
Castleisland
Listowel
Tarbert
Ballybunion
Kilmihill

IRELAND

OFFALY
Tullamore
Birr
Banagher
Portumna

Galway (Gaillimh)
Galway Bay
Aran Islands
Inishmore
Inishmaan
Inisheer

WICKLOW

Lough Derg
Shannon
River Shannon
Mouth of the Shannon

© – John Bartholomew & Son Ltd. Edinburgh

Longitude West 8° of Greenwich

1:1,500,000

Kilometres
0 10 20 30 40 50 60

English Miles
0 5 10 20 30 40

Conic Projection

Railways
Canals
Boundaries

Conic Projection

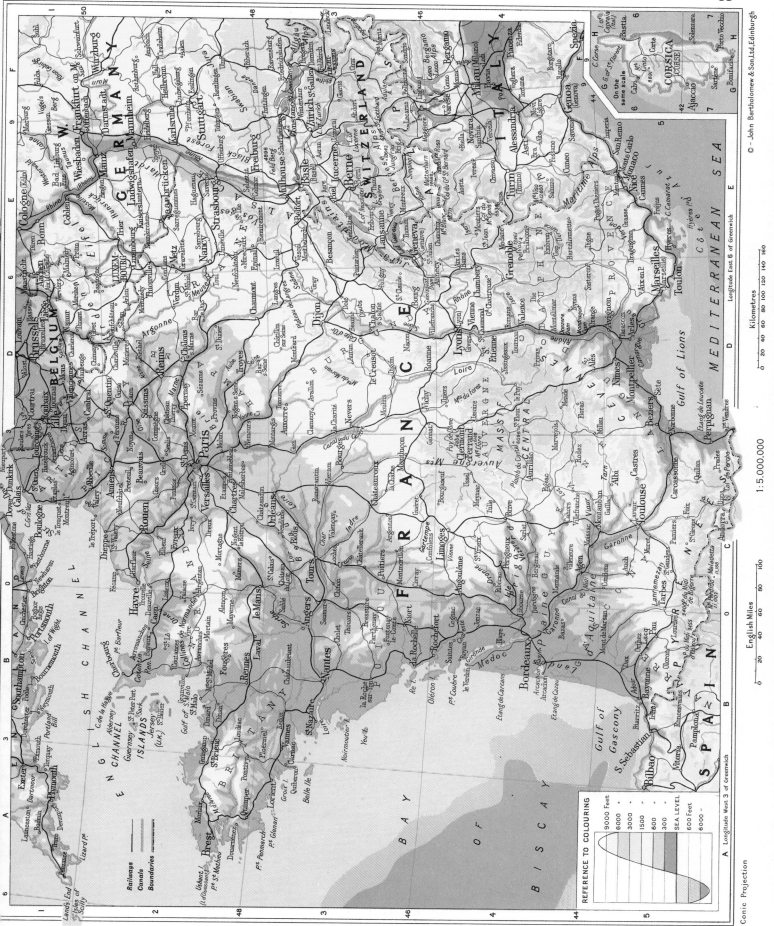

REFERENCE TO COLOURING

9000 Feet
6000 "
3000 "
1500 "
600 "
300 "
SEA LEVEL
600 Feet
6000 "

Railways
Canals
Boundaries

1:5,000,000

Conic Projection

© - John Bartholomew & Son, Ltd., Edinburgh

Kilometres
0 20 40 60 80 100 120 140 160

English Miles
0   20   40   60   80   100

Longitude East 6 of Greenwich

A Longitude West 3 of Greenwich

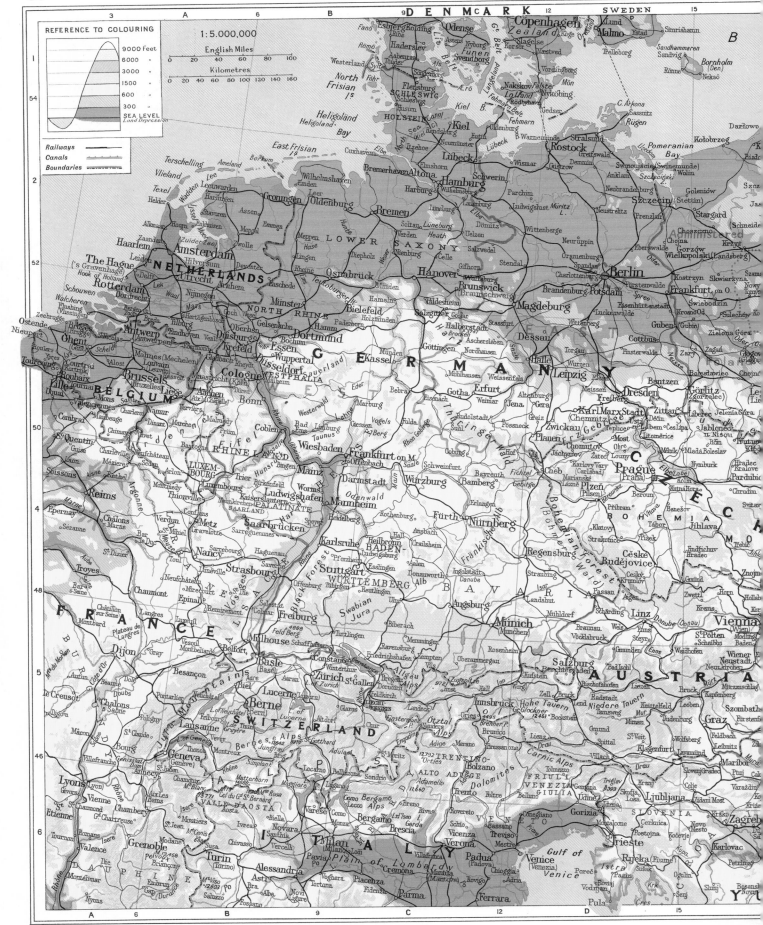

REFERENCE TO COLOURING

1:5,000,000

	9000 Feet
	6000 "
	3000 "
	1500 "
	600 "
	300 "
	SEA LEVEL
	Land Depression

Railways
Canals
Boundaries

English Miles

Kilometres

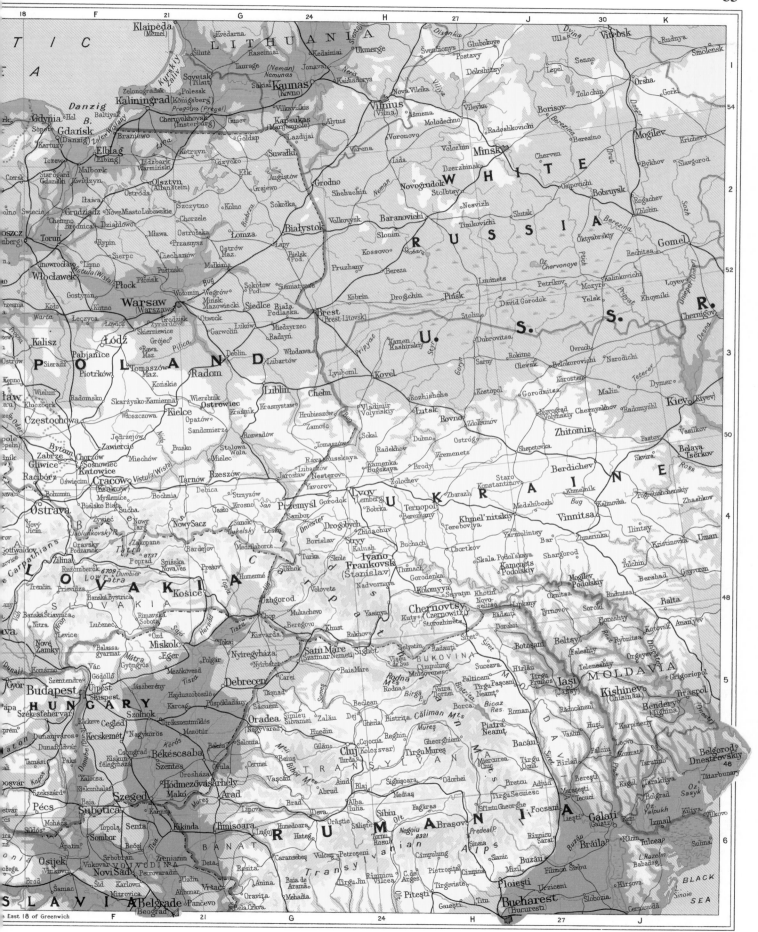

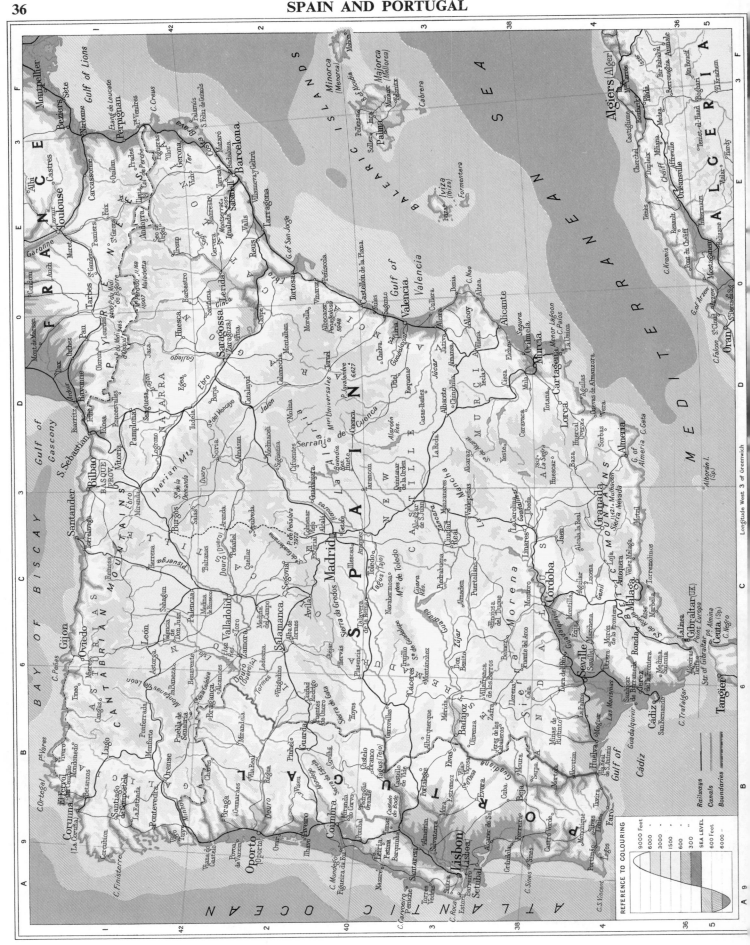

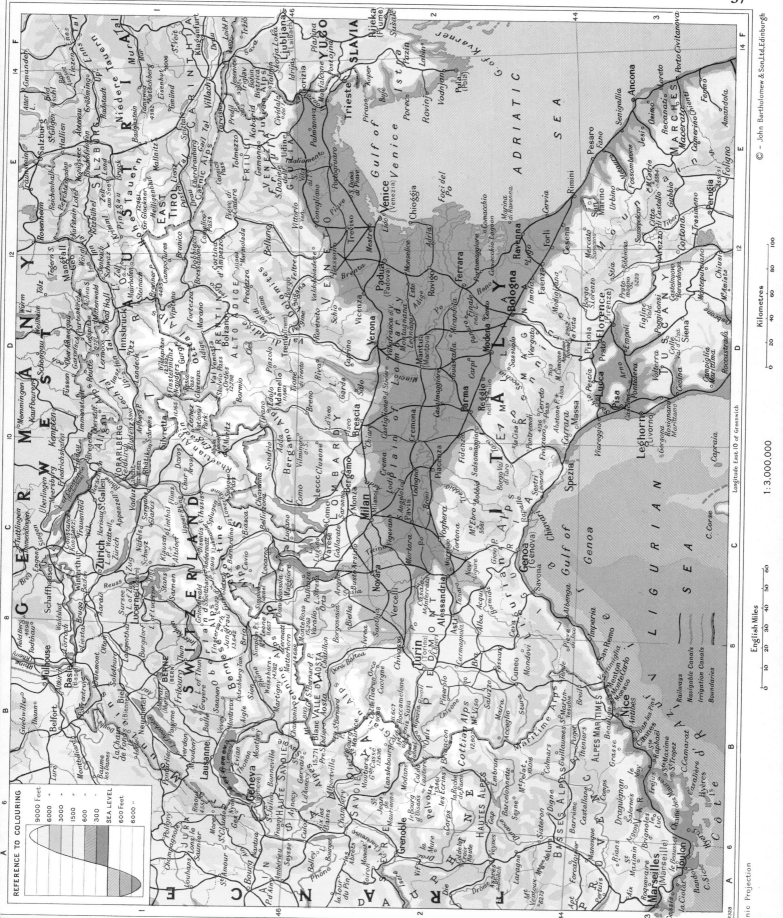

© — John Bartholomew & Son, Ltd., Edinburgh

1 : 3,000,000

Conic Projection

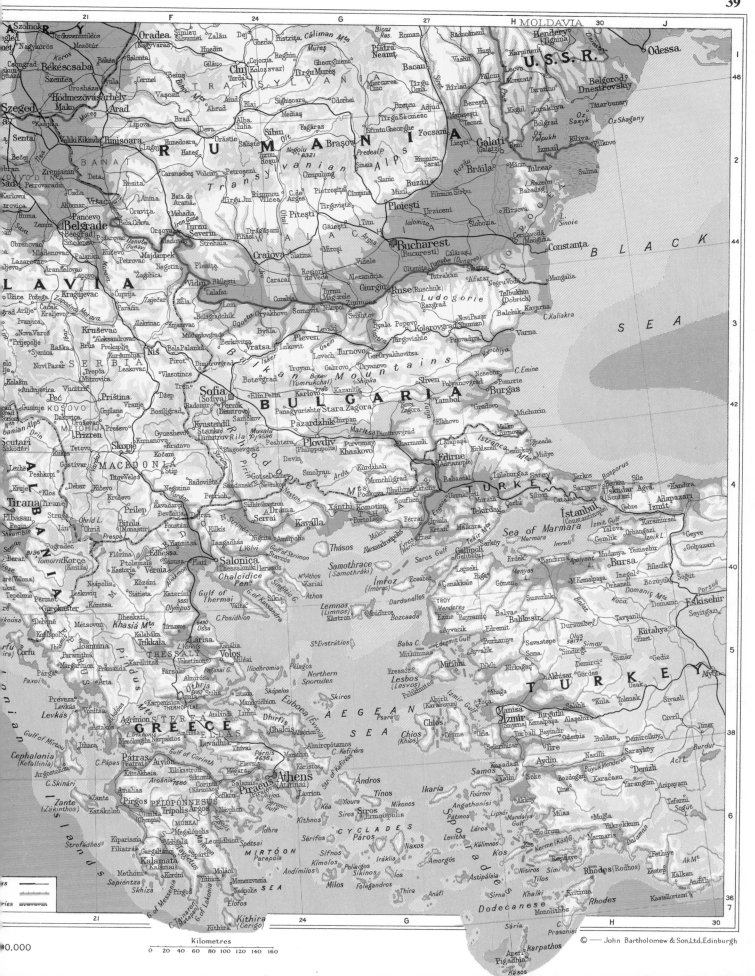

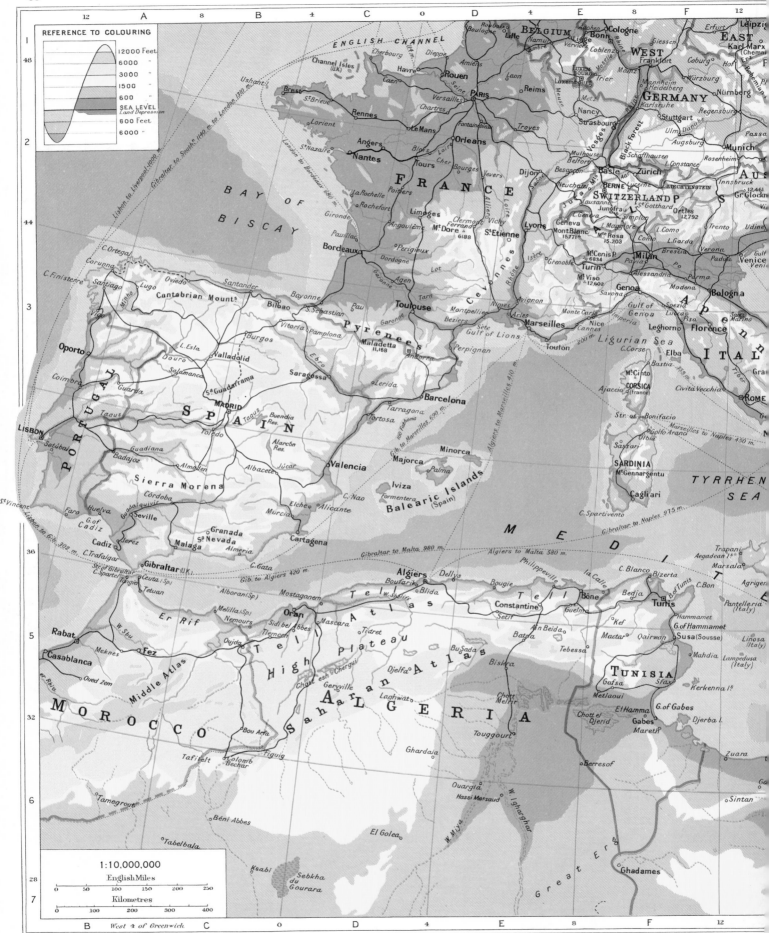

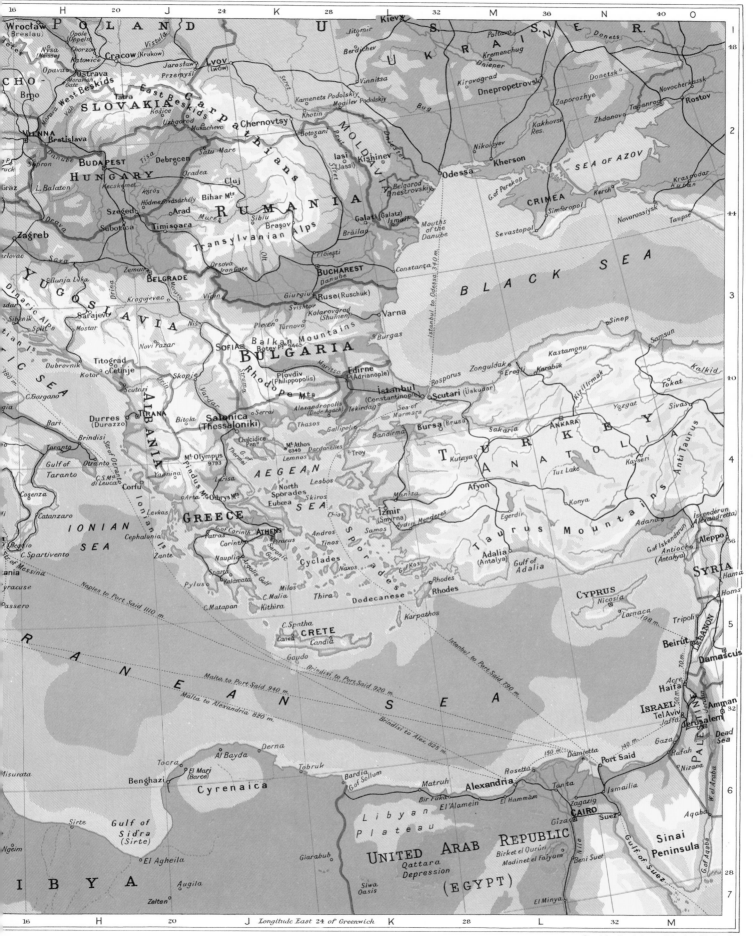

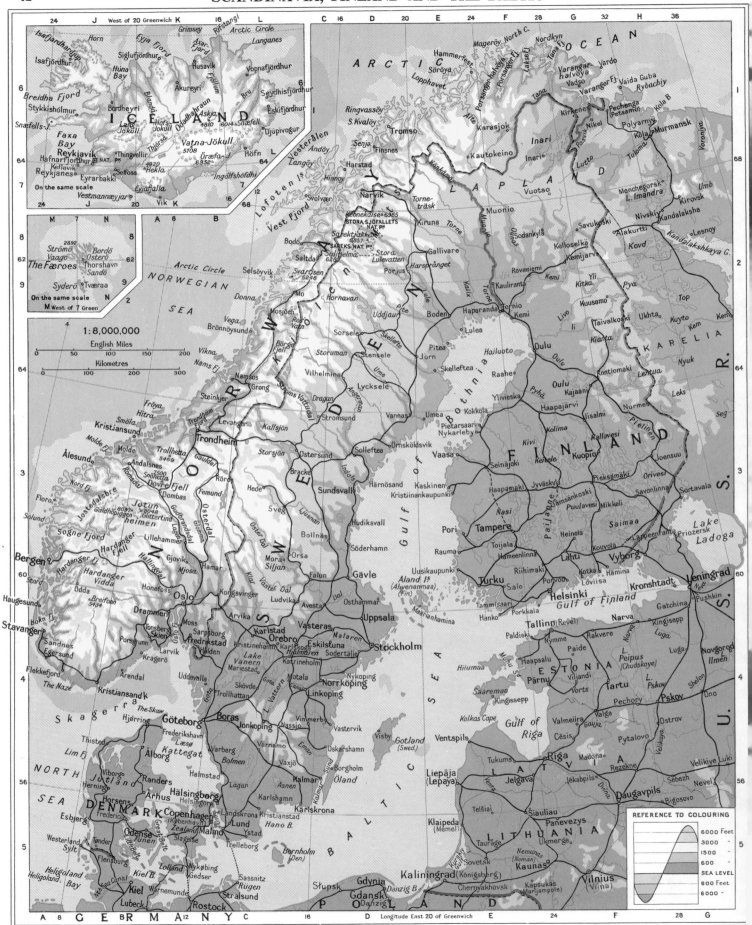

Conic Projection

© — John Bartholomew & Son. Ltd., Edinburgh

Railways   Canals   Ice Caps

Boundaries

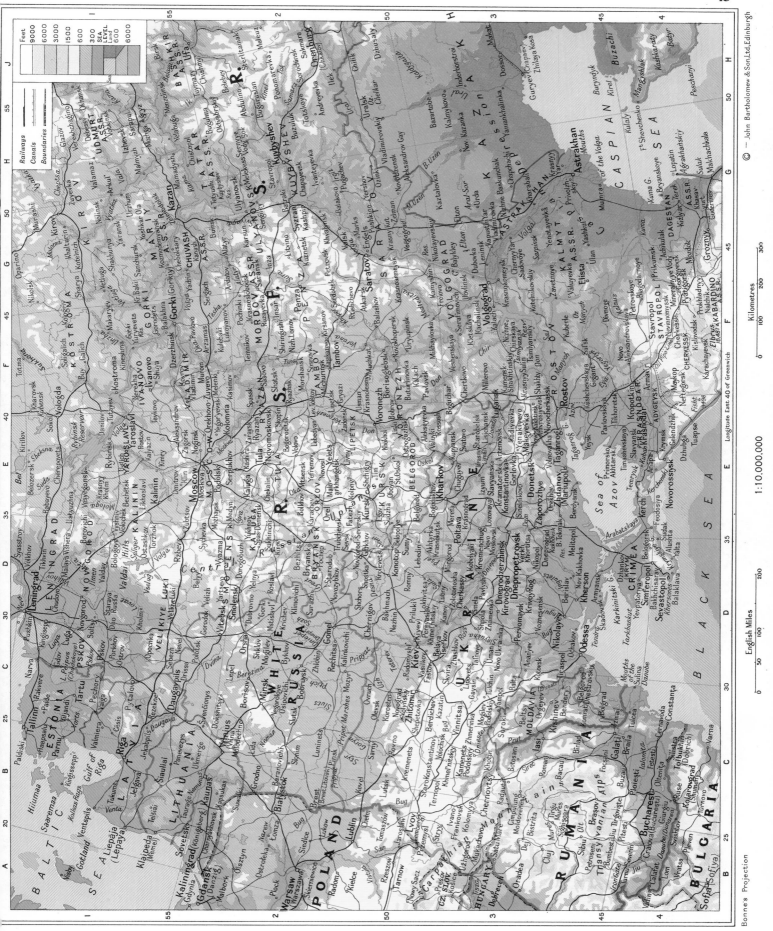

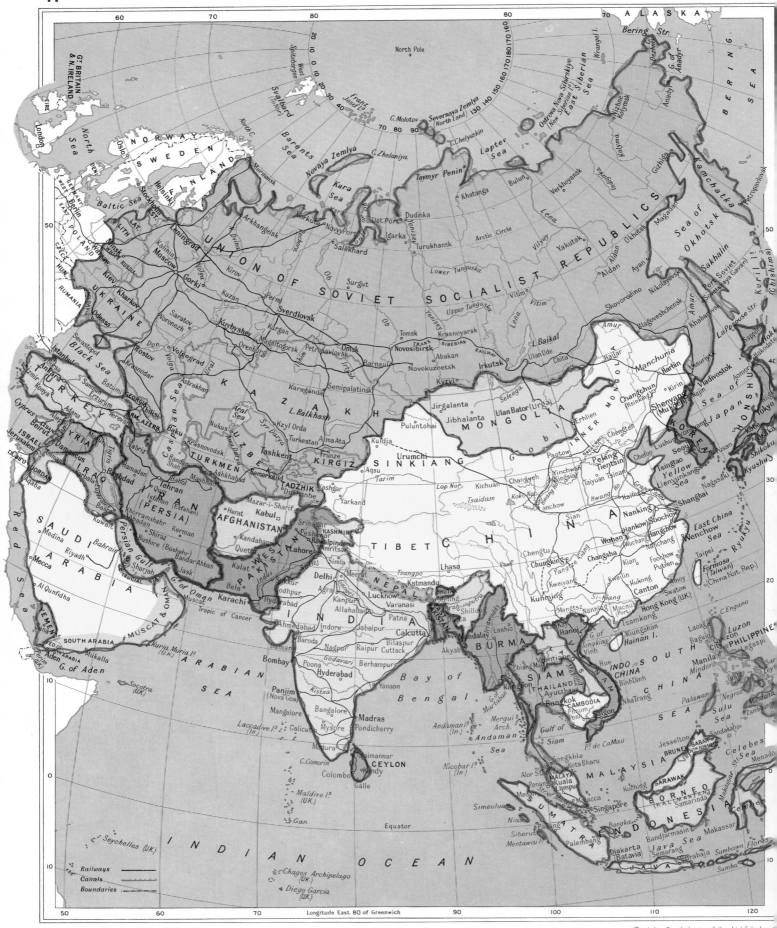

Railways
Canals
Boundaries

Lambert's Zenithal Equal-Area Projection   English Miles   0   200   400   600   800   1000   1:45,000,000   Kilometres   0   200 400 600 800 1000 1200 1400 1600   ©—John Bartholomew & Son,Ltd.,Edinburgh

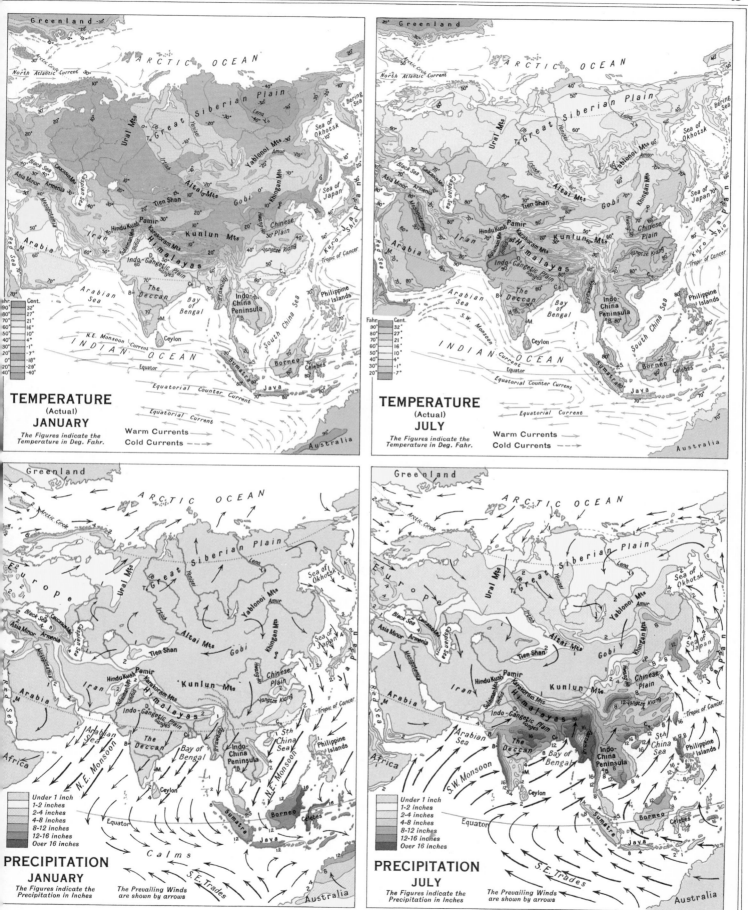

TEMPERATURE
(Actual)
JANUARY

The Figures indicate the
Temperature in Deg. Fahr.

Warm Currents ——→
Cold Currents ---→

TEMPERATURE
(Actual)
JULY

The Figures indicate the
Temperature in Deg. Fahr.

Warm Currents ——→
Cold Currents ---→

PRECIPITATION
JANUARY

The Figures indicate the
Precipitation in Inches

The Prevailing Winds
are shown by arrows

Under 1 inch
1-2 inches
2-4 inches
4-8 inches
8-12 inches
12-16 inches
Over 16 inches

PRECIPITATION
JULY

The Figures indicate the
Precipitation in Inches

The Prevailing Winds
are shown by arrows

Under 1 inch
1-2 inches
2-4 inches
4-8 inches
8-12 inches
12-16 inches
Over 16 inches

English Miles
0   500   1000   1500

1:105,000,000

© — John Bartholomew & Son Ltd. Edinburgh

REFERENCE TO COLOURING

18000 Feet
12000 "
6000 "
3000 "
1500 "
600 "
SEA LEVEL
Land Depression
600 Feet
6000 "

2649

Lambert's Zenithal Equal-Area Projection

Railways ——   Canals ·········   Marshes ···   Boundaries ···········

Longitude East 80 of Green

1:25,000,000
English Miles
0   50 100   200   300   400   500   600
0   100 200   400   600   800   1000
Kilometres

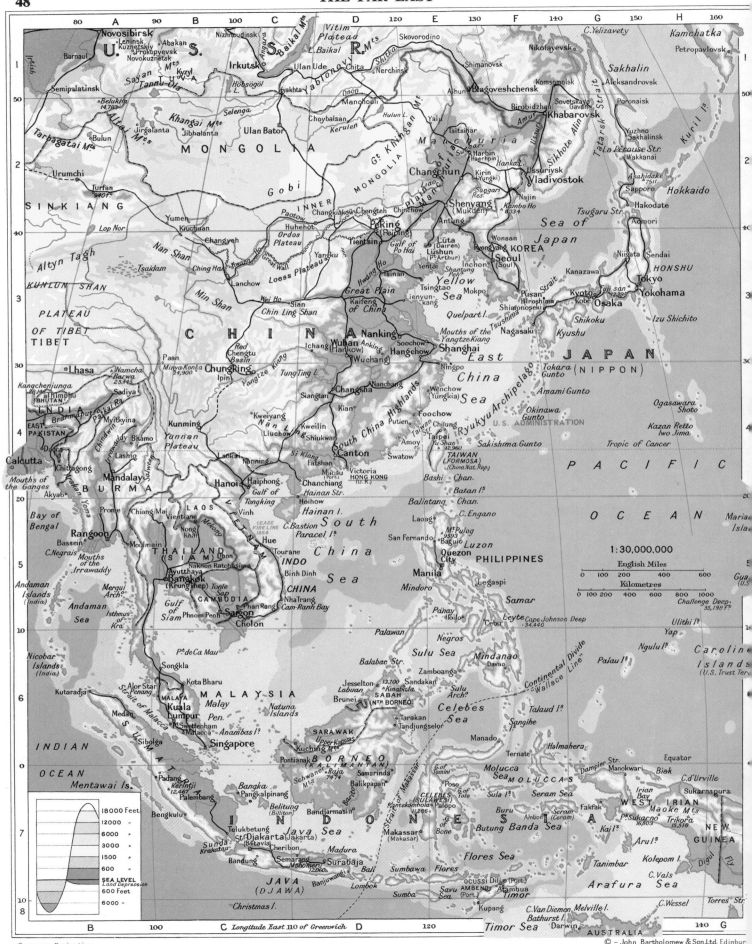

Sanson's Projection

Railways ———   Canals

Boundaries

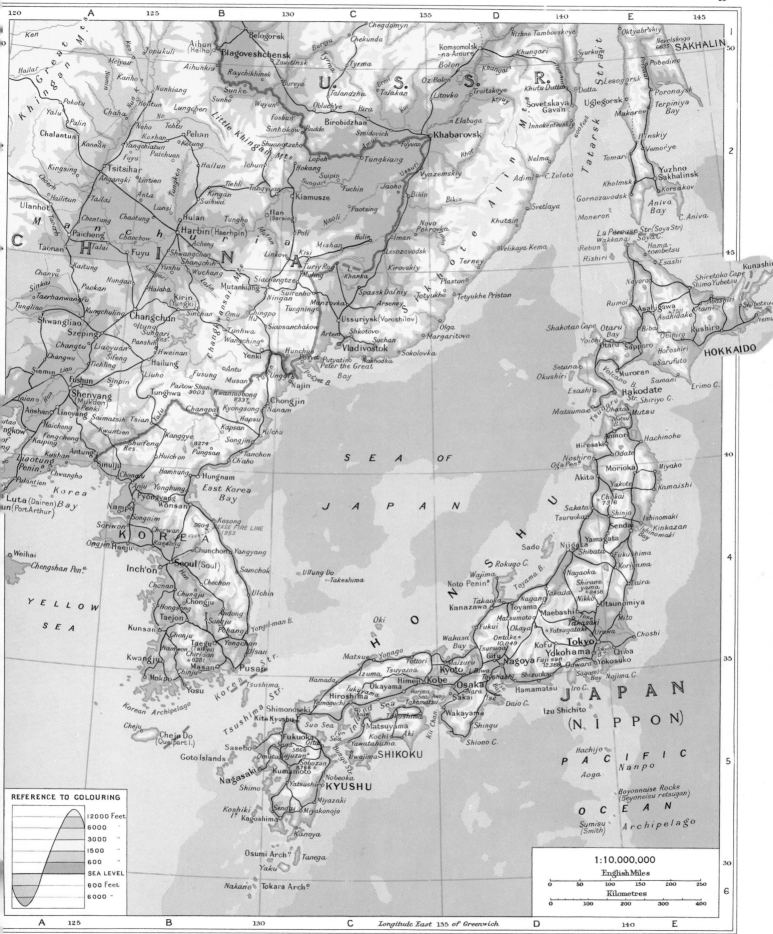

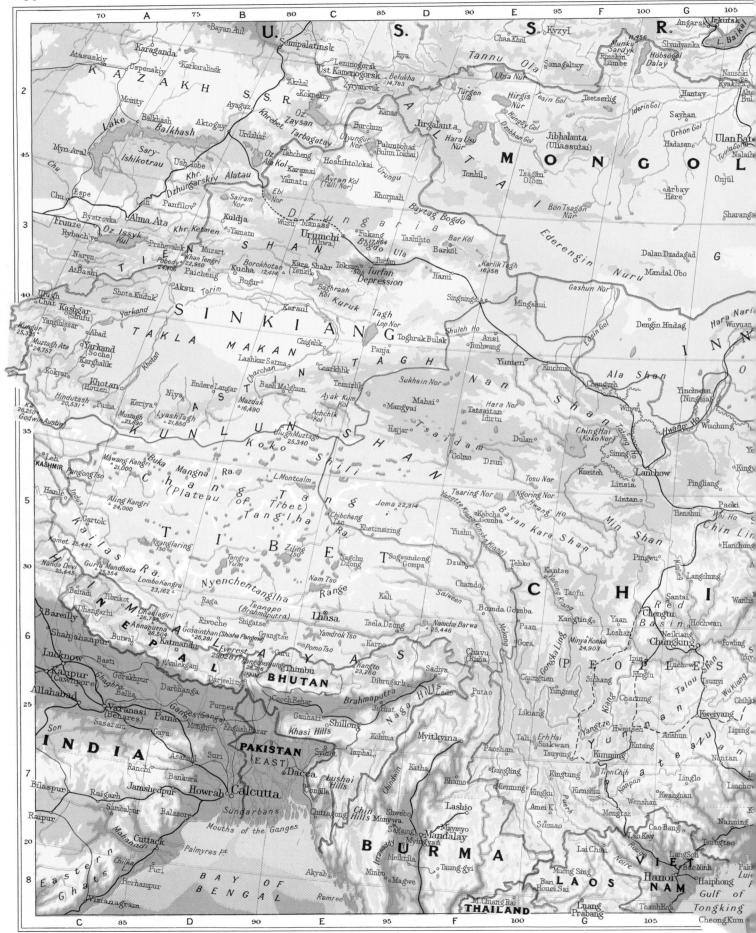

Railways ———　　Canals ┅┅┅　　Boundaries ━━━━━

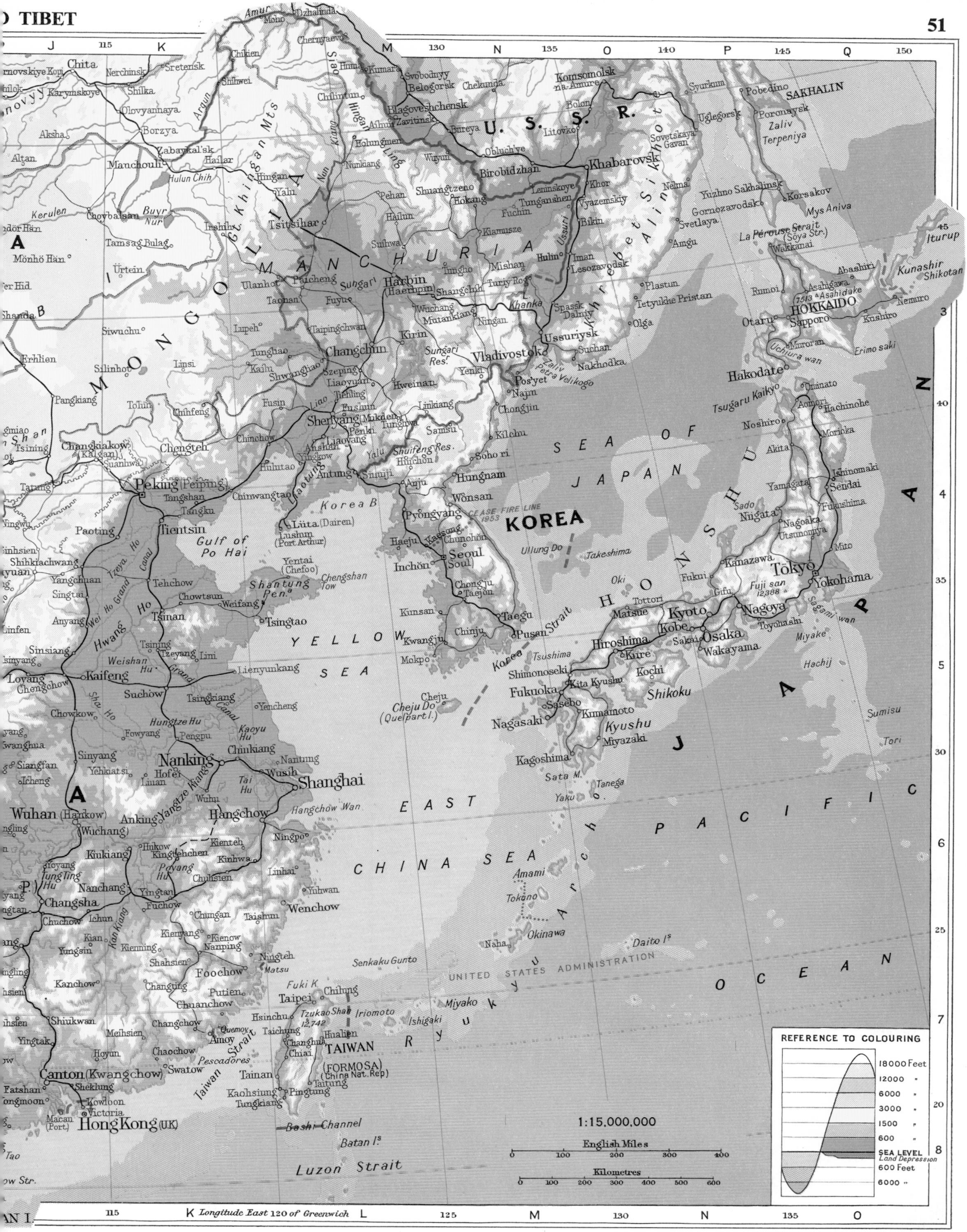

MONGOLIA

MANCHURIA

U.S.S.R.

Amur Moho Dzhalinda
Chita Nerchinsk Sretensk Chikien Shilwei Himan Kumara Svobodnyy Chekunda Komsomolsk na-Amure Syurkum Pobedino SAKHALIN
nyovskiye Kopi Karymskoye Shilka Hinggan Belogorsk Uglegorsk Poronaysk Zaliv
ilok Olovyannaya Borzya Zabaykal'sk Blagoveshchensk Zavitinsk Bureya Litovko Bolon Sovetskaya Terpeniya
Altan Manchouli Hailar Hingan Holungmen Obluch'ye Khabarovsk Gavan Yuzhno Sakhalinsk Korsakov
Kerulen Choybalsan Buyr Tsitsihar Nunkiang Shuangtzeno Hokang Khor Tunganshen Vyazemskiy Svetlaya Gornozavodsk Mys Aniva
dör Hän Tamsag Bulag Taonan Paicheng Sungari Harbin Haerhpin Shangchih Turiy Rog Bikin Iman Amgu La Pérouse Strait (Sōya Str.) Wakkanai
Mönhö Han Ulanhot Fuyu Wuchang Ningan Khanka Spassk Dalniy Plastun Rumoi Asahigawa HOKKAIDO
Shanda B Siwuchu Linsi Tungliao Kirin Mishan Lesozavodsk Olga Asahidake Sapporo Kushiro Nemuro
Erhlien Silinhot Tohin Kailu Shwanghao Szeping Linkiang Samsu Pos'yet Najin Otaru Muroran Hakodate Erimo saki
Pangkiang Changkiakow Chengteh Fusin Shenyang Mukden Penki Tunghwa Chongjin Aomori Hachinohe
Kalgan Suanhwa Hihutao Yingkow Anshan Liaoyang Yalu Hyesan Kilchu Noshiro Morioka
Peking (Peiping) Tangshan Chinwangtao Antung Sinuiju Soho ri Akita Yamagata Sendai
Tientsin Tangku Lüta (Dairen) Korea B Anju Hungnam Sado Niigata Fukushima
Paoting Lushun (Port Arthur) Pyongyang Wonsan CEASE FIRE LINE 1953 KOREA Ullung Do Takeshima Nagaoka Kanazawa Tokyo
Gulf of Po Hai Yentai (Chefoo) Chengshan Tow Haeju Kaesong Chunchon Oki Fukui Gifu Fuji san Yokohama
Shihkiachwang Weihsien Chowtsun Weifang Tsingtao Seoul Soul Inchon Chongju Taejon Tottori Matsue Kyoto Nagoya Mito
Tsinan Shantung Pen. Kunsan Taegu Pusan Strait Hiroshima Kobe Osaka Wakayama Miyake
Tzeyang Lim Yencheng Chinju Kwangju Tsushima Kita Kyushu Kochi Shikoku Sagami wan
Kaifeng Weishan Hu Lienyunkang Mokpo Cheju Shimonoseki Fukuoka Kumamoto Kagoshima
Suchow Tsingkiang Cheju Do (Quelpart I.) Nagasaki Sasebo Kyushu Miyazaki Sata M.

YELLOW SEA

SEA OF JAPAN

HONSHU

JAPAN

EAST CHINA SEA

PACIFIC OCEAN

Nanking Chinkiang Nantung Wusih Shanghai Hangchow Wan Hangchow Ningpo
Wuhan (Hankow) Anking Yangtze Kiang Kienteh Kinhwa Linhai
Changsha Nanchang Yingtan Fuchow Wenchow
Kiukiang Hukow Kingtehchen Chuhsien Yuhwan Amami Tokano
Kian Kienyang Kienow Nanping Shahsien Nungteh Okinawa Daito Is
Yungsin Kienning Chimgan Taishun Naha
Kanchow Changting Putien Foochow Matsu
Meihsien Changchow Chinanchow Fuki K Chilung RYUKYU Miyako Ishigaki
Shiukwan Hoyun Chaochow Swatow Taipei Hsinchu Taichung UNITED STATES ADMINISTRATION
Canton (Kwangchow) Shekung Quemoy St Loi Amoy Pescadores Changhua Chiai Iriomoto Senkaku Gunto
Fatshan Kowloon Victoria TAIWAN (FORMOSA) (China Nat. Rep) Tainan Taitung Hualien
Macau (Port.) Hong Kong (UK) Kaohsiung Pingtung
Bashi Channel Batan Is
Luzon Strait

1:15,000,000

English Miles
0 100 200 300 400

Kilometres
0 100 200 300 400 500 600

© – John Bartholomew & Son.Ltd. Edinburgh

REFERENCE TO COLOURING
18000 Feet
12000 "
6000 "
3000 "
1500 "
600 "
SEA LEVEL
Land Depression
600 Feet
6000 "

Longitude East 120 of Greenwich

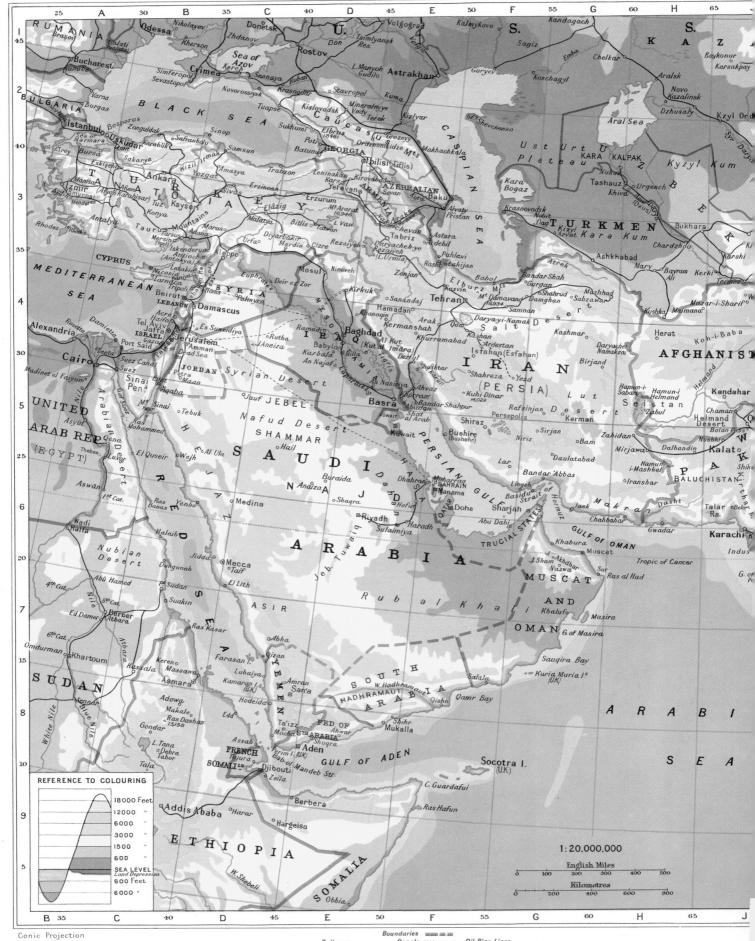

Boundaries
Railways   Canals   Oil Pipe Lines
Dry Salt Lakes   Marshes

1:20,000,000

English Miles
0   100   200   300   400   500

Kilometres
0   200   400   600   800

REFERENCE TO COLOURING

18000 Feet
12000 "
6000 "
3000 "
1500 "
600 "
SEA LEVEL
Land Depression
600 Feet
6000 "

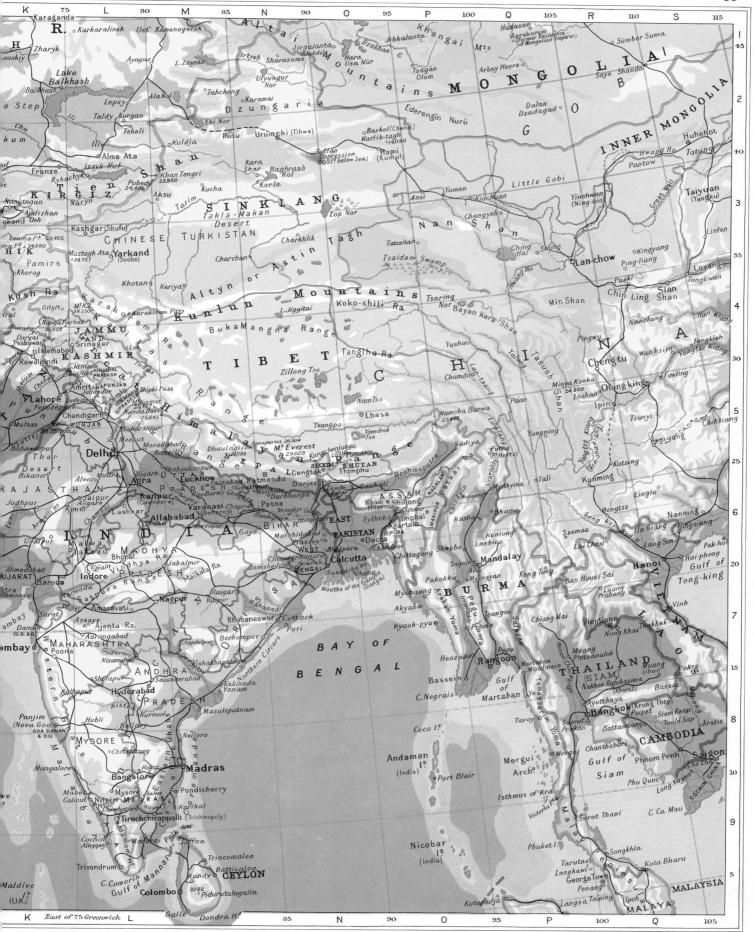

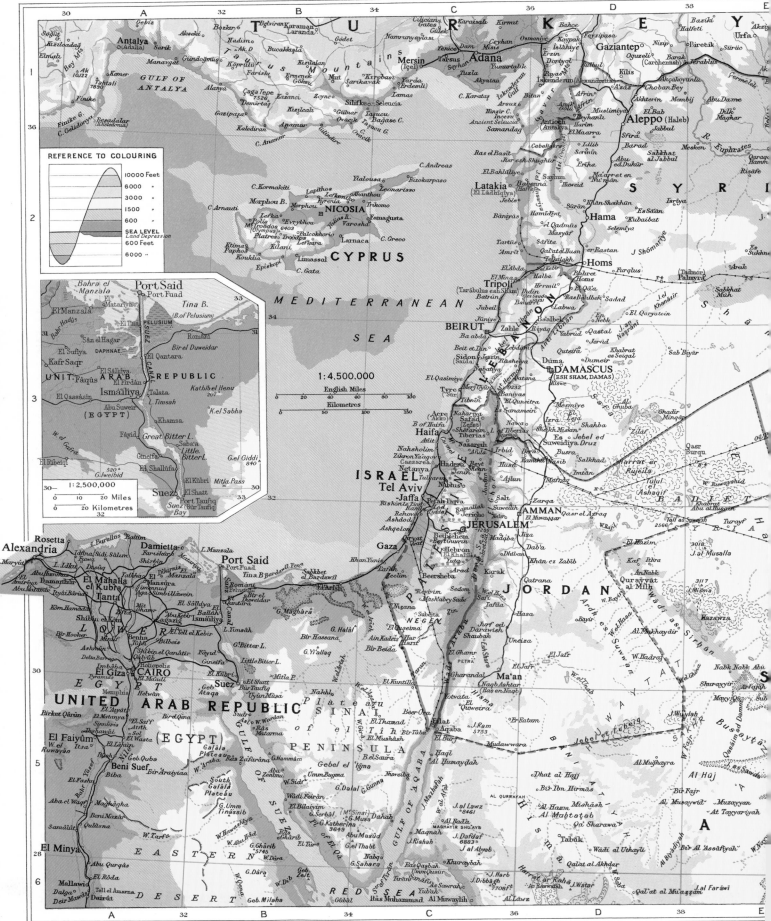

REFERENCE TO COLOURING

10000 Feet
6000 "
3000 "
1500 "
600 "
SEA LEVEL
Land Depression
600 Feet
6000 "

UNIT: Fáqûs

1:2,500,000

30 —
0   10   20 Miles
0   20 Kilometres

1:4,500,000

English Miles
0   20   50   80   100
Kilometres
0   50   100   150

Conic Projection

Boundaries ▬▬▬▪▪▪▪   Railways ▬▬▬   Canals ⌇⌇⌇   Sand Dune Areas ⬡   Rock Escarpments ⌐⌐⌐

Oil Pipe Lines ▬▪▬▪▬   Lava   Wells ˇ

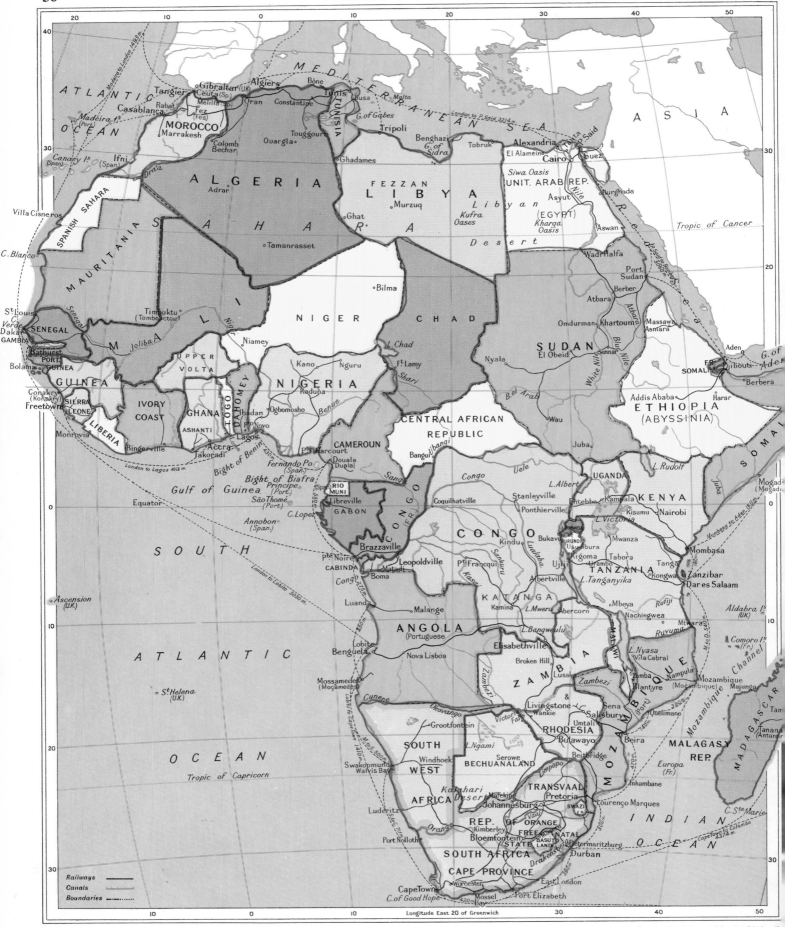

Railways
Canals
Boundaries

Lambert's Zenithal Equal-Area Projection

English Miles

1:35,000,000

Kilometres

©—John Bartholomew & Son.Ltd.,Edinburgh

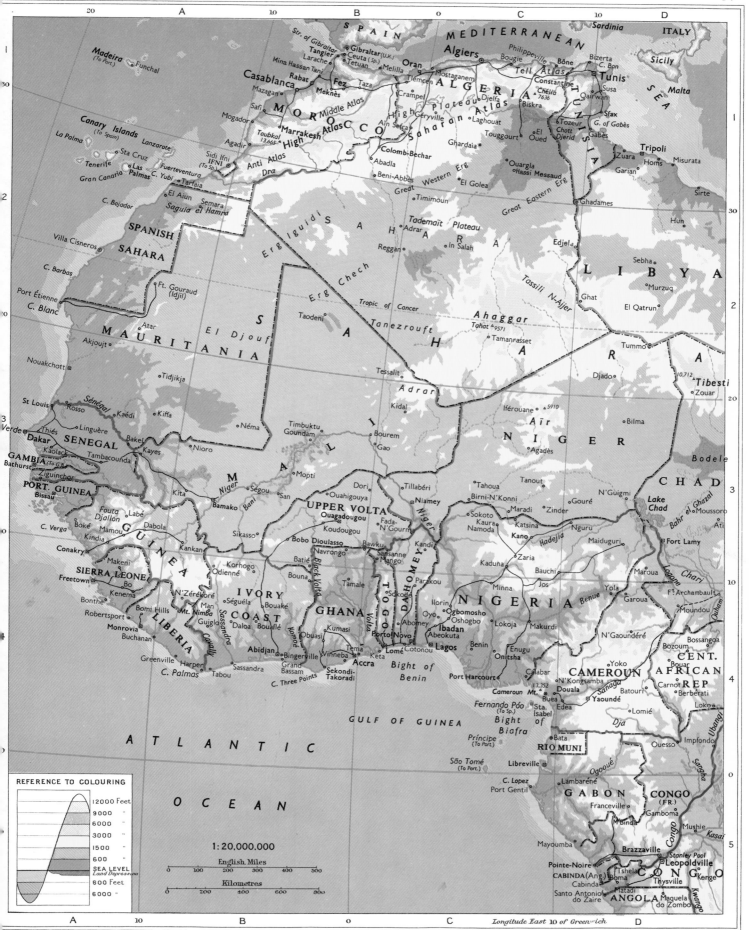

REFERENCE TO COLOURING

12000 Feet
9000 "
6000 "
3000 "
1500 "
600 "
SEA LEVEL
Land Depression
600 Feet
6000 "

1:20,000,000

English Miles
0   100   200   300   400   500

Kilometres
0   200   400   600   800

ller's Prolated Stereographic Projection

Railways ——— Marsh and Flood Areas
Boundaries

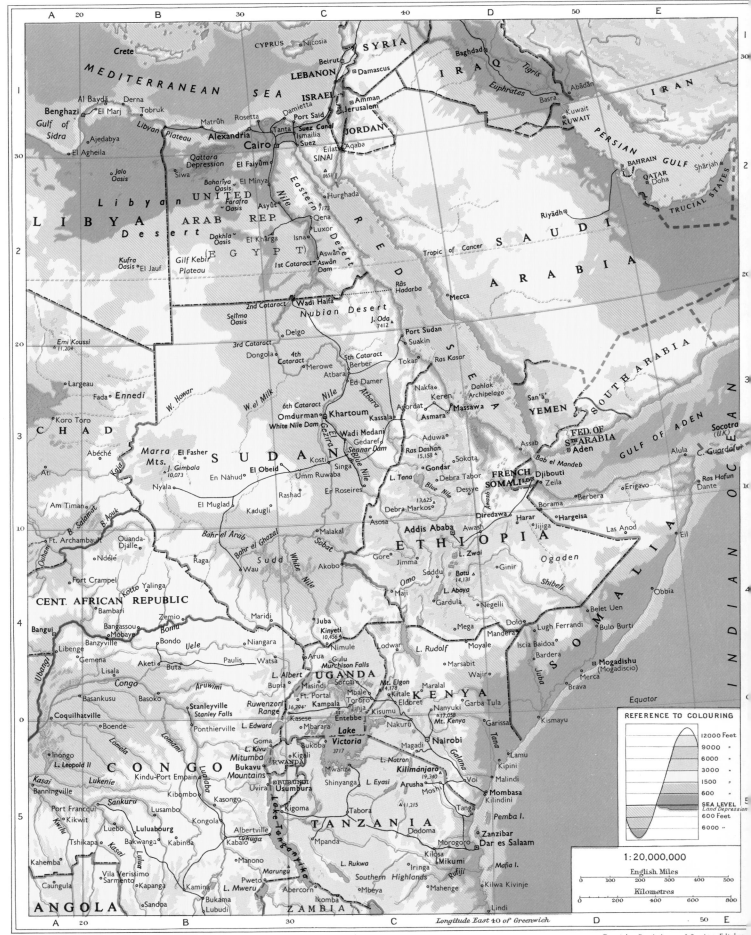

REFERENCE TO COLOURING

12000 Feet
9000
6000
3000
1500
600
SEA LEVEL
Land Depression
600 Feet
6000

1:20,000,000

English Miles

0   100   200   300   400   500

Kilometres

0   200   400   600   800

Longitude East 40 of Greenwich

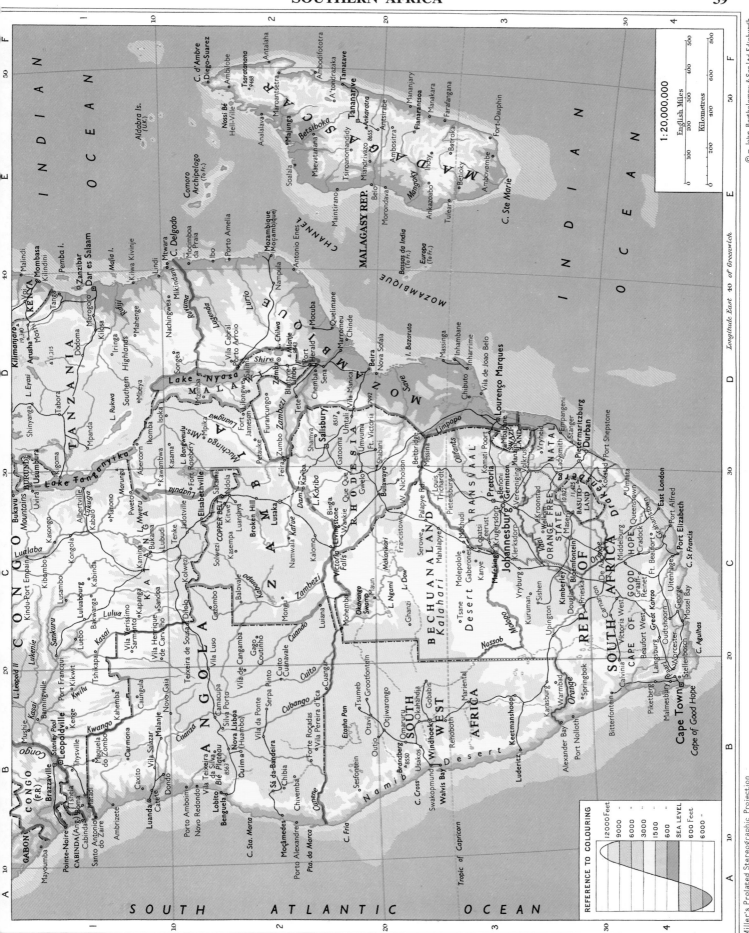

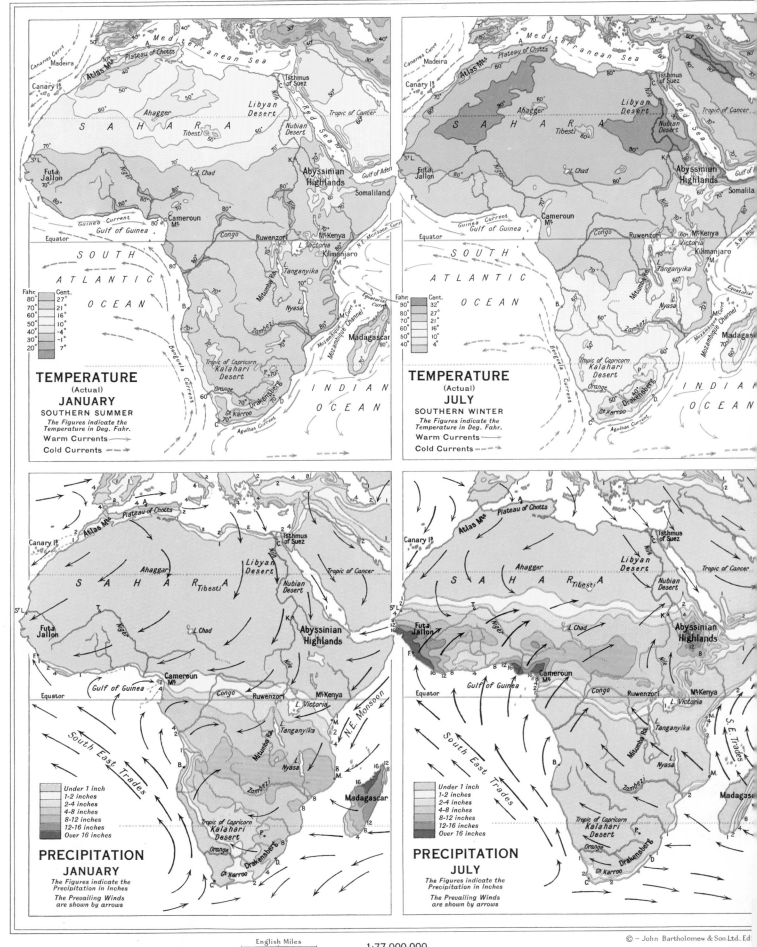

TEMPERATURE
(Actual)
JANUARY
SOUTHERN SUMMER
The Figures indicate the
Temperature in Deg. Fahr.
Warm Currents ——→
Cold Currents – – –→

Fahr.	Cent.
80°	27°
70°	21°
60°	16°
50°	10°
40°	4°
30°	-1°
20°	7°

TEMPERATURE
(Actual)
JULY
SOUTHERN WINTER
The Figures indicate the
Temperature in Deg. Fahr.
Warm Currents ——→
Cold Currents – – –→

Fahr.	Cent.
90°	32°
80°	27°
70°	21°
60°	16°
50°	10°
40°	4°

PRECIPITATION
JANUARY
The Figures indicate the
Precipitation in Inches
The Prevailing Winds
are shown by arrows

Under 1 inch
1-2 inches
2-4 inches
4-8 inches
8-12 inches
12-16 inches
Over 16 inches

PRECIPITATION
JULY
The Figures indicate the
Precipitation in Inches
The Prevailing Winds
are shown by arrows

Under 1 inch
1-2 inches
2-4 inches
4-8 inches
8-12 inches
12-16 inches
Over 16 inches

English Miles
0   500   1000

1:77,000,000

© – John Bartholomew & Son.Ltd.,Ed:

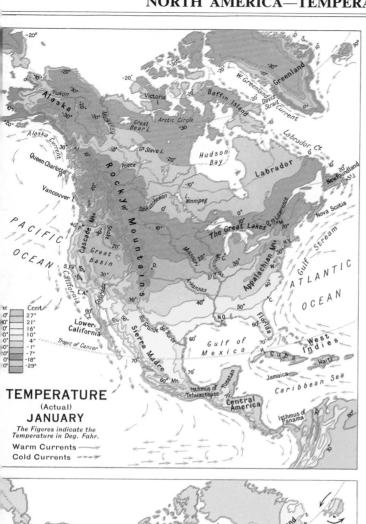

TEMPERATURE
(Actual)
JANUARY
The Figures indicate the
Temperature in Deg. Fahr.

Warm Currents →
Cold Currents →

Fahr.	Cent.
	27°
	21°
	16°
	10°
	4°
	-1°
	-7°
	-18°
	-29°

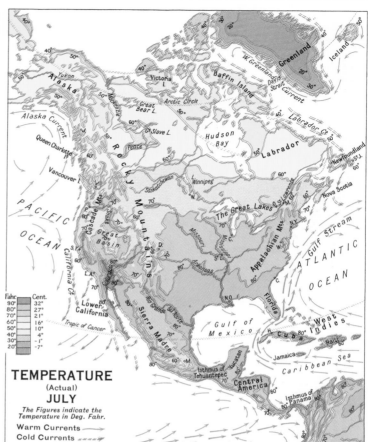

TEMPERATURE
(Actual)
JULY
The Figures indicate the
Temperature in Deg. Fahr.

Warm Currents →
Cold Currents →

Fahr.	Cent.
90°	32°
80°	27°
70°	21°
60°	16°
50°	10°
40°	4°
30°	-1°
20°	-7°

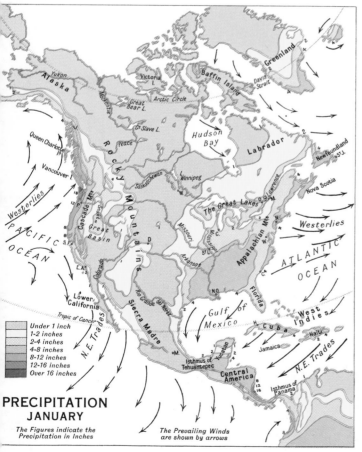

PRECIPITATION
JANUARY
The Figures indicate the
Precipitation in Inches

The Prevailing Winds
are shown by arrows

	Under 1 inch
	1-2 inches
	2-4 inches
	4-8 inches
	8-12 inches
	12-16 inches
	Over 16 inches

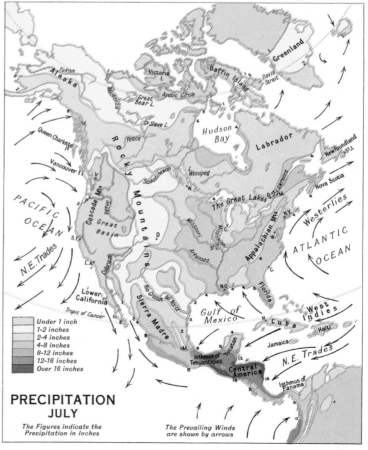

PRECIPITATION
JULY
The Figures indicate the
Precipitation in Inches

The Prevailing Winds
are shown by arrows

	Under 1 inch
	1-2 inches
	2-4 inches
	4-8 inches
	8-12 inches
	12-16 inches
	Over 16 inches

English Miles
0   500   1000

1:75,000,000

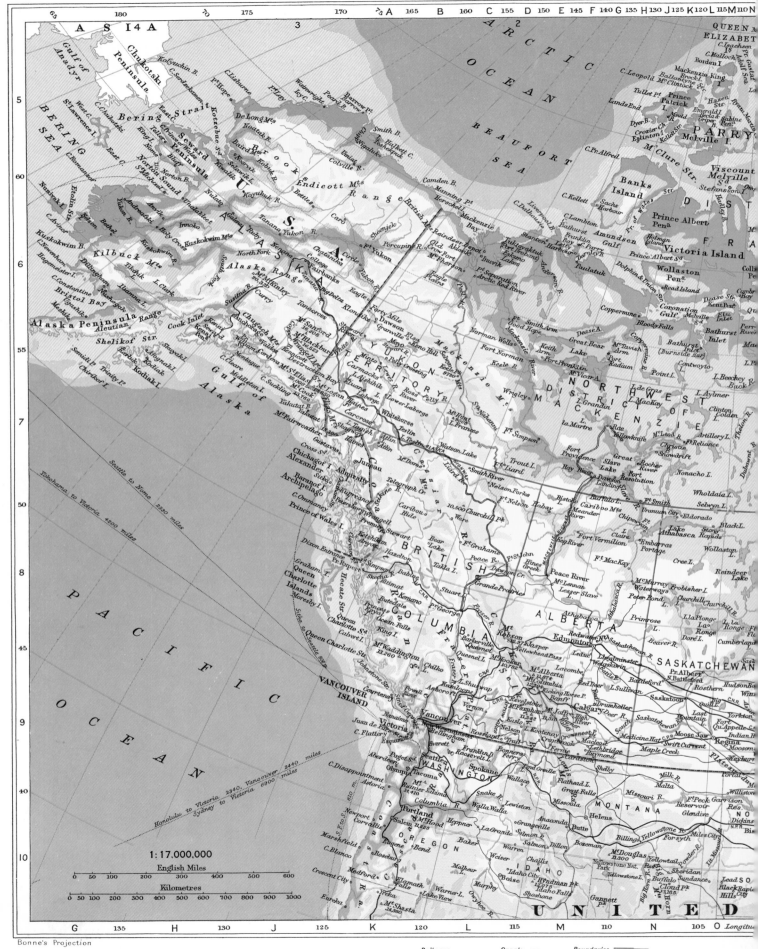

Railways ——— Canals ▭▭▭ ▭▭ Boundaries ▭▭▭▭

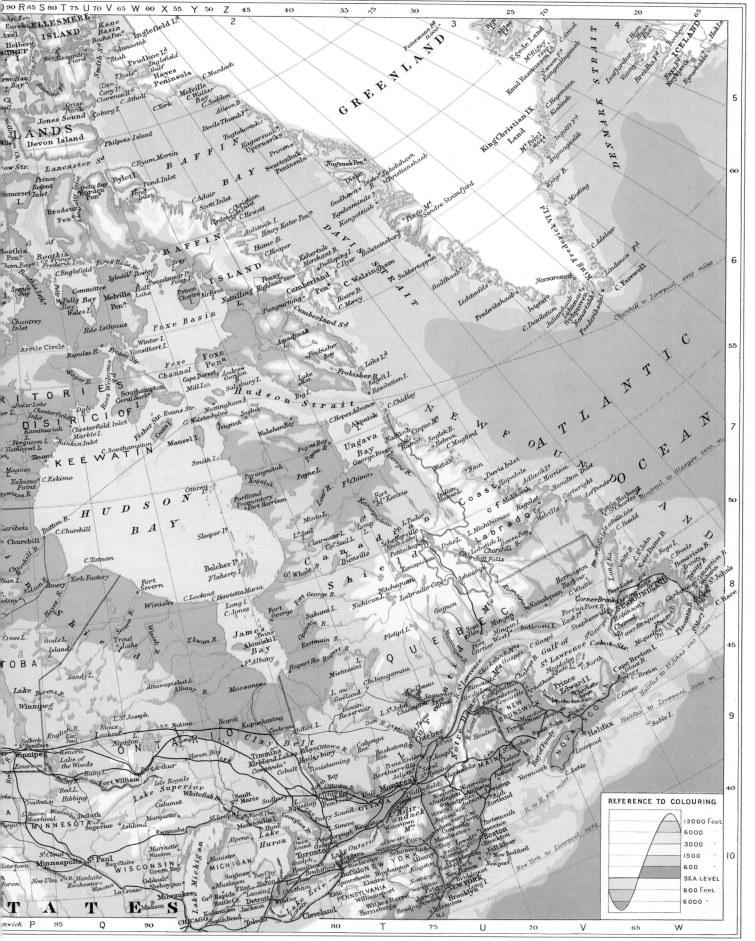

GREENLAND

DENMARK STRAIT

ICELAND

BAFFIN BAY

DAVIS STRAIT

ATLANTIC OCEAN

HUDSON BAY

HUDSON STRAIT

KEEWATIN

Ungava Bay

NEWFOUNDLAND

Labrador

JAMES BAY

QUEBEC

ONTARIO

NEW BRUNSWICK

NOVA SCOTIA

MICHIGAN

WISCONSIN

MINNESOTA

NEW YORK

PENNSYLVANIA

Lake Superior

Lake Huron

Lake Michigan

Lake Erie

Lake Ontario

REFERENCE TO COLOURING

12000 Feet
6000
3000
1500
600
SEA LEVEL
600 Feet
6000

© —John Bartholomew & Son, Ltd., Edinburgh

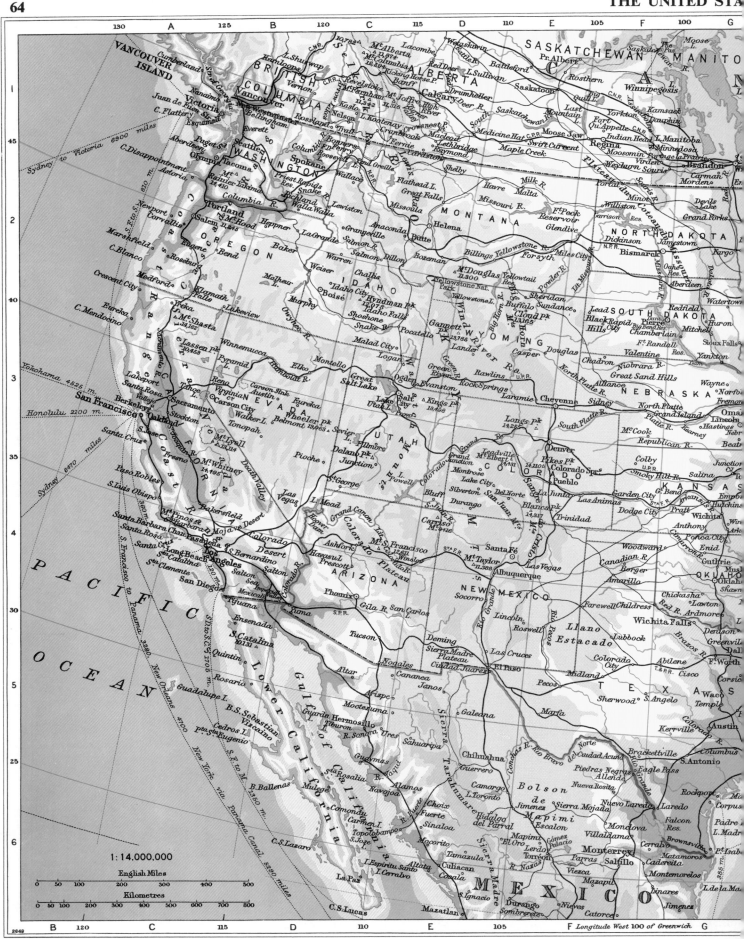

1:14,000,000

English Miles

Kilometres

Railways ——   *Canals* ----   *Boundaries* ———

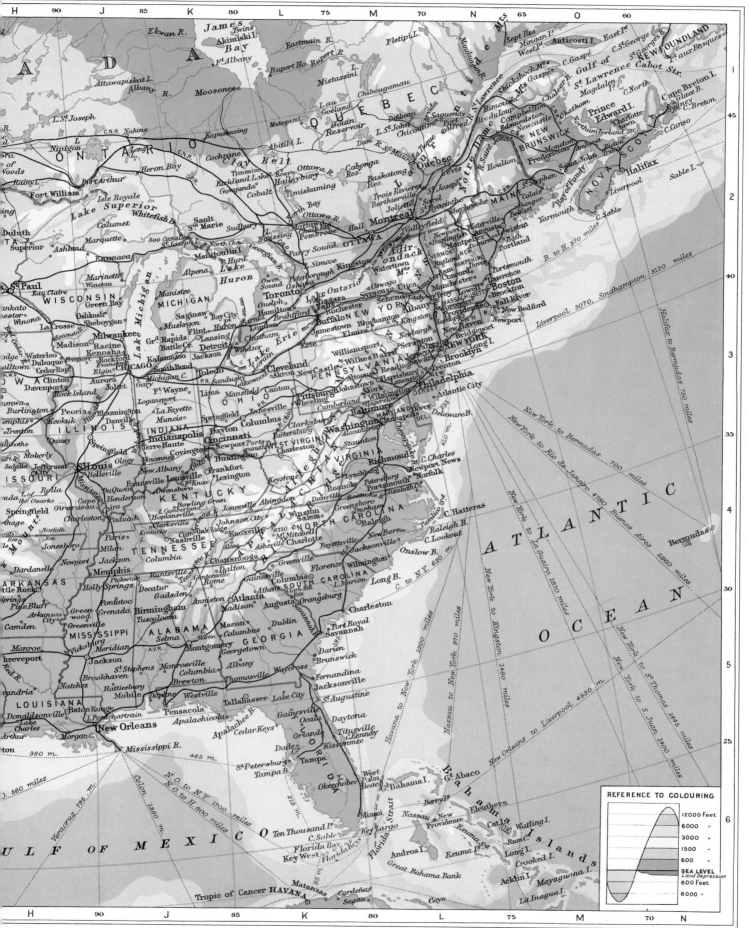

© — John Bartholomew & Son,Ltd.,Edinburgh

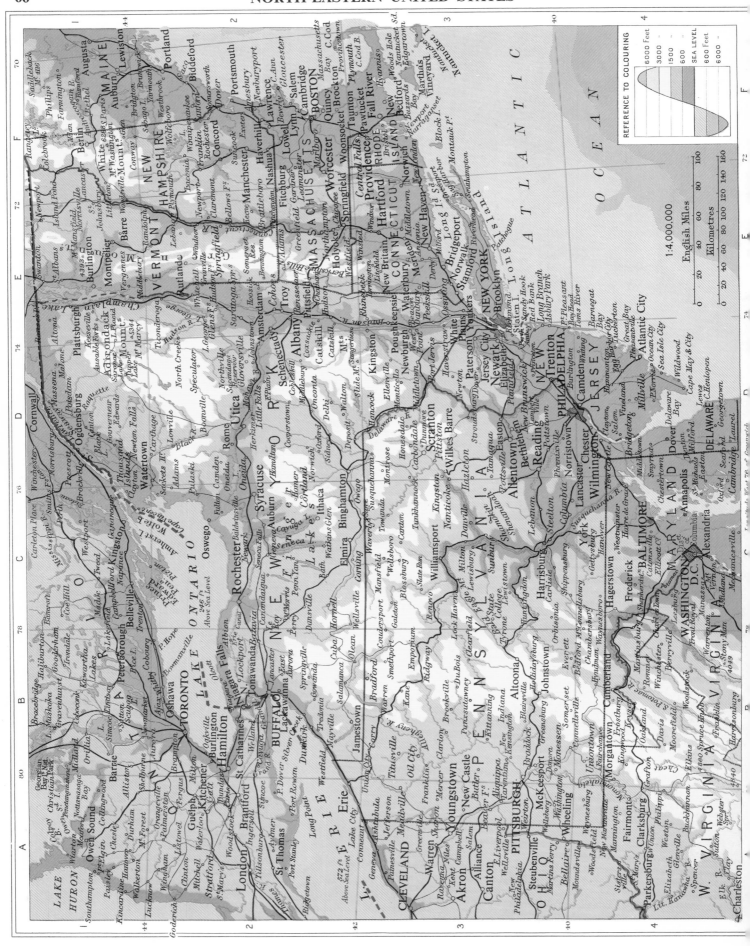

REFERENCE TO COLOURING

6000 Feet
3000
1500
600
SEA LEVEL
600
6000 Feet

1:4,000,000

English Miles
0   20   40   60   80   100
Kilometres
0   20   40   60   80 100 120 140 160

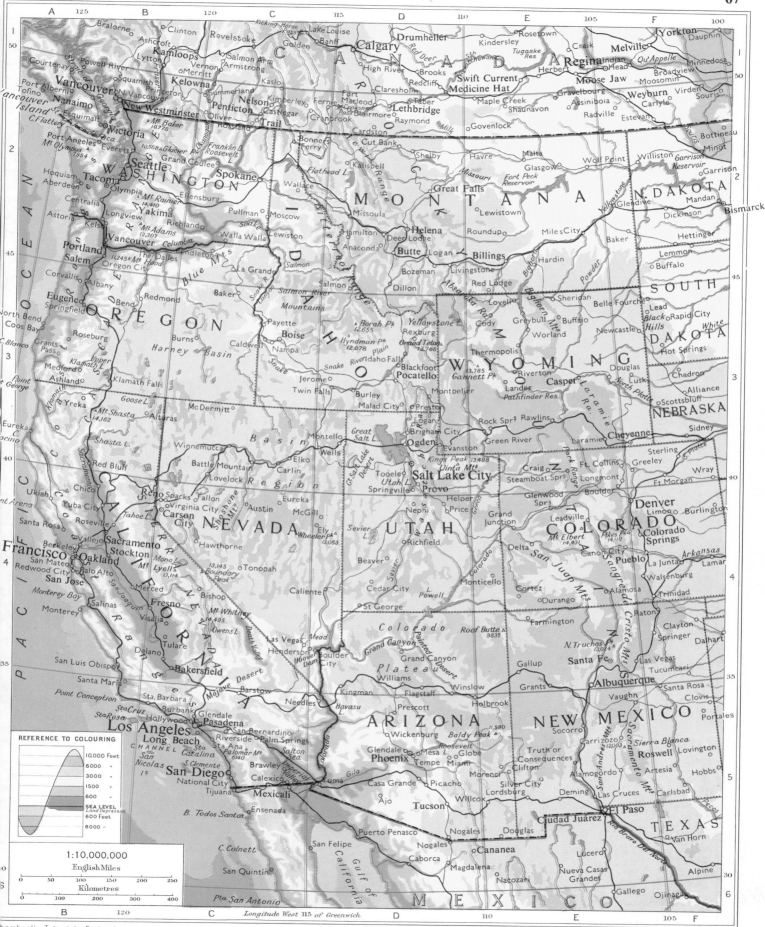

Chamberlin Trimetric Projection

© — John Bartholomew & Son Ltd., Edinburgh

REFERENCE TO COLOURING

10,000 Feet
6000 "
3000 "
1500 "
600 "
SEA LEVEL
Land Depression
600 Feet
6000 "

1:10,000,000
English Miles
0   50   100   150   200   250
Kilometres
0   100   200   300   400

Railways ——— Boundaries ▬▬▬

Longitude West 115 of Greenwich

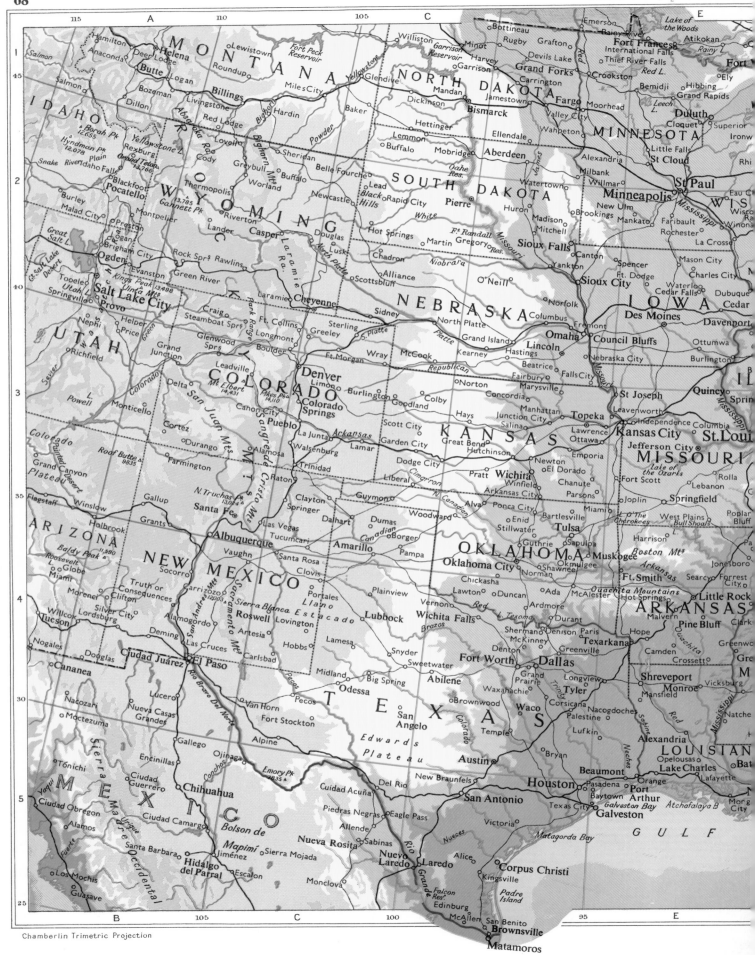

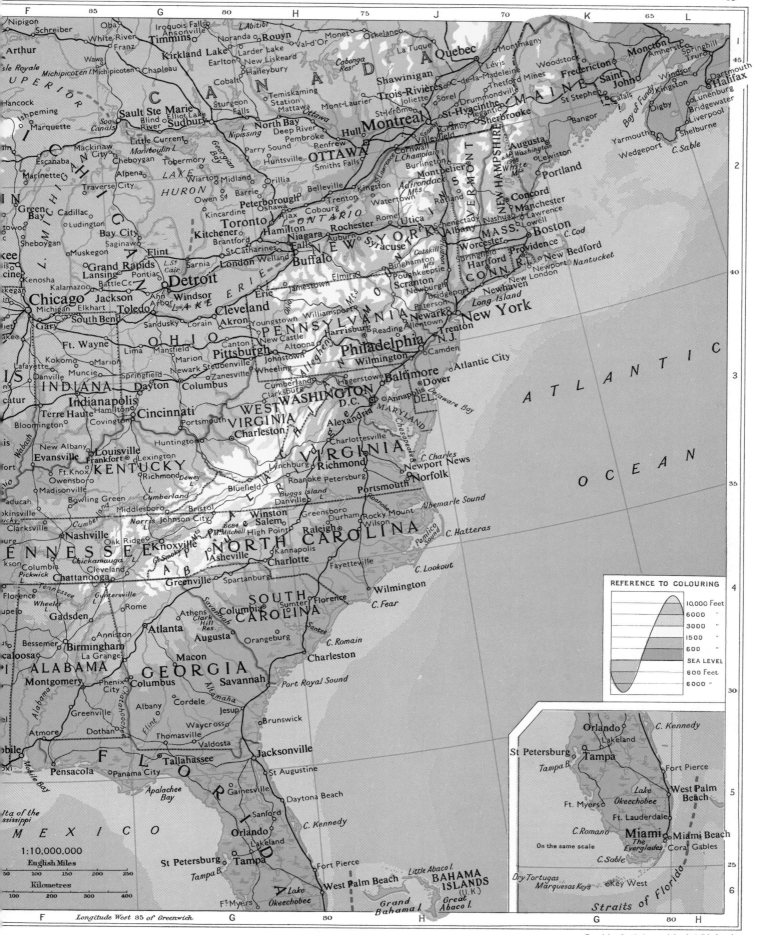

REFERENCE TO COLOURING

10,000 Feet
6000 "
3000 "
1500 "
600 "
SEA LEVEL
600 Feet
6000 "

1:10,000,000
English Miles
50   100   150   200   250
Kilometres
100   200   300   400

Longitude West 85 of Greenwich

Railways ——— Canals – – – Boundaries ———

© – John Bartholomew & Son. Ltd., Edinburgh

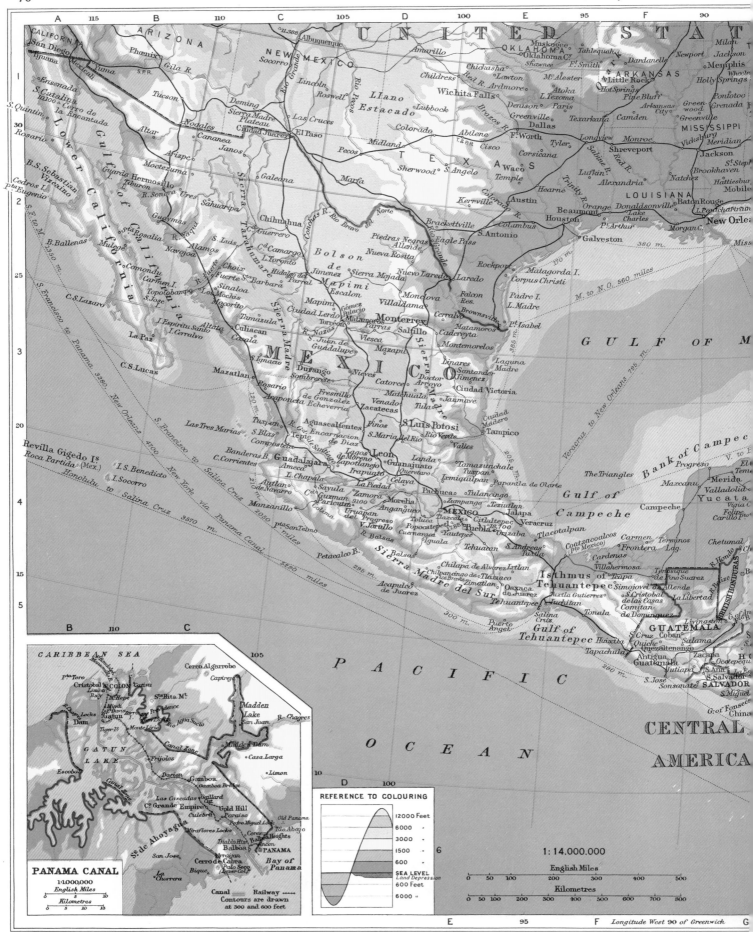

PANAMA CANAL
1:1,000,000
English Miles

Kilometres

REFERENCE TO COLOURING

12000 Feet
6000
3000
1500
600
SEA LEVEL
Land Depression
600 Feet
6000

1 : 14,000,000

English Miles
0 50 100   200   300   400   500

Kilometres
0 50 100 200 300 400 500 600 700 800

Railways ————   Canals ++++++   Boundaries ━━━━

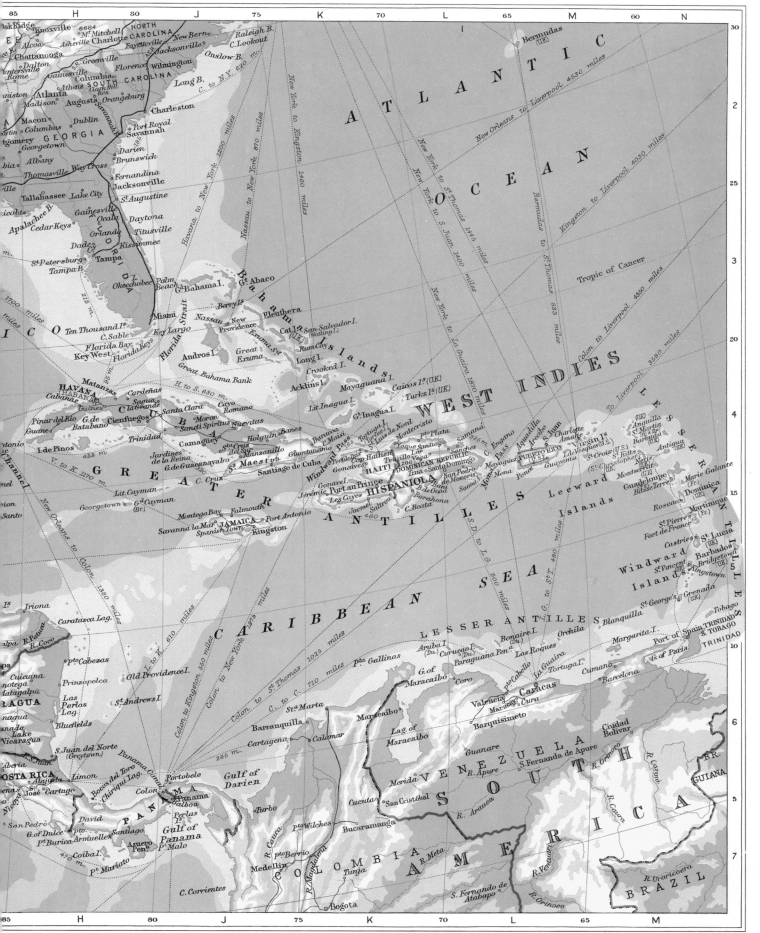

C A R I B B E A N S E A

N O R T H

A T L A N T I C O C E A N

Equator

Panama Canal   Colón   Portobelo   **PANAMA**   Panama   Gulf of Panama   Gulf of Darien

Dominica (UK)   Martinique (Fr)   St Lucia (UK)   Barbados   St Vincent (UK)   Grenada (UK)   **Windward Islands**

Aruba (Neth)   Curaçao   Bonaire (Neth)   Margarita   Tobago   TRINIDAD & TOBAGO   Port of Spain   Trinidad

Pta. Gallinas   Sta Marta   **Barranquilla**   Cartagena   Gulf of Venezuela   L. of Maracaibo   **Maracaibo**   Pto Cabello   La Guaira   **Caracas**   Valencia   Barquisimeto   Barcelona   Cumaná   Cerro de Merida   **VENEZUELA**

Turbo   Valdivia   Medellín   Manizales   Buenaventura   Cali   Popayán   Pasto   **COLOMBIA**   Bucaramanga   Cúcuta   San Cristóbal   Mérida   San Felix   El Pao   Maturín   Tucupita   Ciudad Bolívar   Cerro Bolívar   Orinoco   Arauca   Calabozo   Puerto Ayacucho   San Fernando de Atabapo

Tunja   **Bogotá**   Ibagué   Neiva   Florencia   Magdalena   Magdalena Basin

Paramaribo   **SURINAM (NETH. GUIANA)**   Cayenne   **FRENCH GUIANA**   Moengo   Kabel   **BRITISH GUIANA**   Georgetown   New Amsterdam   Mackenzie   Parika   Kaieteur Falls   Essequibo   Angel Falls 9094   Roraima   G U I A N A   H I G H L A N D S

Maraca I.   Mouths of the Amazon   I. of Marajó   **Belem (Pará)**   Macapá   Terezinha   Amazon   Obidos   Santarem   Fordlandia   Manaus   Manicoré   Negro   Barcelos   Uaupés   Boa Vista   Fonte Boa   Japura   Amazon (Solimões)   Purus   Juruá

São Luis   Parnaiba   Caxias   Pedreiras   Tijoca   Tocantins   Xingú   Tapajós   Teles Pires (São Manuel)   Barra do São Manuel   Canudos   Jurema

Fortaleza   Cascavel   Branca   Camocim   Sousa   Teresina   Floriano   Piripiri   Campo Maior   Natal   C. de São Roque   João Pessoa   **Recife (Pernambuco)**   Campina Grande   Maceió   Aracaju   Paulo Afonso Falls   São Francisco   **Salvador (Bahia)**   Macau   Angical   Juazeiro   Senhor do Bonfim   Feira de Santana   Nazaré   Itabuna   Ilheus   Caravelas

B R A Z I L   Serra Geral de Goiás   Carol   Marabá   Goiás   Goiás Massif   Anápolis   **FEDERAL DISTRICT: Brasília**   Goiânia   Serra do Roncador   Araguaia   Tocantins

Januário   Barra   Montes Claros   Diamantina   Piraporá   **MINAS GERAIS**   São Francisco   Jequitinhonha   Uberlândia   Sdos de Espinhaço   ESPIRITO SANTO

M A T T O G R O S S O   Plateau of Mato Grosso   Cuiabá   Mato Grosso   Serra dos Parecis   Guaporé   Guaporé   Corumbá   Pto. Suarez   San José   Plateau

Porto Velho   Rio Branco   Cruzeiro do Sul   Guajará Mirim   Riberalta   Beni   Madeira   Llanos de Mojos   Trinidad   Sta Ana   Guayos   Santa Cruz   **BOLIVIA**   Cochabamba   Sucre   Mizque   Oruro   **La Paz**   Illampu 23,012   Illimani 22,579   L. Titicaca   Guaqui   Puno   Popo   Sajama 22,214

S e l v a s   Leticia   Río Branco   Madre de Dios   **Cuzco (Cusco)**   Abancay   Machu Picchu   Ayacucho   Arequipa   Matarani   Mollendo   Tacna   Arica

Mitú   Vaupés   Caquetá   Putumayo   Napo   Amazon   Iquitos   Marañón   Ucayali   Pucallpa   Huallaga   Cerro de Pasco   La Oroya   Huánuco   Huancayo   **P E R U**   Montaña   La Montaña   Cordillera Occidental

Quito   Otavalo   Latacunga   Cotopaxi 19,347   Ambato   Chimborazo 20,577   Riobamba   Sangay 17,464   **ECUADOR**   **Guayaquil**   Manta   Cuenca   Loja   Morona   Gulf of Guayaquil   San Lorenzo   Tumaco   Esmeraldas

Paita   Sechura Desert   Piura   Talara   Chiclayo   Pacasmayo   Cajamarca   Trujillo   Chimbote   Huascarán 22,205   Huaraz   Goyllarisquizga   Paramonga   **Lima**   Callao   Pisco   San Juan   Huancavelica   Portuguesa   Cordillera Central

C O R D I L L E R A O C C I D E N T A L   C O R D I L L E R A C E N T R A L   Yungas

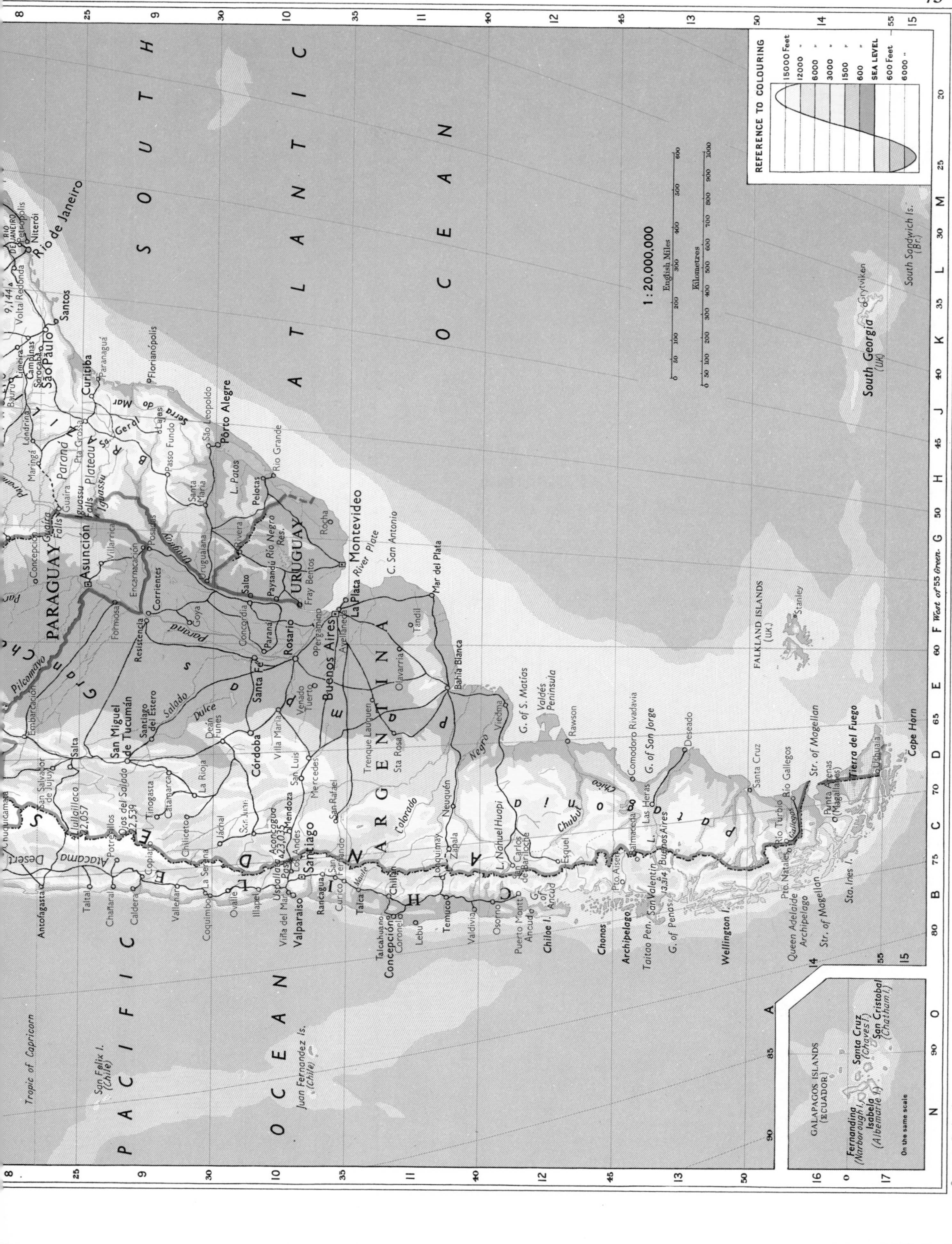

PACIFIC OCEAN

ATLANTIC OCEAN

SOUTH

Rio de Janeiro
RIO DE JANEIRO
Niterói
Petrópolis
Volta Redonda
9,144
Barra
Resende
São Paulo
Santos
Sorocaba
Campinas
Lineira
Bauru
Londrina
Maringá
Curitiba
Paranaguá
Florianópolis
Lajes
São Leopoldo
Pôrto Alegre
Pelotas
Rio Grande
L. Patos
Santa Maria
Passo Fundo
Guaíra Falls
Iguassu Falls
Iguassu
Paraná
Pta. Porá
Paraná Plateau
Serra do Mar
Serra Geral
BRAZIL

PARAGUAY
Asunción
Concepción
Villarrica
Encarnación
Posadas
Corrientes
Resistencia
Formosa
Goya
Gran Chaco
Pilcomayo
Embarcación
San Salvador de Jujuy
Salta
Tullaillaco 22,057
Ojos del Salado 22,539
Antofagasta
Tattal
Chañaral
Caldera
Copiapó
Vallenar
Coquimbo
La Serena
Ovalle
Illapel
Valparaíso
Viña del Mar
Santiago
Rancagua
San Fernando
Curicó
Talca
Chillán
Concepción
Talcahuano
Coronel
Lebu
Temuco
Valdivia
Osorno
Puerto Montt
Ancud
Chiloé I.
G. of Ancud
Chonos Archipelago
Taitao Pen.
San Valentin 13,314
G. of Peñas
Wellington I.
Queen Adelaide Archipelago
Sta. Inés I.
Str. of Magellan
Punta Arenas (Magallanes)
Tierra del Fuego
Ushuaia
Cape Horn

ARGENTINA
San Miguel de Tucumán
Santiago del Estero
Catamarca
Tinogasta
La Rioja
Córdoba
Villa María
San Luis
Mendoza
San Rafael
Aconcagua 23,035
Uspallata
Mercedes
Dean Funes
Dulce
Salado
Rosario
Santa Fe
Paraná
Concordia
Salto
Paysandú
Fray Bentos
Rogha
Rivera
Río Negro Res.
URUGUAY
Montevideo
La Plata River Plate
Buenos Aires
Avellaneda
Pergamino
Olavarría
Tandil
C. San Antonio
Mar del Plata
Bahía Blanca
Trenque Lauquen
Sta. Rosa
General Acha
Neuquén
Zapala
Loncoquimay
L. Nahuel Huapi
San Carlos de Bariloche
Esquel
Colorado
Negro
Chubut
Chubut
Chico
Viedma
Rawson
Valdés Peninsula
G. of S. Matías
G. of San Jorge
Comodoro Rivadavia
Deseado
Las Heras
Balmaceda
Pto. Aisén
Pto. Natales
Río Turbio
Río Gallegos
Santa Cruz
Str. of Magellan

FALKLAND ISLANDS (U.K.)
Stanley

South Georgia (U.K.)
Grytviken

South Sandwich Is. (Br.)

Tropic of Capricorn

San Félix I. (Chile)
Juan Fernandez Is. (Chile)

1 : 20,000,000

REFERENCE TO COLOURING
15000 Feet
12000
6000
3000
1500
600
SEA LEVEL
600 Feet
6000

English Miles
Kilometres

Sanson's Projection

© – John Bartholomew & Son, Ltd., Edinburgh

Railways ——— Canals
Boundaries

West of 55 Green.

GALAPAGOS ISLANDS (ECUADOR)
Fernandina (Narborough I.)
Isabela (Albemarle I.)
Santa Cruz (Chaves I.)
San Cristóbal (Chatham I.)
On the same scale

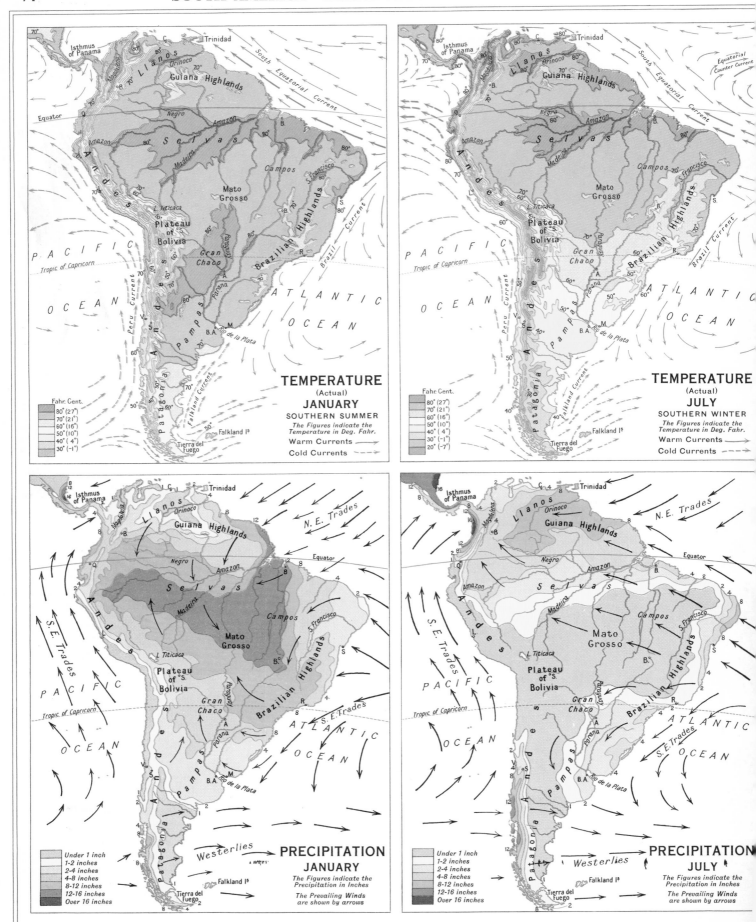

TEMPERATURE
(Actual)
JANUARY
SOUTHERN SUMMER
The Figures indicate the Temperature in Deg. Fahr.
Warm Currents →
Cold Currents ⇢

Fahr. Cent.	
80° (27°)	
70° (21°)	
60° (16°)	
50° (10°)	
40° (4°)	
30° (-1°)	

TEMPERATURE
(Actual)
JULY
SOUTHERN WINTER
The Figures indicate the Temperature in Deg. Fahr.
Warm Currents →
Cold Currents ⇢

Fahr. Cent.	
80° (27°)	
70° (21°)	
60° (16°)	
50° (10°)	
40° (4°)	
30° (-1°)	
20° (-7°)	

PRECIPITATION
JANUARY
The Figures indicate the Precipitation in Inches
The Prevailing Winds are shown by arrows

	Under 1 inch
	1-2 inches
	2-4 inches
	4-8 inches
	8-12 inches
	12-16 inches
	Over 16 inches

PRECIPITATION
JULY
The Figures indicate the Precipitation in Inches
The Prevailing Winds are shown by arrows

	Under 1 inch
	1-2 inches
	2-4 inches
	4-8 inches
	8-12 inches
	12-16 inches
	Over 16 inches

English Miles
0   500   1000

1 : 64,000,000

© — John Bartholomew & Son Ltd. Edin

TEMPERATURE
(Actual)
JULY
SOUTHERN WINTER

The Figures indicate the
Temperature in Deg. Fahr.

Warm Currents
Cold Currents

TEMPERATURE
(Actual)
JANUARY
SOUTHERN SUMMER

The Figures indicate the
Temperature in Deg. Fahr.

Warm Currents
Cold Currents

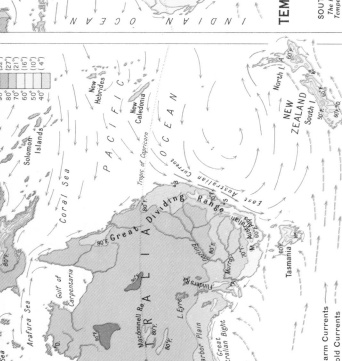

PRECIPITATION
JULY

The Figures indicate the
Precipitation in Inches

The Prevailing Winds
are shown by arrows

PRECIPITATION
JANUARY

The Figures indicate the
Precipitation in Inches

The Prevailing Winds
are shown by arrows

Under 1 inch
1-2 inches
2-4 inches
4-8 inches
8-12 inches
12-16 inches
Over 16 inches

© – John Bartholomew & Son. Ltd. Edinburgh

1:52,000,000

English Miles

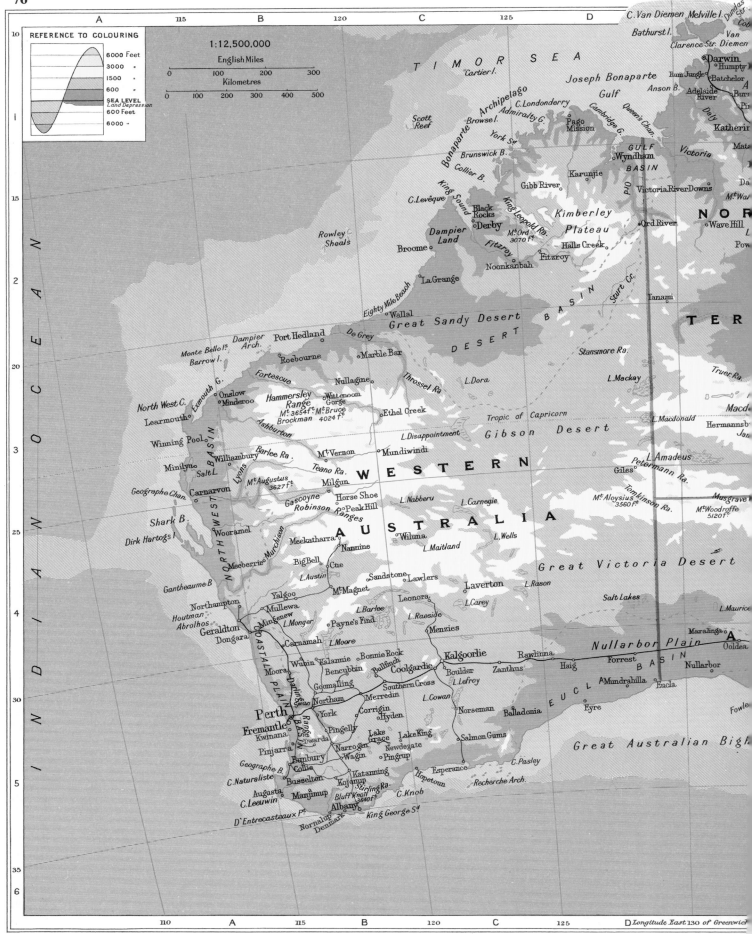

REFERENCE TO COLOURING

6000 Feet
3000 "
1500 "
600 "
SEA LEVEL
Land Depression
600 Feet
6000 "

1:12,500,000

English Miles
0   100   200   300

Kilometres
0   100   200   300   400   500

TIMOR SEA

Cartier I.

C. Van Diemen Melville I. Dundas
Bathurst I.
Clarence Str. Diemen
Van
Darwin
Humpty
Rum Jungle   Batchelor
Adelaide   Pi
River
Katherin
Mata

Joseph Bonaparte
Gulf
Anson B.

Scott Reef
Browse I.   C. Londonderry   Admiralty G.   Pago Mission
Bonaparte   Archipelago
York Sd
Brunswick B.
Collier B.   King Sd   GULF
Cambridge G.   Queen's Chan.   BASIN
Wyndham
Ord
Victoria
C. Levêque   Black Rocks   King Leopold Ra.   Gibb River   Victoria River Downs   Mt Wa
Derby   Mt Ord   Kimberley   Ord River   Mt Wave Hill
Dampier   3070 ft   Plateau   Pow
Land   Halls Creek
Rowley Shoals   Fitzroy   Fitzroy
Broome   Noonkanbah
La Grange   Sturt Cr.   Tanami

N O R
T E R

Eighty Mile Beach   Wallal   Great Sandy Desert   DESERT   BASIN
Stansmore Ra.   Truer Ra
Port Hedland   De Grey
Dampier Arch.   Roebourne   Marble Bar   L. Dora   L. Mackay
Monte Bello Is.   Nullagine   Throssel Ra   L. Macdonald   Macd
Barrow I.   Throssel Ra   Hermannsb
Fortescue   Wittenoom   Tropic of Capricorn   Jan
North West C.   Onslow   Hammersley   Gorge   Ethel Creek   Gibson   Desert
Learmouth   Minderoo   Range   L. Disappointment
Mt 3654ft Mt Bruce   Mt Vernon   L. Amadeus   Petermann Ra.
Brockman   4024 ft   Ashburton   Mundiwindi   Giles   Tomkinson Ra.
Winning Pool   Teano Ra   W E S T E R N   Mt Aloysius   Mt Woodroffe
Williambury   Barlee Ra.   Milgun   3560 ft   5120 ft   Musgrave
Minilya   Salt L.   Mt Augustus   Horse Shoe   L. Nabberu   A U S T R A L I A   Great Victoria Desert
Geographe Chan.   Carnarvon   3627 ft   Gascoyne   Peak Hill   L. Carnegie
Shark B.   Robinson Ranges   Wiluna   L. Wells
Dirk Hartogs I.   Wooramel   Meekatharra   L. Maitland
Gantheaume B   Meeberrie   Murchison   Nannine   Salt Lakes
Big Bell   Sandstone   Lawlers   Laverton   L. Rason
L. Austin   Cue   Leonora   L. Carey   L. Maurice
Houtman   Yalgoo   Mt Magnet   L. Raeside   Maralinga
Abrolhos   Mullewa   L. Barlee   Menzies   Nullarbor Plain   Ooldea
Northampton   Mingenew   Payne's Find   Zanthus   Forrest   Haig   Nullarbor
Geraldton   L. Monger   Kalgoorlie   Rawlinna   EUCL   BASIN
Dongara   Carnamah   L. Moore   Coolgardie   Boulder   BASIN
Wubin   Bonnie Rock   Southern Cross   L. Lefroy   Mundrabilla   Eucla
Moora   Kalannie   Ballfinch   L. Cowan   Norseman   Eyre   Fowle
Bencubbin   Merredin   Balladonia   Great Australian Bigh
Perth   Goomalling   Corrigin   Salmon Gums   C. Pasley
Fremantle   Swan   Northam   Hyden   Recherche Arch.
Kwinana   York   Lake Grace   Lake King   Esperance
Pinjarra   Dwarda   Narrogin   Newdegate   Hopetoun   C. Knob
Geographe B.   Pingelly   Wagin   Pingrup
C. Naturaliste   Collie   Kojonup   Bluff Knoll
Bunbury   Katanning   3640 ft   King George Sd
Busselton   Stirling Ra.
Augusta   Manjimup
C. Leeuwin   Albany
D'Entrecasteaux Pt   Nornalup   Denmark

N O R T H   W E S T   B A S I N
Exmouth G.
Lyons
Darling   Range
COASTAL   PLAIN

I N D I A N   O C E A N

Bonne's Projection

Railways ———   Dry Salt Lakes -----   Artesian Basin Limits ⌒⌒⌒   Boundaries ▬▬▬

D Longitude East 130 of Greenwich
110   A   115   B   120   C   125

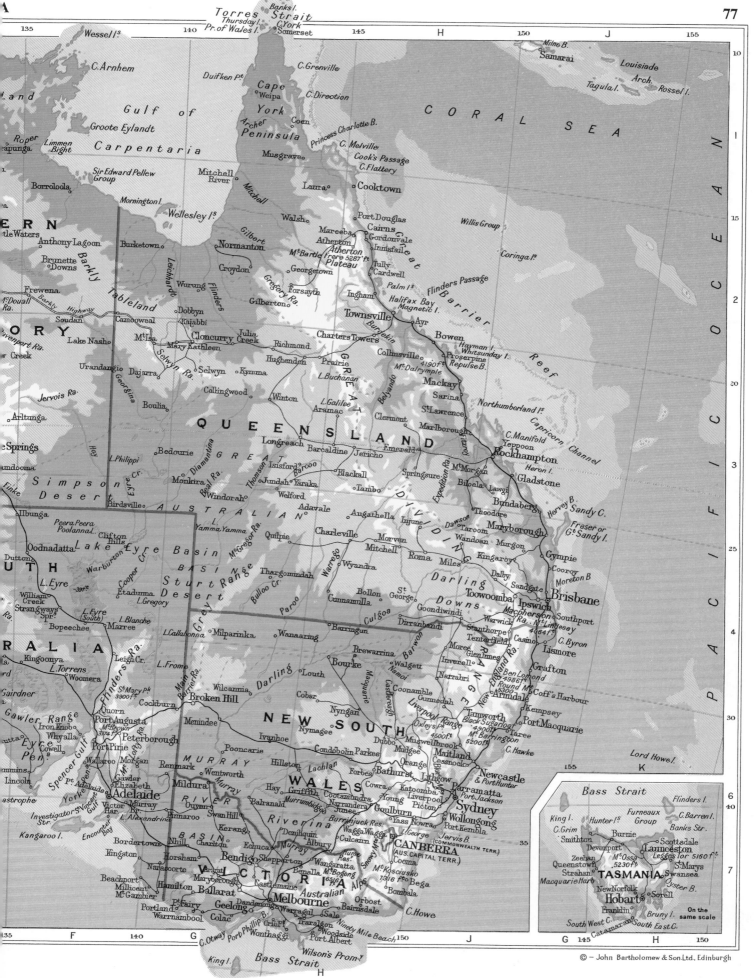

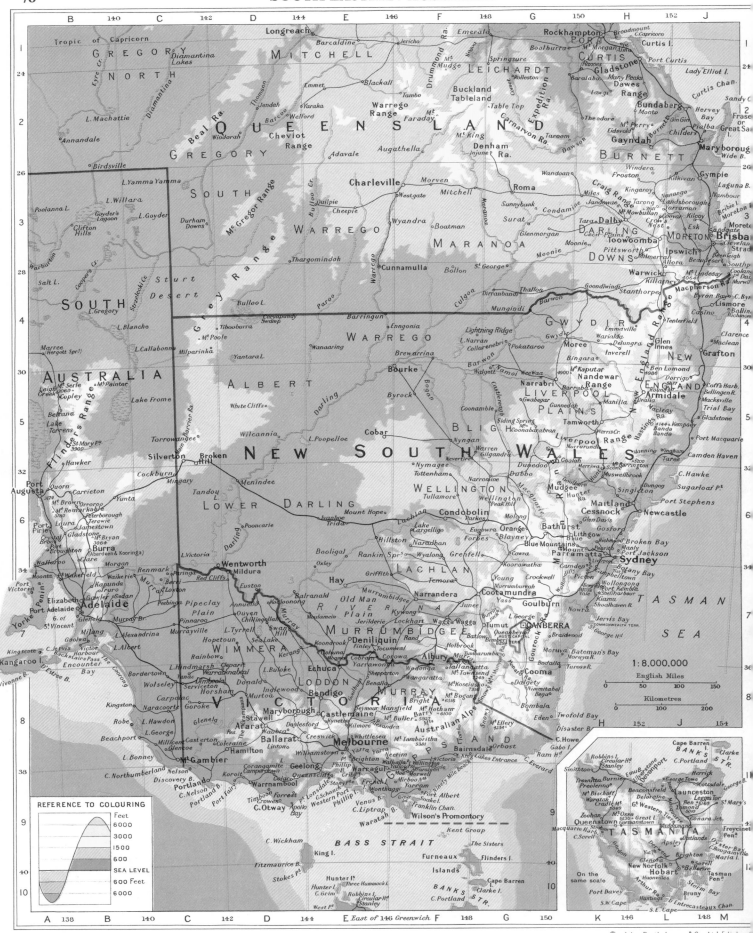

Railways ———

Dry Salt Lakes

Boundaries

© – John Bartholomew & Son Ltd. Edinburgh

THE ANTIPODES
New Zealand names are printed in
heavy lettering thus — Auckland
European and African names are
in light lettering thus — Paris

REFERENCE TO COLOURING

	12000 Feet
	6000 "
	3000 "
	1500 "
	600 "
	SEA LEVEL
	600 Feet
	6000 "

1:6,000,000

English Miles

Kilometres

Statistical Area Boundaries ....   Railways _____   © — John Bartholomew & Son.Ltd. Edinburgh

Polar Regions

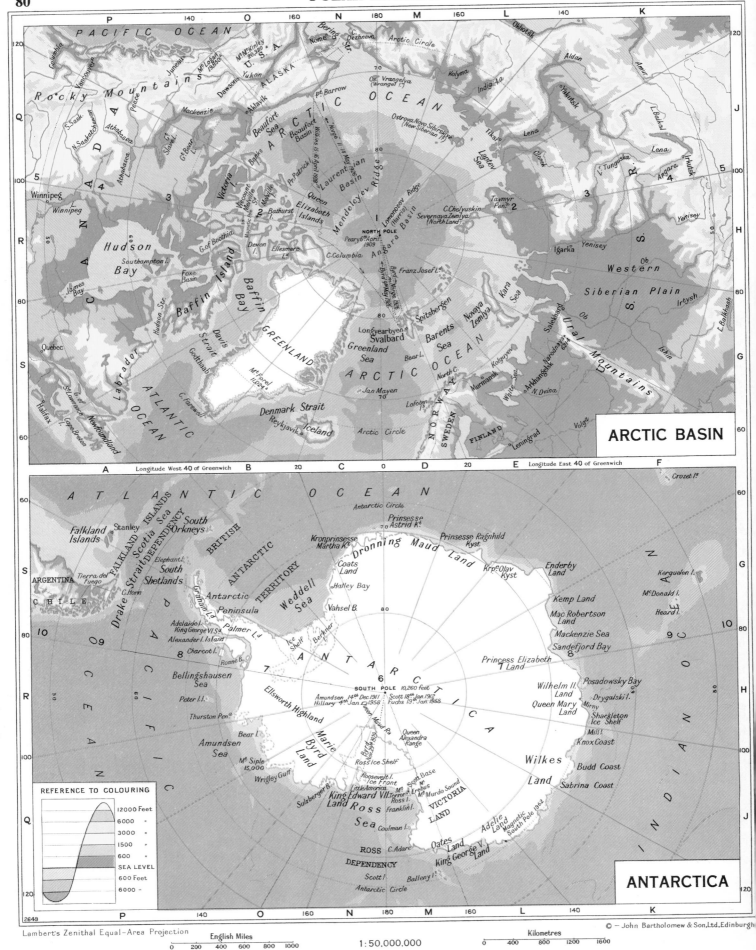

ARCTIC BASIN

PACIFIC OCEAN

Columbia · Juneau · Vancouver I. · Mt. Logan 19,850 · Mt. McKinley 20,300 · U.S.A. · Nome · Bering Str. · C. Dezhneva · Arctic Circle · Okhotsk

Rocky Mountains · Dawson · ALASKA · Yukon · Aklavik · Pt. Barrow · Wilkins 15-16 April 1928 · Os. Vrangelya (Wrangel I.) · Kolyma · Aldan · Amur

CANADA · Peace · Mackenzie · Beaufort Sea · Beaufort Basin · Nansen 21-24 May 1926 · ARCTIC OCEAN · Indigirka · Yakutsk · L. Baikal · Lena · Angara · Irkutsk

S. Sask. · N. Saskatchewan · Athabasca · Gt. Slave L. · Gt. Bear L. · Banks · Melville I. · Pr. Patrick I. · Laurentian Basin · Tiksi · Lena · Olenek · L. Tungiska

Winnipeg · L. Winnipeg · Victoria · Melville Pen. · Bathurst · Elizabeth Islands · Queen · North Pole · Peary 6th April 1909 · Amundsen Basin · Severnaya Zemlya (North Land) · C. Chelyuskin · Taymyr Pen. · Yenisey

Hudson Bay · Southampton I. · G. of Boothia · Devon · Ellesmere Ld. · Byrd & May 1926 · Franz Josef Ld. · Western

James Bay · Foxe Basin · Baffin Island · Davis Strait · Hudson Str. · Greenland · Longyearbyen · Svalbard · Spitsbergen · Barents Sea · Novaya Zemlya · Kara Sea · Igarka · Yenisey · Siberian Plain · Irtysh

Quebec · Labrador · Baffin Bay · Godthaab · Mt. Forel 11,024 · Greenland Sea · Bear I. · North C. · Kolguyev · Salekhard · Narodnaya 6214 · Ural Mountains · L. Balkhash

G. of St. Lawrence · Halifax · Cape Breton I. · Newfoundland · ATLANTIC OCEAN · Denmark Strait · Reykjavik · Iceland · Jan Mayen · Lofoten · Murmansk · White Sea · Arkhangelsk · N. Dvina · Ishim

Arctic Circle · NORWAY · SWEDEN · FINLAND · Leningrad · Volga

Longitude West 40 of Greenwich · Longitude East 40 of Greenwich

ANTARCTICA

ATLANTIC OCEAN · Crozet I.

Falkland Islands · Stanley · FALKLAND ISLANDS DEPENDENCY · Scotia Sea · South Orkneys · South · BRITISH · Antarctic Circle · Prinsesse Astrid Kt. · Prinsesse Ragnhild Kyst · Enderby Land · Kerguelen I.

ARGENTINA · Tierra del Fuego · C. Horn · Drake Strait · Elephant I. · South Shetlands · ANTARCTIC · Kronprinsesse Martha Kt. · Dronning Maud Land · Krp. Olav Kyst · McDonald I.

CHILE · Graham Ld. · Antarctic Peninsula · TERRITORY · Coats Land · Halley Bay · Kemp Land · Heard I.

Adelaide I. · King George VI S. · Palmer Ld. · Weddell Sea · Vahsel B. · Mac Robertson Land · Mackenzie Sea

Alexander I. Island · Charcot I. · Ice Shelf · Berkner I. · Sandefjord Bay · Princess Elizabeth Land

Ronne B. · ANTARCTICA · Wilhelm II. Land · Posadowsky Bay · Drygalski I.

Bellingshausen Sea · SOUTH POLE 10,260 feet · Queen Mary Land · Mirny · Shackleton Ice Shelf

Peter I. I. · Amundsen 14th Dec 1911 · Scott 18th Jan 1912 · Ellsworth Highland · Hillary 4th Jan 1958 · Fuchs 19th Jan 1958 · Mill I. · Knox Coast

Thurston Pen. · Queen Alexandra Range · Wilkes Land

Bear I. · Amundsen Sea · Marie Byrd Land · Budd Coast

Mt. Siple 15,000 · Wrigley Gulf · Ross Ice Shelf · Roosevelt I. · Ice Front · Little America · Mt. Terror · Mt. Erebus · Scott Base · McMurdo Sound · Sabrina Coast

Sulzberger B. · King Edward VII Land · Ross Sea · Franklin I. · VICTORIA LAND · Adelie Land · Magnetic South Pole 1962

ROSS DEPENDENCY · C. Adare · Oates Land · King George V. Land

Scott I. · Balleny I. · Antarctic Circle

PACIFIC OCEAN · INDIAN OCEAN

REFERENCE TO COLOURING

12000 Feet
6000 "
3000 "
1500 "
600 "
SEA LEVEL
600 Feet
6000 "

0 200 400 600 800 1000
0 400 800 1200 1600

ABBREVIATIONS

Afghan. = Afghanistan
Afr. = Africa(n)
Antarct. = Antarctica
Arch. = Archipelago
Arg. = Argentina
Ark. = Arkansas
Aust. = Australia
B. = Bay
B.C. = British Columbia
Br. = British
Braz. = Brazil
C. = Cape
Can. = Canada, Canal
Cent. = Central
Chan. = Channel
Co. = County
Cord. = Cordillera
Cr. = Creek
Czech. = Czechoslovakia
Dep. = Depression
Des. = Desert
Dist. = District
E. = East(ern)
Eng. = England
Fd. = Fiord, Fjord
Fr. = France, French
G. = Gulf
Ger. = Germany
Gt. = Great
Harb. = Harbo(u)r
Hd. = Head
I(s). = Island(s)
Ind. = India
Indon. = Indonesia
Ire. = Ireland
Kazakh. = Kazakhstan
Kirgiz. = Kirgizia
L. = Lac, Laguna, Lake, Loch, Lough
Lit. = Little
Ld. = Land
Lr. = Lower
Man. = Manitoba
Medit. = Mediterranean
Mich. = Michigan
Min. = Minnesota
Mo. = Missouri
Mt(s). = Mont, Mount, Mountain(s)
N. = North(ern)
N.B. = New Brunswick
Neth. = Netherlands
N.S.W. = New South Wales
N.-W. Terr. = North-West Territories (to be designated as Mackenzie and Nunassiaq)
N.Z. = New Zealand
Oc. = Ocean
Okla. = Oklahoma
Ont. = Ontario
Pas. = Passage
Pen. = Peninsula
Pk. = Peak
Plat. = Plateau
Port. = Portugal, Portuguese
Prov. = Province
Pt. = Point
Qnsld. = Queensland
Que. = Quebec
R. = River, Rio
Ra. = Range
Reg. = Region
Rep. = Republic
Res. = Reservoir
S. = South(ern)
Sa. = Serra, Sierra
Sask. = Saskatchewan
Sd. = Sound
Sp. = Spain, Spanish
St(e). = Saint(e)
Str. = Strait
Tadzhik. = Tadzhikistan
Terr. = Territory
Turkmen. = Turkmenistan
Up. = Upper
U.S.S.R. = Union of Soviet Socialist Republics
Uzbek. = Uzbekistan
Val. = Valley
Vict. = Victoria
Vol. = Volcano
W. = West(ern)

Aachen	Germany, W.	34	B3
Aalen	Germany, W.	34	C4
Aalsmeer	Netherlands	32	C2
Aar, R.	Switzerland	37	B1
Aarau	Switzerland	37	C1
Aarschot	Belgium	32	C4
Abaco I., Gt.	Bahamas	71	J2
Abad	Sinkiang	50	B4
Abadan	Iran	52	E4
Abadia	Algeria	57	B1
Abancay	Peru	72	C6
Abashiri	Japan	51	P3
Abaya, L.	Ethiopia	58	C4
Abbeville	France	33	C1
Abbeyfeale	Eire	31	B5
Abbeyleix	Eire	31	D5
Abbey Town	England	25	B2
Abbots Bromley	England	27	F2
Abbotsbury	England	26	E4
Abéché	Chad	58	B3
Abeokuta	Nigeria	57	C4
Aberayron	Wales	26	C2
Aberchirder	Scotland	28	F3
Abercorn	Zambia	59	D1
Aberdare	Wales	26	D3
Aberdeen	Scotland	16	D3
Aberdeen	S. Dakota	64	G1
Aberdeen	Washington	64	B1
Aberdeen L.	N.-W. Terr., Can.	62	O5
Aberdovey	Wales	17	C5
Aberfeldy	Scotland	29	E4
Aberfoyle	Scotland	29	D4
Abergavenny	Wales	17	D6
Abergele	Wales	26	D1
Abernethy	Scotland	29	E4
Aberthaw	Wales	26	D3
Abertillery	Wales	26	D3
Aberystwyth	Wales	17	C5
Abha	Saudi Arabia	52	D7
Abidjan	Ivory Coast	57	B4
Abilene	Texas	64	G4
Abingdon	England	17	E6
Abingdon	Virginia	65	K3
Abington	Scotland	29	E5
Abitibi L.	Ont.-Quebec	63	S8
Abomey	Dahomey	57	C4
Aboyne	Scotland	28	F3
Abruzzi & Molise	Italy	38	C3
Absaroka Ra.	Montana-Wyoming	67	D2
Abu Dabi	Trucial States	52	F6
Abut Hd.	New Zealand	79	C5
Acaponeta	Mexico	70	C3
Acapulco de Juarez	Mexico	70	E4
Accra	Ghana	57	B4
Accrington	England	25	C3
Achill I.	Eire	17	A5
Achinsk	U.S.S.R.	47	K3
Achnasheen	Scotland	28	C3
Acklins I.	Bahamas	71	K3
Aclare	Eire	30	C3
Aconcagua, mt.	Argentina	73	D10
Acre	Israel	54	C3
Ada	Oklahoma	68	D4
Adair, C.	N.-W. Terr., Can.	63	U3
Adalia	Turkey	41	L4
Adamello, mt.	Italy	38	B1
Adams, Mt.	Washington	67	B2
Adana	Turkey	52	C3
Adapazari	Turkey	41	J4
Adare	Eire	31	C5
Adare, C.	Antarctica	80	M7
Adavale	Qnsld.	77	G4
Adda, R.	Italy	38	B2
Addis Ababa	Ethiopia	58	C4
Adelaer, C.	Greenland	63	Z5
Adelaide	S. Australia	77	F5
Adelaide I.	Antarctica	80	S8
Adelaide Pen.	N.-W. Terr., Can.	63	P4
Adelaide River	N. Terr., Aust.	76	E1
Adelie Land	Antarctica	80	L8
Aden	S. Arabia	52	E8
Aden, G. of	Afr.-Arabia	52	E8
Adige, R.	Italy	38	B1
Adirondack Mts.	New York	65	M2
Adlavik Is.	Labrador	63	X6
Admiralty G.	W. Australia	76	D1
Admiralty Inlet	N.-W. Terr., Can.	63	R3
Admiralty I.	Alaska	62	H6
Adrar	Algeria	57	C2
Adrar, reg.	Mali, etc.	57	C3
Adria	Italy	38	C2
Adrianople	Turkey	39	G4
Adriatic Sea	Mediterranean	38	C2
Aduwa	Ethiopia	58	C3
Adygeysk	U.S.S.R.	43	F7
Aegadean Is.	Sicily	38	C6
Aegean Sea	Greece-Turkey	39	G5
Afghanistan	S. Asia	52	H4
Afognak Island	Alaska	62	D6
Africa	—	56	—
Afyon	Turkey	52	B3
Agades	Niger	57	C3
Agadir	Morocco	57	B1
Agartala	Tripura, Ind.	53	O6
Agen	France	33	C4
Agheila	Libya	58	A1
Agincourt	France	33	C1
Agordat	Ethiopia	58	C3
Agra	India	53	L5
Agrigento	Sicily	38	C6
Agrinion	Greece	39	F5
Agropoli	Italy	38	D4
Aguascalientes	Mexico	70	D3
Agulhas, C.	Cape of Good Hope	59	C4
Agulhas Negras, mt.	Brazil	73	H8
Ahaggar, reg.	Algeria	57	C2
Ahipara B.	New Zealand	79	D1
Ahmadi, Al	Kuwait	55	K5
Ahmedabad	India	53	K6
Ahvaz	Iran	52	E4
Ahwar	S. Arabia	52	E8
Aigen	Austria	34	D4
Aigle	Switzerland	37	B1
Aihun	China	48	N1
Aileron	N. Terr., Aust.	77	E3
Ailsa Craig	Scotland	17	C4
Aimorés, Sa. dos, mts.	Brazil	72	J7
Ain Sefra	Algeria	57	B1
Aintree	England	25	C3
Air, mts.	Niger	57	C3
Airdrie	Scotland	29	E5
Aire, R.	England	17	E5
Airedale	England	25	D3
Aishihik, L.	Yukon	62	G5
Aisne, R.	France	33	D2
Aiun, El	Sp. Sahara	57	A2
Aix-en-Provence	France	33	D5
Aix-Les-Bains	France	33	D4
Aiyion	Greece	39	F5
Ajaccio	Corsica	38	A4
Ajanta Ra.	India	53	L6
Ajax, Mt.	New Zealand	79	D5
Ajedabya	Libya	58	B1
Ajmer	India	53	K5
Ajo	Arizona	67	D5
Akaroa	New Zealand	79	D5
Aketi	Congo	58	B4
Akhdhar, Jebel, mt.	Muscat & Oman	52	G6
Akhisar	Turkey	39	H5
Akimiski I.	N.-W. Terr., Can.	63	S7
Akita	Japan	51	O4
Akjoujt	Mauritania	57	A3
Aklavik	N.-W. Terr., Can.	62	G4
Akobo	Sudan	58	C4
Akpatok I.	N.-W. Terr., Can.	63	V5
Akron	Ohio	65	K2
Aksu	Sinkiang	50	C3
Aktyubinsk	Kazakh.	46	F3
Akureyri	Iceland	42	K6
Akyab	Burma	53	O6
Ala Mts.	Kirgiz., etc.	46	H5
Alabama, state	U.S.A.	65	J4
Alabama, R.	Alabama	69	F4
Ala Kol, L.	Kazakh.	46	J4
Alamein, El	Egypt	41	L6
Alamogordo	New Mexico	67	E5
Alamos	Mexico	70	C2
Alamosa	Colorado	67	E4
Aland Is.	Finland	42	D3
Alarcón Res.	Spain	36	D3
Alaska, state	U.S.A.	62	C5
Alaska, G. of	Alaska	62	E6
Alaska Highway	Alaska-Can.	62	J5
Alaska Pen.	Alaska	62	C6
Alaska Ra.	Alaska	62	D5
Ala tau, mts.	Kazakh.	46	H4
Alatri	Italy	38	C4
Alba	Italy	38	A2
Albacete	Spain	36	D3
Albania	S. Europe	39	E4
Albany	Georgia	65	K4
Albany	New York	65	M2
Albany	Oregon	67	B3
Albany	W. Australia	76	B5
Albany R.	Ontario	63	R7
Al Bayda	Libya	41	J5
Albemarle Sd.	N. Carolina	69	H3
Albert, L.	Congo-Uganda	58	C4
Alberta, prov.	Canada	62	L7
Alberta, Mt.	Alberta	62	L7
Albertville	Congo	59	C1
Albi	France	33	C5
Alborg	Denmark	42	B4
Albuquerque	New Mexico	64	E3
Albury	New South Wales	77	H6
Alcanices	Spain	36	B2
Alcester	England	27	F2
Alcoa	Tennessee	65	K3
Alcoy	Spain	36	D3
Alcudia, B. of	Balearic Is.	36	F3
Aldabra Is.	Indian Oc.	59	E1
Aldan	U.S.S.R.	47	N3
Aldan Plat. & R.	U.S.S.R.	47	N3
Aldbrough	England	25	E3
Aldeburgh	England	27	J2
Alderney, I.	Channel Is.	33	B2
Aldershot	England	17	E6
Aleksandrovsk	U.S.S.R.	47	P3
Alençon	France	33	C2
Aleppo	Syria	52	C3
Ales	France	33	D4
Alessandria	Italy	38	A2
Ålesund	Norway	42	A3
Aleutian Is.	Bering Sea	10	D2
Aleutian Ra.	Alaska	62	C6
Alexander Arch.	Alaska	62	G6
Alexander Bay	C. of Good Hope	59	B3
Alexander I. I.	Antarctica	80	S8
Alexandra	New Zealand	79	B6
Alexandra Fiord	N.-W. Terr., Can.	63	T2
Alexandria	Egypt	58	B1
Alexandria	Louisiana	65	H4
Alexandria	Minnesota	68	D1
Alexandria	Scotland	29	D5
Alexandria	Virginia	65	L3
Alexandrina, L.	S. Australia	77	F6
Alexandroapolis	Greece	39	G4
Alford	England	25	F3
Alford	Scotland	28	F3
Alfreton	England	27	F1
Algeciras	Spain	36	C4
Algeria	N.W. Africa	57	C1
Algiers	Algeria	57	C1
Alicante	Spain	36	D3
Alice	Texas	68	D5
Alice Springs	N. Terr., Aust.	77	E3
Aligarh	Rajasthan, India	53	L5
Aligarh	Uttar Pradesh, India	53	L5
Aling Kangri, mt.	Tibet	50	C5
Alkmaar	Netherlands	32	C2
Allahabad	India	53	L5
Allaykha	U.S.S.R.	47	P1
Allegheny Mts.	U.S.A.	65	K3
Allen, Bog of	Eire	17	B5
Allen, L.	Eire	17	A4
Allendale Town	England	25	C2
Allende	Mexico	70	D2
Allentown	Pennsylvania	66	D3
Alleppey	India	53	L9
Alliance	Nebraska	64	F2
Alliance	Ohio	66	A3
Alloa	Scotland	16	D3
Allonby	England	25	B2
Alma Ata	Kazakh.	46	H4
Almelo	Netherlands	32	E2
Almeria & G. of	Spain	36	D4
Aln, R.	England	25	D1
Aless	Scotland	28	D3
Alnmouth	England	25	D1
Alnwick	England	17	E4
Alor Star	Malaya	48	C6
Alost	Belgium	32	C4
Aloysius, Mt.	W. Australia	76	D4
Alpena	Michigan	65	K1
Alphen	Netherlands	32	C2
Alpine	Texas	68	C4
Alps, mts.	Central Europe	33	E3
Alsace	France	33	E3
Alston	England	25	D2
Altai Mts.	U.S.S.R.-Mongolia	47	J3
Altamaha, R.	Georgia	69	G4
Altamura	Italy	38	D4
Altan Bulag	Mongolia	50	H2
Altár	Mexico	70	B1
Altata	Mexico	70	C3

Australia	Australasia	76-77	—
Australian Alps	Victoria-N.S.W.	77	H6
Australian Capital Terr.	Australia	77	H6
Austria	Europe	34	D5
Autun	France	33	D3
Auvergne & Mts.	France	33	C4
Auxerre	France	33	D3
Ava	Burma	53	P6
Avallon	France	33	D3
Avalon Pen.	Newfoundland	63	Y8
Aveiro	Portugal	36	B2
Avellaneda	Argentina	73	F10
Avellino	Italy	38	C4
Avesta	Sweden	42	C3
Avezzano	Italy	38	C3
Aviemore	Scotland	28	E3
Avignon	France	33	D5
Avila	Spain	36	C2
Avoca	Eire	31	E5
Avon, R.	Hants, England	17	E6
Avon, R.	Warwick, England	17	E5
Avon, R.	Scotland	29	E4
Avonmouth	England	26	E3
Avranches	France	33	B2
Awash	Ethiopia	58	D4
Awash R.	Ethiopia	58	D3
Awe, L.	Scotland	16	C3
Ax	France	33	C5
Axar Fd.	Iceland	42	K6
Axbridge	England	26	E3
Axel Heiberg I.	N.-W. Terr., Can.	63	Q2
Axminster	England	26	E4
Ayacucho	Peru	72	C6
Ayaguz	Kazakh.	46	J4
Ayak Kum Köl, L.	Sinkiang	50	D4
Ayan	U.S.S.R.	47	O3
Aycliffe	England	25	D2
Aydin	Turkey	52	A3
Aylesbury	England	17	E6
Aylmer, L.	N.-W. Terr., Can.	62	N5
Aylsham	England	27	J2
Ayr	Queensland	77	H2
Ayr & R.	Scotland	16	C4
Ayre, Pt. of	Isle of Man	17	C4
Ayutthaya	Thailand	53	Q8
Azerbaijan	U.S.S.R.	46	E4
Azov, Sea of	U.S.S.R.	46	D4
Ba'albek	Lebanon	54	D2
Bab-el-Mandeb Str.	Red Sea	52	D8
Babine L.	Br. Columbia	62	J7
Babol	Iran	52	F3
Babylon	Iraq	52	D4
Bacau	Rumania	35	H5
Bac Ninh	Vietnam	50	H7
Bacup	England	25	C3
Badajoz	Spain	36	B3
Bad Ems	Germany, W.	34	B3
Baden	Austria	34	E4
Baden	Switzerland	37	C1
Badenoch	Scotland	29	D4
Baden-Württemberg	Germany, W.	34	C4
Bad Ischl	Austria	34	D5
Baffin B.	Can.-Greenland	63	U3
Baffin I.	N.-W. Terr., Can.	63	T4
Baghdad	Iraq	52	D4
Baghrash Köl, L.	Sinkiang	50	D3
Bagshot	England	27	G3
Baguio	Philippines	48	E5
Bahama Is.	W. Indies	71	J2
Bahariya Oasis	Egypt	58	B2
Bahawalpur	W. Pakistan	53	K5
Bahia	Brazil	72	K6
Bahia Blanca	Argentina	73	E11
Bahrain	Persian Gulf	52	F5
Bahr el Arab, R.	Sudan	58	B4
Bahr el Ghazal, R.	Sudan	58	B4
Baia Mare	Rumania	35	G5
Baikal L. & Mts.	U.S.S.R.	47	L3
Bailieborough	Eire	30	E4
Bairnsdale	Victoria	77	H6
Bakel	Senegal	57	A3
Baker	Montana	67	F2
Baker	Oregon	64	C2
Baker, Mt.	Washington	67	B2
Baker Lake	N.-W. Terr., Can.	63	P5
Bakersfield	California	64	C3
Bakewell	England	27	F1
Baku	U.S.S.R.	46	E4
Bakwanga	Congo	59	C1
Bala	Wales	17	D5
Bala L.	Wales	26	D2
Balabac Str.	Philippines, etc.	48	D6
Balaklava	Ukraine	43	D4
Balashov	U.S.S.R.	43	F2
Balasore	India	50	D7
Balaton, L.	Hungary	35	E5
Balboa	Panama	71	J6
Balbriggan	Eire	17	B5
Balclutha	New Zealand	79	B7
Baldock	England	27	G3
Baldy Peak	Arizona	67	E5
Balearic Is.	Medit. Sea	40	D4
Balerno	Scotland	29	E5
Bali, I.	Indonesia	48	D7
Balikesir	Turkey	39	H5
Balikpapan	Borneo	48	D7
Balintang Chan.	Philippines	48	D5
Balkan Mts.	Bulgaria	39	F3
Balkhash & L.	Kazakh.	46	H4
Ballachulish	Scotland	16	C3
Balladonia	W. Australia	76	C5
Ballaghaderreen	Eire	30	C3
Ballantrae	Scotland	29	C5
Ballarat	Victoria	77	G6
Ballater	Scotland	16	D3
Balleny Is.	Antarctica	80	M8
Ballia	India	50	C6
Ballina	Eire	17	A4
Ballinasloe	Eire	17	A5
Ballindine	Eire	30	C4
Ballingarry	Eire	31	C5
Ballinluig	Scotland	29	E4
Ballinrobe	Eire	17	A5
Ballybay	Eire	30	E3
Ballybofey	Eire	30	D3
Ballybunion	Eire	31	B5
Ballycastle	Eire	17	A4
Ballycastle	N. Ireland	30	E2
Ballyconnell	Eire	30	D3
Ballydull	Eire	31	C5
Ballygar	Eire	30	C4
Ballygawley	N. Ireland	30	D3
Ballyhaise	Eire	30	D3
Ballyhaunis	Eire	30	C4
Ballyjamesduff	Eire	30	D4
Ballymahon	Eire	30	D4
Ballymena	N. Ireland	17	B4
Ballymoney	N. Ireland	17	B4
Ballymote	Eire	30	C3
Ballynahinch	N. Ireland	30	F3
Ballyragget	Eire	31	D5
Ballyshannon	Eire	17	A4
Ballytore	Eire	31	E4
Ballyvaughan	Eire	31	B4
Balmaceda	Chile	73	C13
Balmoral Castle	Scotland	28	E3
Balovale	Zambia	59	C2
Balranald	New South Wales	77	G5
Balsas & R.	Mexico	70	D4
Balta	Ukraine	43	C3
Baltasound	Scotland	28	A1
Baltic Sea	N. Europe	42	D5
Baltimore	Eire	31	B6
Baltimore	Maryland	65	L3
Baltinglass	Eire	31	E5
Baluchistan	W. Pakistan	52	H5
Bam	Iran	52	G5
Bamako	Mali	57	B3
Bambari	Cent. Afr. Rep.	58	B4
Bamberg	Germany, W.	34	C4
Bamburgh	England	25	D1
Bampton	Devon, England	26	D4
Bampton	Oxford, England	27	F3
Banagher	Eire	17	B5
Banat	Rumania	39	F2
Banavie	Scotland	29	C4
Banbridge	N. Ireland	30	E3
Banbury	England	27	F2
Banchory	Scotland	28	F3
Banda Sea	Indonesia	48	E7
Bandar 'Abbas	Iran	52	G5
Bandar Shah	Iran	52	F3
Bandar Shahpur	Iran	52	E4
Bandeira, mt.	Brazil	73	J8
Bandirma	Turkey	41	L3
Bandjarmasin	Borneo	48	D7
Bandon	Eire	17	A6
Bandung	Java	48	C7
Banes	Cuba	71	J3
Banff	Alberta	62	L7
Banff	Scotland	16	D3
Bangalore	India	53	L8
Bangassou	Cent. Afr. Rep.	58	B4
Bangka, I.	Indonesia	48	C7
Bangkok	Thailand	53	Q8
Bangor	Maine	65	N2
Bangor	N. Ireland	17	C4
Bangor	Wales	17	C5
Bangui	Cent. Afr. Rep.	58	A4
Bangweulu, L.	Zambia	59	D2
Ban Houei San	Laos	53	Q6
Bani	Dominican Rep.	71	K4
Bani, R.	Mali	57	B3
Baniyas	Syria	52	C3
Banja Luka	Yugoslavia	38	D2
Banjuwangi	Java	48	D7
Bankipore	India	53	M5
Banks I.	N.-W. Terr., Can.	62	K3
Banks I.	Queensland	77	G1
Banks Pen.	New Zealand	79	D5
Banks Str.	Tasmania	77	H7
Bankura	India	50	D7
Bann, R.	N. Ireland	17	B4
Banningville	Congo	59	B1
Bannockburn	Scotland	29	E4
Banská Bystrica	Czechoslovakia	35	F4
Banská Stiavnica	Czechoslovakia	35	F4
Bantry	Eire	17	A6
Bantry B.	Eire	31	B6
Banzyville	Congo	58	B4
Baraba Steppe	U.S.S.R.	46	H3
Baracoa	Cuba	71	K4
Barahona	Dominican Rep.	71	K4
Baranof I.	Alaska	62	G6
Barbados, I.	West Indies	71	M5
Barbastro	Spain	36	E1
Barbuda, I.	West Indies	71	M4
Barcaldine	Queensland	77	H3
Barcelona	Spain	36	E2
Barcelona	Venezuela	72	E1
Barcelonnette	France	33	E4
Barcelos	Brazil	72	E4
Barcoo R.	Queensland	77	G3
Bardera	Somalia	58	D4
Bardia	Libya	41	K6
Bardsey, I.	Wales	26	C2
Bareilly	India	53	L5
Barents Sea	Arctic Oc.	46	D1
Bargoed	Wales	26	D3
Barguzin	U.S.S.R.	47	L3
Barham	England	27	J3
Bari	Italy	38	D4
Barito, R.	Borneo	48	D7
Barkerville	Br. Columbia	62	K7
Barkly Highway	N. Terr.-Qnsld.	77	F2
Barkly Tableland	N. Terr.-Qnsld.	77	F2
Barköl	Sinkiang	50	E3
Bar-le-Duc	France	33	D2
Barlee, L.	W. Australia	76	B4
Barlee Ra.	W. Australia	76	B3
Barletta	Italy	38	D4
Barmouth	Wales	26	C2
Barnard Castle	England	25	D2
Barnaul	U.S.S.R.	46	J3
Barnet	England	27	G3
Barnsley	England	17	E5
Barnstaple	England	17	C6
Baroda	India	53	K6
Barquisimeto	Venezuela	72	D2
Barra	Brazil	72	J6
Barra Hd.	Scotland	16	B3
Barra, Sd. of	Scotland	16	B3
Barra do São Manuel	Brazil	72	F5
Barranquilla	Colombia	72	B1
Barre	Vermont	66	E1
Barrhill	Scotland	29	D5
Barrington, Mt.	New South Wales	77	J5
Barringun	New South Wales	77	H4
Barrow	Alaska	62	C3
Barrow	England	17	D4
Barrow I.	W. Australia	76	B3
Barrow Pt.	Alaska	62	C3
Barrow, R.	Eire	17	B5
Barrow Str.	N.-W. Terr., Can.	63	P3
Barrow Creek	N. Terr., Aust.	77	E3
Barry	Wales	26	D3
Barstow	California	67	C5
Bar-sur-Seine	France	33	D2
Bartle Frere, Mt.	Queensland	77	G2
Bartlesville	Oklahoma	68	D3
Barton	England	17	E5
Barvas	Scotland	28	B2
Barwon R.	N.S.W.-Qnsld.	77	H4
Basankusu	Congo	58	A4
Bashi Chan.	Taiwan, etc.	48	E4
Bashkir A.S.S.R.	U.S.S.R.	43	H1
Bash Malghun	Sinkiang	50	D4
Basidu	Iran	52	G5
Basildon	England	17	F6
Basilicata	Italy	38	D4
Basingstoke	England	17	E6
Baskatong L.	Quebec	63	T8
Basle	Switzerland	37	B1
Basoko	Congo	58	B4
Basque	Spain	36	D1
Basra	Iraq	52	E4
Bass Rock	Scotland	28	F4
Bass Str.	Tasmania-Victoria	78	E9
Bassac	Laos	53	R8
Bassano	Italy	38	B2
Bassas da India, I.	Mozambique Chan.	59	D3
Bassein	Burma	53	O7
Basse Terre	West Indies	71	M4
Basti	India	50	C6
Bastia	Corsica	38	B3
Bastion, C.	China	48	C5
Bastogne	Belgium	32	D4
Basutoland	S. Africa	59	C3
Bata	Rio Muni	57	C4
Batamay	U.S.S.R.	47	N2
Batan Is.	Philippines	48	E4
Batavia	New York	66	B2
Batchelor	N. Terr., Aust.	76	E1
Bath	England	17	D6
Bath	Maine	65	N2
Bathgate	Scotland	29	E5
Bathurst	Gambia	57	A3
Bathurst	New South Wales	77	H5
Bathurst, C.	N.-W. Terr., Can.	62	J3
Bathurst Inlet	N.-W. Terr., Can.	62	N4
Bathurst I.	N. Terr., Aust.	76	E1
Bathurst I.	N.-W. Terr., Can.	62	O2
Batié	Up. Volta	57	B3
Batley	England	25	D3
Baton Rouge	Louisiana	65	H4
Batouri	Cameroun	57	D4
Battambang	Cambodia	53	Q8
Batticaloa	Ceylon	53	M9
Battle	England	27	H4
Battle R.	Alberta-Sask.	62	M7
Battle Creek	Michigan	65	J2
Battleford	Saskatchewan	62	N7
Battle Harbour	Labrador	63	X7
Battle Mountain	Nevada	67	C3
Batu, mt.	Ethiopia	58	C4
Batumi	Georgia, U.S.S.R.	46	E4
Bauchi	Nigeria	57	C3
Bauld, C.	Newfoundland	63	X7
Bauru	Brazil	73	H8
Bautzen	Germany, E.	34	D3
Bavaria	Germany, W.	34	C4
Bawku	Ghana	57	B3
Bawtry	England	25	D3
Bayan Dzürihe	Mongolia	50	H2
Bayan Kara Shan, mts.	China	50	F5
Bay City	Michigan	65	K2
Bayeux	France	33	B2
Bayonne	France	33	B5
Bayram Ali	Turkmen.	52	H3
Bayreuth	Germany, W.	34	C4
Baytown	Texas	68	E5
Bazaruto, I.	Mozambique	59	D3
Bazas	France	33	B4
Beachport	S. Australia	77	F6
Beachy Hd.	England	17	F6
Beaconsfield	England	27	G3
Beal Ra.	Queensland	77	G3
Beaminster	England	26	E4
Bear I.	Antarctica	80	Q7
Bear I.	Arctic Oc.	46	B1
Bear Lake	Br. Columbia	62	J6
Beatrice	Nebraska	64	G2
Beattock	Scotland	29	E5
Beauce, plain	France	33	C3
Beaufort Sea	Arctic Oc.	62	F3
Beaufort West	C. of Good Hope	59	C4
Beaulieu	England	27	F4
Beauly	Scotland	16	C3
Beauly Firth	Scotland	28	D3
Beaumaris	Wales	17	C5
Beaumont	Texas	65	H4
Beaune	France	33	D3
Beauvais	France	33	C2
Beaver	Utah	67	D4
Beaver R.	Alberta-Sask.	62	N7
Beaver Falls	Pennsylvania	66	A3
Bebra	Germany, W.	34	C3
Beccles	England	27	J2
Bechuanaland	S. Africa	59	C3
Bedale	England	25	D2
Beddgelert	Wales	26	C1
Bedford	England	17	E5
Bedlington	England	25	D1
Bedourie	Queensland	77	F3
Bedworth	England	27	F2
Beersheba	Israel	54	C4

Borris *Eire* **31** E5
Borrisoleigh *Eire* **31** D5
Borroola *N. Terr., Aust.* **77** F2
Borujerd *Iran* **55** K3
Borzya *U.S.S.R.* **47** M3
Boscastle *England* **26** C4
Bosnia *Yugoslavia* **38** D2
Bosporus *Turkey* **39** H4
Bossangoa *Cent. Afr. Rep.* **57** D4
Boston *England* **17** E5
Boston *Massachusetts* **65** M2
Boston Mts. *Arkansas* **68** E3
Botany B. *New South Wales* **78** H7
Bothnia, G. of *Sweden-Finland* **42** D3
Botley *England* **27** F4
Botoşani *Rumania* **35** H5
Bottesford *England* **27** G2
Bottineau *N. Dakota* **68** C1
Bouaflé *Ivory Coast* **57** B4
Bouaké *Ivory Coast* **57** B4
Bouar *Cent. Afr. Rep.* **57** D4
Bougie *Algeria* **57** C1
Boulder *Colorado* **67** E3
Boulder *W. Australia* **76** C5
Boulder City *Nevada* **67** D4
Boulia *Queensland* **77** F3
Boulogne *France* **33** C1
Bouna *Ivory Coast* **57** B4
Bounty I. *S. Pacific Oc.* **10** D7
Bourem *Mali* **57** B3
Bourg *France* **33** D3
Bourganeuf *France* **33** C4
Bourges *France* **33** C3
Bourke *New South Wales* **77** H5
Bourne *England* **27** G2
Bournemouth *England* **17** E6
Bouvet I. *Antarctica* **11** L7
Bovey Tracey *England* **26** D4
Bow *England* **26** D4
Bowen *Queensland* **77** H2
Bowes *England* **25** C2
Bowling Green *Kentucky* **65** J3
Bowmore *Scotland* **29** B5
Boyle *Eire* **17** A5
Boyne, R. *Eire* **17** B5
Bozeman *Montana* **64** D1
Bozoum *Cent. Afr. Rep.* **57** D4
Bra *Italy* **38** A2
Brabant *Belgium* **32** C4
Brac, I. *Yugoslavia* **38** D3
Bracadale, L. *Scotland* **16** B3
Bracke *Sweden* **42** C3
Brackettville *Texas* **64** F5
Brackley *England* **27** F2
Bracknell *England* **27** G3
Braddock *Pennsylvania* **66** B3
Bradford *England* **17** E5
Bradford *Pennsylvania* **66** B3
Bradninch *England* **26** D4
Bradwell *England* **27** H3
Bradworthy *England* **26** C4
Braemar *Scotland* **28** E3
Braeriach, mt. *Scotland* **28** E3
Braga *Portugal* **36** B2
Braganca *Portugal* **36** B2
Brahmaputra R. *India, etc.* **53** O5
Braich-y-pwll *Wales* **17** C5
Brăila *Rumania* **39** H2
Braintree *England* **27** H3
Brampton *England* **25** C2
Branco, R. *Brazil* **72** E4
Brandberg, mt. *S.W. Africa* **59** B3
Brandenburg *Germany, E.* **34** D2
Brander, Pass of *Scotland* **29** C4
Brandon *England* **27** H2
Brandon *Manitoba* **63** P7
Braniewo *Poland* **35** F1
Branston *England* **27** G1
Brantford *Ontario* **63** S9
Brasilia *Brazil* **72** H7
Brasov *Rumania* **39** G2
Bratislava *Czechoslovakia* **35** E4
Bratsk *U.S.S.R.* **47** L3
Brattleboro *Vermont* **66** E2
Braunau *Austria* **34** D4
Braunton *England* **26** C3
Brava *Somalia* **58** D4
Brawley *California* **67** C5
Bray *Eire* **17** B5
Brazil *S. America* **72** E6
Brazil Plat. *Brazil* **72** H7
Brazilian Highlands *Brazil* **73** G9
Brazos R. *Texas* **64** G4
Brazzaville *Rep. of Congo* **57** D5
Breaksea Sd. *New Zealand* **79** A6
Bream B. *New Zealand* **79** E1
Brechin *Scotland* **16** D3
Brecknock *Wales* **17** D6
Brecon *Wales* **26** D3
Brecon Beacons, mts. *Wales* **26** D3
Breda *Netherlands* **32** C3
Bregenz *Austria* **34** C5
Breidha Fd. *Iceland* **42** J6
Breifonn, mt. *Norway* **42** A4
Bremen *Germany, W.* **34** B2
Bremerhaven *Germany, W.* **34** B2
Brendon Hills *England* **26** D3
Brenner, pass *Austria-Italy* **38** B1
Breno *Italy* **38** B2
Brentford *England* **27** G3
Brentwood *England* **27** H3
Brescia *Italy* **38** B2
Breslau *Poland* **35** E3
Bressanone *Italy* **38** B1
Bressay, I. *Scotland* **16** E1
Bressuire *France* **33** B3
Brest *France* **33** A2
Brest *White Russia* **43** B2
Breteuil *France* **33** C2
Breton, C. *Nova Scotia* **63** X8
Breukelen *Netherlands* **32** C2
Brewarrina *New South Wales* **77** H4
Brewton *Alabama* **65** J4
Briançon *France* **33** E4
Bridgend *Wales* **26** D3
Bridge of Orchy *Scotland* **29** D4
Bridgeport *Connecticut* **65** M2
Bridgeton *New Jersey* **66** D4
Bridgetown *West Indies* **71** M5
Bridgnorth *England* **26** E2
Bridgwater & B. *England* **17** D6
Bridlington & B. *England* **17** E4
Bridport *England* **26** E4
Brig *Switzerland* **37** B1
Brigg *England* **25** E3
Brigham City *Utah* **67** D3
Brighouse *England* **25** D3
Brightlingsea *England* **27** J3
Brighton *England* **17** E6
Brigstock *England* **27** G2
Brill *England* **27** F3
Brindisi *Italy* **38** D4
Brisbane *Queensland* **77** J4
Bristol *England* **17** D6
Bristol *Tennessee* **69** G3
Bristol B. *Alaska* **62** C6
Bristol Chan. *Eng.-Wales* **17** C6
British Isles *N.W. Europe* **16-17** —
British Mts. *Alaska-Yukon* **62** F4
British Columbia, prov. *Canada* **62** J6
British Guiana *S. America* **72** F2
British Honduras *Cent. America* **70** G4
British North Borneo (Sabah) *Malaysia* **48** D6
Briton Ferry *Wales* **26** D3
Brive *France* **33** C4
Brixham *England* **26** D4
Brno *Czechoslovakia* **34** E4
Broad B. *Scotland* **16** B2
Broadford *Scotland* **28** C3
Broad Law, hill *Scotland* **16** D4
Broadstairs *England* **27** J3
Brockman, mt. *W. Australia* **76** B3
Brockton *Massachusetts* **65** M2
Brodick *Scotland* **16** C4
Broken Hill *New South Wales* **77** G5
Broken Hill *Zambia* **59** C2
Bromley *England* **27** H3
Bromsgrove *England* **27** E2
Bromyard *England* **26** E2
Brönnöysund *Norway* **42** B2
Brookhaven *Mississippi* **65** H4
Brookings *S. Dakota* **68** D2
Brooklyn *New York* **65** M2
Brooks Ra. *Alaska* **62** B4
Broom, L. *Scotland* **16** C3
Broome *W. Australia* **76** C2
Brora *Scotland* **28** E2
Brough *England* **25** C2
Broughton *England* **25** B2
Broughty Ferry *Scotland* **29** F4
Brown, Mt. *S. Australia* **77** F5
Brownhills *England* **27** F2
Brownsville *Texas* **64** G5
Brownwood *Texas* **68** D4
Browse I. *W. Australia* **76** C1
Bruce, Mt. *W. Australia* **76** B3
Bruck *Austria* **34** D5
Bruck *Austria* **34** E4
Bruck *Austria* **34** E5
Bruff *Eire* **31** C5
Bruges *Belgium* **32** B3
Brugg *Switzerland* **37** C1
Brunei *Borneo* **48** D6
Brunette Downs *N. Terr., Aust.* **77** F2
Brunico *Italy* **38** B1
Brunner, L. *New Zealand* **79** C5
Brunswick *Georgia* **65** K4
Brunswick *Germany, W.* **34** C2
Bruny I. *Tasmania* **77** H7
Brussels *Belgium* **32** C4
Bruton *England* **26** E3
Bryan *Texas* **68** D4
Bryansk *U.S.S.R.* **43** D2
Brynamman *Wales* **26** D3
Brynmawr *Wales* **26** D3
Brzeg *Poland* **35** E3
Bucaramanga *Colombia* **72** C2
Buchan *Scotland* **28** F3
Buchan Ness *Scotland* **16** E3
Buchanan *W. Africa* **57** A4
Buchanan, L. *Queensland* **77** H3
Bucharest *Rumania* **39** G2
Buchlyvie *Scotland* **29** D4
Buckden *England* **27** G2
Buckie *Scotland* **16** D3
Buckingham *England* **17** E5
Budapest *Hungary* **35** F5
Bude *England* **17** C6
Budleigh Salterton *England* **26** D4
Buea *Cameroun* **57** C4
Buenaventura *Colombia* **72** B3
Buendia Res. *Spain* **36** D2
Buenos Aires *Argentina* **73** F10
Buenos Aires, L. *Arg.-Chile* **73** C13
Buffalo *New York* **65** L2
Buffalo *S. Dakota* **68** C1
Buffalo *Wyoming* **64** E2
Buffalo L. *N.-W. Terr., Can.* **62** L5
Bug, R. *Poland-Ukraine* **35** G2
Bug, R. *Ukraine* **43** D3
Buggs Island L. *Virginia* **69** H3
Bugur *Sinkiang* **50** C3
Builth Wells *Wales* **26** D2
Bukama *Congo* **59** C1
Buka Mangna Ra. *Tibet* **50** C5
Bukavu *Congo* **58** B5
Bukhara *Uzbek.* **46** G5
Bukoba *Tanganyika* **58** C5
Bukovina *Rumania* **35** H5
Bulawayo *Rhodesia* **59** C3
Bulgaria *S.E. Europe* **39** G3
Bulle *Switzerland* **37** B1
Buller, R. *New Zealand* **79** D4
Bullfinch *W. Australia* **76** B5
Bulloo Cr. *Qnsld.* **77** G4
Bull Shoals Res. *Missouri-Arkansas* **65** H3
Bulo Burti *Somalia* **58** D4
Bulun *U.S.S.R.* **47** N1
Bulwell *England* **27** F2
Bunbury *W. Australia* **76** B5
Bunclody *Eire* **31** E5
Buncrana *Eire* **30** D2
Bundaberg *Queensland* **77** J3
Bundooma *N. Terr., Aust.* **77** E3
Bundoran *Eire* **30** C3
Bungay *England* **27** J2
Bunia *Congo* **58** C4
Buntingford *England* **27** G3
Buraida *Saudi Arabia* **52** D5
Burbank *California* **67** C5
Burchun *Sinkiang* **50** D2
Burdekin R. *Queensland* **77** H2
Bure, R. *England* **27** J2
Bures *England* **27** H3
Bureya R. *U.S.S.R.* **47** O3
Burford *England* **27** F3
Burg *Netherlands* **32** C1
Burgas *Bulgaria* **39** H3
Burgdorf *Switzerland* **37** B1
Burgess Hill *England* **27** G4
Burghead *Scotland* **28** E3
Burgh-le-Marsh *England* **27** H1
Burgos *Spain* **36** C1
Burgundy *France* **33** D3
Burketown *Queensland* **77** F2
Burley *Idaho* **67** D3
Burlington *Colorado* **67** F4
Burlington *Iowa* **65** H2
Burlington *Vermont* **65** M2
Burma *S.E. Asia* **53** O6
Burnham *Essex, England* **27** H3
Burnham *Somerset, England* **26** D3
Burnham Market *England* **27** H2
Burnie *Tasmania* **77** H7
Burnley *England* **17** D5
Burns *Oregon* **67** C3
Burntisland *Scotland* **29** E4
Burra *S. Australia* **78** B6
Burravoe *Scotland* **28** A1
Burrinjuck Res. *N. S. W.* **77** H5
Burrow Hd. *Scotland* **17** C4
Burrundie *N. Terr., Aust.* **76** E1
Burry Inlet *Wales* **26** C3
Burry Port *Wales* **26** C3
Bursa *Turkey* **52** A2
Burslem *England* **17** D5
Burton-in-Kendal *England* **25** C2
Burton-on-Trent *England* **17** E5
Burtonport *Eire* **30** C3
Buru, I. *Indonesia* **48** E7
Burundi *Cent. Africa* **58** B5
Bury *England* **25** C3
Buryat *U.S.S.R.* **47** M3
Bury St. Edmunds *England* **17** F5
Bushire *Iran* **52** F5
Bushmills *N. Ireland* **30** E2
Buta *Congo* **58** B4
Bute *Scotland* **16** C4
Butedale *Br. Columbia* **62** J7
Butte *Montana* **64** D1
Buttevant *Eire* **31** C5
Butung, I. *Indonesia* **48** E7
Buxton *England* **25** D3
Buy *U.S.S.R.* **46** E3
Buzau *Rumania* **39** G2
Buzuluk *U.S.S.R.* **43** H2
Byam Martin, C. *N.-W. Terr., Can.* **63** T3
Byam Martin Chan. *N.-W. Terr., Can.* **62** N2
Byam Martin I. *N.-W. Terr., Can.* **62** O2
Bydgoszcz *Poland* **35** E2
Bylot I. *N.-W. Terr., Can.* **63** T3
Byron, C. *New South Wales* **77** J4
Bytom *Poland* **35** F3
Caatinga *Brazil* **72** G5
Cabanas *Cuba* **71** H3
Cabinda *Angola* **57** D5
Cabonga Res. *Quebec* **63** T8
Cabot Str. *Canada* **63** W8
Cabrera, I. *Balearic Is.* **36** F3
Cáceres *Spain* **36** B3
Cadereyta *Mexico* **70** E2
Cader Idris, mt. *Wales* **17** D5
Cadillac *Michigan* **69** F2
Cádiz & G. of *Spain* **36** B4
Caen *France* **33** B2
Caergwrle *Wales* **26** D1
Caerleon *Wales* **26** E3
Caernarvon & B. *Wales* **17** C5
Caerphilly *Wales* **26** D3
Caersws *Wales* **26** D2
Caesarea *Israel* **54** C3
Cagliari *Sardinia* **38** B5
Cahir *Eire* **31** D5
Cahirciveen *Eire* **31** A6
Cahors *France* **33** C4
Caicos Is. *W. Indies* **71** K3
Cairn Gorm, mt. *Scotland* **28** E3
Cairngorms, mts. *Scotland* **16** D3
Cairns *Queensland* **77** H2
Cairn Toul, mt. *Scotland* **28** E3
Cairo *Egypt* **58** C1
Cairo *Illinois* **65** J3
Caister *England* **27** J2
Caistor *England* **25** E3
Caithness, co. *Scotland* **16** D2
Cajamarca *Peru* **72** B5
Calabar *Nigeria* **57** C4
Calabozo *Venezuela* **72** D2
Calabria *Italy* **38** D5
Calafat *Rumania* **39** F3
Calais *France* **33** C1
Calais *Maine* **65** N1
Calcutta *India* **53** N6
Caldbeck *England* **25** C2
Calder, R. *England* **25** D3
Caldera *Chile* **73** C9
Calder Hall *England* **25** B2
Caledonian Can. *Scotland* **28** D3
Calexico *California* **67** C5
Calgary *Alberta* **62** M7
Cali *Colombia* **72** B3
Calicut *India* **53** L8
Caliente *Nevada* **67** D4
California, state *U.S.A.* **64** B3
California, G. of *Mexico* **70** B2
Callabonna, L. *S. Australia* **77** G4
Callan *Eire* **31** D5
Callander *Scotland* **29** D4

Callao *Peru* 72 B6
Callington *England* 26 C4
Calne *England* 27 E3
Caltanissetta *Sicily* 38 C6
Calumet *Michigan* 65 J1
Calvi *Corsica* 38 A3
Calvinia *Cape of Good Hope* 59 B4
Camacupa *Angola* 59 B2
Camagüey *Cuba* 71 J3
Camarat, C. *France* 33 E5
Camargue, dist. *France* 33 D5
Ca Mau, Pt. de *Vietnam* 48 C6
Cambay, G. of *India* 53 K6
Cambodia *S.E. Asia* 48 C5
Camborne *England* 26 B4
Cambrai *France* 33 D1
Cambrian Mts. *Wales* 17 D6
Cambridge *England* 17 F5
Cambridge *Maryland* 66 C4
Cambridge *Massachusetts* 66 F2
Cambridge *New Zealand* 79 E2
Cambridge Bay *N.-W. Terr., Can.* 62 O4
Cambridge G. *W. Australia* 76 D1
Camden *Arkansas* 65 H4
Camden *New Jersey* 66 D4
Camelford *England* 26 C4
Cameroun *W. Africa* 57 D4
Cameroun Mt. *Cameroun* 57 C4
Camocim *Brazil* 72 J4
Camooweal *Queensland* 77 F3
Campania *Italy* 38 C4
Campbell I. *S. Pacific Oc.* 10 D7
Campbellpore *W. Pakistan* 53 K4
Campbellton *New Brunswick* 63 V8
Campbeltown *Scotland* 16 C4
Campeche & G. of *Mexico* 70 F4
Campina Grande *Brazil* 72 K5
Campinas *Brazil* 73 H8
Campobasso *Italy* 38 C4
Campo Grande *Brazil* 72 G8
Campos *Brazil* 73 J8
Campsie Fells, hills *Scotland* 29 D4
Cam-Ranh B. *Vietnam* 48 C5
Canada *N. America* 56-57 —
Canadian R. *Texas, etc.* 64 F3
Cananea *Mexico* 70 C1
Canary Is. *Atlantic Oc.* 57 A2
Canberra *Australia* 77 H6
Candia *Crete* 38 L8
Canea *Crete* 38 K8
Canisp, mt. *Scotland* 28 C2
Canna, I. *Scotland* 16 B3
Cannes *France* 33 E5
Cannock *England* 27 E2
Cannock Chase *England* 27 E2
Canonbie *Scotland* 29 E5
Canon City *Colorado* 67 E4
Canso, C. *Nova Scotia* 63 W8
Cantabrian Mts. *Spain* 36 B1
Canterbury *England* 17 F6
Canterbury *New Zealand* 79 C6
Canterbury Bight *N. Z.* 79 C6
Canterbury Plains *N. Z.* 79 C6
Canton *China* 48 D4
Canton *Ohio* 65 K2
Canton *S. Dakota* 68 D2
Canton I. *Pacific Oc.* 10 E5
Canudos *Brazil* 72 F5
Cao Bang *Vietnam* 50 H7
Cape Barren I. *Tasmania* 77 H7
Cape Breton I. *Nova Scotia* 63 W8
Cape Dorset *N.-W. Terr., Can.* 63 T5
Cape Dyer *N.-W. Terr., Can.* 63 W4
Cape Girardeau *Missouri* 65 J3
Cape Johnson Depth *Pacific Oc.* 48 E5
Capel *England* 27 G3
Cape of Good Hope, prov. *South Africa* 59 C4
Cape Kennedy *Florida* 69 G5
Cape Parry *N.-W. Terr., Can.* 62 K3
Cape Town *C. of Good Hope* 59 B4
Cape Verde Is. *Atlantic Oc.* 11 K4
Cape York Pen. *Queensland* 77 G1
Cap-Haitien *Haiti* 71 K4
Cappoquin *Eire* 31 D5
Capráia, I. of *Italy* 38 B3
Capri, I. of *Italy* 38 C4
Capricorn Chan. *Queensland* 77 J3
Caqueta R. *Colombia* 72 C4
Caracas *Venezuela* 72 D1
Caravelas *Brazil* 72 K7
Carbondale *Pennsylvania* 66 D3
Carbonear *Newfoundland* 63 Y8
Carcassonne *France* 33 C5
Carcross *Yukon* 62 G5
Cardamon Hills *India* 53 L8
Cardeñas *Cuba* 71 H3
Cardenas *Mexico* 70 F4
Cardiff *Wales* 17 D6
Cardigan & B. *Wales* 17 C5
Cardston *Alberta* 62 M8
Cardwell *Queensland* 77 H2
Carei *Rumania* 35 G5
Carey, L. *W. Australia* 76 C4
Caribbean Sea *America* 71 J5
Cariboo Mts. *Alberta* 62 L6
Caribou *Manitoba* 63 P6
Caribou Hide *Br. Columbia* 62 J6
Carlin *Nevada* 67 C3
Carlingford *Eire* 30 E3
Carlingford L. *Eire* 17 B4
Carlisle *England* 17 D4
Carlow *Eire* 17 B5
Carloway *Scotland* 28 B2
Carlsbad *New Mexico* 67 F5
Carlton *England* 25 D3
Carluke *Scotland* 29 E5
Carmacks *Yukon* 62 G5
Carman *Manitoba* 63 P7
Carmarthen & B. *Wales* 17 C6
Carmel, Mt. *Israel* 54 C3
Carmen *Mexico* 70 F4
Carmona *Angola* 59 B1
Carnac *France* 33 A3
Carnamah *W. Australia* 76 B4
Carnarvon *Cape of Good Hope* 59 C4
Carnarvon *W. Australia* 76 A3
Carnatic *India* 53 L8
Carndonagh *Eire* 30 D2
Carnegie, L. *W. Australia* 76 C4
Carnforth *England* 25 C2
Carnic Alps *Italy* 38 C1
Carno *Wales* 26 D2
Carnot *Cent. Afr. Rep.* 57 D4
Carnoustie *Scotland* 29 F4
Carnsore Pt. *Eire* 17 B5
Carnwath *Scotland* 29 E5
Caro *Alaska* 62 E4
Carol *Brazil* 72 H5
Caroline I. *Pacific Oc.* 10 F5
Caroline Is. *W. Pacific Oc.* 10 C4
Carpathians, mts. *E. Europe* 41 J1
Carpentaria, G. of *N. Terr.-Qnsld.* 77 F1
Carrantouhill, mt. *Eire* 17 A6
Carrara *Italy* 38 B2
Carrbridge *Scotland* 28 E3
Carrick *Scotland* 29 D5
Carrickfergus *N. Ireland* 17 C4
Carrickmacross *Eire* 30 E4
Carrick-on-Shannon *Eire* 17 A5
Carrick-on-Suir *Eire* 17 B5
Carrington *N. Dakota* 68 D1
Carriso Mt. *Arizona* 64 E3
Carrizozo *New Mexico* 67 E5
Carse of Gowrie *Scotland* 29 E4
Carson City *Nevada* 64 C3
Carson Sink *Nevada* 64 C3
Carsphairn *Scotland* 29 D5
Carstairs *Scotland* 29 E5
Cartagena *Colombia* 72 B1
Cartagena *Spain* 36 D4
Cartago *Costa Rica* 71 H5
Carter Bar, pass *Eng.-Scot.* 29 F5
Carthage *Missouri* 65 H3
Carthage *New York* 66 D2
Cartier I. *Timor Sea* 76 C1
Cartwright *Labrador* 63 X7
Casablanca *Morocco* 57 B1
Casa Grande *Arizona* 67 D5
Cascade Pt. *New Zealand* 79 B5
Cascade Ra. *Oregon, etc.* 64 B2
Cascavel *Brazil* 72 K4
Cashel *Eire* 31 D5
Casino *New South Wales* 77 J4
Casiquiare R. *Braz.-Venez.* 72 D3
Casper *Wyoming* 64 E2
Caspian Sea *Iran-U.S.S.R.* 46 E4
Cassiar Mts. *Br. Columbia* 62 J6
Cassino *Italy* 38 C4
Castellón de la Plana *Spain* 36 D3
Castelo Branco *Portugal* 36 B3
Castlebar *Eire* 17 A5
Castlebay *Scotland* 28 A4
Castlebellingham *Eire* 30 E4
Castleblayney *Eire* 30 E3
Castle Cary *England* 26 E3
Castlecomer *Eire* 31 D5
Castlederg *N. Ireland* 30 D3
Castledermot *Eire* 31 E5
Castle Douglas *Scotland* 17 D4
Castleford *England* 25 D3
Castleisland *Eire* 31 B5
Castlemaine *Eire* 31 B5
Castlemaine *Victoria* 77 G6
Castlepollard *Eire* 30 D4
Castlerea *Eire* 17 A5
Castlereagh R. *N. S. W.* 77 H5
Castletown *Isle of Man* 17 C4
Castletown *Scotland* 28 E2
Castletown Bere *Eire* 31 B6
Castres *France* 33 C5
Castries *West Indies* 71 M5
Castrovillari *Italy* 38 D5
Cat I. *Bahamas* 71 J3
Catalonia *Spain* 36 E2
Catamaran *Tasmania* 77 H7
Catamarca *Argentina* 73 D9
Catania *Sicily* 38 D6
Catanzaro *Italy* 38 D5
Catastrophe, C. *S. Australia* 77 F5
Catete *Angola* 59 B1
Catorce *Mexico* 70 D3
Catskill *New York* 66 E2
Catskill Mts. *New York* 66 D2
Catterick *England* 25 D2
Caucasus, mts. *U.S.S.R.* 46 E4
Caungula *Angola* 59 B1
Cauvery, R. *India* 53 L8
Cavally, R. *Liberia, etc.* 57 B4
Cavan *Eire* 17 B5
Caxias *Brazil* 72 J4
Caxito *Angola* 59 B1
Cayenne *Fr. Guiana* 72 G3
Cayman, Grand, I. *West Indies* 71 H4
Cayman, Little, I. *West Indies* 71 H4
Cazombo *Angola* 59 C2
Ceanannus Mór *Eire* 30 D4
Cebu *Philippines* 48 E5
Cécina *Italy* 38 B3
Cedar City *Utah* 67 D4
Cedar Falls *Iowa* 68 E2
Cedar Keys *Florida* 65 K5
Cedar Rapids *Iowa* 65 H2
Ceduna *S. Australia* 77 E5
Cegléd *Hungary* 35 F5
Celaya *Mexico* 70 D3
Celebes (Sulawesi), I. *Indonesia* 48 D7
Celebes Sea *Indonesia* 48 E6
Celle *Germany, W.* 34 C2
Cemais *Wales* 25 A3
Central African Rep. *Africa* 58 A4
Central America *America* 70 G5
Central Auckland *New Zealand* 79 E2
Central Cordillera, mts. *Colombia* 72 B3
Central Falls *Rhode I.* 66 F2
Centralia *Washington* 67 B2
Cephalonia, I. *Greece* 39 E5
Cerignola *Italy* 38 D4
Cernavoda *Rumania* 39 H2
Cerne Abbas *England* 26 E4
Cerralvo *Mexico* 70 E2
Cerro Bolivar, mt. *Venezuela* 72 E2
Cerro de Pasco *Peru* 72 B6
Cesena *Italy* 38 C2
Cesenatica *Italy* 38 C2
Cēsis *Latvia* 42 F4
České Budějovice *Czechoslovakia* 34 D4
Cessnock *New South Wales* 77 J5
Cetinje *Yugoslavia* 38 E3
Cetraro *Italy* 38 D5
Ceuta *N.W. Africa* 57 B1
Cevennes, mts. *France* 33 D5
Cevio *Switzerland* 37 C1
Ceylon *S. Asia* 53 M9
Chad & L. *Africa* 57 D3
Chadron *Nebraska* 64 F2
Chagos Arch. *Indian Oc.* 11 N5
Chahbahar *Iran* 52 H5
Chalantun *China* 49 A2
Chalcidice Pen. *Greece* 39 F4
Chalcis *Greece* 39 F5
Chaleur B. *N.B.-Quebec* 63 V8
Chalk River *Ontario* 63 T8
Chalky Inlet *New Zealand* 79 A7
Challenger Deep *Pacific Oc.* 48 F5
Challis *Idaho* 64 D2
Chalna *E. Pakistan* 53 N6
Châlons-sur-Marne *France* 33 D2
Chalon-sur-Saône *France* 33 D3
Chaman *W. Pakistan* 52 J4
Chambal R. *India* 53 L5
Chamberlain *S. Dakota* 64 G2
Chambery *France* 33 D4
Chamdo *Tibet* 50 F5
Chamonix *France* 33 E4
Champagne *France* 33 D2
Champaign *Illinois* 69 F2
Chañaral *Chile* 73 C9
Chanchiang *China* 48 D4
Chandernagore *India* 53 N6
Chandigarh *India* 53 L4
Chandpur *E. Pakistan* 53 O6
Changchow *China* 51 K7
Changchun *China* 48 E2
Changhua *Taiwan* 51 L7
Changkiakow *China* 48 D2
Changsha *China* 48 D4
Chang Tang, plat. *Tibet, etc.* 50 C5
Changteh *China* 51 J6
Changting *China* 51 K6
Changyeh *China* 48 C3
Channel *Newfoundland* 63 X8
Channel Is. *California* 67 C5
Channel Is. *England* 33 A2
Chanthaburi *Thailand* 53 Q8
Chanute *Kansas* 68 D3
Chany, L. *U.S.S.R.* 46 H3
Chaochow *China* 51 K7
Chaotung *China* 50 G6
Chapala, L. *Mexico* 70 D3
Chapel-en-le-Frith *England* 25 D3
Chapra *India* 53 M5
Charchan *Sinkiang* 53 N3
Charchan, R. *Sinkiang* 50 D4
Charcot I. *Antarctica* 80 S8
Chard *England* 26 E4
Chardstock *England* 26 D4
Chardzhou *Turkmen.* 46 G5
Chari, R. *Chad* 57 D3
Charing *England* 27 H3
Charité, la *France* 33 D3
Charkhlik *Sinkiang* 50 D4
Charlbury *England* 27 F3
Charleroi *Belgium* 32 C4
Charles, C. *Virginia* 65 L3
Charles City *Iowa* 68 E2
Charleston *Missouri* 65 J3
Charleston *S. Carolina* 65 L4
Charleston *W. Virginia* 65 K3
Charlestown *Eire* 30 C4
Charleville *Eire* 17 A5
Charleville *France* 33 D2
Charleville *Queensland* 77 H4
Charlotte *N. Carolina* 65 K3
Charlotte Amalie *Puerto Rico* 71 L4
Charlottenburg *Germany* 34 D2
Charlottesville *Virginia* 69 H3
Charlottetown *Prince Edward I.* 63 W8
Charlton *Victoria* 77 G6
Charnwood Forest *England* 27 F2
Charters Towers *Queensland* 77 H3
Chartres *France* 33 C2
Chatahoochee, R. *Alabama, etc.* 69 F4
Chatanika *Alaska* 62 E4
Châteaubriant *France* 33 B3
Château-du-Loir *France* 33 C3
Châteaudun *France* 33 C2
Châteauroux *France* 33 C3
Château Thierry *France* 33 D2
Châtellerault *France* 33 C3
Chatham *England* 17 F6
Chatham *New Brunswick* 63 V8
Chatham *Ontario* 63 S9
Chatham Is. *S. Pacific Oc.* 10 E7
Chatham Str. *Alaska* 62 H6
Châtillon-sur-Seine *France* 33 D3
Châtre, la *France* 33 C3
Chattanooga *Tennessee* 65 J3
Chatteris *England* 27 H2
Chaumont *France* 33 D2
Chawton *England* 27 G3
Chayu *Tibet* 50 F6
Cheadle *England* 27 F2
Cheb *Czechoslovakia* 34 D3
Cheboksary *U.S.S.R.* 43 G1
Cheboygan *Michigan* 69 G1
Cheddar *England* 26 E3
Chélia, mt. *Algeria* 57 C1
Chelkar *Kazakh.* 52 G1
Chelm *Poland* 35 G3
Chelmno *Poland* 35 F2
Chelmsford *England* 17 F6
Cheltenham *England* 17 D6
Chelyabinsk *U.S.S.R.* 46 G3
Chelyuskin, C. *U.S.S.R.* 47 L1
Chemba *Mozambique* 59 D2
Chenab, R. *W. Pakistan, etc.* 53 K4
Chengchow *China* 51 J5
Chengteh *China* 48 D2

Chengtu	China	48	C3
Chenhsien	China	51	J6
Cheong Kum	China	50	H8
Chepstow	Wales	26	E3
Cher, R.	France	33	C3
Cherbourg	France	33	B2
Cheremkhovo	U.S.S.R.	47	L3
Cheribon	Java	48	C7
Cherkassy	Ukraine	43	D3
Cherkessk	U.S.S.R.	43	F4
Chernigov	Ukraine	43	D2
Chernovtsy	Ukraine	46	C4
Chernyakhovsk	U.S.S.R.	42	E5
Cherokee	Iowa	64	G2
Cherokees, L. O' The	Oklahoma	68	E3
Cherskogo Mts.	U.S.S.R.	47	P2
Chertsey	England	27	G3
Cherwell, R.	England	27	F3
Chesapeake B.	Maryland, etc.	65	L3
Chesham	England	27	G3
Chesil Bank	England	17	D6
Cheshire	England	26	E1
Cheshire Plain	England	25	C3
Chester	England	17	D5
Chester	Pennsylvania	66	D4
Chesterfield	England	17	E5
Chesterfield Inlet	N.-W. Terr., Can.	63	Q5
Chester-le-Street	England	25	D2
Chetumal & B.	Mexico	70	G4
Cheviot, The, hill	England	16	D4
Cheviot Hills	Scot.-Eng.	17	D4
Cheyenne	Wyoming	64	F2
Chiai	Taiwan	51	L7
Chiang Mai	Thailand	53	P7
Chibia	Angola	59	B2
Chibougamau	Quebec	63	U7
Chibuto	Mozambique	59	D3
Chicago	Illinois	65	J2
Chichagof I.	Alaska	62	G6
Chichester	England	17	E6
Chickamauga L.	Tennessee	69	F3
Chickasha	Oklahoma	64	G4
Chiclayo	Peru	72	A5
Chico	California	67	B4
Chico R.	Argentina	73	D12
Chicoutimi	Quebec	63	U8
Chidley, C.	Quebec	63	W5
Chieti	Italy	38	C3
Chigelik	Sinkiang	50	D4
Chigwell	England	27	H3
Chihfeng	China	51	K3
Chihkiang	China	50	H6
Chihuahua	Mexico	70	C2
Chikien	China	51	L1
Chilapa de Alvarez	Mexico	70	E4
Chilbolton	England	27	F3
Childress	Texas	64	F4
Chile	S. America	73	C12
Chilham	England	27	H3
Chiliceto	Argentina	73	D9
Chilintun	China	51	M1
Chilko L.	Br. Columbia	62	K7
Chillan	Chile	73	C11
Chillicothe	Missouri	65	H3
Chiloe, I.	Chile	73	C12
Chiltern Hills	England	17	E6
Chilung	Taiwan	48	E4
Chilwa, L.	Malawi	59	D2
Chimban	Uzbek.	46	G4
Chimborazo, mt	Ecuador	72	B4
Chimbote	Peru	72	B5
Chimkent	Kazakh.	46	G4
Chin Hills	Burma	50	E7
China	E. Asia	48	C3
China, Great Plain of	China	48	D3
Chinandega	Nicaragua	70	G5
Chinchow	China	48	E2
Chinde	Mozambique	59	D2
Chindwin R.	Burma	53	P6
Chinese Turkistan	Sinkiang	53	L3
Ching Hai, L.	China	48	C3
Chinju	Korea	51	M4
Chinkiang	China	51	K5
Chin Ling Shan, mts.	China	48	C3
Chinon	France	33	C3
Chinwangtao	China	51	K4
Chioggia	Italy	38	C2
Chios & I.	Greece	39	G5
Chippenham	England	27	E3
Chipping Campden	England	27	F2
Chipping Norton	England	17	E6
Chipping Sodbury	England	26	E3
Chiquito Plat.	Bolivia	72	E7
Chirk	Wales	26	D2
Chirnside	Scotland	29	F5
Chisledon	England	27	F3
Chita	U.S.S.R.	47	M3
Chitaldroog	India	53	L8
Chitral	W. Pakistan	53	K3
Chittagong	E. Pakistan	53	O6
Chiusi	Italy	38	B3
Chivasso	Italy	38	A2
Chivemba	Angola	59	B2
Choix	Mexico	70	C2
Chojnice	Poland	35	E2
Cholet	France	33	B3
Cholon	Vietnam	48	C5
Cholsey	England	27	F3
Cholu	Honduras	70	G5
Chomutov	Czechoslovakia	34	D3
Chongjin	Korea	51	M3
Chongju	Korea	51	M4
Chonos Arch.	Chile	73	C12
Chorley	England	25	C3
Chorzów	Poland	35	F3
Chowkow	China	51	J5
Chowstun	China	51	K4
Choybalsan	Mongolia	48	D2
Christchurch	England	27	F4
Christchurch	New Zealand	79	D5
Christianshaab	Greenland	63	Y4
Christmas I.	Indian Oc.	10	B5
Christmas I.	Pacific Oc.	10	E4
Chu, R.	Kazakh.	46	H4
Chuanchow	China	51	K6
Chuanhsien	China	51	J6
Chubut R.	Argentina	73	D12
Chuchow	China	51	J6
Chudleigh	England	26	D4
Chugach mts.	Alaska	62	E5
Chuhsien	China	51	K6
Chukotsk Sea	Arctic Oc.	10	E1
Chukotskiy Mts. & Pen.	U.S.S.R.	47	T2
Chulmleigh	England	26	D4
Chulym	U.S.S.R.	46	J3
Chulym R.	U.S.S.R.	47	J3
Chuna R.	U.S.S.R.	47	K3
Chunchon	Korea	51	M4
Chungan	China	51	K6
Chungking	China	48	C4
Chungtien	China	50	F6
Chuquicamata	Chile	73	D8
Chur	Switzerland	37	C1
Churchill & C.	Manitoba	63	Q6
Churchill Falls & R.	Labrador	63	W7
Churchill L.	Saskatchewan	62	N6
Churchill Pk.	Br. Columbia	62	J6
Churchill R.	Man.-Sask.	63	P6
Church Stretton	England	26	E2
Chuvash A.S.S.R.	U.S.S.R.	43	G1
Ciengfuegos	Cuba	71	H3
Cimarron R.	Oklahoma, etc.	64	G3
Cimone, Mte.	Italy	38	B2
Cîmpulung Moldovenesc	Rumania	35	H5
Cinca ,R.	Spain	36	E2
Cincinnati	Ohio	65	K3
Cinderford	England	26	E3
Cinto, Mt.	Corsica	38	A3
Circle	Alaska	62	F4
Cirencester	England	27	F3
Ciro	Italy	38	D5
Cisco	Texas	64	G4
Citlaltepec, mt.	Mexico	70	E4
Cittanova	Italy	38	D5
Ciudad Bolivar	Venezuela	72	E2
Ciudad Camargo	Mexico	70	C2
Ciudad Guzman	Mexico	70	D4
Ciudad Juarez	Mexico	70	C1
Ciudad Lerdo	Mexico	70	D2
Ciudad Madero	Mexico	70	E3
Ciudad Real	Spain	36	C3
Ciudad Rodrigo	Spain	36	B2
Ciudad Victoria	Mexico	70	E3
Civitavécchia	Italy	38	B3
Civray	France	33	C3
Cizre	Turkey	52	D3
Clackmannan	Scotland	29	E4
Clacton on Sea	England	27	J3
Claire, L.	Alberta	62	M6
Clamecy	France	33	D3
Clara	Eire	31	D4
Clare, co.	Eire	17	A5
Clare	England	27	H2
Clarecastle	Eire	31	C5
Claremorris	Eire	30	C4
Clarence, R.	New Zealand	79	D5
Clarence Sd.	Alaska-B.C.	62	H6
Clarence Str.	N. Terr., Aust.	76	E1
Clark, L.	Alaska	62	C5
Clark Hill Res.	Georgia-S. Car.	65	K4
Clarksburg	W. Virginia	65	K3
Clarksdale	Mississippi	68	E4
Clarksville	Tennessee	65	J3
Claydon	England	27	J2
Clayton	New Mexico	67	F4
Clear, C.	Eire	17	A6
Cleare, C.	Alaska	62	E6
Cleddau, R.	Wales	26	C3
Cleethorpes	England	25	E3
Clent Hills	England	27	E2
Cleobury Mortimer	England	26	E2
Clermont	France	33	D4
Clermont	Queensland	77	H3
Clevedon	England	26	E3
Cleveland	Ohio	65	K2
Cleveland	Tennessee	69	G3
Cleveland Hills	England	17	E4
Clew B.	Eire	17	A5
Clifden	Eire	17	A5
Cliffe	England	27	H3
Clifton	Arizona	67	E5
Clifton Hills	S. Australia	77	F4
Clinton	Iowa	65	H2
Clinton Colden L.	N.-W. Terr., Can.	62	N5
Clipperton I.	Pacific Oc.	10	G4
Clitheroe	England	25	C3
Cloghan	Eire	31	D4
Clogher	N. Ireland	30	D3
Clonakilty & B.	Eire	17	A6
Cloncurry	Queensland	77	G3
Clondalkin	Eire	31	E4
Clonegall	Eire	31	E5
Clonmel	Eire	17	B5
Clones	Eire	17	B4
Cloquet	Minnesota	68	E1
Cloud Pk.	Wyoming	64	E2
Clova, & Glen	Scotland	29	E4
Clovelly	England	26	C4
Clovis	New Mexico	67	F5
Cloyne	Eire	31	C6
Cluj	Rumania	35	G5
Clun	England	26	D2
Clun Forest	Wales	26	D2
Clunie, L.	Scotland	28	C3
Clutha, R.	New Zealand	79	B6
Clwyd, R.	Wales	26	D1
Clyde	N.-W. Terr., Can.	63	V3
Clyde, Firth of	Scotland	16	C4
Clyde, R	Scotland	16	D4
Coalville	England	27	F2
Coast Ra.	Can.-U.S.A.	62	H6
Coastal Plain Basin	W. Australia	76	B4
Coast of Labrador	Newfoundland	63	W6
Coatbridge	Scotland	16	C4
Coats I.	N.-W. Terr., Can.	63	S5
Coats Land	Antarctica	80	C7
Coatzacoalcos	Mexico	70	F4
Cobalt	Ontario	63	S8
Coban	Guatemala	70	F4
Cobar	New South Wales	77	H5
Cobh	Eire	17	A6
Coblenz	Germany, W.	34	B3
Cobourg Pen.	N. Terr., Aust.	76	E1
Coburg	Germany, W.	34	C3
Cochabamba	Bolivia	72	D7
Cochin	India	53	L9
Cochin China	Vietnam	53	R9
Cochrane	Ontario	63	S8
Cock Bridge	Scotland	28	E3
Cockburn	S. Australia	77	G5
Cockburnspath	Scotland	29	F5
Cockermouth	England	25	B2
Cocos Is.	Pacific Oc.	11	H4
Cocos Keeling Is.	Indian Oc.	10	B5
Cod, C.	Massachusetts	66	F2
Codfish I.	New Zealand	79	A7
Cody	Wyoming	67	E3
Coen	Queensland	77	G1
Coevorden	Netherlands	32	E2
Coff's Harbour	N. S. W.	77	J5
Cognac	France	33	B4
Cohoes	New York	66	E2
Coiba I.	Panama	71	H6
Coimbatore	India	53	L8
Coimbra	Portugal	36	B2
Colac	Victoria	77	G6
Colatina	Brazil	72	J7
Colby	Kansas	64	F3
Colchester	England	17	F6
Coldingham	Scotland	29	F5
Coldstream	Scotland	16	D4
Coleraine	N. Ireland	17	B4
Coleridge, L.	New Zealand	79	C5
Colima	Mexico	70	D4
Coll, I.	Scotland	16	B3
College	Alaska	62	E5
Collie	W. Australia	76	B5
Collingwood	Queensland	77	G3
Collinson Pen.	N.-W. Terr., Can.	62	O3
Collinstown	Eire	31	E4
Collinsville	Queensland	77	H3
Collooney	Eire	30	C3
Colmar	France	33	E2
Colmonell	Scotland	29	D5
Colne	England	25	C3
Colne, R.	England	27	H3
Cologne	Germany, W.	34	B3
Colomb-Bechar	Algeria	57	B1
Colombia	S. America	72	B3
Colombo	Ceylon	53	L9
Colon	Panama	71	H6
Colonsay, I.	Scotland	16	B3
Colorado, state	U.S.A.	64	E3
Colorado Des.	California	64	C4
Colorado Plat.	Arizona	64	D3
Colorado R.	Argentina	73	D11
Colorado R.	Texas	64	G4
Colorado R.	U.S.A.	64	D3
Colorado City	Texas	64	F4
Colorado Springs	Colorado	64	F3
Colsterworth	England	27	G2
Columbia	Alabama	65	J4
Columbia	Missouri	68	E3
Columbia	Pennsylvania	66	C3
Columbia	S. Carolina	65	K4
Columbia	Tennessee	65	J3
Columbia, Dist. of (D.C.)	U.S.A.	69	H3
Columbia, Mt.	Br. Columbia	62	L7
Columbia, R.	Oregon, etc.	64	B1
Columbus	Georgia	65	K4
Columbus	Mississippi	69	F4
Columbus	Nebraska	68	D2
Columbus	Ohio	65	K3
Columbus	Texas	64	G5
Colville, C.	New Zealand	79	E2
Colville R.	Alaska	62	D4
Colwyn Bay	Wales	26	D1
Colyton	England	26	D4
Comacchio	Italy	38	C2
Comay	Honduras	70	G5
Comber	N. Ireland	30	F3
Comeragh Mts.	Eire	31	D5
Comilla	E. Pakistan	50	E7
Comitan de Dominguez	Mexico	70	F4
Committee B.	N.-W. Terr., Can.	63	R4
Como & L.	Italy	38	B2
Comodoro Rivadavia	Argentina	73	D13
Comondu	Mexico	70	B2
Comorin, C.	India	53	L9
Comoro Arch.	Indian Oc.	59	E2
Compiègne	France	33	C2
Compostela	Mexico	70	C3
Comrie	Scotland	29	E4
Conakry	Guinea	57	A4
Concepción	Chile	73	C11
Concepción	Paraguay	73	F8
Conception B.	Newfoundland	63	Y8
Conchas R.	Mexico	70	C2
Concord	New Hampshire	65	M2
Concordia	Argentina	73	F10
Concordia	Kansas	68	D3
Condamine R.	Queensland	78	G2
Condobolin	New South Wales	77	H5
Condom	France	33	C5
Conegliano	Italy	38	C2
Conflans	France	33	D2
Confolens	France	33	C3
Cong	Eire	30	B4
Congleton	England	27	E1
Congo	Africa	59	C1
Congo, Rep. of	Cent. Africa	57	D5
Congo R.	Congo	57	D5
Coniston	England	17	D4
Conn, L.	Eire	17	A4
Connacht	Eire	30	B4
Connecticut, state	U.S.A.	65	M2
Connel Ferry	Scotland	29	C4
Connemara Mts.	Eire	17	A5
Consall	England	27	F1
Consett	England	25	D2
Constance	Germany, W.	34	C5
Constance, L.	Germany-Switz.	34	C5
Constanta	Rumania	39	H2
Constantine	Algeria	57	C1
Constantinople	Turkey	41	L3

Denilquin *New South Wales* **77** H6
Denison *Texas* **64** G4
Denizli *Turkey* **39** H6
Denmark *N.W. Europe* **42** B5
Denmark *W. Australia* **76** B6
Denmark Str. *Iceland-Greenland* **11** J1
Denny *Scotland* **29** E4
Denton *Texas* **68** D4
D'Entrecasteaux Pt. *W. Australia* **76** B5
Denver *Colorado* **64** F3
Deptford *England* **27** F3
Dera Ghazi Khan *W. Pakistan* **53** K4
Dera Ismail Khan *W. Pakistan* **53** K4
Derby *England* **17** E5
Derby *W. Australia* **76** C2
Derg, L. *Eire* **17** A5
Derna *Libya* **58** B1
Derrynasaggart Mts. *Eire* **17** A6
Derryveagh Mts. *Eire* **17** A4
Derwent, R. *Durham, Eng.* **25** C2
Derwent, R. *Yorks., Eng.* **25** E3
Derwent Water *England* **25** B2
Desaguadero, R. *Bolivia* **72** D7
Desborough *England* **27** G2
Deseado *Argentina* **73** D13
Des Moines *Iowa* **65** H2
Des Moines R. *Iowa, etc.* **65** H2
Desna R. *U.S.S.R.* **46** D3
Desolation, C. *Greenland* **63** Z5
Dessau *Germany, E.* **34** D3
Dessye *Ethiopia* **58** C3
Destruction Bay *Yukon* **62** G5
Detroit *Michigan* **65** K2
Deventer *Netherlands* **32** E2
Devil River Pk. *New Zealand* **79** D4
Devil's Bridge *Wales* **26** D2
Devil's Elbow *Scotland* **29** E4
Devils Lake *N. Dakota* **64** G1
Devizes *England* **17** E6
Devon, co. *England* **17** C6
Devon I. *N.-W. Terr., Can.* **63** Q2
Devonport *England* **17** C6
Devonport *New Zealand* **79** E2
Devonport *Tasmania* **77** H7
Dewey L. *Kentucky* **69** G3
Dewsbury *England* **25** D3
Dezful *Iran* **52** E4
Dezhneva, C. *U.S.S.R.* **47** T2
Dhahran *Saudi Arabia* **52** E5
Dhaulagiri, mt. *Nepal* **53** M5
Diamantina *Brazil* **72** J7
Diamantina R. *Qnsld.-S. Aust.* **77** G3
Dibrugarh *India* **50** E6
Dickinson *N. Dakota* **64** F1
Die *France* **33** D4
Diego-Suarez *Malagasy Rep.* **59** E2
Diepholz *Germany, W.* **34** B2
Dieppe *France* **33** C2
Diest *Belgium* **32** D4
Digne *France* **33** E4
Digom *France* **33** D3
Dijon *France* **33** D3
Dili *Timor I.* **48** E7
Dillingham *Alaska* **62** C6
Dillon *Montana* **64** D1
Dilolo *Congo* **59** C2
Dinan *France* **33** B2
Dinant *Belgium* **32** C4
Dinard *France* **33** B2
Dinaric Alps *Yugoslavia* **38** D2
Dinas Mawddwy *Wales* **26** D2
Dingle *Eire* **17** A5
Dingwall *Scotland* **16** C3
Diredawa *Ethiopia* **58** D4
Dirk Hartog's I. *W. Australia* **76** A4
Dirranbandi *Queensland* **77** H4
Disappointment, C. *Washington* **64** B1
Disappointment, L. *W. Australia* **76** C3
Disentis *Switzerland* **37** C1
Disko I. *Greenland* **63** Y4
Diss *England* **27** J2
Distington *England* **25** B2
District of Columbia (D.C.) *U.S.A.* **66** C4
Diu I. *India* **53** K6
Dixon Entrance *Br. Columbia* **62** H7
Diyālā *Iraq* **55** H3
Diyarbakir *Turkey* **52** D3
Djado *Niger* **57** D2
Djakarta *Java* **48** C7
Djelfa *Algeria* **57** C1
Djerid, Chott, L. *Tunisia* **57** C1
Djibouti *Fr. Somaliland* **58** D3
Djouf, El, reg. *Mauritania* **57** B2
Djúpivogur *Iceland* **42** L6
Dneprodzerzhinsk *Ukraine* **43** D3
Dneprograd *Ukraine* **43** D3
Dnepropetrovsk *Ukraine* **46** D4
Dnieper, R. *Ukraine, etc.* **46** D4
Dniester, R. *Ukraine, etc.* **46** C4
Dobbyn *Queensland* **77** F2
Dobrogea *Rumania* **39** H2
Docking *England* **27** H2
Dodecanese Is. *Greece* **39** G6
Dodge City *Kansas* **64** F3
Dodman Pt. *England* **26** C4
Dodoma *Tanzania* **58** C5
Doha *Qatar* **52** F5
Dokkum *Netherlands* **32** E1
Dolbeau *Quebec* **63** U8
Dole *France* **33** D3
Dolgelley *Wales* **17** D5
Dollar *Scotland* **29** E4
Dolo *Ethiopia* **58** D4
Dolomites, mts. *Italy* **38** B1
Dombas *Norway* **42** B3
Dominica, I. *West Indies* **71** M4
Dominican Rep. *Hispaniola* **71** K4
Dömitz *Germany, E.* **34** C2
Don, R. *England* **25** D3
Don, R. *Scotland* **16** D3
Don, R. *U.S.S.R.* **46** E3
Donaghadee *N. Ireland* **17** C4
Donaldsonville *Louisiana* **65** H4
Donard *Eire* **31** E4
Donauworth *Germany, W.* **34** C4
Doncaster *England* **17** E5
Dondo *Angola* **59** B1
Dondra Hd. *Ceylon* **53** M9
Donegal & B. *Eire* **17** A4
Doneraile *Eire* **31** C5
Donets R. *U.S.S.R.* **43** E3
Donetsk *Ukraine* **46** D4
Dongara *W. Australia* **76** A4
Dongola *Sudan* **58** C3
Donington *England* **27** G2
Doon, L. & R. *Scotland* **29** D5
Dorchester *England* **17** D6
Dordogne, R. *France* **33** B4
Dordrecht *Netherlands* **32** C3
Doré L. *Saskatchewan* **62** N7
Dore, Mt. *France* **33** C4
Dores do Indaiá *Brazil* **72** H7
Dori *Up. Volta* **57** B3
Dorking & Gap *England* **27** G3
Dornbirn *Austria* **34** C5
Dornie *Scotland* **28** C3
Dornoch *Scotland* **16** C3
Dornoch Firth *Scotland* **16** D3
Dorset, co. *England* **17** D6
Dortmund *Germany, W.* **34** B3
Dossor *Kazakh.* **43** H3
Dothan *Alabama* **69** F4
Douai *France* **33** D1
Douala *Cameroun* **57** D4
Douarnenez *France* **33** A2
Doubs, R. *France* **33** D3
Doubtful Sd. *New Zealand* **79** A6
Doubtless B. *New Zealand* **79** D1
Douglas *Arizona* **67** E5
Douglas *Cape of Good Hope* **59** C3
Douglas *Isle of Man* **17** C4
Douglas *Scotland* **29** E5
Douglas *Wyoming* **64** E2
Douglas, Mt. *Montana* **64** D1
Doune *Scotland* **29** D4
Dounreay *Scotland* **16** D2
Douro, R. *Portugal-Spain* **36** B2
Dover *Delaware* **65** L3
Dover *England* **17** F6
Dover *New Hampshire* **65** M2
Dovercourt *England* **27** J3
Dovre Fjell, mts. *Norway* **42** B3
Dow, L. *Bechuanaland* **59** C3
Dowlais *Wales* **26** D3
Down, co. *N. Ireland* **17** B4
Downham *England* **17** F5
Downpatrick *N. Ireland* **17** C4
Downton *England* **27** F4
Dra, R. *Morocco* **57** B2
Drachten *Netherlands* **32** E1
Draguignan *France* **33** E5
Drake Str. *Antarctica* **80** S9
Drakensberg, mts. *S. Africa* **59** C4
Drama *Greece* **39** G4
Drammen *Norway* **42** B4
Drau, R. *Austria* **34** D5
Drava, R. *Yugoslavia, etc.* **38** D1
Drem *Scotland* **29** F4
Drenthe *Netherlands* **32** E2
Dresden *Germany, E.* **34** D3
Dreux *France* **33** C2
Drimoleague *Eire* **31** B6
Drin, R. *Albania* **41** J3
Drina, R. *Yugoslavia* **38** E3
Drogheda *Eire* **17** B5
Droitwich *England* **27** E2
Dromore *Eire* **30** C3
Dromore *Down, N. Ire.* **30** E3
Dromore *Tyrone, N. Ire.* **30** D3
Dronfield *England* **25** D3
Dronne, R. *France* **33** C4
Drumheller *Alberta* **62** M7
Drumlish *Eire* **30** D4
Drummore *Scotland* **29** D6
Drumnadrochit *Scotland* **28** D3
Drumochter Pass *Scotland* **29** D4
Drumod *Eire* **30** D4
Drumshanbo *Eire* **30** C3
Druzhina *U.S.S.R.* **47** P2
Drymen *Scotland* **29** D4
Dubawnt L. & R. *N.-W. Terr., Can.* **62** O5
Dubbo *New South Wales* **77** H5
Dubh Artach *Scotland* **16** B3
Dublin *Eire* **17** B5
Dublin *Georgia* **65** K4
Dublin B. *Eire* **17** B5
Dubrovnik *Yugoslavia* **38** E3
Dubuque *Iowa* **65** H2
Ducie I. *Pacific Oc.* **10** F6
Dudinka *U.S.S.R.* **47** J2
Dudley *England* **17** D5
Dufftown *Scotland* **16** D3
Duifken Pt. *Queensland* **77** G1
Duisburg *Germany, W.* **34** B3
Dulan *China* **50** F4
Dulce, R. *Argentina* **73** E9
Duluth *Minnesota* **65** H1
Dulverton *England* **26** D3
Duma *Syria* **54** D3
Dumas *Texas* **68** C3
Dumbarton *Scotland* **16** C4
Dumfries *Scotland* **17** D4
Dunbar *Scotland* **16** D4
Dunbarton, co. *Scotland* **16** C3
Dunblane *Scotland* **16** D3
Dunboyne *Eire* **31** E4
Duncan *Oklahoma* **68** D4
Duncannon *Eire* **31** E5
Duncansby Hd. *Scotland* **16** D2
Dundalk *Eire* **17** B4
Dundalk B. *Eire* **17** B5
Dundas Str. *N. Terr., Aust.* **76** E1
Dundee *Scotland* **16** D3
Dundrum *N. Ireland* **30** F3
Dundrum B. *N. Ireland* **17** C4
Dunedin *New Zealand* **79** C6
Dunfanaghy *Eire* **30** D2
Dunfermline *Scotland* **16** D3
Dungannon *N. Ireland* **17** B4
Dungarvan & Harb. *Eire* **17** B5
Dungeness *England* **17** F6
Dungiven *N. Ireland* **30** E3
Dungloe *Eire* **30** C3
Dunkeld *Scotland* **16** D3
Dunkery Beacon *England* **26** D3
Dunkirk *France* **33** C1
Dunkirk *New York* **66** B2
Dunlaoghaire *Eire* **17** B5
Dunlavin *Eire* **31** E4
Dunleer *Eire* **30** E4
Dunmanway *Eire* **17** A6
Dunmara *N. Terr., Aust.* **77** E2
Dunmore *Eire* **30** C4
Dunnet Hd. *Scotland* **16** D2
Dunoon *Scotland* **29** D5
Duns *Scotland* **16** D4
Dunstable *England* **27** G3
Dunster *England* **26** D3
Dunvegan *Scotland* **28** B3
Dunvegan, L. *Scotland* **16** B3
Du Quoin *Illinois* **65** J3
Durango *Colorado* **64** E3
Durant *Oklahoma* **68** D4
Durban *Natal* **59** D3
Düren *Germany, W.* **34** B3
Durham *England* **17** E4
Durham *N. Carolina* **65** L3
Durness *Scotland* **28** D2
Durrës *Albania* **39** E4
Durrow *Eire* **31** D5
Dursley *England* **26** E3
Durston *England* **26** D3
D'Urville I. *New Zealand* **79** D4
Dushanbe *Tadzhik.* **46** G5
Dusky Sd. *New Zealand* **79** A6
Düsseldorf *Germany, W.* **34** B3
Dutch Harbor *Alaska* **10** E2
Dvina R. *White Russia, etc.* **43** C1
Dvina, N., R. *U.S.S.R.* **46** E2
Dvina, W., R. *U.S.S.R.* **46** C3
Dyce *Scotland* **28** F3
Dyersburg *Tennessee* **69** F3
Dyfi, *Wales* **26** D2
Dyke L. *Labrador* **63** V7
Dymchurch *England* **27** J3
Dysart *Scotland* **29** E4
Dzamin Ude *Mongolia* **51** J3
Dzerhinsk *U.S.S.R.* **43** F1
Dzhalal Abad *Kirgiz.* **46** H4
Dzhalinda *U.S.S.R.* **47** N3
Dzhambul *Kazakh.* **53** K2
Dzhugdzhur Mts. *U.S.S.R.* **47** O3
Dzun *China* **50** F4
Dzun *Tibet* **50** F5
Dzungaria, reg. *Sinkiang* **50** C3
Dzungarian Gap *Sinkiang* **46** J4
Eagle *Alaska* **62** F5
Eagle Pass *Texas* **64** F5
Eagle Plains *Yukon* **62** G4
Ealing *England* **27** G3
Eardisley *England* **26** D2
Earith *England* **27** H2
Earlestown *England* **25** C3
Earls Colne *England* **27** H3
Earlston *Scotland* **29** F5
Earn, L. *Scotland* **29** D4
Earn, R. *Scotland* **29** E4
Eas-Coul-Aulin *Scotland* **28** D2
Easington *England* **25** D2
Easingwold *England* **25** D2
East C. *New Zealand* **79** G2
East Aurora *New York* **66** B2
Eastbourne *England* **17** F6
East China Sea *China, etc.* **48** E3
East Coast *New Zealand* **79** F3
East Dereham *England* **27** H2
Easter I. *S. Pacific Oc.* **10** G6
Eastern Ghats *India* **53** L8
East Flanders *Belgium* **32** B4
East Frisian Is. *Germany, W.* **34** B2
East Grinstead *England* **27** G3
East Harling *England* **27** H2
East Kilbride *Scotland* **29** D5
Eastleigh *England* **27** F4
East London *Cape of Good Hope* **59** C4
East Looe *England* **26** C4
East Lothian, co. *Scotland* **16** D4
Eastmain R. *Quebec* **63** T7
Easton *Pennsylvania* **66** D3
East Pakistan *Pakistan* **53** N6
East Retford *England* **17** E5
Eastry *England* **27** J3
East St. Louis *Illinois* **68** F3
East Siberian Sea *Arctic Oc.* **47** Q1
Eau Claire *Wisconsin* **65** H2
Ebbw Vale *Wales* **17** D6
Eberswalde *Germany, E.* **34** D2
Ebi Nor, L. *Sinkiang* **50** C2
Ebro, R. *Spain* **36** C1
Ecclefechan *Scotland* **29** E5
Eccles *England* **25** C3
Eccleshall *England* **26** E2
Echt *Scotland* **28** F3
Echuca *Victoria* **77** G6
Eck, L. *Scotland* **29** C4
Eckington *England* **25** D3
Ecuador *S. America* **72** B4
Eday, I. *Scotland* **28** F1
Eddystone Lt. Ho. *England* **26** C4
Edea *Cameroun* **57** D4
Eden, R. *England* **17** D4
Edenberry *Eire* **31** D4
Edenbridge *England* **27** H3
Eder, R. *Germany, W.* **34** B3
Ederengin Nuru, mts. *Mongolia* **50** F3
Edge Hill *England* **27** F2
Edgeworthstown *Eire* **30** D4
Edgware *England* **27** G3
Edhessa *Greece* **39** F4
Edievale *New Zealand* **79** B6
Edinburg *Texas* **68** D5
Edinburgh *Scotland* **16** D4
Edirne *Turkey* **39** G4
Edjele *Algeria* **57** C2
Edmonton *Alberta* **62** M7
Edmundston *New Brunswick* **63** V8
Edrachillis B. *Scotland* **16** C2
Edward, L. *Congo-Uganda* **58** B5
Edwards Plat. *Texas* **68** C4

Edzell	*Scotland*	**29**	F4
Eecloo	*Belgium*	**32**	B3
Egede Land	*Greenland*	**63**	Z4
Egedesminde	*Greenland*	**63**	Y4
Egerdir	*Turkey*	**41**	L4
Egersund	*Norway*	**42**	A4
Egilsay, I.	*Scotland*	**28**	F1
Eglinton I.	*N.-W. Terr., Can.*	**62**	L2
Egmond-aan-Zee	*Netherlands*	**32**	C2
Egmont, C.	*New Zealand*	**79**	D3
Egmont, Mt.	*New Zealand*	**79**	E3
Egremont	*England*	**25**	B2
Egton	*England*	**25**	E2
Egypt (U.A.R.)	*N.E. Africa*	**58**	B2
Eigg, I.	*Scotland*	**16**	B3
Eighty Mile Beach	*W. Australia*	**76**	C2
Eil	*Somalia*	**58**	D4
Eil, L.	*Scotland*	**29**	C4
Eilat	*Israel*	**54**	C5
Eindhoven	*Netherlands*	**32**	D3
Eire	*British Isles*	**17**	A5
Eisenach	*Germany, E.*	**34**	C3
Eisenhüttenstadt	*Germany, E.*	**34**	D2
Eisenstadt	*Austria*	**34**	E5
Eketahuna	*New Zealand*	**79**	E4
Elâzig	*Turkey*	**52**	C3
Elba, I.	*Italy*	**38**	B3
Elbasan	*Albania*	**39**	E4
Elbe, R.	*Germany*	**34**	B2
Elbert, Mt.	*Colorado*	**64**	E3
Elbeuf	*France*	**33**	C2
Elblag	*Poland*	**35**	F1
Elbrus, mt.	*U.S.S.R.*	**46**	E4
Elburz Mts.	*Iran*	**52**	F3
El Cuyo	*Mexico*	**70**	G3
El Dorado	*Kansas*	**68**	D3
Eldorado	*Saskatchewan*	**62**	N6
Eldoret	*Kenya*	**58**	C4
Eleuthera, I.	*Bahamas*	**71**	J2
El Ferrol del Caudillo	*Spain*	**36**	B1
El'gen	*U.S.S.R.*	**47**	P2
Elgin	*Illinois*	**65**	J2
Elgin	*Scotland*	**16**	D3
Elgon, mt.	*Kenya-Uganda*	**58**	C4
Elham	*England*	**27**	J3
Elie	*Scotland*	**29**	F4
Elisabethville	*Congo*	**59**	C2
Elista	*U.S.S.R.*	**46**	E4
Elizabeth	*New Jersey*	**66**	D3
Elizabeth	*S. Australia*	**77**	F5
Elizabeth City	*N. Carolina*	**65**	L3
Elk	*Poland*	**35**	G2
Elkhart	*Indiana*	**69**	F2
Elko	*Nevada*	**64**	C2
Ellef Ringnes I.	*N.-W. Terr., Can.*	**62**	O2
Ellendale	*N. Dakota*	**68**	D1
Ellensburg	*Washington*	**67**	B2
Ellesmere	*England*	**26**	E2
Ellesmere I.	*N.-W. Terr., Can.*	**63**	S1
Ellesmere, L.	*New Zealand*	**79**	D5
Ellesmere Port	*England*	**25**	C3
Ellice Is.	*Pacific Oc.*	**10**	D5
Elliot	*N. Terr., Aust.*	**77**	E2
Ellon	*Scotland*	**28**	F3
Ellsworth Highland	*Antarctica*	**80**	R7
Elmira	*New York*	**65**	L2
Elmshorn	*Germany, W.*	**34**	C2
El Pao	*Venezuela*	**72**	E2
El Paso	*Texas*	**64**	E4
Elphin	*Eire*	**30**	C4
El Portugues	*Peru*	**72**	B5
Elsa	*Yukon*	**62**	G5
Eltham	*New Zealand*	**79**	E3
Elvas	*Portugal*	**36**	B3
Ely	*England*	**17**	F5
Ely	*Minnesota*	**68**	E1
Ely	*Nevada*	**67**	D4
Emba, R.	*Kazakh.*	**46**	F4
Embarcación	*Argentina*	**73**	E8
Embarras Portage	*Alberta*	**62**	M6
Embleton	*England*	**25**	D1
Embrun	*France*	**33**	E4
Emden	*Germany, W.*	**34**	B2
Emerald	*Queensland*	**77**	H3
Emerson	*Manitoba*	**63**	P7
Emi Koussi, mt.	*Chad*	**58**	A3
Emilia Romagna	*Italy*	**38**	B2
Emmen	*Netherlands*	**32**	E2
Empangeni	*Natal*	**59**	D3
Empoli	*Italy*	**38**	B3
Emporia	*Kansas*	**64**	G3
Emporium	*Pennsylvania*	**66**	B2
Ems, R.	*Germany, W.*	**34**	B2
Emsworth	*England*	**27**	G4
Encantada, Cerro de la, mt.	*Mexico*	**70**	A1
Encarnación	*Paraguay*	**73**	F9
Encarnacion de Diaz	*Mexico*	**70**	D3
Encounter B.	*S. Australia*	**77**	F6
Enderby Land	*Antarctica*	**80**	F8
Endere Langar	*Sinkiang*	**50**	C4
Endicott Mts.	*Alaska*	**62**	D4
Enfield	*England*	**27**	G3
Engadin	*Switzerland*	**37**	C1
Engano, C.	*Philippines*	**48**	E5
Engels	*U.S.S.R.*	**46**	E3
England	*British Isles*	**17**	D5
English R.	*Ontario*	**63**	Q7
English Bazar	*India*	**50**	D6
Enid	*Oklahoma*	**64**	G3
Enkhuizen	*Netherlands*	**32**	D2
Ennadai	*N.-W. Terr., Can.*	**62**	O5
Ennedi, plat.	*Chad*	**58**	B3
Ennis	*Eire*	**17**	A5
Enniscorthy	*Eire*	**17**	B5
Enniskillen	*N. Ireland*	**17**	B4
Ennistimon	*Eire*	**17**	A5
Enns	*Austria*	**34**	D4
Enns, R.	*Austria*	**34**	D5
Ens	*Netherlands*	**32**	D2
Enschede	*Netherlands*	**32**	E2
Ensenada	*Mexico*	**70**	A1
Enshih	*China*	**50**	H5
Entebbe	*Uganda*	**58**	C4
Enugu	*Nigeria*	**57**	C4
Epernay	*France*	**33**	D2
Epinal	*France*	**33**	E2
Epirus	*Greece*	**39**	E5
Epping	*England*	**27**	H3
Epping Forest	*England*	**27**	H3
Epsom	*England*	**17**	E6
Epworth	*England*	**25**	E3
Erebus, Mt.	*Antarctica*	**80**	M7
Erech	*Iraq*	**55**	H4
Eregli	*Turkey*	**41**	L3
Erfurt	*Germany, E.*	**34**	C3
Erg Chech, sand dunes	*Algeria-Mali*	**57**	B2
Erg, Gt., E. & W., sand dunes	*Algeria*	**57**	C2
Erg Iguidi, sand dunes	*Algeria-Mauritania*	**57**	B2
Erhlien	*China*	**51**	J3
Ericht, L.	*Scotland*	**16**	C3
Erie	*Pennsylvania*	**65**	L2
Erie, L.	*U.S.A.-Canada*	**65**	K2
Erigavo	*Somalia*	**58**	D3
Eriskay, I.	*Scotland*	**28**	A3
Erlangen	*Germany, W.*	**34**	C4
Erne, L.	*N. Ireland*	**17**	B4
Erne, R.	*Eire-N. Ire.*	**30**	C3
Erne, Upr. L.	*N. Ireland*	**17**	B4
Erriboll, L.	*Scotland*	**16**	C2
Errigal, mt.	*Eire*	**17**	A4
Erris Hd.	*Eire*	**30**	A3
Erz Gebirge, mts.	*Germany*	**34**	D3
Erzincan	*Turkey*	**52**	C3
Erzurum	*Turkey*	**52**	D3
Esashi	*Japan*	**49**	E3
Esbjerg	*Denmark*	**42**	B5
Escalon	*Mexico*	**70**	D2
Escanaba	*Michigan*	**65**	J1
Escorial, E.	*Spain*	**36**	C2
Esk, R.	*Scotland*	**29**	E5
Esk, N. & S., Rs.	*Scotland*	**29**	F4
Eskifjördhur	*Iceland*	**42**	L6
Eskilstuna	*Sweden*	**42**	D4
Eskimo, C.	*N.-W. Terr., Can.*	**63**	Q5
Eskimo Point	*N.-W. Terr., Can.*	**63**	Q5
Eskişehir	*Turkey*	**52**	B3
Esla Res.	*Spain*	**36**	C2
Esperance	*W. Australia*	**76**	C5
Espinhaco, Sa. do, mts.	*Brazil*	**72**	J7
Espirito Santo	*Brazil*	**72**	J8
Esquel	*Argentina*	**73**	C12
Esquimalt	*Br. Columbia*	**62**	K8
Essen	*Germany, W.*	**34**	B3
Essequibo R.	*Br. Guiana*	**72**	F3
Essex, co.	*England*	**17**	F6
Esslingen	*Germany, W.*	**34**	C4
Estonia	*U.S.S.R.*	**46**	C2
Estremadura	*Spain*	**36**	B3
Etadunna	*S. Australia*	**77**	F4
Etah	*Greenland*	**63**	U2
Etampes	*France*	**33**	C2
Etaples	*France*	**33**	C1
Ethel Creek	*W. Australia*	**76**	C3
Ethiopia	*E. Africa*	**58**	C4
Etive, L.	*Scotland*	**29**	C4
Etna, mt.	*Sicily*	**38**	C6
Etolin Str.	*Alaska*	**62**	A5
Eton	*England*	**27**	G3
Ettrick, R.	*Scotland*	**29**	E5
Ettrick Pen, hill	*Scotland*	**17**	D4
Euboea, I.	*Greece*	**39**	G5
Eucla	*W. Australia*	**76**	D5
Eucla Basin	*S. & W. Australia*	**76**	D5
Eugene	*Oregon*	**64**	B2
Eugowra	*New South Wales*	**78**	G6
Eupen	*Belgium*	**32**	E4
Euphrates, R.	*Iraq, etc.*	**52**	D4
Eureka	*California*	**64**	B2
Eureka	*Nevada*	**64**	C3
Eureka	*N.-W. Terr., Can.*	**63**	R1
Europa, I.	*Mozambique Chan.*	**59**	E3
Europa, Pt.	*Spain*	**36**	C4
Europe	—	**12-13**	—
Eutin	*Germany, W.*	**34**	C1
Evanston	*Illinois*	**65**	J2
Evanston	*Wyoming*	**64**	D2
Evansville	*Indiana*	**65**	J3
Everard, L.	*S. Australia*	**77**	E5
Everest, Mt.	*Nepal-Tibet*	**53**	N5
Everett	*Washington*	**64**	B1
Evesham	*England*	**27**	F2
Evesham, Vale of	*England*	**27**	F2
Evora	*Portugal*	**36**	B3
Evreux	*France*	**33**	C2
Ewe, L.	*Scotland*	**28**	C3
Ewijcksluis	*Netherlands*	**32**	C2
Exe, R.	*England*	**17**	D6
Exeter	*England*	**17**	D6
Exminster	*England*	**26**	D4
Exmoor	*England*	**17**	D6
Exmouth	*England*	**17**	D6
Exmouth G.	*W. Australia*	**76**	A3
Expedition Ra.	*Queensland*	**77**	H3
Exton	*England*	**26**	D3
Exuma Sd.	*Bahamas*	**71**	J3
Exuma, Gt., I.	*Bahamas*	**71**	J3
Eyasi, L.	*Tanzania*	**58**	C5
Eye	*England*	**27**	J2
Eye Pen.	*Scotland*	**16**	B2
Eyemouth	*Scotland*	**16**	D4
Eyja Fd.	*Iceland*	**42**	K6
Eyjafjalla	*Iceland*	**42**	K7
Eyrarbakki	*Iceland*	**42**	J7
Eyre	*W. Australia*	**76**	D5
Eyre Cr.	*Qnsld.-S. Aust.*	**77**	F4
Eyre, L.	*S. Australia*	**77**	F4
Eyre Pen.	*S. Australia*	**77**	F5
Eyrecourt	*Eire*	**31**	C4
Fada	*Chad*	**58**	B3
Fada-N'Gourma	*Up. Volta*	**57**	C3
Faenza	*Italy*	**38**	B2
Faeroes, The, is.	*N.W. Europe*	**46**	A2
Fair Hd.	*N. Ireland*	**17**	B4
Fair I.	*Scotland*	**16**	E2
Fairbanks	*Alaska*	**62**	E5
Fairbury	*Nebraska*	**68**	D2
Fairford	*England*	**27**	F3
Fairlie	*New Zealand*	**79**	C6
Fairmont	*W. Virginia*	**66**	A4
Fairweather, mt.	*Alaska-B.C.*	**62**	G6
Faizabad	*India*	**53**	M5
Fakenham	*England*	**27**	H2
Falaise	*France*	**33**	B2
Falcon Res.	*Mex.-U.S.A.*	**64**	G5
Falkirk	*Scotland*	**16**	D3
Falkland	*Scotland*	**29**	E4
Falkland Is.	*S. Atlantic Oc.*	**73**	F14
Falkland Islands Dependency	*Antarctica*	**80**	A8
Fallon	*Nevada*	**67**	C4
Fall River	*Massachusetts*	**65**	M2
Falls City	*Nebraska*	**68**	D2
Falmouth	*England*	**17**	C6
Falmouth	*Jamaica*	**71**	J4
Falmouth B.	*England*	**26**	B4
Falun	*Sweden*	**42**	C3
Famagusta	*Cyprus*	**54**	C2
Fannich, L.	*Scotland*	**28**	C3
Fanning I.	*Pacific Oc.*	**10**	E4
Fano	*Italy*	**38**	C3
Farafangana	*Malagasy Rep.*	**59**	E3
Farafra Oasis	*Egypt*	**58**	B2
Farasan I.	*Red Sea*	**52**	D7
Fareham	*England*	**27**	F4
Farewell	*Texas*	**64**	F4
Farewell, C.	*Greenland*	**63**	Z6
Farewell, C.	*New Zealand*	**79**	D4
Fargo	*N. Dakota*	**64**	G1
Faribault	*Minnesota*	**68**	E2
Faringdon	*England*	**27**	F3
Farmington	*New Mexico*	**67**	E4
Farnborough	*Hants, England*	**27**	G3
Farnborough	*Kent, England*	**27**	H3
Farne Is.	*England*	**25**	D1
Farnham	*England*	**27**	G3
Farnham, Mt.	*Br. Columbia*	**62**	L7
Farnworth	*England*	**25**	C3
Faro	*Portugal*	**36**	B4
Fasano	*Italy*	**38**	D4
Fasher, El	*Sudan*	**58**	B3
Fatshan	*China*	**48**	D4
Faversham	*England*	**27**	H3
Fawley	*England*	**27**	F4
Faxa B.	*Iceland*	**42**	J6
Fayetteville	*Arkansas*	**65**	H3
Fayetteville	*N. Carolina*	**65**	L3
Fayûm, El	*Egypt*	**58**	C2
Fear, C.	*N. Carolina*	**69**	H4
Fécamp	*France*	**33**	C2
Fehmarn, I.	*Germany, W.*	**34**	C1
Feilding	*New Zealand*	**79**	E4
Feira	*Zambia*	**59**	D2
Feira de Santana	*Brazil*	**72**	K6
Feldbach	*Austria*	**34**	E5
Feldkirch	*Austria*	**34**	C5
Felipe Carillo Puerto	*Mexico*	**70**	G4
Felixstowe	*England*	**17**	F6
Feltre	*Italy*	**38**	B1
Fengkieh	*China*	**50**	H5
Fenit	*Eire*	**31**	B5
Fenny Stratford	*England*	**27**	G2
Fens, The	*England*	**27**	G2
Fenyang	*China*	**51**	J4
Ferguson L.	*N.-W. Terr., Can.*	**63**	P5
Fermanagh, co.	*N. Ireland*	**17**	B4
Fermo	*Italy*	**38**	C3
Fermoy	*Eire*	**17**	A5
Fernandina	*Florida*	**65**	K4
Fernandina, I.	*Galapagos Is.*	**73**	N17
Fernando Póo, I.	*W. Africa*	**57**	C4
Fernhurst	*England*	**27**	G3
Fernie	*Br. Columbia*	**62**	M8
Ferns	*Eire*	**31**	E5
Ferozepore	*India*	**53**	K4
Ferrand	*France*	**33**	C4
Ferrara	*Italy*	**38**	B2
Fethard	*Eire*	**31**	D5
Fetlar, I.	*Scotland*	**16**	E1
Fez	*Morocco*	**57**	B1
Ffestiniog	*Wales*	**26**	D2
Fianarantsoa	*Malagasy Rep.*	**59**	E3
Fichtel Geb., mts.	*Germany, W.*	**34**	C3
Fidenza	*Italy*	**38**	B2
Fife, co.	*Scotland*	**16**	D3
Fife Ness	*Scotland*	**16**	D3
Figeac	*France*	**33**	C4
Fiji Is.	*Pacific Oc.*	**10**	D5
Filey	*England*	**17**	E4
Fillmore	*Utah*	**64**	D3
Findhorn	*Scotland*	**28**	E3
Findhorn, R.	*Scotland*	**16**	C3
Findon	*England*	**27**	G4
Finger Ls.	*New York*	**66**	C2
Finglas	*Eire*	**31**	E4
Finisterre, C.	*Spain*	**36**	A1
Finke R.	*N. Terr., Aust.*	**77**	E4
Finland	*N.W. Europe*	**42**	F3
Finland, G. of	*Finland, etc.*	**42**	F4
Finnart	*Scotland*	**29**	D4
Finsnes	*Norway*	**42**	D1
Finsteraarhorn, mt.	*Switzerland*	**37**	C1
Finsterwalde	*Germany, E.*	**34**	D3
Fintona	*N. Ireland*	**30**	D3
Fisher Str.	*N.-W. Terr., Can.*	**63**	R5
Fishguard	*Wales*	**17**	C6
Fitchburg	*Massachusetts*	**66**	E2
Fitzroy	*W. Australia*	**76**	D2
Fitzroy R.	*Queensland*	**77**	H3
Fitzroy R.	*W. Australia*	**76**	C2
Fiume	*Yugoslavia*	**38**	C2
Fivemiletown	*N. Ireland*	**30**	D3
Fjöllum, R.	*Iceland*	**42**	K6
Flagstaff	*Arizona*	**67**	D4
Flaherty I.	*N.-W. Terr., Can.*	**63**	S6
Flamborough Hd.	*England*	**17**	E4
Flannan Is.	*Scotland*	**16**	B2
Flathead L.	*Montana*	**64**	D1
Flattery, C.	*Queensland*	**77**	H1
Flattery, C.	*Washington*	**64**	B1
Fleet	*England*	**27**	G3
Fleetwood	*England*	**17**	D5
Flekkefjord	*Norway*	**42**	A4
Flensburg	*Germany, W.*	**34**	C1
Flims	*Switzerland*	**37**	C1
Flinders I.	*S. Australia*	**77**	E5
Flinders I.	*Tasmania*	**78**	G9
Flinders Pas.	*Queensland*	**77**	H2
Flinders Ra.	*S. Australia*	**77**	F5
Flinders R.	*Queensland*	**77**	G2

Flin Flon *Manitoba* **62** O7
Flint *Michigan* **65** K2
Flint *Wales* **17** D5
Flint, R. *Georgia* **69** G4
Flodden *England* **16** D4
Florac *France* **33** D4
Florence *Alabama* **69** F4
Florence *Italy* **38** B3
Florence *S. Carolina* **65** L4
Florencia *Colombia* **72** B3
Flores, I. *Indonesia* **48** E7
Flores Sea *Indonesia* **48** E7
Floriano *Brazil* **72** J5
Florianópolis *Brazil* **73** H9
Florida, state *U.S.A.* **65** K5
Florida B. *Florida* **65** K6
Florida Keys *Florida* **65** K6
Florida Str. *U.S.A.* **65** L6
Floro *Norway* **42** A3
Flushing *Netherlands* **32** B3
Fochabers *Scotland* **28** E3
Focşani *Rumania* **39** H2
Foggia *Italy* **38** D4
Fogo I. *Newfoundland* **63** Y8
Föhr, I. *Germany, W.* **34** B1
Foix *France* **33** C5
Foligno *Italy* **38** C3
Folkestone *England* **17** F6
Folkingham *England* **27** G2
Fond du Lac *Wisconsin* **69** F2
Fontainebleau *France* **33** C2
Fonte Boa *Brazil* **72** D4
Fontenay-le-Comte *France* **33** B3
Foochow *China* **48** D4
Forbes *New South Wales* **77** H5
Fordingbridge *England* **27** F4
Fordlandia *Brazil* **72** F4
Forel, mt. *Greenland* **63** Z4
Foreland Pt. *England* **26** D3
Forfar *Scotland* **16** D3
Forli *Italy* **38** C2
Formby *England* **25** B3
Formby Hd. *England* **17** D5
Formentera, I. *Balearic Is.* **36** E3
Formia *Italy* **38** C4
Formosa *Argentina* **73** F9
Formosa (Taiwan), I. *S.E. Asia* **48** E4
Forres *Scotland* **28** E3
Forrest *W. Australia* **76** D5
Forrest City *Arkansas* **68** E3
Forsayth *Queensland* **77** G2
Forsyth *Montana* **64** E1
Fort Albany *Ontario* **63** S7
Fortáleza *Brazil* **72** K4
Fort Archambault *Chad* **58** A4
Fort Augustus *Scotland* **16** C3
Fort Beaufort *Cape of Good Hope* **59** C4
Fort Chimo *Quebec* **63** V6
Fort Chipewyan *Alberta* **62** M6
Fort Collins *Colorado* **67** E3
Fort Crampel *Cent. Afr. Rep.* **58** A4
Fort-Dauphin *Malagasy Rep.* **59** E3
Fort de France *West Indies* **71** M5
Fort Dodge *Iowa* **65** H2
Forte Roçadas *Angola* **59** B2
Fortescue R. *W. Australia* **76** B3
Fort Franklin *N.-W. Terr., Can.* **62** K4
Fort George *Quebec* **63** T7
Fort George *Scotland* **28** D3
Fort George R. *Quebec* **63** T7
Fort Good Hope *N.-W. Terr., Can.* **62** J4
Fort Gouraud *Mauritania* **57** A2
Fort Grahame *Br. Columbia* **62** K6
Forth, Firth of *Scotland* **16** D3
Forth, R. *Scotland* **16** C3
Fort Jameson *Zambia* **59** D2
Fort Knox *Kentucky* **65** J3
Fort Lamy *Chad* **57** D3
Fort Liard *N.-W. Terr., Can.* **62** K5
Fort MacKay *Alberta* **62** M6
Fort McKenzie *Quebec* **63** V6
Fort Macleod *Alberta* **62** M8
Fort McPherson *N.-W. Terr., Can.* **62** G4
Fort Morgan *Colorado* **67** F3
Fort Myers *Florida* **69** G5
Fort Nelson *Br. Columbia* **62** K6
Fort Norman *N.-W. Terr., Can.* **62** J5
Fort Portal *Uganda* **58** C4
Fort Peck Res. *Montana* **64** E1
Fort Pierce *Florida* **69** G5
Fort Providence *N.-W. Terr., Can.* **62** L5
Fort Qu'Appelle *Saskatchewan* **62** O7
Fort Randall Res. *S. Dakota* **64** G2
Fort Reliance *N.-W. Terr., Can.* **62** N5
Fort Resolution *N.-W. Terr., Can.* **62** M5
Fortrose *Scotland* **28** D3
Fort Roseberry *Zambia* **59** C2
Fort St. John *Br. Columbia* **62** K6
Fort Scott *Kansas* **65** H3
Fort Severn *Ontario* **63** R6
Fort Shevchenko *Kazakh.* **46** F4
Fort Simpson *N.-W. Terr., Can.* **62** K5
Fort Smith *Arkansas* **65** H3
Fort Smith *N.-W. Terr., Can.* **62** M5
Fort Stockton *Texas* **68** C4
Fortune B. *Newfoundland* **63** X8
Fort Vermilion *Alberta* **62** L6
Fort Victoria *Rhodesia* **59** D2
Fort Wayne *Indiana* **65** J2
Fort William *Ontario* **63** R8
Fort William *Scotland* **16** C3
Fort Worth *Texas* **64** G4
Forty Mile *Yukon* **62** F5
Fort Yukon *Alaska* **62** F4
Fossano *Italy* **38** A2
Fotheringhay *England* **27** G2
Fougères *France* **33** B2
Foula, I. *Scotland* **16** D1
Foulness I. *England* **17** F6
Foulsham *England* **27** H2
Foulwind, C. *New Zealand* **79** C4
Fouta Djallon, mts. *Guinea* **57** A3
Fovant *England* **27** F3
Foveaux Str. *New Zealand* **79** A7
Fowey *England* **26** C4
Fowler B. *S. Australia* **76** E5
Fowling *China* **50** H6
Fowyang *China* **51** K5
Foxe Basin *N.-W. Terr., Can.* **63** S4
Foxe Chan. *N.-W. Terr., Can.* **63** S4
Foxe Pen. *N.-W. Terr., Can.* **63** T4
Foxford *Eire* **30** B4
Foxton *New Zealand* **79** E4
Foyers & Falls of *Scotland* **28** D3
Foyle, L. *N. Ireland* **17** B4
Foyle, R. *N. Ireland* **30** D3
Foynes *Eire* **17** A5
Framlingham *England* **27** J2
France *W. Europe* **33** C3
Frances, L. *Yukon* **62** J5
Franceville *Gabon* **57** D5
Francistown *Bechuanaland* **59** C3
Franeker *Netherlands* **32** D1
Frankfort *Kentucky* **65** K3
Frankfurt-on-Main *Germany, W.* **34** B3
Frankfurt-on-Oder *Germany, E.* **34** D2
Franklin *New Hampshire* **66** F2
Franklin *Tasmania* **77** H7
Franklin Bay *N.-W. Terr., Can.* **62** J3
Franklin, Dist. of *N.-W. Terr., Can.* **62** M3
Franklin I. *Antarctica* **80** M7
Franklin Str. *N.-W. Terr., Can.* **63** P3
Franklin D. Roosevelt L. *Washington* **64** C1
Franklyn, Mt. *New Zealand* **79** D5
Franz Josef Land, Is. *Arctic Oc.* **46** E1
Frascati *Italy* **38** C4
Fraser I. *Queensland* **77** J4
Fraser Plat. *Br. Columbia* **62** K7
Fraser R. *Br. Columbia* **62** K7
Fraserburgh *Scotland* **16** E3
Frauenfeld *Switzerland* **37** C1
Fray Bentos *Uruguay* **73** F10
Fredericia *Denmark* **42** B5
Frederick *Maryland* **66** C4
Fredericton *New Brunswick* **63** V8
Frederiksdal *Greenland* **63** Z6
Frederikshaab *Greenland* **63** Y5
Frederikshavn *Denmark* **42** B4
Fredrikstad *Norway* **42** B4
Freeport *Illinois* **65** J2
Freetown *Sierra Leone* **57** A4
Freiberg *Germany, E.* **34** D3
Freiburg *Germany, W.* **34** B4
Fréjus *France* **33** E5
Fremantle *W. Australia* **76** B5
Fremont *Nebraska* **64** G2
French Guiana *S. America* **72** G3
Frenchpark *Eire* **30** C4
French Somaliland *N.E. Africa* **58** D3
Freshford *Eire* **31** D5
Fresno *California* **64** C3
Frewena *N. Terr., Aust.* **77** F2
Fribourg *Switzerland* **37** B1
Friedrichshafen *Germany, W.* **34** C5
Friesland *Netherlands* **32** D1
Frinton-on-Sea *England* **27** J3
Friuli Venezia Giulia *Italy* **38** C1
Frobisher L. *Saskatchewan* **62** N6
Frobisher Bay *N.-W. Terr., Can.* **63** V5
Frockheim *Scotland* **29** F4
Frome *England* **17** D6
Frome, L. *S. Australia* **77** G5
Frome, R. *England* **27** E4
Frontera *Mexico* **70** F4
Frosinone *Italy* **38** C4
Frunze *Kirgiz.* **46** H4
Fuchin *China* **51** N2
Fuchow *China* **51** K6
Fuerte, R. *Mexico* **70** C2
Fuerteventura, I. *Canary Is.* **57** A2
Fuji san, mt. *Japan* **48** F3
Fukang *Sinkiang* **50** D3
Fukui *Japan* **51** O4
Fukuoka *Japan* **51** N5
Fukushima *Japan* **51** P4
Fulda *Germany, W.* **34** C3
Funchal *Madeira* **57** A1
Fundy, B. of *N.B.-Nova Scotia* **63** V8
Fünen, I. *Denmark* **42** B5
Funzie *Scotland* **28** B1
Furancungo *Mozambique* **59** D2
Furka Pass *Switzerland* **37** C1
Furneaux Is. *Tasmania* **78** F9
Furness *England* **25** B2
Fürstenfeld *Austria* **34** E5
Fürth *Germany, W.* **34** C4
Fushun *China* **51** L3
Fusin *China* **51** L3
Fuyu *China* **51** L2
Fyne, L. *Scotland* **15** C3
Gaberones *Bechuanaland* **59** C3
Gabès & G. of *Tunisia* **57** D1
Gabon *Cent. Africa* **57** D5
Gadsden *Alabama* **65** J4
Gaerwen *Wales* **26** C1
Gaeta & G. of *Italy* **38** C4
Gagnon *Quebec* **63** V7
Gago Coutinho *Angola* **59** C2
Gaillac *France* **33** C5
Gainesville *Florida* **65** K5
Gainesville *Georgia* **65** K4
Gairdner, L. *S. Australia* **77** E5
Gairloch *Scotland* **16** C3
Gala, R. *Scotland* **29** F5
Galana R. *Kenya* **58** C5
Galapagos Is. *Pacific Oc.* **73** N16
Galashiels *Scotland* **16** D4
Galaţi *Rumania* **39** H2
Galdhöpiggen, mt. *Norway* **42** A3
Galeana *Mexico* **70** C1
Galena *Alaska* **62** C5
Galesburg *Illinois* **68** E2
Galgate *England* **25** C3
Galic *Spain* **36** B1
Galich *U.S.S.R.* **43** F1
Galilee, L. *Queensland* **77** H3
Galle *Ceylon* **53** M9
Gallegos R. *Argentina* **73** C14
Gallinas, Pta. *Colombia* **72** C1
Gallipoli *Turkey* **39** G4
Gallivare *Sweden* **42** E2
Galloway *Scotland* **29** D6
Galloway, Mull of *Scotland* **17** C4
Gallup *New Mexico* **67** E4
Galston *Scotland* **29** D5
Galty Mts. *Eire* **31** C5
Galveston *Texas* **65** H5
Galveston B. *Texas* **68** E5
Galway & B. *Eire* **17** A5
Gambia *W. Africa* **57** A3
Gamboma *Congo Rep.* **57** D5
Gander *Newfoundland* **63** Y8
Ganges, R. *India* **53** M5
Gangtok *Sikkim* **53** N5
Gannat *France* **33** D3
Gannett Pk. *Wyoming* **64** E2
Gantheaume B. *W. Australia* **76** A4
Ganton *England* **25** E2
Gao *Mali* **57** B3
Gap *France* **33** E4
Gara, L. *Eire* **17** A5
Garba Tula *Kenya* **58** C4
Garda, L. *Italy* **38** B2
Garden City *Kansas* **64** F3
Gardula *Ethiopia* **58** C4
Garelochhead *Scotland* **29** D4
Gargano, Mte. *Italy* **38** D4
Garian *Libya* **57** D1
Garissa *Kenya* **58** C5
Garnett *Kansas* **64** G3
Garonne, R. *France* **33** C5
Garoua *Cameroun* **57** D4
Garrison *N. Dakota* **68** C1
Garrison Res. *N. Dakota* **64** F1
Garron Pt. *N. Ireland* **17** C4
Garrovillas *Spain* **36** B3
Garry, L. *N.-W. Terr., Can.* **63** P4
Garstang *England* **25** C3
Garth *Wales* **26** D2
Gartok *Tibet* **50** C5
Garvagh *N. Ireland* **30** E3
Garve *Scotland* **28** D3
Gary *Indiana* **65** J2
Gascony *France* **33** B4
Gascony, G. of *France* **33** B5
Gascoyne R. *W. Australia* **76** B4
Gaserta *Italy* **38** C4
Gaspé & C. *Quebec* **63** W8
Gata, C. *Spain* **36** D4
Gatehouse-of-Fleet *Scotland* **29** D6
Gateshead *England* **17** E4
Gatooma *Rhodesia* **59** D2
Gatun & L. *Panama* **70** B5
Gauhati *India* **53** O5
Gauldal, valley *Norway* **42** B3
Gävle *Sweden* **42** D3
Gawler *S. Australia* **77** F5
Gawler Ra. *S. Australia* **77** F5
Gaya *India* **53** M6
Gayndah *Queensland* **78** H1
Gaza *Egypt* **54** C4
Gaziantep *Turkey* **54** D1
Gdańsk *Poland* **35** F1
Gdynia *Poland* **35** F1
Gedaref *Sudan* **58** C3
Gedser *Denmark* **42** C5
Geel *Belgium* **32** C3
Geelong *Victoria* **77** G6
Gelderland *Netherlands* **32** D2
Gelsenkirchen *Germany, W.* **34** B3
Gemena *Congo* **58** A4
Gemona *Italy* **38** C1
Geneva & L. of *Switzerland* **37** B1
Genk *Belgium* **32** D4
Gennargentu, mt. *Sardinia* **38** B5
Genoa & G. of *Italy* **38** A2
Geographe B. *W. Australia* **76** B5
Geographe Chan. *W. Australia* **76** A3
George *Cape of Good Hope* **59** C4
George, L. *New South Wales* **77** H6
George Sd. *New Zealand* **79** A6
George River *Quebec* **63** V6
Georgetown *Br. Guiana* **72** F2
Georgetown *Georgia* **65** K4
George Town *Malaya* **53** Q9
Georgetown *Queensland* **77** G2
Georgetown *W. Indies* **71** H4
Georgia *U.S.S.R.* **46** E4
Georgia, state *U.S.A.* **65** K4
Georgia, Str. of *Br. Columbia* **62** K8
Georgian B. *Ontario* **63** S8
Georgina R. *N. Terr.-Qnsld.* **77** F3
Georgiyevsk *U.S.S.R.* **43** F4
Gera *Germany, E.* **34** D3
Geral, Sa., mts. *Brazil* **73** G9
Geral de Goias, Sa., mts. *Brazil* **72** H6
Geraldton *W. Australia* **76** A4
Germany, East *Europe* **34** D3
Germany, West *Europe* **34** B3
Germiston *Traansvaal* **59** C3
Gerona *Spain* **36** E1
Géryville *Algeria* **57** C1
Gezira, El *Sudan* **58** C3
Ghadames *Libya* **57** D1
Ghaghra R. *India* **53** M5
Ghana *W. Africa* **57** B4
Ghanzi *Bechuanaland* **59** C3
Ghardaia *Algeria* **57** C1
Ghat *Libya* **57** D2
Ghazni *Afghanistan* **52** J4
Ghent *Belgium* **32** B3
Giant's Causeway *N. Ireland* **30** E2
Gibb River *W. Australia* **76** D2
Gibraltar *S.W. Europe* **36** C4
Gibraltar, Str. of *Spain-Africa* **36** C5

Gibson Des.	*W. Australia*	**76**	C3
Gien	*France*	**33**	C3
Giessen	*Germany, W.*	**34**	B3
Gifford	*Scotland*	**29**	F5
Gifhorn	*Germany, W.*	**34**	C2
Gifu	*Japan*	**51**	O4
Gigha, I.	*Scotland*	**29**	C5
Giglio, I.	*Italy*	**38**	B3
Gijon	*Spain*	**36**	C1
Gila R.	*Arizona*	**64**	D4
Gilbert Is.	*Pacific Oc.*	**10**	D4
Gilbert R.	*Queensland*	**77**	G2
Gilberton	*Queensland*	**77**	G2
Giles	*W. Australia*	**76**	D4
Gilf Kebir Plat.	*Egypt*	**58**	B2
Gilgit	*Kashmir*	**53**	K3
Gill, L.	*Eire*	**17**	A4
Gillingham	*England*	**17**	F6
Gilyui R.	*U.S.S.R.*	**47**	N3
Gimbala, Jebel, mt.	*Sudan*	**58**	B3
Gin Gin	*Queensland*	**78**	J2
Ginir	*Ethiopia*	**58**	D4
Girdle Ness	*Scotland*	**16**	D3
Gironde, R.	*France*	**33**	B4
Girvan	*Scotland*	**17**	C4
Gisborne	*New Zealand*	**79**	G3
Gisors	*France*	**33**	C2
Giulianova	*Italy*	**38**	C3
Giurgiu	*Rumania*	**39**	G3
Givors	*France*	**33**	D4
Gîza	*Egypt*	**41**	L6
Gizhiga & B.	*U.S.S.R.*	**47**	Q2
Gizycko	*Poland*	**35**	G1
Gjirokaster	*Albania*	**39**	E4
Gjoa Haver	*N.-W. Terr., Can.*	**63**	P4
Gjovik	*Norway*	**42**	B3
Glace Bay	*Nova Scotia*	**63**	X8
Glacier Pk.	*Washington*	**67**	B2
Gladstone	*Queensland*	**77**	J3
Glamis	*Scotland*	**29**	F4
Glamorgan, co.	*Wales*	**17**	D6
Glarus	*Switzerland*	**37**	C1
Glasgow	*Montana*	**67**	E2
Glasgow	*Scotland*	**16**	C4
Glastonbury	*England*	**26**	E3
Glazov	*U.S.S.R.*	**43**	H1
Glen Affric, valley	*Scotland*	**28**	D3
Glenarm	*N. Ireland*	**30**	F3
Glen Cannich, valley	*Scotland*	**28**	D3
Glen Carron, valley	*Scotland*	**28**	C3
Glen Coe, valley	*Scotland*	**29**	D4
Glendale	*Arizona*	**67**	D5
Glendale	*California*	**67**	C5
Gleneagles	*Scotland*	**29**	E4
Glenelg	*Scotland*	**28**	C3
Glenfinnan	*Scotland*	**29**	C4
Glengariff	*Eire*	**31**	B6
Glen Garry, val.	*Perth, Scot.*	**29**	D4
Glen Garry, val.	*Inverness, Scot.*	**28**	D3
Glenhope	*New Zealand*	**79**	D4
Glen Innes	*New South Wales*	**77**	J4
Glenluce	*Scotland*	**29**	D6
Glen Lyon, valley	*Scotland*	**29**	D4
Glen More, valley	*Scotland*	**16**	C3
Glen Moriston, valley	*Scotland*	**28**	D3
Glennamaddy	*Eire*	**30**	C4
Glenora	*Tasmania*	**78**	L12
Glenrothes	*Scotland*	**16**	D3
Glens Falls	*New York*	**66**	E2
Glen Shee, valley	*Scotland*	**29**	E4
Glenties	*Eire*	**17**	A4
Glenwood Springs	*Colorado*	**67**	E4
Gletsch	*Switzerland*	**37**	C1
Glin	*Eire*	**31**	B5
Glittertind, mt.	*Norway*	**42**	B3
Gliwice	*Poland*	**35**	F3
Globe	*Arizona*	**67**	D5
Glógów	*Poland*	**34**	E3
Glomach, Falls of	*Scotland*	**28**	C3
Glomma, R.	*Norway*	**42**	B3
Glossop	*England*	**25**	D3
Gloucester	*England*	**17**	D6
Gloversville	*New York*	**66**	D2
Glyndebourne	*England*	**27**	H4
Gmünd	*Austria*	**34**	E4
Gmünd	*Austria*	**34**	D5
Gmunden	*Austria*	**34**	D5
Gniezno	*Poland*	**35**	E2
Goa	*India*	**53**	K7
Goa, Daman & Diu	*India*	**53**	K7
Goat Fell, mt.	*Scotland*	**29**	C5
Gobabis	*S.W. Africa*	**59**	B3
Gobi, des.	*Mongolia*	**48**	C2
Goch	*Germany, W.*	**34**	B3
Godalming	*England*	**27**	G3
Godavari R.	*India*	**53**	L7
Godhavn	*Greenland*	**63**	Y4
Godmanchester	*England*	**27**	G2
Gods, L.	*Manitoba*	**63**	Q7
Godshill	*England*	**27**	F4
Godthaab	*Greenland*	**63**	Y5
Goéland, L. au	*Quebec*	**63**	T8
Goeree, I.	*Netherlands*	**32**	B3
Gog Magog Hills	*England*	**27**	H2
Goiânia	*Brazil*	**72**	H7
Goiás	*Brazil*	**72**	G7
Goiás Massif, mts.	*Brazil*	**72**	H6
Goil, L.	*Scotland*	**29**	D4
Golchikha	*U.S.S.R.*	**47**	J1
Goldap	*Poland*	**35**	G1
Golden B.	*New Zealand*	**79**	D4
Golden Vale	*Eire*	**31**	C5
Golea, El	*Algeria*	**57**	C1
Golmo	*China*	**50**	F4
Golodnaya Step	*Kazakh.*	**52**	J1
Golspie	*Scotland*	**28**	E3
Goma	*Congo*	**58**	B5
Gomel	*White Russia*	**46**	D3
Gómez Palacio	*Mexico*	**70**	D2
Gonaives	*Haiti*	**71**	K4
Gondar	*Ethiopia*	**58**	C3
Good Hope, C. of	*Cape of Good Hope*	**59**	B4
Goodland	*Kansas*	**68**	C3
Goodwin Sands	*England*	**27**	J3
Goole	*England*	**17**	E5
Goomalling	*W. Australia*	**76**	B5
Goondiwindi	*Queensland*	**77**	J4
Goose Bay	*Labrador*	**63**	W7
Gora	*Tibet*	**50**	F6
Gorakhpur	*India*	**53**	M5
Gordonvale	*Queensland*	**77**	H2
Gore	*Ethiopia*	**58**	C4
Gore	*New Zealand*	**79**	B7
Gorebridge	*Scotland*	**29**	F5
Gorey	*Eire*	**31**	E5
Goring	*England*	**27**	F3
Gorizia	*Italy*	**38**	C2
Gorki	*U.S.S.R.*	**46**	E3
Gorki Res.	*U.S.S.R.*	**43**	F1
Gorleston	*England*	**27**	J2
Görlitz	*Germany, E.*	**34**	E3
Gorlovka	*Ukraine*	**43**	E3
Gorno Altaysk	*U.S.S.R.*	**47**	J3
Gorredijk	*Netherlands*	**32**	E1
Gort	*Eire*	**31**	C4
Gorzów Wielkopolski	*Poland*	**34**	E2
Gosainthan (Shisha Pangma), mt.	*Tibet*	**50**	D6
Gosforth	*Cumberland, Eng.*	**25**	B2
Gosforth	*Northumberland, Eng.*	**25**	D1
Goslar	*Germany, W.*	**34**	C3
Gosport	*England*	**27**	F4
Gota Can.	*Sweden*	**42**	C4
Gota, R.	*Sweden*	**42**	C4
Göteborg	*Sweden*	**42**	B4
Gotha	*Germany, E.*	**34**	C3
Gotland, I.	*Sweden*	**42**	D4
Göttingen	*Germany, W.*	**34**	C3
Gottwaldov	*Czechoslovakia*	**35**	E4
Gouda	*Netherlands*	**32**	C2
Gough I.	*S. Atlantic Oc.*	**11**	K7
Gouin Res.	*Quebec*	**63**	T8
Goulburn	*New South Wales*	**77**	H5
Goundam	*Mali*	**57**	B3
Gouré	*Niger*	**57**	D3
Gourock	*Scotland*	**29**	D5
Gower	*Wales*	**26**	C3
Gowganda	*Ontario*	**63**	S8
Goya	*Argentina*	**73**	F9
Goyllarisquizga	*Peru*	**72**	B6
Graaff-Reinet	*Cape of Good Hope*	**59**	C4
Grafton	*New South Wales*	**77**	J4
Grafton	*N. Dakota*	**68**	D1
Graham I.	*Br. Columbia*	**62**	H7
Graham Land	*Antarctica*	**80**	A8
Grahamstown	*Cape of Good Hope*	**59**	C4
Grain	*England*	**27**	H3
Grampian Mts.	*Scotland*	**16**	C3
Grampound	*England*	**26**	C4
Granada	*Nicaragua*	**71**	G5
Granada	*Spain*	**36**	C4
Granard	*Eire*	**30**	D4
Gran Canaria, I.	*Canary Is.*	**57**	A2
Gran Chaco, plain	*Arg.-Paraguay*	**73**	E8
Grand Can.	*Eire*	**31**	D4
Grand, R.	*Colorado*	**64**	E3
Grand Bahama I.	*Bahamas*	**71**	J2
Grand Bassam	*Ivory Coast*	**57**	B4
Grand Canyon	*Arizona*	**67**	D4
Grand Coulee	*Washington*	**67**	C2
Grande, R.	*New Mexico*	**64**	E4
Grande Chartreuse	*France*	**33**	D4
Grand Falls	*Newfoundland*	**63**	X8
Grand Forks	*N. Dakota*	**64**	G1
Grandin, L.	*N.-W. Terr., Can.*	**62**	L5
Grand Island	*Nebraska*	**64**	G2
Grand Junction	*Colorado*	**64**	E3
Grand Prairie	*Texas*	**68**	D4
Grand Rapids	*Michigan*	**65**	J2
Grand Rapids	*Minnesota*	**68**	E1
Grand St. Bernard Pass	*Switz.-Italy*	**37**	B2
Grangemouth	*Scotland*	**29**	E4
Grange-over-Sands	*England*	**25**	C2
Grangeville	*Idaho*	**64**	C1
Gran Sasso, mt.	*Italy*	**38**	C3
Grantham	*England*	**17**	E5
Granton	*Scotland*	**29**	E5
Grantown	*Scotland*	**16**	D3
Grants	*New Mexico*	**67**	E4
Grants Pass	*Oregon*	**67**	B3
Granville	*France*	**33**	B2
Granville	*Yukon*	**62**	G5
Grasmere	*England*	**25**	B2
Grassano	*Italy*	**38**	D4
Grasse	*France*	**33**	E5
Gravelotte	*France*	**33**	E2
Gravesend	*England*	**27**	H3
Gray	*France*	**33**	D3
Grays	*England*	**27**	H3
Graz	*Austria*	**34**	E5
Gt. Australian Basin	*Queensland*	**77**	G3
Gt. Australian Bight	*S. & W. Australia*	**76**	D5
Gt. Bahama Bank	*Bahamas*	**71**	J3
Great Barrier I.	*New Zealand*	**79**	E2
Gt. Barrier Reef	*Queensland*	**77**	H2
Great Bear L.	*N.-W. Terr., Can.*	**62**	K4
Great Belt, str.	*Denmark*	**42**	B5
Great Bend	*Kansas*	**64**	G3
Great Britain, I.	*British Isles*	**11**	K2
Great Crosby	*England*	**25**	B3
Gt. Dividing Ra.	*N.S.W.-Qnsld.*	**77**	H3
Great Driffield	*England*	**17**	E4
Great Dunmow	*England*	**27**	H3
Great Falls	*Montana*	**64**	D1
Great Grimsby	*England*	**17**	E5
Great Karroo, reg.	*Cape of Good Hope*	**59**	C4
Great Malvern	*England*	**26**	E2
Great Ormes Hd.	*Wales*	**17**	D5
Great Rowsley	*England*	**27**	F1
Great Salt L.	*Utah*	**64**	D2
Great Salt Lake Des.	*Utah*	**67**	D3
Great Sand Hills	*Nebraska*	**64**	F2
Great Sandy Des.	*W. Australia*	**76**	C3
Gt. Sandy I.	*Queensland*	**77**	J4
Great Slave L.	*N.-W. Terr., Can.*	**62**	M5
Great Smoky Mts.	*Tennessee, etc.*	**69**	G3
Great Torrington	*England*	**26**	C4
Great Victoria Des.	*S. & W. Australia*	**76**	D4
Great Whernside, mt.	*England*	**25**	D2
Great Yarmouth	*England*	**17**	F5
Greece	*S.E. Europe*	**39**	F5
Greelye	*Colorado*	**67**	F3
Green Mts.	*Vermont*	**66**	E2
Green R.	*Wyoming*	**64**	E2
Green Bay	*Wisconsin*	**65**	J2
Green Island	*New Zealand*	**79**	C6
Greenland, I.	*N. America*	**11**	J1
Greenlaw	*Scotland*	**16**	D4
Greenock	*Scotland*	**16**	C4
Greenore	*Eire*	**17**	B4
Greenore Pt.	*Eire*	**31**	E5
Green River	*Wyoming*	**64**	E2
Greensboro	*N. Carolina*	**65**	L3
Greenville	*Alabama*	**69**	F4
Greenville	*Liberia*	**57**	B4
Greenville	*Mississippi*	**65**	H4
Greenville	*S. Carolina*	**65**	K4
Greenville	*Texas*	**64**	G4
Greenwich	*England*	**17**	F6
Greenwood	*Mississippi*	**65**	H4
Gregory	*S. Dakota*	**68**	D2
Gregory, L.	*S. Australia*	**77**	F4
Gregory Ra.	*Queensland*	**77**	G2
Greifswald	*Germany, E.*	**34**	D1
Greiz	*Germany, E.*	**34**	D3
Grenada	*Mississippi*	**65**	J4
Grenada, I.	*West Indies*	**71**	M5
Grenoble	*France*	**33**	D4
Grenville, C.	*Queensland*	**77**	G1
Gretna Green	*Scotland*	**29**	E6
Grey Ra.	*N.S.W.-Qnsld.*	**77**	G4
Grey, R.	*New Zealand*	**79**	C5
Greybull	*Wyoming*	**67**	E3
Greymouth	*New Zealand*	**79**	C5
Greystones	*Eire*	**31**	E4
Greytown	*New Zealand*	**79**	E4
Gries	*Austria*	**34**	C5
Griffith	*New South Wales*	**77**	H5
Grijpskerk	*Netherlands*	**32**	E1
Grim, C.	*Tasmania*	**77**	G7
Grimsby, Gt.	*England*	**17**	E5
Grind, I.	*Netherlands*	**32**	D1
Grindelwald	*Switzerland*	**37**	C1
Grise Fiord	*N.-W. Terr., Can.*	**63**	S2
Gris Nez, C.	*France*	**33**	C1
Grodno	*White Russia*	**43**	B2
Grodzisk	*Poland*	**35**	F2
Grong	*Norway*	**42**	C2
Groningen	*Netherlands*	**32**	E1
Groote Eylandt, I.	*N. Terr., Aust.*	**77**	F1
Grootfontein	*S.W. Africa*	**59**	B2
Grosseto	*Italy*	**38**	B3
Gross Glockner, mt.	*Austria*	**34**	D5
Groznyy	*U.S.S.R.*	**43**	G4
Grudziądz	*Poland*	**35**	F2
Gruinard B.	*Scotland*	**28**	C3
Grutness	*Scotland*	**28**	A2
Gruyère, L. of	*Switzerland*	**37**	B1
Grytviken	*S. Georgia*	**73**	K14
Guadalajara	*Mexico*	**70**	D3
Guadalajara	*Spain*	**36**	C2
Guadalquivir, R.	*Spain*	**36**	B4
Guadarrama, Sa de, mts.	*Spain*	**36**	C2
Guadeloupe, I.	*West Indies*	**71**	M4
Guadiana, R.	*Spain, etc.*	**36**	C3
Guaíra & Falls	*Brazil*	**73**	G8
Guajará Mirim	*Brazil*	**72**	E6
Gualdo Tadino	*Italy*	**38**	C3
Guam, I.	*Pacific Oc.*	**10**	C4
Guanajuato	*Mexico*	**70**	D3
Guane	*Cuba*	**71**	H3
Guapore R.	*Bolivia-Brazil*	**72**	E6
Guaqui	*Bolivia*	**72**	D7
Guarayos, Llanosdi,	*Bolivia*	**72**	E7
Guarda	*Portugal*	**36**	B2
Guardafui, C.	*Somalia*	**58**	E3
Guatemala	*Cent. America*	**70**	F4
Guatemala	*Guatemala*	**70**	F5
Guaviare R.	*Colombia*	**72**	C3
Guayaquil & G. of	*Ecuador*	**72**	A4
Guaymas	*Mexico*	**70**	B2
Gubbio	*Italy*	**38**	C3
Guben	*Germany, E.*	**34**	D3
Gudbrandsdal, valley	*Norway*	**42**	B3
Guelph	*Ontario*	**63**	S9
Guéret	*France*	**33**	C3
Guernsey, I.	*Channel Is.*	**33**	B2
Guiana Highlands	*S. America*	**72**	D3
Guiglo	*Ivory Coast*	**57**	B4
Guildford	*England*	**17**	E6
Guinea	*W. Africa*	**57**	A3
Guinea, G. of	*W. Africa*	**57**	C4
Guiries	*Cuba*	**71**	H3
Guingamp	*France*	**33**	A2
Guisborough	*England*	**25**	D2
Guise	*France*	**33**	D2
Gujarat, state	*India*	**53**	K6
Gulf Basin	*N. Terr.-W. Aust.*	**76**	D2
Gullane	*Scotland*	**29**	F4
Gulu	*Uganda*	**58**	C4
Gunnedah	*New South Wales*	**77**	J5
Gunnislake	*England*	**26**	C4
Guntersville L.	*Alabama*	**65**	J4
Gurgan	*Iran*	**52**	F3
Gurla Mandhata, mt.	*Tibet*	**50**	C5
Guru	*Tibet*	**50**	D6
Guryev	*Kazakh.*	**46**	F4
Gustavus	*Alaska*	**62**	G6
Güstrow	*Germany, E.*	**34**	D2
Guthrie	*Oklahoma*	**64**	G3
Guyenne	*France*	**33**	C4
Guyhirne	*England*	**27**	H2
Guymon	*Oklahoma*	**68**	C3
Gwadar	*W. Pakistan*	**52**	H6
Gweebarra B.	*Eire*	**17**	A4
Gwelo	*Rhodesia*	**59**	C2

Gyangtse	*Tibet*	**50**	D6
Gympie	*Queensland*	**77**	J4
Györ	*Hungary*	**35**	E5
Haapajärvi	*Finland*	**42**	F3
Haapamaki	*Finland*	**42**	E3
Haapsalu	*Estonia*	**42**	E4
Haarlem	*Netherlands*	**32**	C2
Haarlemmer Meer	*Netherlands*	**32**	C2
Haast R.	*New Zealand*	**79**	B5
Habay	*Alberta*	**62**	L6
Habbaniyah	*Iraq*	**55**	G3
Hachinohe	*Japan*	**49**	E3
Had, Ras al, pt.	*Muscat & Oman*	**52**	H6
Hadarba, Râs, pt.	*Sudan*	**58**	C2
Hadasan	*Mongolia*	**50**	G2
Haddington	*Scotland*	**16**	D4
Hadejia, R.	*Nigeria*	**57**	C3
Hadera	*Jordan*	**54**	C3
Hadhramaut	*S. Arabia*	**52**	E7
Hadleigh	*England*	**27**	H2
Haeju	*Korea*	**51**	M4
Hafnarfjordhur	*Iceland*	**42**	J6
Hagerstown	*Maryland*	**65**	L3
Hague, The	*Netherlands*	**32**	C2
Haguenau	*France*	**33**	E2
Haifa	*Israel*	**54**	C3
Haig	*W. Australia*	**76**	D5
Hail	*Saudi Arabia*	**52**	D5
Hailar	*China*	**51**	K2
Haileybury	*Ontario*	**63**	T8
Hailsham	*England*	**27**	H4
Hailun	*China*	**51**	M2
Hailung	*China*	**49**	B3
Hainan I.	*China*	**48**	D5
Hainan Str.	*China*	**48**	D4
Hainaut	*Belgium*	**32**	B4
Haines	*Alaska*	**62**	G6
Haines Junction	*Yukon*	**62**	G5
Haiphong	*Vietnam*	**48**	C4
Haiti	*Hispaniola*	**71**	K4
Hajjar	*China*	**50**	E4
Hakodate	*Japan*	**48**	G2
Halberstadt	*Germany, E.*	**34**	C3
Halden	*Norway*	**42**	B4
Halesworth	*England*	**27**	J2
Halifax	*England*	**17**	E5
Halifax	*Nova Scotia*	**63**	W9
Halifax B.	*Queensland*	**77**	H2
Halkett, C.	*Alaska*	**62**	D3
Halkirk	*Scotland*	**28**	E2
Hall	*Austria*	**34**	C5
Hall	*Germany, W.*	**34**	C4
Halle	*Germany, E.*	**34**	D3
Hallingdal, valley	*Norway*	**42**	B3
Hall Lake	*N.-W. Terr., Can.*	**63**	S4
Halls Creek	*W. Australia*	**76**	D2
Halmahera, I.	*Indonesia*	**48**	E6
Halmstad	*Sweden*	**42**	C4
Hälsingborg	*Sweden*	**42**	C4
Halstead	*England*	**27**	H3
Haltwhistle	*England*	**25**	C2
Hama	*Syria*	**54**	D2
Hamadan	*Iran*	**52**	E4
Hamamatsu	*Japan*	**49**	D5
Hamar	*Norway*	**42**	B3
Hamatombetsu	*Japan*	**49**	E2
Hamburg	*Germany, W.*	**34**	C2
Hameenlinna	*Finland*	**42**	E3
Hameln	*Germany, W.*	**34**	C2
Hamilton	*Montana*	**67**	D2
Hamilton	*New Zealand*	**79**	E2
Hamilton	*Ohio*	**69**	G3
Hamilton	*Ontario*	**63**	S9
Hamilton	*Scotland*	**16**	C4
Hamilton	*Victoria*	**77**	G6
Hamilton Inlet	*Labrador*	**63**	X7
Hamina	*Finland*	**42**	F3
Hamm	*Germany, W.*	**34**	B3
Hammerfest	*Norway*	**42**	E1
Hammersley Ra.	*W. Australia*	**76**	B3
Hampden	*New Zealand*	**79**	C6
Hampshire, co.	*England*	**17**	E6
Ham Street	*England*	**27**	H3
Hamun-i-Helmand	*Afghan.-Iran*	**52**	H4
Hamun-i-Mashkel, L.	*Pakistan-Iran*	**52**	H5
Hamun-i-Sabari	*Afghan.-Iran*	**52**	H4
Hanchung	*China*	**50**	H5
Hancock	*Michigan*	**69**	F1
Hancock	*New York*	**66**	D3
Handley	*England*	**27**	E4
Hangchow	*China*	**48**	E3
Hanka L.	*China-U.S.S.R.*	**48**	F2
Hanko	*Finland*	**42**	E4
Hanley	*England*	**17**	D5
Hammer	*New Zealand*	**79**	D5
Hanoi	*Vietnam*	**48**	C4
Hantay	*Mongolia*	**50**	G2
Haparanda	*Sweden*	**42**	E2
Hami	*Sinkiang*	**50**	E3
Hamilton Inlet & R.	*Labrador*	**63**	W7
Haradh	*Saudi Arabia*	**52**	E6
Harar	*Ethiopia*	**58**	D4
Hara Usu Nür, L.	*Mongolia*	**50**	E2
Harbin	*China*	**48**	E2
Harburg	*Germany, W.*	**34**	C2
Hardanger Fd.	*Norway*	**42**	A3
Hardanger Fjell, mts	*Norway*	**42**	A3
Hardanger Vidda, plat.	*Norway*	**42**	A3
Harderwijk	*Netherlands*	**32**	D2
Hardin	*Montana*	**67**	E2
Harfleur	*France*	**33**	C2
Hargeisa	*Somalia*	**58**	D4
Harlech	*Wales*	**26**	C2
Harleston	*England*	**27**	J2
Harlingen	*Netherlands*	**32**	D1
Harlow	*England*	**17**	F6
Harmelen	*Netherlands*	**32**	C2
Harmerhill	*England*	**26**	E2
Härnösand	*Sweden*	**42**	D3
Haroldswick	*Scotland*	**28**	B1
Harpenden	*England*	**27**	G3
Harper	*Liberia*	**57**	B4
Harrington Harbour	*Quebec*	**63**	X7
Harris & Sd. of	*Scotland*	**16**	B3
Harrisburg	*Pennsylvania*	**65**	L2
Harrison	*Arkansas*	**68**	E3
Harrogate	*England*	**17**	E4
Harrold	*England*	**27**	G2
Harrow	*England*	**27**	G3
Harsprånget	*Sweden*	**42**	E2
Harstad	*Norway*	**42**	D1
Hart Fell, hill	*Scotland*	**17**	D4
Hartford	*Connecticut*	**65**	M2
Hartland	*England*	**26**	C4
Hartland Pt.	*England*	**17**	C6
Hartlepool	*England*	**17**	E4
Harvey	*N. Dakota*	**68**	C1
Harwell	*England*	**17**	E6
Harwich	*England*	**17**	F6
Harz, mts.	*Germany*	**34**	C3
Hasa	*Saudi Arabia*	**52**	E5
Hase, R.	*Germany, W.*	**34**	B2
Haseke, El	*Syria*	**55**	F1
Haslemere	*England*	**27**	G3
Hasselt	*Belgium*	**32**	D4
Hastings	*England*	**17**	F6
Hastings	*Nebraska*	**64**	G2
Hastings	*New Zealand*	**79**	F3
Hatfield	*Herts, England*	**27**	G3
Hatfield	*Yorks, England*	**25**	D3
Hatherleigh	*England*	**26**	C4
Hathersage	*England*	**25**	D3
Hatteras, C.	*N. Carolina*	**65**	L3
Hattiesburg	*Mississippi*	**65**	J4
Haugesund	*Norway*	**42**	A4
Hauraki G.	*New Zealand*	**79**	E2
Hauroko, L.	*New Zealand*	**79**	A6
Havana	*Cuba*	**71**	H3
Havant	*England*	**27**	G4
Havasu L.	*California*	**64**	D4
Haverfordwest	*Wales*	**17**	C6
Haverhill	*England*	**27**	H2
Havre	*France*	**33**	C2
Havre	*Montana*	**64**	E1
Hawaiian Is.	*Pacific Oc.*	**10**	E3
Hawarden	*Wales*	**26**	D1
Hawea, L.	*New Zealand*	**79**	B6
Hawera	*New Zealand*	**79**	E3
Hawes	*England*	**25**	C2
Hawick	*Scotland*	**16**	D4
Hawke B.	*New Zealand*	**79**	F3
Hawke, C.	*New South Wales*	**77**	J5
Hawke's Bay	*New Zealand*	**79**	F3
Hawkhurst	*England*	**27**	H3
Hawkshead	*England*	**25**	B2
Hawthorne	*Nevada*	**67**	C4
Hay	*New South Wales*	**77**	G5
Hay	*Wales*	**17**	D5
Hay R.	*N. Terr., Aust.*	**77**	F3
Hayes Pen.	*Greenland*	**63**	V2
Hayes R.	*Manitoba*	**63**	Q6
Hayle	*England*	**26**	B4
Hayling I.	*England*	**27**	G4
Hayman I.	*Queensland*	**77**	H3
Hay River	*N.-W. Terr., Can.*	**62**	L5
Hays	*Kansas*	**68**	D3
Hayy, Al	*Iraq*	**55**	H3
Hazebrouck	*France*	**33**	C1
Hazelton	*Br. Columbia*	**62**	J6
Hazen Str.	*N.-W. Terr., Can.*	**62**	M2
Hazleton	*Pennsylvania*	**66**	C3
Headcorn	*England*	**27**	H3
Headford	*Eire*	**31**	B4
Heard I.	*S. Indian Oc.*	**11**	N7
Hearne	*Texas*	**64**	G4
Hearst	*Ontario*	**63**	S7
Heathfield	*England*	**27**	H4
Hebrides, Outer, Is.	*Scotland*	**28**	A3
Hebron	*Jordan*	**54**	C4
Hebron	*Labrador*	**63**	W6
Hecate Str.	*Br. Columbia*	**62**	H7
Hede	*Sweden*	**42**	C3
Hedon	*England*	**25**	E3
Heerenveen	*Netherlands*	**32**	D2
Hegemann, C.	*Greenland*	**63**	Z4
Heidelberg	*Germany, W.*	**34**	B4
Heilbronn	*Germany, W.*	**34**	C4
Heinola	*Finland*	**42**	F3
Hejaz	*Saudi Arabia*	**52**	C5
Hekla, mt.	*Iceland*	**42**	K7
Helder	*Netherlands*	**32**	C2
Helena	*Arkansas*	**68**	E4
Helena	*Montana*	**64**	D1
Helensburgh	*Scotland*	**29**	D4
Helensville	*New Zealand*	**79**	E2
Heligoland B. & I.	*Germany, W.*	**34**	B1
Heliopolis	*Egypt*	**54**	A4
Hell-Ville	*Malagasy Rep.*	**59**	E2
Helper	*Utah*	**67**	D4
Helmand Des.	*Afghanistan*	**52**	H4
Helmand R.	*Afghanistan*	**52**	H4
Helmdon	*England*	**27**	F2
Helmsdale	*Scotland*	**16**	D2
Helmsley	*England*	**25**	D2
Helsingor	*Denmark*	**42**	B4
Helsinki	*Finland*	**42**	F3
Helston	*England*	**26**	B4
Helvellyn, mt.	*England*	**17**	D4
Hemel Hempstead	*England*	**27**	G3
Henderson	*Kentucky*	**65**	J3
Henderson	*Nevada*	**67**	C4
Hengelo	*Netherlands*	**32**	E2
Henghsien	*China*	**50**	H7
Hengyang	*China*	**51**	J6
Henley	*England*	**17**	E6
Henrietta Maria, C.	*Ontario*	**63**	S6
Henzado	*Burma*	**53**	P7
Heppner	*Oregon*	**64**	C1
Herat	*Afghanistan*	**52**	H4
Herceg Novi	*Yugoslavia*	**38**	E3
Hercegovina	*Yugoslavia*	**38**	D3
Hereford	*England*	**17**	D5
Herisau	*Switzerland*	**37**	C1
Herma Ness	*Scotland*	**28**	A1
Hermannsburg	*N. Terr., Aust.*	**76**	E3
Hermon, Mt.	*Lebanon-Syria*	**54**	C3
Hermosillo	*Mexico*	**70**	B2
Herne Bay	*England*	**27**	J3
Herning	*Denmark*	**42**	B4
Heron Bay	*Ontario*	**63**	R8
Heron I.	*Queensland*	**77**	J3
Herschel I.	*Yukon*	**62**	G4
Herstmonceux	*England*	**27**	H4
Hertford	*England*	**17**	E6
s'Hertogenbosch	*Netherlands*	**32**	D3
Hervey B.	*Queensland*	**77**	J3
Hesse	*Germany, W.*	**34**	B4
Hettinger	*N. Dakota*	**68**	C1
Hetton-le-Hole	*England*	**25**	D2
Heughlin, Mt.	*N. Terr., Aust.*	**76**	E3
Hexham	*England*	**17**	D4
Heysham	*England*	**17**	D4
Heytesbury	*England*	**27**	E3
Hibbing	*Minnesota*	**65**	H1
Hidalgo del Parral	*Mexico*	**70**	C2
High Atlas, mts.	*Morocco*	**57**	B1
High Point	*N. Carolina*	**69**	G3
High River	*Alberta*	**62**	M7
High Wycombe	*England*	**27**	G3
Hiiumaa, I.	*Estonia*	**42**	E4
Hikurangi	*New Zealand*	**79**	E1
Hikurangi, Mt.	*New Zealand*	**79**	G2
Hildesheim	*Germany, W.*	**34**	C2
Hilla	*Iraq*	**52**	E4
Hillegom	*Netherlands*	**32**	C2
Hillston	*New South Wales*	**77**	H5
Hillswick	*Scotland*	**28**	A1
Hilversum	*Netherlands*	**32**	D2
Himachal Pradesh, terr.	*India*	**53**	L4
Himalayan Ra.	*India-Tibet*	**53**	M4
Himeji	*Japan*	**49**	C5
Hinckley	*England*	**27**	F2
Hindley	*England*	**25**	C3
Hindon	*England*	**27**	E3
Hindubagh	*W. Pakistan*	**52**	J4
Hindu Kush Ra.	*Afghanistan, etc.*	**53**	K3
Hindutash, mt.	*Sinkiang*	**50**	B4
Hines Creek	*Alberta*	**62**	L6
Hingan	*China*	**51**	L2
Hingham	*England*	**27**	H2
Hinnoy, I.	*Norway*	**42**	C1
Hirosaki	*Japan*	**49**	E3
Hiroshima	*Japan*	**48**	F3
Hispaniola, I.	*West Indies*	**71**	K4
Hitcham	*England*	**27**	H2
Hitchin	*England*	**27**	G3
Hitra, I.	*Norway*	**42**	B3
Hjälmaren, L.	*Sweden*	**42**	C4
Hjorring	*Denmark*	**42**	B4
Hobart	*Tasmania*	**77**	H7
Hobbs	*New Mexico*	**67**	F5
Höbsögol Dalay, L.	*Mongolia*	**50**	G2
Hochwan	*China*	**50**	H5
Hodder, R.	*England*	**25**	C3
Hoddesdon	*England*	**27**	H3
Hodeida	*Yemen*	**52**	D8
Hódmezövásarhely	*Hungary*	**35**	F5
Hof	*Germany, W.*	**34**	C3
Hofei	*China*	**51**	K5
Höfn	*Iceland*	**42**	L6
Hofs Jökull, mt.	*Iceland*	**42**	K6
Hofuf	*Saudi Arabia*	**52**	E5
Hohe Tauern, mts.	*Austria*	**34**	D5
Hoihong	*China*	**50**	J7
Hoihow	*China*	**48**	D5
Hokang	*China*	**51**	N2
Hokiange Harb.	*New Zealand*	**79**	D1
Hokitika	*New Zealand*	**79**	C5
Hokkaido, I.	*Japan*	**48**	G2
Holbeach	*England*	**27**	H2
Holbeach Marsh	*England*	**27**	H2
Holbrook	*Arizona*	**67**	D5
Hollabrunn	*Austria*	**34**	E4
Holland, *see* Netherlands			
Holland	*England*	**17**	E5
Holland, Hook of	*Netherlands*	**32**	C3
Holly Springs	*Mississippi*	**65**	J4
Hollywood	*California*	**67**	C5
Holman Island	*N.-W. Terr., Can.*	**62**	L3
Holme	*England*	**27**	G2
Holmfirth	*England*	**25**	D3
Holsteinsborg	*Greenland*	**63**	Y4
Holsworthy	*England*	**26**	C4
Holt	*England*	**27**	J2
Holt	*Wales*	**26**	E1
Holungmen	*China*	**51**	M2
Holy I.	*England*	**16**	E4
Holy I.	*Wales*	**17**	C5
Holy L.	*Scotland*	**29**	D4
Holy Cross	*Alaska*	**62**	C5
Holyhead	*Wales*	**17**	C5
Holyoke	*Massachusetts*	**66**	E2
Holywell	*Wales*	**26**	D1
Holywood	*N. Ireland*	**30**	F3
Holzminden	*Germany, W.*	**34**	C3
Homs	*Libya*	**57**	D1
Homs	*Syria*	**52**	C4
Honduras	*Cent. America*	**70**	G5
Honefoss	*Norway*	**42**	B3
Hong Kong	*China (Br.)*	**48**	D4
Honiton	*England*	**17**	D6
Honolulu	*Hawaii*	**10**	E3
Honshu, I.	*Japan*	**48**	G3
Hood, Mt.	*Oregon*	**64**	B1
Hoogezand	*Netherlands*	**32**	E1
Hook Hd.	*Eire*	**17**	B5
Hooker, Mt.	*B.C.-Alberta*	**62**	L7
Hoorn	*Netherlands*	**32**	D2
Hoover Dam	*Nevada-Arizona*	**64**	D3
Hope	*Arkansas*	**68**	E4
Hopedale	*Labrador*	**63**	W6
Hopetoun	*W. Australia*	**76**	C5
Hopkinsville	*Kentucky*	**65**	J3
Hoquiam	*Washington*	**67**	B2
Horley	*England*	**27**	G3
Hormuz, Str. of	*Persian Gulf*	**52**	G5
Horn	*Austria*	**34**	E4
Horn, C.	*Chile*	**73**	D15
Hornavan, L.	*Sweden*	**42**	D2
Horncastle	*England*	**27**	G1
Horndean	*England*	**27**	F4
Hornell	*New York*	**66**	C2
Hornsea	*England*	**25**	E3
Horsens	*Denmark*	**42**	B5

Horse Shoe	*W. Australia*	**76**	B4
Horsham	*Norfolk, England*	**27**	J2
Horsham	*Sussex, England*	**27**	G3
Horsham	*Victoria*	**77**	G6
Horwich	*England*	**25**	C3
Hoshihtolokai	*Sinkiang*	**50**	D2
Hot Springs	*Arkansas*	**65**	H4
Hot Springs	*S. Dakota*	**68**	C2
Houlton	*Maine*	**65**	N1
Hounslow	*England*	**27**	G3
Houston	*Texas*	**64**	G5
Houtman Abrolhos, Is.	*W. Australia*	**76**	A4
Hove	*England*	**17**	E6
Howar, Wadi, val.	*Chad*	**58**	B3
Howden	*England*	**25**	E3
Howden Res.	*England*	**25**	D3
Howe, C.	*N.S.W.-Vict.*	**77**	J5
Howrah	*India*	**53**	N6
Howth	*Eire*	**31**	E4
Howth Hd.	*Eire*	**17**	B5
Hoy, I.	*Scotland*	**16**	D2
Hoylake	*England*	**25**	B3
Hoyun	*China*	**51**	J7
Hradec Kralove	*Czechoslovakia*	**34**	E3
Hsinchu	*Taiwan*	**51**	L7
Hualien	*Taiwan*	**51**	L7
Huallaga, R.	*Peru*	**72**	B5
Huancavelica	*Peru*	**72**	B6
Huancayo	*Peru*	**72**	B6
Huanuco	*Peru*	**72**	B5
Huaras	*Peru*	**72**	B5
Huascaran, mt.	*Peru*	**72**	B5
Hubli	*India*	**53**	L7
Hucknall Torkard	*England*	**27**	F1
Huddersfield	*England*	**17**	E5
Hudiksvall	*Sweden*	**42**	D3
Hudson	*New York*	**66**	E2
Hudson B.	*Canada*	**63**	R6
Hudson, R.	*New York*	**65**	M2
Hudson Str.	*N.-W. Terr., Can.*	**63**	U5
Hudson Bay	*Saskatchewan*	**62**	O7
Hue	*Vietnam*	**48**	C5
Huelva	*Spain*	**36**	B4
Huesca	*Spain*	**36**	D1
Hughenden	*Queensland*	**77**	G3
Hugh Town	*Scilly Is.*	**17**	B6
Huhehot	*China*	**48**	D2
Huichon	*Korea*	**51**	M3
Huixtla	*Mexico*	**70**	F4
Hukow	*China*	**51**	K6
Hulin	*China*	**51**	N2
Hull	*England*	**17**	E5
Hull	*Quebec*	**63**	T8
Hull, R.	*England*	**25**	E3
Hulun L.	*China*	**48**	D2
Hulutao	*China*	**51**	L3
Huma	*China*	**51**	M1
Humber, R.	*England*	**17**	E5
Humboldt R.	*Nevada*	**64**	C2
Hume Res.	*New South Wales*	**77**	H6
Humpty Doo	*N. Terr., Aust.*	**76**	E1
Hun	*Libya*	**57**	D2
Húna B.	*Iceland*	**42**	J6
Hungary	*Europe*	**35**	F5
Hungerford	*England*	**27**	F3
Hungersteppe	*Kazakh.*	**46**	G4
Hungkiang	*China*	**50**	H6
Hungnam	*Korea*	**51**	M4
Hunmanby	*England*	**25**	E2
Hunsruck, mts.	*Germany, W.*	**34**	B4
Hunstanton	*England*	**27**	H2
Hunt, Mt.	*Yukon*	**62**	J5
Hunte, R.	*Germany, W.*	**34**	B2
Hunter Is.	*Tasmania*	**77**	H7
Huntingdon	*England*	**17**	E5
Huntington	*W. Virginia*	**65**	K3
Huntly	*New Zealand*	**79**	E2
Huntly	*Scotland*	**16**	D3
Huntsville	*Alabama*	**65**	J4
Hurd, C.	*Ontario*	**63**	S8
Hurgnada	*Egypt*	**58**	C2
Hurliness	*Scotland*	**28**	E2
Huron	*S. Dakota*	**64**	G2
Huron, L.	*U.S.A.-Canada*	**65**	K2
Husavik	*Iceland*	**42**	K6
Husum	*Germany, W.*	**34**	C1
Hutchinson	*Kansas*	**64**	G3
Hutton Rudby	*England*	**25**	D2
Huy	*Belgium*	**32**	D4
Hvar, I.	*Yugoslavia*	**38**	D3
Hwang Ho, R.	*China*	**48**	C3
Hweinan	*China*	**51**	M3
Hweitseh	*China*	**50**	G6
Hyde	*England*	**25**	C3
Hyden	*W. Australia*	**76**	B5
Hyderabad	*India*	**53**	L7
Hyderabad	*W. Pakistan*	**52**	J5
Hyères	*France*	**33**	E5
Hyndman Pk.	*Idaho*	**64**	D2
Hythe	*Hampshire, Eng.*	**27**	F4
Hythe	*Kent, Eng.*	**27**	J3
Iaşi	*Rumania*	**35**	J5
Ibadan	*Nigeria*	**57**	C4
Ibague	*Colombia*	**72**	B3
Iberian Mts.	*Spain*	**36**	D1
Ibo	*Mozambique*	**59**	E2
Ica	*Peru*	**72**	B6
Iceland	*N.W. Europe*	**11**	K1
Ichang	*China*	**48**	D3
Ichun	*China*	**51**	J6
Ida, mt.	*Crete*	**38**	L8
Idaho, state	*U.S.A.*	**64**	C2
Idaho City	*Idaho*	**64**	C2
Idaho Falls	*Idaho*	**64**	D2
Idirtu	*China*	**50**	F4
Iférouane	*Niger*	**57**	C3
Ifni	*N.W. Africa*	**57**	A2
Igarka	*U.S.S.R.*	**47**	J2
Iglesias	*Sardinia*	**38**	A5
Igloolik	*N.-W. Terr., Can.*	**63**	S4
Iguala	*Mexico*	**70**	E4
Iguassu Falls & R.	*Brazil, etc.*	**73**	G9
Ihosy	*Malagasy Rep.*	**59**	E3
Iisalmi	*Finland*	**42**	F3
Ijmuiden	*Netherlands*	**32**	C2
Ijssel Meer, sea	*Netherlands*	**32**	D2
Ijssel, R.	*Netherlands*	**32**	E2
Ikaria, I.	*Greece*	**39**	G6
Ikomba	*Zambia*	**59**	D1
Ilam	*Iran*	**55**	J3
Ilan	*China*	**49**	B2
Ilawa	*Poland*	**35**	F2
Ilbunga	*S. Australia*	**77**	F4
Ilchester	*England*	**26**	E4
Ilford	*England*	**27**	H3
Ilfracombe	*England*	**17**	C6
Ilheus	*Brazil*	**72**	K7
Ili & R.	*Kazakh.*	**46**	H4
Iliamna L.	*Alaska*	**62**	C6
Ilim	*U.S.S.R.*	**47**	L3
Ilkeston	*England*	**27**	F2
Ilkley	*England*	**25**	D3
Illampu, mt.	*Bolivia*	**72**	D7
Illapel	*Chile*	**73**	C10
Illimani, mt.	*Bolivia*	**72**	D7
Illinois, state	*U.S.A.*	**65**	H2
Illinois R.	*Illinois*	**65**	J2
Ilmen, L.	*U.S.S.R.*	**43**	D1
Ilminster	*England*	**26**	E4
Iloilo	*Philippines*	**48**	E5
Ilorin	*W. Africa*	**57**	C4
Immingham	*England*	**17**	E5
Imperia	*Italy*	**38**	A3
Imperial Valley	*California*	**64**	C4
Impfondo	*Congo Rep.*	**57**	D4
Imphal	*Manipur, Ind.*	**53**	O6
Imros, I.	*Turkey*	**39**	G4
Imst	*Austria*	**34**	C5
Inagua I., Gr. & Little	*W. Indies*	**71**	K3
Inari & L.	*Finland*	**42**	F1
Inchkeith, I.	*Scotland*	**29**	E4
Inchnadamph	*Scotland*	**28**	D2
Inchon	*Korea*	**48**	E3
Indals, R.	*Sweden*	**42**	D3
Independence	*Missouri*	**68**	E3
India	*S. Asia*	**53**	L6
Indian Oc.	—	**11**	N5
Indiana, state	*U.S.A.*	**65**	J3
Indianapolis	*Indiana*	**65**	J3
Indian Head	*Saskatchewan*	**62**	O7
Indian House L.	*Quebec*	**63**	W6
Indigirka R.	*U.S.S.R.*	**47**	P2
Indo China	*S.E. Asia*	**48**	C5
Indonesia	*S.E. Asia*	**48**	C7
Indore	*India*	**53**	L6
Indre, R.	*France*	**33**	C3
Indus R.	*W. Pakistan, etc.*	**53**	K5
Ingatestone	*England*	**27**	H3
Ingham	*Queensland*	**77**	H2
Ingleborough, mt.	*England*	**17**	D4
Inglefield G.	*Greenland*	**63**	V2
Inglefield Land	*Greenland*	**63**	W2
Ingleton	*England*	**25**	C2
Ingolstadt	*Germany, W.*	**34**	C4
Inhambane	*Mozambique*	**59**	D3
Inharrime	*Mozambique*	**59**	D3
Inishowen, pen.	*Eire*	**30**	D2
Inishowen Hd.	*Eire*	**17**	B4
Inishtrahull Sd.	*Eire*	**30**	D2
Injuni	*Queensland*	**77**	H4
Inn, R.	*Austria*	**34**	C5
Inner Sd.	*Scotland*	**16**	C3
Innerleithen	*Scotland*	**29**	E5
Inner Mongolia	*China*	**48**	D2
Inniscrone	*Eire*	**30**	B3
Innisfail	*Queensland*	**77**	H2
Innoko R.	*Alaska*	**62**	C5
Innsbruck	*Austria*	**34**	C5
Inongo	*Congo*	**58**	A5
Inowroclaw	*Poland*	**35**	F2
In Salah	*Algeria*	**57**	C2
Insch	*Scotland*	**28**	F3
Interlaken	*Switzerland*	**37**	B1
Inuvik	*N.-W. Terr., Can.*	**62**	H4
Inveraray	*Scotland*	**16**	C3
Inverbervie	*Scotland*	**29**	F4
Invercargill	*New Zealand*	**79**	B7
Inverell	*New South Wales*	**77**	J4
Invergordon	*Scotland*	**28**	D3
Inverkeithing	*Scotland*	**29**	E4
Inverness	*Scotland*	**16**	C3
Invershin	*Scotland*	**28**	D3
Inverurie	*Scotland*	**28**	F3
Investigator Str.	*S. Australia*	**77**	F6
Ioannina	*Greece*	**39**	E5
Iona, I.	*Scotland*	**16**	B3
Ionian Is.	*Greece*	**39**	E5
Ionian Sea	*Mediterranean*	**38**	D5
Iowa, state	*U.S.A.*	**65**	H2
Ipin	*China*	**50**	G6
Ipoh	*Malaya*	**53**	Q10
Ipswich	*England*	**17**	F5
Ipswich	*Queensland*	**77**	J4
Iquique	*Chile*	**72**	C8
Iquitos	*Peru*	**72**	C4
Iran (Persia)	*S.W. Asia*	**52**	F4
Iranshar	*Iran*	**52**	H5
Irapuato	*Mexico*	**70**	D3
Iraq	*S.W. Asia*	**52**	D4
Ireland, I.	*British Isles*	**17**	B5
Ireland, Rep. of (Eire)	*N.W. Europe*	**31**	C4
Ireland's Eye, I.	*Eire*	**31**	E4
Irgiz	*Kazakh.*	**46**	G4
Irian Barat, *see* West Irian			
Iringa	*Tanzania*	**58**	C5
Iriona	*Mexico*	**71**	H4
Irish Sea	*Ire.-Eng.*	**17**	C5
Irkutsk	*U.S.S.R.*	**47**	L3
Ironbridge	*England*	**26**	E2
Iron Gate	*Yugoslavia-Rumania*	**41**	J2
Iron Knob	*S. Australia*	**77**	F5
Iron Mountain	*Michigan*	**69**	F1
Ironwood	*Michigan*	**68**	E1
Irrawaddy R.	*Burma*	**53**	P6
Irshih	*China*	**51**	K2
Irtysh, R.	*U.S.S.R.*	**46**	G3
Irvine	*Scotland*	**16**	C4
Irvinestown	*N. Ireland*	**30**	D3
Isabela, I.	*Galapagos Is.*	**73**	N17
Isafjördhur	*Iceland*	**42**	J6
Isar, R.	*Germany*	**34**	D4
Isbister	*Scotland*	**28**	A1
Ischia, I. d'	*Italy*	**38**	C4
Iscia Baioda	*Somalia*	**58**	D4
Iseo, L. d'	*Italy*	**38**	B2
Isère, R.	*France*	**33**	D4
Isernia	*Italy*	**38**	C4
Isfahan	*Iran*	**52**	F4
Ishan	*China*	**50**	H7
Ishim, R.	*Kazakh.*	**46**	G3
Ishinomaki	*Japan*	**51**	P4
Ishpeming	*Michigan*	**69**	F1
Isisford	*Queensland*	**77**	G3
Iskenderun	*Turkey*	**52**	C3
Islamabad	*W. Pakistan*	**53**	K4
Island L.	*Manitoba*	**63**	Q7
Island Magee	*N. Ireland*	**30**	F3
Islands, B. of	*New Zealand*	**79**	E1
Islay, I.	*Scotland*	**16**	B4
Isle, R.	*France*	**33**	C4
Ismailia	*Egypt*	**58**	C1
Isna	*Egypt*	**58**	C2
Isoka	*Zambia*	**59**	D2
Israel	*W. Asia*	**54**	C3
Issoire	*France*	**33**	D4
Issyk Kul, L.	*Kirgiz.*	**46**	H4
Istanbul	*Turkey*	**52**	A2
Itabira	*Brazil*	**72**	J7
Itabuna	*Brazil*	**72**	K6
Italy	*S. Europe*	**38**	B2
Itasca, L.	*Minnesota*	**64**	G1
Ithaca	*Greece*	**39**	E5
Ithaca	*New York*	**66**	C2
Iturup I.	*Kuril Is.*	**47**	P4
Itzehoe	*Germany, W.*	**34**	C2
Ivanhoe	*New South Wales*	**77**	G5
Ivanovo	*U.S.S.R.*	**46**	E3
Ivigtut	*Greenland*	**63**	Z5
Iviza, I.	*Balearic Is.*	**36**	E3
Ivory Coast	*W. Africa*	**57**	B4
Ivrea	*Italy*	**38**	A2
Ivry	*France*	**33**	C2
Ivugivik	*Quebec*	**63**	T5
Ivybridge	*England*	**26**	D4
Ixmiquilpan	*Mexico*	**70**	E3
Ixtlan	*Mexico*	**70**	E4
Izhevsk	*U.S.S.R.*	**46**	F3
Izmail	*Ukraine*	**43**	C3
Izmir	*Turkey*	**52**	A3
Izmit	*Turkey*	**52**	A2
Jabalpur	*India*	**53**	L6
Jablonec nad Nisou	*Czechoslovakia*	**34**	E3
Jáchal	*Argentina*	**73**	D10
Jáchymov	*Czechoslovakia*	**34**	D3
Jackson	*Michigan*	**65**	K2
Jackson	*Mississippi*	**65**	H4
Jackson	*Tennessee*	**65**	J3
Jackson B.	*New Zealand*	**79**	B5
Jacksonville	*Florida*	**65**	K4
Jacksonville	*N. Carolina*	**65**	L4
Jacmel	*Haiti*	**71**	K4
Jadotville	*Congo*	**59**	C2
Jaen	*Spain*	**36**	C4
Jaffa	*Israel*	**54**	C3
Jaffna	*Ceylon*	**53**	M9
Jagdalpur	*India*	**53**	M7
Jaipur	*India*	**53**	L5
Jakobshavn	*Greenland*	**63**	Y4
Jalalabad	*W. Pakistan*	**53**	K4
Jalapa	*Mexico*	**70**	E4
Jalo Oasis	*Libya*	**58**	B2
Jamaica	*West Indies*	**71**	J4
James B.	*Canada*	**63**	S7
James Ras	*N. Terr., Aust.*	**76**	E3
James, R.	*S. Dakota*	**68**	D1
Jamestown	*New York*	**65**	L2
Jamestown	*N. Dakota*	**64**	G1
Jammu	*India*	**53**	L4
Jammu & Kaskmir	*India-Pakistan*	**53**	L4
Jamnagar	*India*	**52**	J6
Jämsänkoski	*Finland*	**42**	F3
Jamshedpur	*India*	**53**	N6
Jan Mayen, I.	*Atlantic Oc.*	**11**	K1
Janos	*Mexico*	**70**	C1
Japan	*E. Asia*	**48**	F3
Japan, Sea of	*Japan, etc.*	**48**	F2
Japura R.	*Brazil*	**72**	D4
Jardines de la Reina Is.	*Cuba*	**71**	J3
Jarosław	*Poland*	**35**	G3
Jarrow	*England*	**25**	D2
Jarvis I.	*Pacific Oc.*	**10**	E5
Jask	*Iran*	**52**	G5
Jasper	*Alberta*	**62**	L7
Jauf	*Saudi Arabia*	**52**	C5
Jauf, El	*Libya*	**58**	B2
Java, I.	*Indonesia*	**48**	C7
Java Sea	*Indonesia*	**48**	D7
Javari, R.	*Braz.-Peru*	**72**	C5
Jebel Shammar	*Saudi Arabia*	**52**	D5
Jedburgh	*Scotland*	**16**	D4
Jefferson City	*Missouri*	**65**	H3
Jēkabpils	*Latvia*	**42**	F4
Jelgava	*Latvia*	**42**	E4
Jena	*Germany, E.*	**34**	C3
Jequié	*Brazil*	**72**	J6
Jequitinhonha, R.	*Brazil*	**72**	J7
Jerez de la Frontera	*Spain*	**36**	B4
Jericho	*Jordan*	**54**	C4
Jericho	*Queensland*	**77**	H3
Jerome	*Idaho*	**67**	D3
Jersey, I.	*Channel Is.*	**33**	B2
Jersey City	*New Jersey*	**65**	M2
Jerusalem	*Israel-Jordan*	**54**	C4
Jervis B.	*Australia*	**77**	J5
Jervois Ra.	*N. Terr., Aust.*	**77**	F3
Jesselton	*Sabah*	**48**	D6
Jesup	*Georgia*	**69**	G4
Jewish Autonomous Prov.	*U.S.S.R.*	**47**	O4
Jhansi	*India*	**53**	L5
Jhelum R.	*W. Pakistan*	**53**	K4
Jibhalanta	*Mongolia*	**48**	B2
Jidda	*Saudi Arabia*	**52**	C6
Jihlava & R.	*Czechoslovakia*	**34**	E4
Jijiga	*Ethiopia*	**58**	D4
Jimenez	*Mexico*	**70**	D2

Jimma	*Ethiopia*	**58**	C4
Jinja	*Uganda*	**58**	C4
Jinotega	*Nicaragua*	**71**	G5
Jirgalanta	*Mongolia*	**48**	B2
João Pessoa	*Brazil*	**72**	K5
Jodhpur	*India*	**53**	K5
Joensuu	*Finland*	**42**	G3
Joffre, Mt.	*Br. Columbia*	**62**	L7
Johannesburg	*Transvaal*	**59**	C3
John o' Groats	*Scotland*	**16**	D2
Johnson City	*Tennessee*	**65**	K3
Johnston I.	*Pacific Oc.*	**10**	E4
Johnstone	*Scotland*	**29**	D5
Johnstone Str.	*Br. Columbia*	**62**	J7
Johnstown	*Eire*	**31**	E4
Johnstown	*Pennsylvania*	**65**	L2
Joliet	*Illinois*	**65**	J2
Joliette	*Quebec*	**63**	U8
Joma, mt.	*China*	**50**	E5
Jones Sd.	*N.-W. Terr., Can.*	**63**	R2
Jonesboro	*Arkansas*	**65**	H3
Jonesville	*Virginia*	**65**	K3
Jonkoping	*Sweden*	**42**	C4
Jonzac	*France*	**33**	B4
Joplin	*Missouri*	**65**	H3
Jordan	*S.W. Asia*	**52**	C4
Jordan, R.	*Israel-Jordan*	**54**	C3
Jorhat	*India*	**50**	E6
Jörn	*Sweden*	**42**	E2
Jorullo, Vol.	*Mexico*	**70**	D4
Jos	*W. Africa*	**57**	C4
Joseph Bonaparte G.	*N. Terr., W. Aust.*	**76**	D1
Jostedalsbre, glacier	*Norway*	**42**	A3
Jotunheimen, mts.	*Norway*	**42**	B3
Juan de Fuca Str.	*B.C.-Washington*	**62**	K8
Juan Fernandez Is.	*Pacific Oc.*	**73**	A10
Juazeiro	*Brazil*	**72**	J5
Juba	*Sudan*	**58**	C4
Juba R.	*Ethiopia-Somalia*	**58**	D4
Juchitan	*Mexico*	**70**	F4
Judenburg	*Austria*	**34**	D5
Juiz de Fora	*Brazil*	**73**	J8
Julia Creek	*Queensland*	**77**	G3
Julianehaab	*Greenland*	**63**	Z5
Julianstown	*Eire*	**30**	E4
Jullundur	*India*	**53**	L4
Junction	*Utah*	**64**	D3
Junction City	*Kansas*	**64**	G3
Jundah	*Queensland*	**77**	G3
Juneau	*Alaska*	**62**	H6
Junee	*New South Wales*	**77**	H5
Jungfrau, mt.	*Switzerland*	**37**	B1
Jura, I.	*Scotland*	**16**	C4
Jura Mts.	*France-Switz.*	**37**	B1
Jura, Sd. of	*Scotland*	**16**	C4
Juruá, R.	*Brazil*	**72**	D5
Juruena R.	*Brazil*	**72**	F5
Jutiapa	*Guatemala*	**70**	F5
Jutland, pen.	*Denmark*	**42**	B4
Jyväskyla	*Finland*	**42**	F3
K2, mt.	*Kashmir*	**53**	L3
Kabalo	*Congo*	**59**	C1
Kabardino A.S.S.R.	*U.S.S.R.*	**43**	F4
Kabel	*Surinam*	**72**	F3
Kabinda	*Congo*	**59**	C1
Kabompo, R.	*Zambia*	**59**	C2
Kabul	*Afghanistan*	**52**	J4
Kachuga	*U.S.S.R.*	**47**	L3
Kadugli	*Sudan*	**58**	B3
Kaduna	*Nigeria*	**57**	C3
Kaédi	*Mauritania*	**57**	A3
Kaesong	*Korea*	**51**	M4
Kafue, R.	*Zambia*	**59**	C2
Kagoshima	*Japan*	**51**	N5
Kagsersuak	*Greenland*	**63**	X3
Kahemba	*Congo*	**59**	B1
Kahutara Pt.	*New Zealand*	**79**	G3
Kai Is.	*Indonesia*	**48**	F7
Kaiapoi	*New Zealand*	**79**	D5
Kaifeng	*China*	**48**	D3
Kaikohe	*New Zealand*	**79**	D1
Kaikoura & Ra.	*New Zealand*	**79**	D5
Kailas Ra.	*Tibet, etc.*	**50**	B5
Kailu	*China*	**51**	L3
Kaimanawa Ra.	*New Zealand*	**79**	E3
Kaipara Harb.	*New Zealand*	**79**	E2
Kaiserslautern	*Germany, W.*	**34**	B4
Kaitaia	*New Zealand*	**79**	D1
Kaitangata	*New Zealand*	**79**	B7
Kaiteur Falls	*Br. Guiana*	**72**	F2
Kajaani	*Finland*	**42**	F2
Kajabbi	*Queensland*	**77**	G3
Kakhovsk Res.	*Ukraine*	**43**	D3
Kakinada	*India*	**53**	M7
Kalahari Des.	*Bechuanaland*	**59**	C3
Kalamata	*Greece*	**39**	F6
Kalamazoo	*Michigan*	**65**	J2
Kalannie	*W. Australia*	**76**	B5
Kalat	*W. Pakistan*	**52**	J5
Kalgoorlie	*W. Australia*	**76**	C5
Kalhapur	*India*	**53**	K7
Kali	*Tibet*	**50**	E5
Kalinin	*U.S.S.R.*	**46**	D3
Kaliningrad	*U.S.S.R.*	**46**	C3
Kalispell	*Montana*	**67**	D2
Kalisz	*Poland*	**35**	F3
Kallavesi, L.	*Finland*	**42**	F3
Kalmar	*Sweden*	**42**	C4
Kalmar Sd.	*Sweden*	**42**	D4
Kalmykovo	*Kazakh.*	**52**	F1
Kalmyt A.S.S.R.	*U.S.S.R.*	**43**	G3
Kalomo	*Zambia*	**59**	C2
Kaluga	*U.S.S.R.*	**43**	E2
Kama, R.	*U.S.S.R.*	**46**	F3
Kamaran I.	*Yemen*	**52**	D7
Kambo Ho, mt.	*Korea*	**48**	E2
Kamchatka, pen.	*U.S.S.R.*	**47**	Q3
Kamenets Podolskiy	*Ukraine*	**43**	C3
Kamenskoye	*U.S.S.R.*	**47**	R2
Kamet, mt.	*Tibet*	**50**	B5
Kamina	*Congo*	**59**	C1
Kaminuriak L.	*N.-W. Terr., Can.*	**63**	Q5
Kamloops	*Br. Columbia*	**62**	K7
Kampala	*Uganda*	**58**	C4
Kamsack	*Saskatchewan*	**62**	O7
Kamyshin	*U.S.S.R.*	**43**	G2
Kanakee	*Illinois*	**69**	F2
Kanas	*Sinkiang*	**50**	D2
Kanazawa	*Japan*	**48**	F3
Kanchow	*China*	**51**	J6
Kandagach	*Kazakh.*	**52**	G1
Kandahar	*Afghanistan*	**52**	J4
Kandi	*Dahomey*	**57**	C3
Kandia	*India*	**53**	K6
Kandy	*Ceylon*	**53**	M9
Kane Basin	*N.-W. Terr., Can.*	**63**	U2
Kangaroo I.	*S. Australia*	**77**	F6
Kangatsiak	*Greenland*	**63**	Y4
Kangchenjunga, mt.	*Nepal, etc.*	**53**	N5
Kangting	*China*	**50**	G5
Kangto, mt.	*India-Tibet*	**50**	E6
Kaniapiskau, L.	*Quebec*	**63**	V7
Kaniapiskau R.	*Quebec*	**63**	V6
Kankan	*Guinea*	**57**	B3
Kannapolis	*N. Carolina*	**69**	G3
Kano	*Nigeria*	**57**	C3
Kanpur	*India*	**53**	L5
Kansas, state	*U.S.A.*	**64**	G3
Kansas R.	*Kansas*	**64**	G3
Kansas City	*Missouri*	**65**	H3
Kansk	*U.S.S.R.*	**47**	K3
Kantse	*China*	**50**	F5
Kanturk	*Eire*	**31**	C5
Kanye	*Bechuanaland*	**59**	C3
Kaohsiung	*Taiwan*	**51**	L7
Kaolack	*Senegal*	**57**	A3
Kapanga	*Congo*	**59**	C1
Kapfenberg	*Austria*	**34**	E5
Kaposvár	*Hungary*	**35**	E5
Kapsukas	*Lithuania*	**42**	E5
Kapuskasing	*Ontario*	**63**	S8
Kara Sea	*Arctic Oc.*	**46**	G1
Kara Str.	*U.S.S.R.*	**46**	F1
Kara Bogas, G. of	*Turkmen.*	**46**	F4
Karabük	*Turkey*	**52**	B2
Karachi	*W. Pakistan*	**52**	J6
Karaganda	*Kazakh.*	**46**	H3
Karak	*Jordan*	**54**	C4
Kara Kalpak	*U.S.S.R.*	**46**	F4
Karakoram Pass	*Kashmir-Sinkiang*	**53**	L3
Karakoram Ra.	*S. Asia*	**53**	L3
Karakorum	*Mongolia*	**53**	Q1
Kara Kum	*Turkmen.*	**46**	F5
Karamai	*Sinkiang*	**50**	C2
Karamea Bight	*New Zealand*	**79**	C4
Karapiro, L.	*New Zealand*	**79**	E3
Karasburg	*S.W. Africa*	**59**	B3
Kara Shahr	*Sinkiang*	**50**	D3
Karasjok	*Norway*	**42**	F1
Karaul	*Sinkiang*	**50**	D3
Karbala	*Iraq*	**52**	D4
Karcag	*Hungary*	**35**	F5
Karelia	*U.S.S.R.*	**46**	D2
Karghalik	*Sinkiang*	**50**	B4
Kariba	*Zambia*	**59**	C2
Kariba, L.	*Zambia-Rhodesia*	**59**	C2
Karikal	*India*	**53**	M8
Karkaralinsk	*Kazakh.*	**46**	H4
Karlik Tagh	*Sinkiang*	**50**	E3
Karl Marx Stadt	*Germany, E.*	**34**	D3
Karlovac	*Yugoslavia*	**38**	D2
Karlovy Vary	*Czechoslovakia*	**34**	D3
Karlshamn	*Sweden*	**42**	C4
Karlskoga	*Sweden*	**42**	C4
Karlskrona	*Sweden*	**42**	C4
Karlsruhe	*Germany, W.*	**34**	B4
Karlstad	*Sweden*	**42**	C4
Karluk	*Alaska*	**62**	D6
Karpathos, I.	*Greece*	**39**	H7
Karpo	*Tibet*	**50**	E6
Kars	*Turkey*	**52**	D2
Karsakpay	*Kazakh.*	**46**	G4
Karshi	*Uzbek.*	**46**	G5
Kartuzy	*Poland*	**35**	F1
Karun R.	*Iran*	**52**	E4
Karunjie	*W. Australia*	**76**	D2
Kasai, R.	*Congo*	**59**	C1
Kasama	*Zambia*	**59**	D2
Kasar, Ras, pt.	*Sudan*	**58**	C3
Kasba L.	*N.-W. Terr., Can.*	**62**	O5
Kasempa	*Zambia*	**59**	C2
Kasese	*Uganda*	**58**	C4
Kashan	*Iran*	**52**	F4
Kashgar	*Sinkiang*	**50**	B4
Kashmar	*Iran*	**52**	G4
Kashmir, *see* Jammu & Kashmir			
Kaskinen	*Finland*	**42**	E3
Kaslo	*Br. Columbia*	**62**	L7
Kasongo	*Congo*	**59**	C1
Kassala	*Sudan*	**58**	C3
Kassel	*Germany, W.*	**34**	C3
Kastamonu	*Turkey*	**41**	M3
Katanga	*Congo*	**59**	C1
Katanning	*W. Australia*	**76**	B5
Katha	*Burma*	**53**	P6
Katherine	*N. Terr., Aust.*	**76**	E1
Katmandu	*Nepal*	**53**	N5
Katoomba	*New South Wales*	**77**	J4
Katowice	*Poland*	**35**	F3
Katrine, L.	*Scotland*	**29**	D4
Katrineholm	*Sweden*	**42**	C4
Katsina	*Nigeria*	**57**	C3
Katta Kurgan	*Uzbek.*	**46**	G5
Kattegat, chan.	*Denmark*	**42**	B4
Katun R.	*U.S.S.R.*	**47**	J3
Kaunas	*Lithuania*	**46**	C3
Kaura Namoda	*Nigeria*	**57**	C3
Kautokeino	*Norway*	**42**	E1
Kaválla	*Greece*	**39**	G4
Kawambwa	*Zambia*	**59**	C1
Kawerau	*New Zealand*	**79**	F3
Kawhia Harb.	*New Zealand*	**79**	E3
Kawran	*U.S.S.R.*	**47**	Q3
Kayes	*Mali*	**57**	A3
Kayseri	*Turkey*	**52**	C3
Kazakhstan (Kazakh S.S.R.)	*U.S.S.R.*	**46**	G4
Kazalinsk	*Kazakh.*	**46**	G4
Kazan	*U.S.S.R.*	**46**	E3
Kazan R.	*N.-W. Terr., Can.*	**62**	O5
Kazbek, mt.	*U.S.S.R.*	**46**	E4
Kazvin	*Iran*	**52**	F3
Kearney	*Nebraska*	**64**	G2
Kebnekaise, mt.	*Sweden*	**42**	D2
Kecskemét	*Hungary*	**35**	F5
Keele Pk.	*Yukon*	**62**	H5
Keele R.	*N.-W. Terr., Can.*	**62**	J5
Keetmanshoop	*S.W. Africa*	**59**	B3
Keewatin, Dist. of	*N.-W. Terr., Can.*	**63**	Q5
Keflavik	*Iceland*	**42**	J7
Keg River	*Alberta*	**62**	L6
Keighley	*England*	**17**	E5
Keitele, L.	*Finland*	**42**	F3
Keith	*Scotland*	**16**	D3
Kekertük	*N.-W. Terr., Can.*	**63**	W4
Kellett Str.	*N.-W. Terr., Can.*	**62**	L2
Kelloselkä	*Finland*	**42**	F2
Kells	*Eire*	**17**	B5
Kells Ra.,	*Scotland*	**29**	D5
Kelsey	*Manitoba*	**63**	P6
Kelso	*Scotland*	**16**	D4
Kelso	*Washington*	**67**	B2
Kelvedon	*England*	**27**	H3
Kemerovo	*U.S.S.R.*	**46**	J3
Kemi & R.	*Finland*	**42**	F2
Kemijarvi	*Finland*	**42**	F2
Kemp Land	*Antarctica*	**80**	G8
Kempten	*Germany, W.*	**34**	C5
Kenai	*Alaska*	**62**	D5
Kendal	*England*	**17**	D4
Kenema	*Sierra Leone*	**57**	A4
Kenge	*Congo*	**59**	B1
Keng Tung	*Burma*	**53**	P6
Kenilworth	*England*	**27**	F2
Kenmare	*Eire*	**17**	A6
Kenmare R.	*Eire*	**31**	A6
Kenmore	*Scotland*	**29**	E4
Kennet, R.	*England*	**27**	F3
Kennet, Vale of	*England*	**27**	F3
Kennicott	*Alaska*	**62**	F5
Keno Hill	*Yukon*	**62**	G5
Kenora	*Ontario*	**63**	Q8
Kenosha	*Wisconsin*	**65**	J2
Kent, co.	*England*	**17**	F6
Kent, Vale of	*England*	**27**	H3
Kentford	*England*	**27**	H2
Kentucky, state	*U.S.A.*	**65**	J3
Kentucky L.	*Tennessee*	**65**	J3
Kenya	*E. Africa*	**58**	C4
Kenya, Mt.	*Kenya*	**58**	C5
Keokuk	*Iowa*	**65**	H2
Kerala, state	*India*	**53**	L8
Kerang	*Victoria*	**77**	G6
Kerch	*Ukraine*	**43**	E3
Keren	*Ethiopia*	**58**	C3
Kerguelen I.	*S. Indian Oc.*	**11**	N7
Kerintji, mt.	*Sumatra*	**48**	C7
Keriya	*Sinkiang*	**50**	C4
Kerki	*Turkmen.*	**46**	G5
Kermadec Is.	*Pacific Oc.*	**10**	E6
Kersan	*Iran*	**52**	G4
Kermanshah	*Iran*	**52**	E4
Kerrville	*Texas*	**64**	G4
Kerry, co.	*Eire*	**17**	A5
Kerulen, R.	*Mongolia*	**48**	D2
Kesteven	*England*	**17**	E5
Keswick	*England*	**17**	D4
Keta	*Ghana*	**57**	C4
Ketshikan	*Alaska*	**62**	H6
Kettering	*England*	**17**	E5
Key Largo	*Florida*	**65**	K5
Keynsham	*England*	**26**	E3
Keystone	*W. Virginia*	**65**	K3
Key West	*Florida*	**65**	K6
Khabarovsk	*U.S.S.R.*	**47**	O4
Khabura	*Muscat & Oman*	**52**	G6
Khairpur	*W. Pakistan*	**52**	J5
Khaluf	*Muscat & Oman*	**52**	G6
Khanaqin	*Iraq*	**52**	E4
Khangai Mts.	*Mongolia*	**48**	B2
Khan Tengri, mt.	*Kirgiz.-Sinkiang*	**53**	M2
Khanty Mansiysk	*U.S.S.R.*	**46**	H2
Khârga, El	*Egypt*	**58**	C2
Kharkov	*Ukraine*	**46**	D3
Khartoum	*Sudan*	**58**	C3
Khasi Hills	*India*	**53**	O5
Khaskovo	*Bulgaria*	**39**	G4
Khatanga & R.	*U.S.S.R.*	**47**	L1
Kherson	*Ukraine*	**43**	D3
Khetinsiring	*China*	**50**	E5
Khingan Mts., Gt.	*China*	**49**	A2
Khingan Mts., Little	*China*	**49**	B2
Khiva	*Uzbek.*	**46**	G4
Khonu	*U.S.S.R.*	**47**	P2
Khormali	*Sinkiang*	**50**	D2
Khorog	*Tadzhik.*	**53**	K3
Khotan	*Sinkiang*	**50**	B4
Khotan, R.	*Sinkiang*	**50**	C4
Khotin	*Ukraine*	**43**	C3
Khurram	*Iran*	**52**	E4
Khurramabad	*Iran*	**52**	E4
Khyber Pass	*W. Pakistan*	**53**	K4
Kialinek	*Greenland*	**63**	Z4
Kiamusze	*China*	**51**	N2
Kian	*China*	**48**	D4
Kiangling	*China*	**51**	J5
Kibombo	*Congo*	**59**	C1
Kicking Horse Pass	*Alberta-B.C.*	**62**	L7
Kidal	*Mali*	**57**	C3
Kidderminster	*England*	**17**	D5
Kidnappers, C.	*New Zealand*	**79**	F3
Kidwelly	*Wales*	**26**	C3
Kiel & B.	*Germany, W.*	**34**	C1
Kielce	*Poland*	**35**	F3
Kienning	*China*	**51**	K6
Kienow	*China*	**51**	K6
Kienshui	*China*	**50**	G7
Kienteh	*China*	**51**	K6
Kienyang	*China*	**51**	K6
Kiev	*Ukraine*	**46**	D3
Kiffa	*Mauritania*	**57**	A3
Kigali	*Rwanda*	**58**	C5
Kigoma	*Tanzania*	**58**	B5
Kikwit	*Congo*	**59**	B1
Kilbeggan	*Eire*	**31**	D4
Kilchiga	*U.S.S.R.*	**47**	R3
Kilchu	*Korea*	**51**	M3
Kilcormac	*Eire*	**31**	D4

Kilcoy *Queensland* **78** J3
Kilcullen *Eire* **31** E4
Kildare *Eire* **17** B5
Kilfinnane *Eire* **31** C5
Kilgarvan *Eire* **31** B6
Kilimanjaro, mt. *Tanzania* **58** C5
Kilindini *Kenya* **58** C5
Kilkee *Eire* **17** A5
Kilkeel *N. Ireland* **30** F3
Kilkenny *Eire* **17** B5
Kill *Eire* **31** E4
Killala *Eire* **30** B3
Killala B. *Eire* **17** A4
Killaloe *Eire* **31** C5
Killarney *Eire* **17** A5
Killiecrankie, Pass of *Scotland* **29** E4
Killimor *Eire* **31** C4
Killin *Scotland* **16** C3
Killorglin *Eire* **31** B5
Killybegs *Eire* **17** A4
Kilmacthomas *Eire* **31** D5
Kilmallock *Eire* **31** C5
Kilmarnock *Scotland* **16** C4
Kilosa *Tanzania* **58** C5
Kilrea *N. Ireland* **30** E3
Kilrush *Eire* **31** B5
Kilsyth *Scotland* **29** D5
Kiltamagh *Eire* **30** C4
Kilwa Kivinje *Tanzania* **58** C5
Kilwinning *Scotland* **29** D5
Kimberley *Cape of Good Hope* **59** C3
Kimberley Plat. *W. Australia* **76** D2
Kimbolton *England* **27** G2
Kinabalu, mt. *Sabah* **48** D6
Kincardine, co. *Scotland* **16** D3
Kincardine-on-Forth *Scotland* **29** E4
Kincraig *Scotland* **28** E3
Kindía *Guinea* **57** A3
Kindu-Port Empain *Congo* **58** B5
Kineton *England* **27** F2
King I. *Tasmania* **78** E9
King Sd. *W. Australia* **76** C2
Kingaroy *Queensland* **77** J4
King Christian IX Land *Greenland* **63** Z4
King Edward VII Land *Antarctica* **80** O7
King Frederick VI Ld. *Greenland* **63** Z5
Kingfu *China* **50** G6
King George Sd. *W. Australia* **76** B6
King George V Land *Antarctica* **80** M8
King George VI Sd. *Antarctica* **80** S8
Kingissepp *Estonia* **42** E4
Kingku *China* **50** G7
King Leopold Ra. *W. Australia* **76** C2
Kingman *Arizona* **67** D4
Kingoonya *S. Australia* **77** F5
Kings Pk. *Utah* **64** D2
Kingsbarns *Scotland* **29** F4
Kingsbridge *England* **26** D4
Kingsclere *England* **27** F3
Kingscourt *Eire* **17** B5
King's Lynn *England* **17** F5
Kingston *England* **17** E6
Kingston *Jamaica* **71** J4
Kingston *New York* **65** M2
Kingston *New Zealand* **79** B6
Kingston *Ontario* **63** T9
Kingston *S. Australia* **77** F6
Kingstown *West Indies* **71** M5
Kingsville *Texas* **68** D5
Kingswear *England* **26** D4
Kingtehchen *China* **51** K6
Kington *England* **26** D2
Kingtung *China* **50** G7
Kingussie *Scotland* **16** C3
King William I. *N.-W. Terr., Can.* **63** P4
King William I Ld. *Greenland* **11** K1
Kingyang *China* **50** H4
Kinhwa *China* **51** K6
Kinleith *New Zealand* **79** E3
Kinlochewe *Scotland* **28** C3
Kinlochleven *Scotland* **16** C3
Kinloch Rannoch *Scotland* **29** D4
Kinnaird Hd. *Scotland* **16** D3
Kinross *Scotland* **16** D3
Kinsale & Harb. *Eire* **17** A6
Kintyre *Scotland* **16** C4
Kintyre, Mull of *Scotland* **17** C4
Kinvarra *Eire* **31** C4
Kinyeti, mt. *Sudan* **58** C4
Kipini *Kenya* **58** D5
Kirby Moorside *England* **25** E2
Kirensk *U.S.S.R.* **47** L3
Kirgiz Steppe *Kazakh.* **46** F4
Kirgizia (Kirgiz S.S.R.) *U.S.S.R.* **46** H4
Kirin *China* **48** E2
Kirkby Lonsdale *England* **25** C2
Kirkby Stephen *England* **25** C2
Kirkcaldy *Scotland* **16** D3
Kirkcolm *Scotland* **29** C6
Kirkconnel *Scotland* **29** D5
Kirkcudbright *Scotland* **17** C4
Kirkenes *Norway* **42** G1
Kirkham *England* **25** C3
Kirkintilloch *Scotland* **29** D5
Kirkliston Ra. *New Zealand* **79** C6
Kirkoswald *England* **25** C2
Kirkuk *Iraq* **52** D3
Kirkwall *Scotland* **16** D2
Kirov *U.S.S.R.* **46** F3
Kirovograd *Ukraine* **43** D3
Kirriemuir *Scotland* **29** E4
Kirthar mts. *W. Pakistan* **52** J5
Kirton *England* **25** E3
Kiruna *Sweden* **42** E2
Kishinev *Moldavia* **46** C4
Kiska I. *Aleutian Is.* **10** D2
Kiskunhalas *Hungary* **35** F5
Kismayu *Somalia* **58** D5
Kispest *Hungary* **35** F5
Kissimmee *Florida* **65** K5
Kistna R. *India* **53** L7
Kisumu *Kenya* **58** C4
Kisvárda *Hungary* **35** G4
Kita *Mali* **57** B3
Kitab *Uzbek.* **46** G5
Kita Kyushu *Japan* **51** N5
Kitale *Kenya* **58** C4
Kithira & I. *Greece* **39** F6
Kitimat *Br. Columbia* **62** J7
Kitwe *Zambia* **59** C2
Kityang *China* **51** K7
Kiuchuan *China* **48** B2
Kiukiang *China* **51** K6
Kiungchow Str. *China* **51** J7
Kiungshan *China* **51** J8
Kivu, L. *Congo, etc.* **58** B5
Kiwalik *Alaska* **62** B4
Kizil Irmak, R. *Turkey* **52** B2
Kizyl Arvat *Turkmen.* **46** F5
Kjöge B. *Greenland* **63** Z5
Klagenfurt *Austria* **34** D5
Klaipeda *Lithuania* **42** E5
Klamath Falls *Oregon* **64** B2
Klausen Pass *Switzerland* **37** C1
Klerksdorp *Transvaal* **59** C3
Klondike *Yukon* **62** G5
Kluane, L. *Yukon* **62** G5
Klyuchev Vol. *U.S.S.R.* **47** R3
Knaresborough *England* **25** D2
Knarsdale *England* **25** C2
Knighton *Wales* **26** D2
Knin *Yugoslavia* **38** D3
Knittelfeld *Austria* **34** D5
Knockmealdown Mts. *Eire* **17** A5
Knottingley *England* **25** D3
Knox Coast *Antarctica* **80** J8
Knoxville *Tennessee* **65** K3
Knud Rasmussen Ld. *Greenland* **63** Z4
Knutsford *England* **25** C3
Kobe *Japan* **48** F3
Kobuk R. *Alaska* **62** C4
Kochi *Japan* **51** N5
Kodiak & I. *Alaska* **62** D6
Koh-i-Baba, mts. *Afghanistan* **52** J4
Kohima *India* **50** E6
Kojonup *Western Australia* **76** B5
Kokand *Uzbek.* **46** H4
Kokkola *Finland* **42** E3
Kokomo *Indiana* **69** F2
Koko Nor, L. *China* **50** G4
Koko Shili, mts. *Tibet* **50** D4
Kokpety *Kazakh.* **46** J4
Kokstad *Cape of Good Hope* **59** C4
Kokyar *Sinkiang* **50** B4
Kola Pen. *U.S.S.R.* **12** G2
Kolar *India* **53** L8
Kolarovgrad *Bulgaria* **39** G3
Kolguyev I. *U.S.S.R.* **46** E2
Kolkas C. *Latvia* **42** E4
Kolobrzeg *Poland* **34** E1
Kolomna *U.S.S.R.* **43** E1
Kolpakova *U.S.S.R.* **47** Q3
Kolpashevo *U.S.S.R.* **46** J3
Kolwezi *Congo* **59** C2
Kolyma R. *U.S.S.R.* **47** Q2
Kolymskiy Mts. *U.S.S.R.* **47** Q2
Komandorskiye Is. *U.S.S.R.* **47** R3
Komárno *Czechoslovakia* **35** F5
Komati Poort *Transvaal* **59** D3
Kommunizma Pk. *Tadzhik., U.S.S.R.* **46** H5
Komoé, R. *Ivory Coast* **57** B4
Komotiní *Greece* **39** G4
Komsomolets I. *U.S.S.R.* **47** K1
Komsomol'sk na Amure *U.S.S.R.* **47** O3
Kongmoon *China* **51** J7
Kongola *Congo* **59** C1
Kongsvinger *Norway* **42** C3
Konotop *Ukraine* **43** D2
Konstantinovka *Ukraine* **43** E3
Kontiomaki *Finland* **42** G2
Konya *Turkey* **52** B3
Kootenay, L. *Br. Columbia* **62** L8
Korangi *W. Pakistan* **52** J6
Korce *Albania* **39** E4
Korea *E. Asia* **48** E3
Korea B. *China-Korea* **51** L4
Korhogo *Ivory Coast* **57** B4
Korla *Sinkiang* **53** N2
Korneuburg *Austria* **34** E4
Koro Toro *Chad* **58** A3
Koryaken Mts. *U.S.S.R.* **47** R2
Kos & I. *Greece* **39** G6
Kosciusko, Mt. *New South Wales* **77** H6
Košice *Czechoslovakia* **35** G4
Kosti *Sudan* **58** C3
Kostroma *U.S.S.R.* **43** F1
Kostrzÿn *Poland* **34** D2
Köszalin *Poland* **34** E1
Kota Bharu *Malaya* **48** C6
Kotelnich *U.S.S.R.* **43** G1
Kotelnyy I. *U.S.S.R.* **47** O1
Kotka *Finland* **42** F3
Kotlas *U.S.S.R.* **46** E2
Kotor *Yugoslavia* **38** E3
Kotzebue Sd. *Alaska* **62** A4
Koudougou *Up. Volta* **57** B3
Kouvola *Finland* **42** F3
Kovel *Ukraine* **43** B2
Kowloon *Hong Kong* **51** J7
Koyukuk R. *Alaska* **62** C4
Kra, Isthmus of *Burma-Thailand* **53** P8
Kragerö *Norway* **42** B4
Kragujevac *Yugoslavia* **39** E3
Kramatorsk *Ukraine* **43** E3
Krasnik *Poland* **35** G3
Krasnodar *U.S.S.R.* **46** D4
Krasnovodsk *Turkmen.* **46** F4
Krasnoyarsk *U.S.S.R.* **47** K3
Kratie *Cambodia* **53** R8
Krefeld *Germany, W.* **34** B3
Kremenchug *Ukraine* **43** D3
Krems *Austria* **34** E4
Kristiansand *Norway* **42** B4
Kristianstad *Sweden* **42** C5
Kristiansund *Norway* **42** A3
Kristiinankaupunki *Finland* **42** E3
Kristinehamn *Sweden* **42** C4
Krivoy Rog *Ukraine* **46** D4
Krk, I. *Yugoslavia* **38** C2
Kroonstad *O.F.S.* **59** C3
Kropotkin *U.S.S.R.* **43** E3
Krugersdorp *Transvaal* **59** C3
Kruševac *Yugoslavia* **39** F3
Kuala Lumpur *Malaya* **48** C6
Kuban, R. *U.S.S.R.* **46** D4
Kucha *Sinkiang* **50** C3
Kuching *Sarawak* **48** D6
Kudymkar *U.S.S.R.* **46** F3
Kueiteh *China* **50** G4
Kufra Oasis *Libya* **58** B2
Kufstein *Austria* **34** D5
Kuhi Dinar, mt. *Iran* **52** F4
Kuldja *Sinkiang* **50** C3
Kulgera *N. Terr., Aust.* **77** E4
Kumamoto *Japan* **51** N5
Kumara *New Zealand* **79** C5
Kumasi *Ghana* **57** B4
Kunashir, I. *Kuril Is.* **47** P4
Kunduz *Afghanistan* **52** J3
Kungrad *Uzbek.* **46** F4
Kungur, mt. *Sinkiang* **50** B4
Kunlong *Burma* **53** P6
Kunlun Mts. *Tibet, etc.* **53** M3
Kunming *China* **48** C4
Kunsan *Korea* **51** M4
Kuopio *Finland* **42** F3
Kupang *Timor I.* **48** E8
Kupreanof I. *Alaska* **62** H6
Kura R. *Azerbaijan* **46** E4
Kurdistan, S. *Iraq* **55** H2
Kure *Japan* **51** N5
Kurgan *U.S.S.R.* **46** G3
Kuria Muria Is. *Arabian Sea* **52** G7
Kuril Is. *U.S.S.R.* **47** P4
Kurnool *India* **53** L7
Kurow *New Zealand* **79** C6
Kursk *U.S.S.R.* **46** D3
Kuruk Tagh, mts. *Sinkiang* **50** D3
Kuruman *Cape of Good Hope* **59** C3
Kushiro *Japan* **51** P3
Kushka *Turkmen.* **52** H3
Kuskokwim Mts. & R. *Alaska* **62** C5
Kustanay *Kazakh.* **46** G3
Kut, Al *Iraq* **52** E4
Kütahya *Turkey* **39** J5
Kutaradja *Sumatra* **48** B6
Kutaya *Turkey* **41** L4
Kutch & G. of *India* **52** J6
Kutno *Poland* **35** F2
Kutsing *China* **50** G6
Kuusamo *Finland* **42** G2
Kuwait *Persian Gulf* **52** E5
Kuybyshev *U.S.S.R.* **46** F3
Kuybyshev Res. *U.S.S.R.* **43** G2
Kuznetsk *U.S.S.R.* **43** G2
Kvarner, G. of *Yugoslavia* **38** C2
Kwanghua *China* **51** J5
Kwangju *Korea* **51** M4
Kwangnan *China* **50** H7
Kwango *Congo* **59** B1
Kweilin *China* **48** D4
Kweiping *China* **50** H7
Kweiyang *China* **48** C4
Kwilu, R. *Congo* **59** B1
Kwinana *W. Australia* **76** B5
Kyakhta *U.S.S.R.* **47** L3
Kyancutta *S. Australia* **77** F5
Kyauk-pyo *Burma* **53** O7
Kyle *Scotland* **29** D5
Kyleakin *Scotland* **28** C3
Kyle of Lochalsh *Scotland* **16** C3
Kynuna *Queensland* **77** G3
Kyoto *Japan* **48** F3
Kyushu, I. *Japan* **48** F3
Kyustendil *Bulgaria* **39** F3
Kyzyl *U.S.S.R.* **47** K3
Kyzyl Kum *Uzbek.* **46** G4
Kzyl Orda *Kazakh.* **46** G4
Labé *Guinea* **57** A3
Laberge, L. *Yukon* **62** G5
Labrador, Coast of *Newfoundland* **63** W7
Labrador City *Labrador* **63** V7
Labuan, I. *Sabah* **48** D6
Laccadive Is. *India* **53** K8
La Ceiba *Honduras* **70** G4
La Chaux de Fonds *Switzerland* **37** B1
Lachlan R. *New South Wales* **77** H5
Lackawanna *New York* **66** B2
Lacken Res. *Eire* **31** E4
Lacombe *Alberta* **62** M7
Lacq *France* **33** B5
La Crosse *Wisconsin* **65** H2
Ladoga, L. *U.S.S.R.* **46** D2
Ladysmith *Natal* **59** C3
Lae *New Guinea* **10** C5
Læsø, I. *Denmark* **42** B4
Lafayette *Indiana* **69** F2
Lafayette *Louisiana* **68** E4
Lagan, R. *N. Ireland* **17** C4
Lagen, R. *Norway* **42** B3
Laggan *Scotland* **28** D3
Laggan, L. *Scotland* **16** C3
Laghouat *Algeria* **57** C1
Lagos *Nigeria* **57** C4
Lagos *Portugal* **36** B4
Lagos de Moreno *Mexico* **70** D3
La Grande *Oregon* **64** C1
La Grange *Georgia* **69** F4
La Grange *W. Australia* **76** C2
La Guaira *Venezuela* **72** D1
Lahijan *Iran* **52** E3
Lahne, R. *Germany, W.* **34** B3
Lahore *W. Pakistan* **53** K4
Lahti *Finland* **42** F3
Lai Chau *Vietnam* **50** G7
Laingsburg *Cape of Good Hope* **59** C4
Lairg *Scotland* **28** D2
La Junta *Colorado* **64** F3
Lake Charles *Louisiana* **65** H4
Lake City *Colorado* **64** E3
Lake City *Florida* **65** K4
Lake District *England* **25** B2
Lake Eyre Basin *S. Australia* **77** F4
Lake Grace *W. Australia* **76** B5
Lake Harbour *N.-W. Terr., Can.* **63** V5

LAKE

LLUL

Lake King	W. Australia	**76**	B5
Lakeland	Florida	**69**	G5
Lake Nash	N. Terr., Aust.	**77**	F3
Lakeport	California	**64**	B3
Lakeview	Oregon	**64**	B2
Lakewood	Ohio	**65**	K2
Lakse Fd..	Norway	**42**	F1
La Libertad	Guatemala	**70**	F4
La Linea	Spain	**36**	C4
La Mancha	Spain	**36**	C3
Lamar	Colorado	**57**	F4
Lambaréné	Gabon	**57**	D5
Lambay I.	Eire	**30**	E4
Lambourn	England	**27**	F3
Lamesa	Texas	**68**	C4
Lamia	Greece	**39**	F5
Lamington	Scotland	**29**	E5
Lamlash	Scotland	**29**	C5
Lammermuir Hills	Scotland	**29**	F5
Lampeter	Wales	**17**	C5
Lamu	Kenya	**58**	D5
Lanark	Scotland	**16**	D4
Lancashire, co.	England	**17**	D5
Lancaster	England	**17**	D4
Lancaster	New York	**66**	B2
Lancaster	Pennsylvania	**65**	L2
Lancaster Sd.	N.-W. Terr., Can.	**63**	R3
Lanchow	China	**48**	C3
Landa	Mexico	**70**	E3
Landeck	Austria	**34**	C5
Lander	Wyoming	**64**	E2
Landi Kotal	W. Pakistan	**53**	K4
Land's End	England	**17**	C6
Landshut	Germany, W.	**34**	D4
Landskrona	Sweden	**42**	C5
Langanes, pen.	Iceland	**42**	L6
Langchung	China	**50**	H5
Langenthal	Switzerland	**37**	B1
Langharne	Wales	**26**	C3
Langholm	Scotland	**17**	D4
Lang-Jökull, mt.	Iceland	**42**	J6
Langkawi, I.	Thailand	**53**	P9
Langöy, I.	Norway	**42**	C1
Langport	England	**26**	E3
Langres	France	**33**	D3
Langsa	Sumatra	**53**	P10
Lang Son	Vietnam	**50**	H7
Languedoc	France	**33**	C5
Lannemezan, plat.	France	**33**	C5
Lansing	Michigan	**65**	K2
Lanzarote, I.	Canary Is.	**57**	A2
Laoag	Philippines	**48**	E5
Laokai	Vietnam	**48**	C4
Laon	France	**33**	D2
La Oroya	Peru	**72**	B6
Laos	S.E. Asia	**53**	Q7
La Palma, I.	Canary Is.	**57**	A2
La Paz	Bolivia	**72**	D7
La Paz	Mexico	**70**	B3
La Pérouse Str.	Japan, etc.	**49**	E2
Lapford	England	**26**	D4
La Piedad	Mexico	**70**	D3
La Plata	Argentina	**73**	F11
Lappeenranta	Finland	**42**	G3
Lappland	Sweden-Finland	**42**	E1
Laptev Sea	Arctic Oc.	**47**	N1
Lar	Iran	**52**	F5
Larache	Morocco	**57**	B1
Laramie	Wyoming	**64**	E2
Laramie Ra.	Wyoming	**67**	E3
Larbert	Scotland	**29**	E4
Laredo	Texas	**64**	G5
Largeau	Chad	**58**	A3
Largo	Scotland	**29**	F4
Largs	Scotland	**29**	D5
La Rioja	Argentina	**73**	D9
Larisa	Greece	**39**	F5
Larnaca	Cyprus	**54**	B2
Larne	N. Ireland	**17**	C4
La Roda	Spain	**36**	D3
La Ronge	Saskatchewan	**62**	N6
Larrimah	N. Terr., Aust.	**77**	E2
Larvik	Norway	**42**	B4
Las Animas	Colorado	**64**	F3
Las Anod	Somalia	**58**	D4
Las Cruces	New Mexico	**64**	E4
La Serena	Chile	**73**	C9
Las Heras	Argentina	**73**	C13
Lashio	Burma	**53**	P6
Lashkar	India	**53**	L5
Lashkar Satma	Sinkiang	**50**	D4
Las Palmas	Canary Is.	**57**	A2
Lassen Pk.	California	**64**	B2
Last Mountain L.	Saskatchewan	**62**	N7
Las Vegas	Nevada	**64**	C3
Las Vegas	New Mexico	**64**	E3
Latacunga	Ecuador	**72**	B4
Latakia	Syria	**52**	C3
Latheron	Scotland	**28**	E2
Latina	Italy	**38**	C4
Latium	Italy	**38**	B3
La Tuque	Quebec	**63**	U8
Latvia	U.S.S.R.	**46**	C3
Lauder	Scotland	**29**	F5
Lauenburg	Germany, W.	**34**	C2
Launceston	England	**17**	C6
Launceston	Tasmania	**77**	H7
Laura	Queensland	**77**	G2
Laurel	Mississippi	**69**	F4
Laurencekirk	Scotland	**29**	F4
Laurentide Mts.	Quebec	**63**	U8
Lauria	Italy	**38**	D4
Lausanne	Switzerland	**37**	B1
Lauwers Zee	Netherlands	**32**	E1
Laval	France	**33**	B2
Lavamünd	Austria	**34**	D5
Lavaur	France	**33**	C5
Laverton	W. Australia	**76**	C4
Lawlers	W. Australia	**76**	C4
Lawrence	Kansas	**64**	G3
Lawrence	Massachusetts	**65**	M2
Lawton	Oklahoma	**64**	G4
Laxey	Isle of Man	**25**	A2
Laxo	Scotland	**28**	A1
Laxton	England	**27**	G1
Lea, R.	England	**17**	F6
Lead	S. Dakota	**64**	F2
Leadhills	Scotland	**29**	E5
Leadville	Colorado	**64**	E3
Leaf R.	Quebec	**63**	U6
Leagrave	England	**27**	G3
Leamington	England	**17**	E5
Learmouth	W. Australia	**76**	A3
Leatherhead	England	**27**	G3
Leavenworth	Kansas	**68**	E3
Lebanon	Missouri	**68**	E3
Lebanon	Pennsylvania	**66**	C3
Lebanon	S.W. Asia	**54**	C3
Lebanon Ra.	Lebanon-Syria	**52**	C4
Lebu	Chile	**73**	C11
Lecco	Italy	**38**	B2
Lechlade	England	**27**	F3
Ledbury	England	**26**	E2
Leduc	Alberta	**62**	M7
Lee, R.	Eire	**17**	A6
Leech L.	Minnesota	**68**	E1
Leeds	England	**17**	E5
Leek	England	**27**	E1
Leer	Germany, W.	**34**	B2
Leeuwarden	Netherlands	**32**	D1
Leeuwin, C.	W. Australia	**76**	A5
Leeward Is.	West Indies	**71**	M4
Lefroy, L.	W. Australia	**76**	C5
Legaspi	Philippines	**48**	E5
Legges Tor, mt.	Tasmania	**77**	H7
Leghorn	Italy	**38**	B3
Legnica	Poland	**34**	E3
Leh	Kashmir	**53**	L4
Leibnitz	Austria	**34**	E5
Leicester	England	**17**	E5
Leichhardt R.	Queensland	**77**	F2
Leichlinbridge	Eire	**31**	E5
Leiden	Netherlands	**32**	C2
Leigh	England	**25**	C3
Leigh Creek	S. Australia	**77**	F5
Leighton Buzzard	England	**27**	G3
Leinster	Eire	**31**	D4
Leipzig	Germany, E.	**34**	D3
Leiria	Portugal	**36**	B3
Leiston	England	**27**	J2
Leith	Scotland	**16**	D4
Leith Hill	England	**17**	E6
Leitrim, co.	Eire	**17**	A4
Leix, co.	Eire	**17**	B5
Leixlip	Eire	**31**	E4
Lek, R.	Netherlands	**32**	C3
Lemmon	S. Dakota	**68**	C1
Lemnos, I.	Greece	**39**	G5
Lena, R.	U.S.S.R.	**47**	N2
Lend	Austria	**34**	D5
Lenina Pk.	Tadzhik., etc.	**53**	K3
Leninabad	Tadzhik.	**46**	G4
Leningrad	U.S.S.R.	**46**	D3
Lens	France	**33**	C1
Leoben	Austria	**34**	E5
Leominster	England	**26**	E2
Leon	Mexico	**70**	D3
Leon	Nicaragua	**70**	G5
León	Spain	**36**	C1
Leonora	W. Australia	**76**	C4
Leopold II, L.	Congo	**58**	A5
Leopoldville	Congo	**59**	B1
Lepontine Alps	Switz.-Italy	**37**	C1
Lepsy	Kazakh.	**53**	L1
Lerida	Spain	**36**	E2
Lerwick	Scotland	**16**	E1
Lesbos, I.	Greece	**39**	G5
Les Cayes	Haiti	**71**	K4
Lesser Antilles, arch.	West Indies	**71**	M4
Lesser Slave L.	Alberta	**62**	L6
Leszno	Poland	**34**	E3
Letchworth	England	**27**	G3
Lethbridge	Alberta	**62**	M8
Leticia	Colombia	**72**	D4
Letterfrack	Eire	**30**	B4
Letterkenny	Eire	**17**	B4
Letty Harbour	N.-W. Terr., Can.	**62**	J4
Leuchars	Scotland	**29**	F4
Levadhia	Greece	**39**	F5
Levanger	Norway	**42**	B3
Leven	Scotland	**29**	F4
Leven, L.	Scotland	**16**	D3
Levêque, C.	W. Australia	**76**	C2
Leverburgh	Scotland	**28**	B3
Levin	New Zealand	**79**	E4
Lévis	Quebec	**63**	U8
Levkás & I.	Greece	**39**	E5
Lewes	England	**17**	F6
Lewis	Scotland	**16**	B2
Lewis, Butt of	Scotland	**16**	B2
Lewis Pass	New Zealand	**79**	D5
Lewis Ra.	Montana	**64**	D1
Lewis R.	Yukon	**62**	G5
Lewiston	Idaho	**64**	C1
Lewiston	Maine	**65**	M2
Lewistown	Montana	**67**	E2
Lexington	Kentucky	**65**	K3
Leyburn	England	**25**	D2
Leyte, I.	Philippines	**48**	E5
Lhasa	Tibet	**50**	E6
Liao, R.	China	**48**	E2
Liaoyang	China	**51**	L3
Liaoyuan	China	**51**	M3
Liard R.	Br. Columbia, etc.	**62**	J6
Libenge	Congo	**58**	A4
Liberal	Kansas	**68**	C3
Liberec	Czechoslovakia	**34**	E3
Liberia	Costa Rica	**71**	G5
Liberia	W. Africa	**57**	A4
Libourne	France	**33**	B4
Libreville	Gabon	**57**	C4
Libya	N. Africa	**58**	A2
Libyan Des.	Egypt-Libya	**58**	B2
Libyan Plat.	Egypt-Libya	**58**	B1
Lichfield	England	**17**	E5
Lichtenfels	Greenland	**63**	Y5
Liddel, R.	Scotland	**29**	F5
Liddesdale	Scotland	**29**	F5
Lido di Ostia	Italy	**38**	C4
Liechtenstein	Europe	**34**	C5
Liège	Belgium	**32**	D4
Lienyunkang	China	**48**	D3
Lienz	Austria	**34**	D5
Liepāja	Latvia	**42**	E4
Lier	Belgium	**32**	C3
Liestal	Switzerland	**37**	B1
Liezen	Austria	**34**	D5
Liffey, R.	Eire	**17**	B5
Lifford	Eire	**17**	B4
Lifton	England	**26**	C4
Liguria	Italy	**38**	A2
Ligurian Sea	Italy	**38**	A3
Lihsien	China	**51**	J6
Likiang	China	**50**	G6
Lille	France	**33**	D1
Lillehammer	Norway	**42**	B3
Lilongwe	Malawi	**59**	D2
Lim Fd.	Denmark	**42**	B4
Lima	Ohio	**65**	K2
Lima	Peru	**72**	B6
Limassol	Cyprus	**54**	B2
Limavady	N. Ireland	**30**	E2
Limbourg	Belgium	**32**	D3
Limburg	Germany, W.	**34**	B3
Limburg	Netherlands	**32**	D3
Limeira	Brazil	**73**	H8
Limerick	Eire	**17**	A5
Limmen Bight	N. Terr., Aust.	**77**	F1
Limoges	France	**33**	C4
Limon	Colorado	**67**	F4
Limon	Costa Rica	**71**	H6
Limpopo, R.	Mozambique, etc.	**59**	D3
Linares	Mexico	**70**	E3
Linares	Spain	**36**	C3
Lincoln	England	**17**	E5
Lincoln	Nebraska	**64**	G2
Lincoln	New Mexico	**64**	E4
Lincoln Wolds, hills	England	**17**	E5
Lindesay, Mt.	Queensland	**77**	J4
Lindi	Tanzania	**59**	D1
Lindsey	England	**17**	E5
Line Is.	Pacific Oc.	**10**	E4
Linfen	China	**51**	J4
Lingeh	Iran	**52**	F5
Lingen	Germany, W.	**34**	B2
Lingling	China	**51**	J6
Linglo	China	**50**	H7
Linguère	Senegal	**57**	A3
Linhai	China	**51**	L6
Linhsien	China	**51**	J7
Lini	China	**51**	K4
Linkoping	Sweden	**42**	C4
Linlithgow	Scotland	**16**	D4
Linnhe, L.	Scotland	**16**	C3
Linsi	China	**51**	K3
Linsia	China	**50**	G4
Lintan	China	**50**	G5
Linthal	Switzerland	**37**	C1
Linz	Austria	**34**	D4
Lions, G. of	France	**33**	D5
Lipari Is.	Italy	**38**	C5
Lipetsk	U.S.S.R.	**43**	E2
Liping	China	**50**	H6
Lisala	Congo	**58**	B4
Lisbon	Portugal	**36**	A3
Lisburn	N. Ireland	**17**	B4
Lisburne, C.	Alaska	**62**	A4
Lisieux	France	**33**	C2
Liskeard	England	**26**	C4
Lismore	Eire	**17**	B5
Lismore	New South Wales	**77**	J4
Lismore, I.	Scotland	**29**	C4
Listowel	Eire	**17**	A5
Litchfield	England	**27**	F3
Lith, El	Saudi Arabia	**52**	D6
Lithgow	New South Wales	**77**	J4
Lithuania	U.S.S.R.	**46**	C3
Litoměrice	Czechoslovakia	**34**	D3
Little America	Antarctica	**80**	N7
Little Barrier I.	New Zealand	**79**	E2
Little Belt, str.	Denmark	**42**	B5
Little Colorado R.	Arizona	**64**	D3
Little Falls	Minnesota	**68**	E1
Little Falls	New York	**66**	D2
Littlehampton	England	**27**	G4
Little Minch, str.	Scotland	**16**	B3
Little Missouri R.	Montana, etc.	**64**	F1
Little Ouse, R.	England	**27**	H2
Little Petherick	England	**26**	C4
Littleport	England	**27**	H2
Little River	New Zealand	**79**	D5
Little Rock	Arkansas	**65**	H4
Little Walsingham	England	**27**	H2
Liuan	China	**51**	K5
Liuchow	China	**48**	C4
Liverpool	England	**17**	D5
Liverpool	New South Wales	**77**	J5
Liverpool	Nova Scotia	**63**	W9
Liverpool B.	England	**17**	D5
Liverpool Ra.	N.S.W.	**77**	H5
Livingston	Guatemala	**70**	G4
Livingstone	Montana	**67**	D2
Livingstone	Zambia	**59**	C2
Lizard	England	**26**	B5
Lizard Hd.	England	**17**	C6
Ljubljana	Yugoslavia	**38**	C1
Llandaff	Wales	**26**	D3
Llandilo	Wales	**26**	C3
Llandovery	Wales	**17**	D5
Llandrindod Wells	Wales	**26**	D2
Llandudno	Wales	**17**	D5
Llandyssul	Wales	**26**	C2
Llanelly	Wales	**17**	C6
Llanerchymedd	Wales	**25**	A3
Llanfair Caereinion	Wales	**26**	D2
Llanfyllin	Wales	**26**	D2
Llangadock	Wales	**26**	D3
Llangefni	Wales	**26**	C1
Llangerniew	Wales	**26**	D1
Llangollen	Wales	**26**	D2
Llanidloes	Wales	**26**	D2
Llanllyfni	Wales	**26**	C1
Llano Estacado, plat.	New Mex.-Texas	**64**	F4
Llanos	Colomb.-Venez.	**72**	C2
Llanrhaiadr	Wales	**26**	D2
Llanrhystyd	Wales	**26**	C2
Llanrwst	Wales	**26**	D1
Llantrisant	Wales	**26**	D3
Llanwrtyd Wells	Wales	**26**	D2
Llanymynech	England	**26**	D2
Llerena	Spain	**36**	B3
Lleyn Pen.	Wales	**26**	C2
Lloydminster	Alberta	**62**	M7
Llullaillaco, mt.	Arg.-Chile	**73**	D8

Llwyngwril *Wales* **26** C2
Lobatsi *Bechuanaland* **59** C3
Lobito *Angola* **59** B2
Lobstick L. *Labrador* **63** W7
Locarno *Switzerland* **37** C1
Lochaber *Scotland* **29** C4
Lochaline *Scotland* **29** C4
Lochboisdale *Scotland* **28** A3
Lochcarron *Scotland* **28** C3
Lochearnhead *Scotland* **29** D4
Loches *France* **33** C3
Lochgelly *Scotland* **29** E4
Lochgilphead *Scotland* **16** C3
Lochgoilhead *Scotland* **29** D4
Lochinver *Scotland* **16** C2
Lochmaben *Scotland* **29** E5
Lochmaddy *Scotland* **28** A3
Lochnagar, mt. *Scotland* **16** D3
Lochranza *Scotland* **29** C5
Lochy, L. *Scotland* **16** C3
Lockerbie *Scotland* **29** E5
Lockport *New York* **66** B2
Locle, le *Switzerland* **37** B1
Loddon *England* **27** J2
Lodi *Italy* **38** B2
Lodwar *Kenya* **58** C4
Łódź *Poland* **35** F3
Lofoten Is. *Norway* **42** C2
Loftus *England* **25** E2
Logan *Montana* **67** D2
Logan *Utah* **64** D2
Logan, Mt. *Yukon* **62** F5
Logansport *Indiana* **65** J2
Logone, R. *Chad, etc.* **57** D3
Logrono *Spain* **36** D1
Loire, R. *France* **33** C3
Loja *Ecuador* **72** B4
Loko *Cent. Afr. Rep.* **57** D4
Lokoja *Nigeria* **57** C4
Lolland, I. *Denmark* **42** B5
Lom *Bulgaria* **39** F3
Lomami R. *Congo* **58** B5
Lombardy & Plain of *Italy* **38** B2
Lombok, I. *Indonesia* **48** D7
Lombo Kangra, mt. *Tibet* **50** C6
Lomé *Togo* **57** C4
Lomela R. *Congo* **58** B5
Lomié *Cameroun* **57** D4
Lomond Hills *Scotland* **29** E4
Lomond, L. *Scotland* **16** C3
Łomza *Poland* **35** G2
London *England* **17** E6
London *Ontario* **63** S9
Londonderry *N. Ireland* **17** B4
Londrina *Brazil* **73** G8
Long B. *S. Carolina* **65** L4
Long I. *Bahamas* **71** K3
Long I. *New York* **65** M2
Long L. *Ontario* **63** R8
Long, L. *Scotland* **29** D4
Long Ra. *Newfoundland* **63** X7
Long Beach *California* **64** C4
Long Branch *New Jersey* **66** D3
Long Compton *England* **27** F2
Long Eaton *England* **27** F2
Longford *Eire* **17** B5
Longhorsley *England* **25** D1
Long Kuyen *Vietnam* **53** R8
Long Melford *England* **27** H2
Longmont *Colorado* **67** E3
Longnor *England* **27** F1
Longreach *Queensland* **77** G3
Longs Pk. *Colorado* **64** E2
Longships Lt. Ho. *England* **26** B4
Long Stratton *England* **27** J2
Long Sutton *England* **27** H2
Longton *England* **27** E2
Longtown *England* **25** C1
Longview *Texas* **65** H4
Longview *Washington* **67** B2
Lonquimay *Chile* **73** C11
Looe, E. & W. *England* **26** C4
Lookout, C. *N. Carolina* **65** L4
Lopatka, C. *U.S.S.R.* **47** Q3
Lop Nor, L. *Sinkiang* **50** E3
Lopphavet *Norway* **42** E1
Lorain *Ohio* **65** K2
Lorca *Spain* **36** D4
Lord Howe I. *Pacific Oc.* **77** K5
Lordsburg *New Mexico* **67** E5
Lorient *France* **33** A3
Lorne *Scotland* **29** C4
Lorne, Firth of *Scotland* **16** C3
Lorraine *France* **33** D2
Los Andes *Chile* **73** C10
Los Angeles *California* **64** C4
Loshan *China* **50** G6
Los Mochis *Mexico* **70** C2
Lossiemouth *Scotland* **16** D3
Lostwithiel *England* **26** C4
Loudéac *France* **33** B2
Loughborough *England* **27** F2
Loughor *Wales* **26** C3
Loughrea *Eire* **17** A5
Louisiade Arch. *Pacific Oc.* **77** J1
Louisiana, state *U.S.A.* **65** H4
Louis Trichardt *Transvaal* **59** C3
Louisville *Kentucky* **65** J3
Lourdes *France* **33** B5
Lourenço Marques *Mozambique* **59** D3
Louth *England* **17** F5
Louth *New South Wales* **77** H5
Louth, co. *Eire* **17** B5
Louvain *Belgium* **32** C4
Lovell *Wyoming* **67** E3
Lovelock *Nevada* **67** C3
Loviisa *Finland* **42** F3
Lovington *New Mexico* **67** F5
Lowdham *England* **27** G1
Lowell *Massachusetts* **65** M2
Lower California *Mexico* **70** A1
Lower Hutt *New Zealand* **79** E4
Lower Laberge *Yukon* **62** H5
Lower Saxony *Germany, W.* **34** B2
Lowestoft *England* **17** F5
Lowick *England* **25** D1
Loyang *China* **51** J5
Lualaba R. *Congo* **58** B5
Luanda *Angola* **59** B1
Luang Prabang *Laos* **53** Q6
Luangwa, R. *Zambia* **59** D2
Luanshya *Zambia* **59** C2
Lubartów *Poland* **35** G3
Lubbock *Texas* **64** F4
Lübeck *Germany, W.* **34** C2
Lübeck B. *Germany* **34** C1
Lublin *Poland* **35** G3
Lubnaig, L. *Scotland* **29** D4
Lubudi *Congo* **59** C1
Lucan *Eire* **31** E4
Lucca *Italy* **38** B3
Luce B. *Scotland* **17** C4
Lucera *Italy* **38** D4
Lucerne & L. of *Switzerland* **37** C1
Luchow *China* **50** H6
Luckenwalde *Germany, E.* **34** D2
Lucknow *India* **53** M5
Luderitz *S.W. Africa* **59** B3
Ludgershall *England* **27** F3
Ludhiana *India* **53** L4
Ludington *Michigan* **69** F2
Ludlow *England* **26** E2
Ludvika *Sweden* **42** C3
Ludwigsburg *Germany, W.* **34** C4
Ludwigshafen *Germany, W.* **34** B4
Ludwigslust *Germany, E.* **34** C2
Luebo *Congo* **59** C1
Lufkin *Texas* **65** H4
Luga & R. *U.S.S.R.* **43** C1
Lugano *Switzerland* **37** C1
Lugano, L. *Switzerland* **37** C2
Lugansk *Ukraine* **43** E3
Lugenda, R. *Mozambique* **59** D2
Lugg, R. *England* **17** D5
Lugh Ferrandi *Somalia* **58** D4
Lugnaquilla, mt. *Eire* **31** E5
Lugo *Spain* **36** B1
Luhaiya *Yemen* **52** D7
Luiana *Angola* **59** C2
Luichow Pen. *China* **50** H7
Lukenie, R. *Congo* **59** C1
Lukmanier Pass *Switzerland* **37** C1
Łuków *Poland* **35** G3
Lukuga, R. *Congo* **59** C1
Lule, R. *Sweden* **42** E2
Lulea *Sweden* **42** E2
Luluabourg *Congo* **59** C1
Lumsden *New Zealand* **79** B6
Lumsden *Scotland* **29** F3
Lund *Sweden* **42** C5
Lundy, I. *England* **17** C6
Lune, R. *England* **17** D4
Lüneburg *Germany, W.* **34** C2
Luneville *France* **33** E2
Lungling *China* **50** F7
Luni R. *India* **53** K5
Lunna *Scotland* **28** A1
Lupeh *China* **51** L3
Lurgan *N. Ireland* **17** B4
Lurio, R. *Mozambique* **59** D2
Lusaka *Zambia* **59** C2
Lusambo *Congo* **59** C1
Lushai Hills *India* **50** E7
Lüshun *China* **48** E3
Lusk *Eire* **17** B5
Lusk *Wyoming* **67** F3
Luss *Scotland* **29** D4
Lut Des. *Iran* **52** G4
Luta, pen. *China* **51** L4
Luton *England* **17** E6
Lutsk *Ukraine* **43** C2
Lutterworth *England* **27** F2
Luxembourg *Belgium* **32** D5
Luxembourg *Luxembourg* **32** E5
Luxembourg *N.W. Europe* **32** D5
Luxeuil *France* **33** E3
Luxor *Egypt* **58** C2
Luzon, I. *Philippines* **48** E5
Luzon Str. *Philippines* **51** L7
Lvov *Ukraine* **46** C4
Lyakhovskiy Is., Gt. *U.S.S.R.* **47** P1
Lyall, Mt. *New Zealand* **79** A6
Lyash Tagh, mt. *Sinkiang* **50** C4
Lybster *Scotland* **16** D2
Lycksele *Sweden* **42** D2
Lydd *England* **27** H4
Lydford *England* **26** C4
Lydney *England* **26** E3
Lye *England* **27** E2
Lyell, Mt. *California* **64** C3
Lyell Ra. *New Zealand* **79** D4
Lyme B. *England* **26** E4
Lyme Regis *England* **17** D6
Lymington *England* **27** F4
Lynchburg *Virginia* **65** L3
Lyndhurst *England* **27** F4
Lynn *Massachusetts* **66** F2
Lynn Lake *Manitoba* **62** O6
Lynton *England* **26** D3
Lyons *France* **33** D4
Lyons R. *W. Australia* **76** B3
Lys, R. *Belgium* **32** B4
Lytham St. Annes *England* **17** D5
Lyttelton *New Zealand* **79** D5
Ma'an *Jordan* **54** C4
Maarianhamina *Finland* **42** D3
Maas, R. *Netherlands* **32** D3
Maaseik *Belgium* **32** D3
Maastricht *Netherlands* **32** D4
Mablethorpe *England* **25** F3
McAlester *Oklahoma* **64** G4
McAllen *Texas* **68** D5
Macapá *Brazil* **72** G3
Macau *Brazil* **72** K5
Macau *China (Port.)* **48** D4
Macchu Picchu *Peru* **72** C6
Macclesfield *England* **17** D5
McClintock Chan. *N.-W. Terr., Can.* **62** O3
M'Clure Str. *N.-W Terr., Can.* **62** K3
McCook *Nebraska* **64** F2
McDame *Br. Columbia* **62** J6
McDermitt *Nevada* **67** C3
McDonald I. *S. Indian Oc.* **80** G9
Macdonald, L. *W. Aust.-N. Terr.* **76** D3
Macdonnell Ras. *N. Terr., Aust.* **76** E3
McDouall Ra. *N. Terr., Aust.* **77** E2
Macduff *Scotland* **16** D3
Macedonia *Greece-Yugoslavia* **39** F4
Maceió *Brazil* **72** K5
Macerata *Italy* **38** C3
McGill *Nevada* **67** D4
Macgillicuddys Reeks *Eire* **17** A5
McGregor Ra. *Qnsld.* **77** G4
Machrihanish *Scotland* **29** C5
Machynlleth *Wales* **26** D2
Mackay *Queensland* **77** H3
MacKay, L. *N.-W. Terr., Can.* **62** M5
Mackay, L. *W. Aust.-N. Terr.* **76** D3
McKeesport *Pennsylvania* **66** B3
Mackenzie *Br. Guiana* **72** F2
Mackenzie B. *Yukon-N.-W. Terr.* **62** G4
Mackenzie, Dist. of *N.-W. Terr., Can.* **62** K5
Mackenzie Highway *Alberta-N.-W.T.* **62** L6
Mackenzie Plains *New Zealand* **79** C6
Mackenzie Mts. *N.-W. Terr.-Yukon* **62** H5
Mackenzie R. *N.-W. Terr., Can.* **62** J4
Mackenzie Sea *Antarctica* **80** G8
Mackenzie King I. *N.-W. Terr., Can.* **62** M2
McKinley, Mt. *Alaska* **62** D5
McKinney *Texas* **68** D4
McLennan *Alberta* **62** L6
McMurray *Alberta* **62** M6
Mâcon *France* **33** D3
Macon *Georgia* **65** K4
Macpherson Ra. *Queensland-N.S.W.* **77** J4
Macquarie Harbour *Tasmania* **77** H7
Macquarie I. *S. Pacific Oc.* **10** D7
Macquarie R. *New South Wales* **77** H5
MacRobertson Land *Antarctica* **80** G8
Macroom *Eire* **31** C6
Madagascar, I. *Indian Oc.* **59** E2
Madang *New Guinea* **10** C5
Madeira, I. *Atlantic Oc.* **57** A1
Madeira, R. *Brazil* **72** E5
Madhya Pradesh, state *India* **53** L6
Madison *Georgia* **65** K4
Madison *S. Dakota* **68** D2
Madison *Wisconsin* **65** J2
Madisonville *Kentucky* **69** F3
Madona *Latvia* **42** F4
Madras *India* **53** M8
Madre, L. *Mexico* **70** E3
Madre, L. *Texas* **64** G5
Madre, Sa, mts. *Mexico* **70** C3
Madre de Dios, R. *Peru-Bolivia* **72** C6
Madre del Sur, Sa, mts. *Mexico* **70** E4
Madrid *Spain* **36** C2
Madura, I. *Indonesia* **48** D7
Madurai *India* **53** L9
Maevatanana *Malagasy Rep.* **59** E2
Mafeking *Cape of Good Hope* **59** C3
Mafia I. *Tanzania* **58** D5
Magadan *U.S.S.R.* **47** Q3
Magadi *Kenya* **58** C5
Magallanes *Chile* **73** C14
Magdalen Is. *Canada* **63** W8
Magdalena Basin & R. *Colombia* **72** C2
Magdeburg *Germany, E.* **34** C2
Magellan, Str. of *Chile* **73** D14
Mageröy, I. *Norway* **42** F1
Maggiore, L. *Italy* **38** A1
Maghera *N. Ireland* **17** B4
Magherafelt *N. Ireland* **30** E3
Magnetic I. *Queensland* **77** H2
Magnitogorsk *U.S.S.R.* **46** F3
Maguse L. *N.-W. Terr., Can.* **63** P6
Magwe *Burma* **50** F7
Mahābād *Iran* **55** H1
Mahai *China* **50** E4
Mahalapye *Bechuanaland* **59** C3
Mahalla el Kubra, El *Egypt* **54** A4
Mahanadi R. *India* **53** M6
Maharashtra, state *India* **53** K7
Mahé *India* **53** L8
Mahenge *Tanzania* **58** C5
Mahia Pen. *New Zealand* **79** G3
Maidenhead *England* **27** G3
Maiden Newton *England* **26** E4
Maidstone *England* **17** F6
Maiduguri *Nigeria* **57** D3
Maikala Ra. *India* **53** M6
Maimana *Afghanistan* **52** H3
Main, R. *Germany* **34** C4
Main Barrier Ra. *N.S.W.-S. Aust.* **77** G5
Maine, state *U.S.A.* **65** N1
Maintirano *Malagasy Rep.* **59** E2
Mainz *Germany, W.* **34** B4
Maitland *New South Wales* **77** J5
Majdanpek *Yugoslavia* **39** F2
Maji *Ethiopia* **58** C4
Majorca, I. *Balearic Is.* **36** F3
Majunga *Malagasy Rep.* **59** E2
Makarikari, saltpan *Bechuanaland* **59** C3
Makassar & Str. of *Celébes* **48** D7
Makeni *Sierra Leone* **57** A4
Makeyevka *Ukraine* **43** E3
Makhach Kala *U.S.S.R.* **46** E4
Makkovik *Labrador* **63** X7
Makkum *Netherlands* **32** D1
Makó *Hungary* **35** F5
Makorako, mt. *New Zealand* **79** F3
Makran *Pakistan-Iran* **52** G5
Makurdi *Nigeria* **57** C4

Mal B.	*Eire*	**17**	A5
Malabar	*India*	**53**	K8
Malacca	*Malaya*	**48**	C6
Malacca, Str. of	*Malaya-Sumatra*	**48**	B6
Malad City	*Idaho*	**64**	D2
Maladetta, mt.	*Spain*	**36**	E1
Malaga	*Spain*	**36**	C4
Malagasy Rep.	*Madagascar*	**59**	E2
Malahide	*Eire*	**31**	E4
Malakal	*Sudan*	**58**	C4
Malanje	*Angola*	**59**	B1
Malaren, L.	*Sweden*	**42**	D4
Malatya	*Turkey*	**52**	C3
Malawi	*Cent. Africa*	**59**	D2
Malay Pen.	*S. Asia*	**48**	C6
Malaya	*Malaysia*	**48**	C6
Malayer	*Iran*	**55**	K2
Malaysia	*S. Asia*	**48**	C6
Malbork	*Poland*	**35**	F2
Malden I.	*Pacific Oc.*	**10**	E5
Maldive Is.	*Indian Oc.*	**53**	K9
Maldon	*England*	**27**	H3
Malesherbes	*France*	**33**	C2
Malheur L.	*Oregon*	**64**	C2
Mali	*W. Africa*	**57**	B3
Malin Hd.	*Eire*	**17**	B4
Malindi	*Kenya*	**58**	D5
Malin More	*Eire*	**30**	C3
Mallaig	*Scotland*	**16**	C3
Mallawi	*Egypt*	**54**	A6
Mallow	*Eire*	**17**	A5
Malmesbury	*Cape of Good Hope*	**59**	B4
Malmesbury	*England*	**27**	E3
Malmo	*Sweden*	**42**	C5
Malpas	*England*	**26**	E1
Malta	*Montana*	**64**	E1
Malta Chan.	*Medit. Sea*	**38**	C6
Malta, I.	*Mediterranean Sea*	**41**	G5
Maltby	*England*	**25**	D3
Malton	*England*	**17**	E4
Malvern	*Arkansas*	**68**	E4
Malvern Hills	*England*	**26**	E2
Malwa Plat.	*India*	**53**	K6
Mamers	*France*	**33**	C2
Mamoa	*Guinea*	**57**	A3
Mamore, R.	*Bolivia*	**72**	D6
Mam Soul, mt.	*Scotland*	**28**	C3
Man	*Ivory Coast*	**57**	B4
Man, Calf of	*Isle of Man*	**17**	C4
Man, Isle of	*Irish Sea*	**17**	C4
Manado	*Celebes*	**48**	E6
Managua & L.	*Nicaragua*	**71**	G5
Manakara	*Malagasy Rep.*	**59**	E3
Manama	*Bahrain*	**52**	F5
Mananjary	*Malagasy Rep.*	**59**	E3
Manapouri, L.	*New Zealand*	**79**	A6
Manass	*Sinkiang*	**50**	D3
Manaus	*Brazil*	**72**	F4
Manchester	*England*	**17**	D5
Manchester	*New Hampshire*	**65**	M2
Manchouli	*China*	**51**	K2
Manchuria & Plain of	*China*	**48**	E2
Mandalay	*Burma*	**53**	P6
Mandal Obo	*Mongolia*	**50**	G3
Mandan	*N. Dakota*	**68**	C1
Mandera	*Kenya*	**58**	D4
Manfredonia & G. of	*Italy*	**38**	D4
Mangalore	*India*	**53**	K8
Mangerton, mt.	*Eire*	**31**	B6
Mangoky, R.	*Malagasy Rep.*	**59**	E3
Mangyai	*China*	**50**	E4
Manhattan	*Kansas*	**68**	D3
Manicoré	*Brazil*	**72**	E5
Manicuagan R.	*Quebec*	**63**	V7
Manifold, C.	*Queensland*	**77**	J3
Manihiki Is.	*Pacific Oc.*	**10**	E5
Manila	*Philippines*	**48**	E5
Manipur, terr.	*India*	**53**	O6
Manisa	*Turkey*	**52**	A3
Manistee	*Michigan*	**65**	J2
Manitoba, prov.	*Canada*	**63**	P7
Manitoba, L.	*Manitoba*	**63**	P7
Manitoulin I.	*Ontario*	**63**	S8
Manitowoc	*Wisconsin*	**69**	F2
Manizales	*Colombia*	**72**	B2
Manjimup	*W. Australia*	**76**	B5
Mankato	*Minnesota*	**65**	H2
Mannar, G. of	*Ceylon-India*	**53**	L9
Mannheim	*Germany, W.*	**34**	B4
Manningtree	*England*	**27**	J3
Manokwari	*W. Irian*	**48**	F7
Manono	*Congo*	**59**	C1
Manresa	*Spain*	**36**	E2
Mans, le	*France*	**33**	C2
Mansel I.	*N.-W. Terr., Can.*	**63**	S5
Mansfield	*England*	**17**	E5
Mansfield	*Louisiana*	**68**	E4
Mansfield	*Ohio*	**65**	K2
Manta	*Ecuador*	**72**	A4
Mantua	*Italy*	**38**	B2
Manukau Harb.	*New Zealand*	**79**	E2
Manych L. & R.	*U.S.S.R.*	**43**	F3
Manzanillo	*Cuba*	**71**	J3
Manzanillo	*Mexico*	**70**	D4
Manzini	*Swaziland*	**59**	D3
Maoke, mts.	*W. Irian*	**48**	F7
Mapimi	*Mexico*	**70**	D2
Maple Creek	*Saskatchewan*	**62**	N8
Ma'qil, Al	*Iraq*	**55**	J4
Maquela do Zombo	*Angola*	**59**	B1
Mar, Sa do, mts.	*Brazil*	**73**	H9
Marabá	*Brazil*	**72**	H5
Maraca I.	*Brazil*	**72**	H3
Maracaibo & L. of	*Venezuela*	**72**	C1
Maracay	*Venezuela*	**72**	D1
Maradi	*Niger*	**57**	C3
Marajo, I. of	*Brazil*	**72**	H4
Maralal	*Kenya*	**58**	C4
Maralinga	*S. Aust.*	**76**	E5
Marañón R.	*Peru*	**72**	B4
Maras	*Turkey*	**52**	C3
Marathon	*Greece*	**39**	F5
Marazion	*England*	**26**	B4
Marble Bar	*W. Australia*	**76**	B3
Marburg	*Germany, W.*	**34**	B3
March	*England*	**27**	H2
Marche	*Belgium*	**32**	D4
Marches	*Italy*	**38**	C3
Marcus I.	*Pacific Oc.*	**10**	D3
Mar del Plata	*Argentina*	**73**	F11
Marden	*England*	**26**	E2
Mardin	*Turkey*	**52**	D3
Maree, L.	*Scotland*	**16**	C3
Mareeba	*Queensland*	**77**	H2
Marfa	*Texas*	**64**	F4
Margam	*Wales*	**26**	D3
Margarita, I.	*Venezuela*	**72**	E1
Margate	*England*	**17**	F6
Marianas Is.	*Pacific Oc.*	**10**	C4
Marianské Lázne	*Czechoslovakia*	**34**	D4
Maria van Diemen, C.	*New Zealand*	**79**	D1
Maribor	*Yugoslavia*	**38**	D1
Maridi	*Sudan*	**58**	B4
Marie Byrd Land	*Antarctica*	**80**	P6
Marie Galante, I.	*West Indies*	**71**	M4
Mariental	*S.W. Africa*	**59**	B3
Mariestad	*Sweden*	**42**	C4
Mariinsk	*U.S.S.R.*	**47**	J3
Mariinsk	*U.S.S.R.*	**47**	O3
Marinette	*Wisconsin*	**65**	J1
Maringá	*Brazil*	**73**	G8
Marion	*Indiana*	**69**	F2
Marion	*Ohio*	**69**	G2
Marion I.	*Indian Oc.*	**11**	M7
Marion, L.	*S. Carolina*	**65**	K4
Maritime Alps	*Italy, etc.*	**38**	A2
Maritsa R.	*Bulgaria, etc.*	**39**	G3
Mariy A.S.S.R.	*U.S.S.R.*	**43**	G1
Marj, El	*Libya*	**58**	B1
Market Deeping	*England*	**27**	G2
Market Drayton	*England*	**26**	E2
Market Harborough	*England*	**27**	G2
Markethill	*N. Ireland*	**30**	E3
Market Rasen	*England*	**25**	E3
Market Weighton	*England*	**25**	E3
Markha R.	*U.S.S.R.*	**47**	M2
Markinch	*Scotland*	**29**	E4
Marlboro	*Massachusetts*	**66**	F2
Marlborough	*England*	**27**	F3
Marlborough	*New Zealand*	**79**	D4
Marlborough	*Queensland*	**77**	H3
Marlow	*England*	**27**	G3
Marmande	*France*	**33**	C4
Marmara, Sea of	*Turkey*	**39**	H4
Marne, R.	*France*	**33**	D2
Maroantsetra	*Malagasy Rep.*	**59**	E2
Maroua	*Cameroon*	**57**	D3
Marquesas Is.	*Pacific Oc.*	**10**	F5
Marquette	*Michigan*	**65**	J1
Marra Mts.	*Sudan*	**58**	B3
Marrakesh	*Morocco*	**57**	B1
Marree	*S. Australia*	**77**	F4
Marromeu	*Mozambique*	**59**	D2
Marsabit	*Kenya*	**58**	C4
Marsala	*Sicily*	**38**	C6
Marseilles	*France*	**33**	D5
Marshall Is.	*Pacific Oc.*	**10**	D4
Marshalltown	*Iowa*	**65**	H2
Marshfield	*England*	**26**	E3
Marshfield	*Oregon*	**64**	B2
Martaban & G. of	*Burma*	**53**	P7
Martha's Vineyard	*Massachusetts*	**66**	F3
Martigny	*Switzerland*	**37**	B1
Martin	*S. Dakota*	**68**	C2
Martin, L.	*Alabama*	**65**	J4
Martinique, I.	*West Indies*	**71**	M5
Martock	*England*	**26**	E4
Marton	*New Zealand*	**79**	E4
Martre, L. la	*N.-W. Terr., Can.*	**62**	L5
Marungu, mt.	*Congo*	**59**	C1
Marvejols	*France*	**33**	D4
Mary	*Queensland*	**77**	F3
Mary	*Turkmen.*	**46**	G5
Maryborough	*Queensland*	**77**	J4
Maryborough	*Victoria*	**77**	G6
Maryland, state	*U.S.A.*	**65**	L3
Maryport	*England*	**25**	B2
Marysville	*Kansas*	**68**	D3
Maseru	*Basutoland*	**59**	C3
Masham	*England*	**25**	D2
Mashhad	*Iran*	**52**	G3
Masindi	*Uganda*	**58**	C4
Masira, G. of	*Muscat & Oman*	**52**	G7
Masira, I.	*Muscat & Oman*	**52**	G6
Mask, L.	*Eire*	**17**	A5
Mason City	*Iowa*	**65**	H2
Massachusetts, state	*U.S.A.*	**65**	M2
Massafra	*Italy*	**38**	D4
Massawa	*Ethiopia*	**58**	C3
Massinga	*Mozambique*	**59**	D3
Masterton	*New Zealand*	**79**	E4
Masulipatnam	*India*	**53**	M7
Matadi	*Congo*	**59**	B1
Matagalpa	*Nicaragua*	**71**	G5
Matagorda B.	*Texas*	**68**	D5
Matagorda I.	*Texas*	**64**	G5
Matamoros	*Mexico*	**70**	E2
Matanzas	*Cuba*	**71**	H3
Matapan, C.	*Greece*	**41**	J4
Matarani	*Peru*	**72**	C7
Mataranka	*N. Terr., Aust.*	**76**	E2
Mataura	*New Zealand*	**79**	B7
Matawai	*New Zealand*	**79**	F3
Matehuala	*Mexico*	**70**	D3
Matera	*Italy*	**38**	D4
Mathry	*Wales*	**26**	B3
Matlock	*England*	**17**	E5
Mato Grosso & Plat. of	*Brazil*	**72**	E7
Matrûh	*Egypt*	**58**	B1
Matsue	*Japan*	**51**	N4
Matsuyama	*Japan*	**49**	C5
Mattawa	*Ontario*	**63**	T8
Matterhorn, mt.	*Switzerland*	**37**	B2
Maturin	*Venezuela*	**72**	E2
Maubeuge	*France*	**33**	D1
Mauchline	*Scotland*	**29**	D5
Maule R.	*Chile*	**73**	C11
Maun	*Bechuanaland*	**59**	C2
Maurice, L.	*S. Aust.*	**76**	E4
Mauritania	*N.W. Africa*	**57**	A2
Mauritius, I.	*Indian Oc.*	**11**	M6
Mawang Kangri, mt.	*Tibet*	**50**	C5
Maxcanu	*Mexico*	**70**	F3
Maxwelltown	*Scotland*	**29**	E5
May, I. of	*Scotland*	**16**	D3
Mayagüez	*Puerto Rico*	**71**	L4
Maybole	*Scotland*	**17**	C4
Mayenne	*France*	**33**	B2
Maykop	*U.S.S.R.*	**43**	F4
Maymyo	*Burma*	**50**	F7
Maynooth	*Eire*	**17**	B5
Mayo	*Yukon*	**62**	G5
Mayo, co.	*Eire*	**17**	A5
Mayoumba	*Gabon*	**57**	D5
Mazagan	*Morocco*	**57**	B1
Mazapil	*Mexico*	**70**	D3
Mazar-i-sharif	*Afghanistan*	**52**	J3
Mazatlán	*Mexico*	**70**	C3
Mazdak, mt.	*Sinkiang*	**50**	D4
Mbabane	*Swaziland*	**59**	D3
Mbale	*Uganda*	**58**	C4
Mbarara	*Uganda*	**58**	C5
Mbeya	*Tanzania*	**58**	C5
M'Binda	*Congo (Fr.)*	**57**	D5
Mead, L.	*Nevada*	**64**	D3
Meadville	*Pennsylvania*	**66**	A3
Meander River	*Alberta*	**62**	L6
Mearns	*Scotland*	**29**	F4
Measach Falls	*Scotland*	**28**	C3
Meath, co.	*Eire*	**17**	B5
Meaux	*France*	**33**	C2
Mecca	*Saudi Arabia*	**52**	D6
Mechelen	*Belgium*	**32**	C3
Medan	*Sumatra*	**48**	B6
Medecine Hat	*Alberta*	**62**	M7
Medellin	*Colombia*	**72**	B2
Medford	*Oregon*	**64**	B2
Medina	*Saudi Arabia*	**52**	D6
Medina Sidonia	*Spain*	**36**	C4
Mediterranean Sea	*Europe, etc.*	**40**	E4
Medway, R.	*England*	**27**	H3
Meeberrie	*W. Australia*	**76**	B4
Meekatharra	*W. Australia*	**76**	B4
Meerut	*India*	**53**	L5
Mega	*Ethiopia*	**58**	C4
Megara	*Greece*	**39**	F5
Meihsien	*China*	**51**	K7
Meiktila	*Burma*	**50**	F7
Meissen	*Germany, E.*	**34**	D3
Meknès	*Morocco*	**57**	B1
Mekong R.	*S.E. Asia*	**53**	R8
Melanesia, arch.	*Pacific Oc.*	**10**	C5
Melbourne	*Derby, England*	**27**	F2
Melbourne	*Yorks, England*	**25**	E3
Melbourne	*Victoria*	**77**	H6
Melilla	*Morocco*	**57**	B1
Melitopol	*Ukraine*	**43**	E3
Melksham	*England*	**27**	E3
Melrose	*Scotland*	**16**	D4
Melton Constable	*England*	**27**	J2
Melton Mowbray	*England*	**17**	E5
Melun	*France*	**33**	C2
Melvich	*Scotland*	**28**	E2
Melville B.	*Greenland*	**63**	W2
Melville, C.	*Queensland*	**77**	G1
Melville I.	*N. Terr., Aust.*	**76**	E1
Melville I.	*N.-W. Terr., Can.*	**62**	L2
Melville, L.	*Labrador*	**63**	X7
Melville Pen.	*N.-W. Terr., Can.*	**63**	S4
Melville Sd.	*N.-W. Terr., Can.*	**62**	M4
Melvin, L.	*Eire*	**17**	A4
Memmingen	*Germany, W.*	**34**	C5
Memphis	*Egypt*	**54**	A5
Memphis	*Missouri*	**65**	H2
Memphis	*Tennessee*	**65**	J3
Menai Bridge	*Wales*	**26**	C1
Menai Str.	*Wales*	**17**	C5
Menam Chao Phraya, R.	*Thailand*	**53**	P7
Mende	*France*	**33**	D4
Menderes R.	*Turkey*	**52**	A3
Mendip Hills	*England*	**17**	D6
Mendocino, C.	*California*	**64**	B2
Mendoza	*Argentina*	**73**	D10
Mengtsz	*China*	**50**	G7
Menin	*Belgium*	**32**	B4
Menindee	*New South Wales*	**77**	G5
Mentawai Is.	*Indonesia*	**48**	B7
Menton	*France*	**33**	E5
Menzies	*W. Australia*	**76**	C4
Meppel	*Netherlands*	**32**	E2
Meppen	*Germany, W.*	**34**	B2
Merano	*Italy*	**38**	B1
Merca	*Somalia*	**58**	D4
Merced	*California*	**67**	B4
Mercedes	*Argentina*	**73**	D10
Merchant B.	*N.-W. Terr., Can.*	**63**	W4
Mercury Is.	*New Zealand*	**79**	E2
Mere	*England*	**27**	E3
Mergui & Arch.	*Burma*	**53**	P8
Merida	*Mexico*	**70**	G3
Mérida	*Spain*	**36**	B3
Merida & Cord. de	*Venezuela*	**72**	C2
Meriden	*Connecticut*	**66**	E3
Meridian	*Mississippi*	**65**	J4
Merioneth, co.	*Wales*	**17**	D5
Merowe	*Sudan*	**58**	C3
Merredin	*W. Australia*	**76**	B5
Merrick, mt.	*Scotland*	**17**	C4
Merse	*Scotland*	**29**	F5
Mersey, R.	*England*	**17**	D5
Mersin	*Turkey*	**52**	B3
Merthyr Tydfil	*Wales*	**17**	D6
Merton	*England*	**26**	C4
Mesa	*Arizona*	**67**	D5
Mesangè	*Italy*	**38**	D4
Meshik	*Alaska*	**62**	C6
Mesopotamia	*Iraq*	**52**	D4
Messina	*Sicily*	**38**	D5
Messina	*Transvaal*	**59**	C3
Messina, Str. of	*Italy-Sicily*	**38**	D5
Mestre	*Italy*	**38**	C2
Methil	*Scotland*	**16**	D3
Methven	*New Zealand*	**79**	C5
Methven	*Scotland*	**29**	E4
Metz	*France*	**33**	E2
Meuse, R.	*France*	**33**	D2
Mevagissey	*England*	**26**	C4
Mexborough	*England*	**25**	D3

Name	Location	Page	Grid
Mexicali	*Mexico*	**70**	A1
Mexico	*Mexico*	**70**	E4
Mexico	*N. America*	**70**	C3
Mexico, G. of	*Mexico, etc.*	**70**	F2
Meyadin	*Syria*	**55**	E2
Meymac	*France*	**33**	C4
Mézieres	*France*	**33**	D2
Miami	*Arizona*	**67**	D5
Miami	*Florida*	**65**	K5
Miami	*Oklahoma*	**68**	D3
Miāndow āb	*Iran*	**55**	J1
Miandrivazo	*Malagasy Rep.*	**59**	E2
Michigan, state	*U.S.A.*	**65**	J2
Michigan, L.	*U.S.A.*	**65**	J2
Michigan City	*Indiana*	**65**	J2
Michikamau, L.	*Labrador*	**63**	W7
Michipicoten	*Ontario*	**69**	G1
Michurinsk	*U.S.S.R.*	**43**	F2
Micronesia, arch.	*Pacific Oc.*	**10**	C4
Middelburg	*Cape of Good Hope*	**59**	C4
Middelburg	*Netherlands*	**32**	B3
Middelkerke	*Belgium*	**32**	A3
Middle Atlas, mts.	*Morocco*	**57**	B1
Middleham	*England*	**25**	D2
Middlesboro	*Kentucky*	**69**	G3
Middlesbro'	*England*	**17**	E4
Middleton	*England*	**25**	C2
Middleton-in-Teesdale	*England*	**25**	C2
Middletown	*New York*	**66**	D3
Middlewick	*England*	**26**	E1
Midhurst	*England*	**27**	G4
Midland	*Texas*	**64**	F4
Midleton	*Eire*	**31**	C6
Midlothian, co.	*Scotland*	**16**	D4
Midway Is.	*Pacific Oc.*	**10**	E3
Mienning	*China*	**50**	F7
Mikhaylovka	*U.S.S.R.*	**43**	F2
Mikindani	*Tanzania*	**59**	D2
Mikkeli	*Finland*	**42**	F3
Mikumi	*Tanzania*	**58**	C5
Milan	*Italy*	**38**	B2
Milan	*Tennessee*	**65**	J3
Milbank	*S. Dakota*	**68**	D1
Milborne Port	*England*	**26**	E4
Mildenhall	*England*	**27**	H2
Mildura	*Victoria*	**77**	G5
Miles	*Queensland*	**77**	H4
Miles City	*Montana*	**64**	E1
Milford	*Eire*	**17**	B4
Milford Sd.	*New Zealand*	**79**	A6
Milford Haven	*Wales*	**17**	C6
Milgun	*W. Australia*	**76**	B3
Milk R.	*Montana*	**64**	E1
Milk, Wadi el	*Sudan*	**58**	B3
Mill I.	*Antarctica*	**80**	J8
Millau	*France*	**33**	D4
Millerovo	*U.S.S.R.*	**43**	F3
Millicent	*S. Australia*	**77**	G6
Millom	*England*	**25**	B2
Millport	*Scotland*	**29**	D5
Millstreet	*Eire*	**31**	B5
Millville	*New Jersey*	**66**	D4
Milne Land	*Greenland*	**63**	Z3
Milos, I.	*Greece*	**39**	G6
Milparinka	*New South Wales*	**77**	G4
Milton	*New Zealand*	**79**	B7
Miltown Malbay	*Eire*	**17**	A5
Milwaukee	*Wisconsin*	**65**	J2
Minā al Ahmadi	*Kuwait*	**55**	K5
Mina Hassan Tani	*Morocco*	**57**	B1
Minaragra	*Peru*	**72**	B6
Minas de Riotinto	*Spain*	**36**	B4
Minas Gerias	*Brazil*	**72**	H7
Minbu	*Burma*	**50**	E7
Mindanao, I.	*Philippines*	**48**	E6
Minden	*Germany, W.*	**34**	B2
Minderoo	*W. Australia*	**76**	B3
Mindoro, I.	*Philippines*	**48**	E5
Minehead	*England*	**26**	D3
Mingan & I.	*Quebec*	**63**	W7
Mingenew	*W. Australia*	**76**	B4
Mingshui	*China*	**50**	F3
Minho, R.	*Spain, etc.*	**36**	B1
Minilya	*W. Australia*	**76**	A3
Minna	*Nigeria*	**57**	C4
Minneapolis	*Minnesota*	**65**	H1
Minnedosa	*Manitoba*	**62**	O7
Minnesota, state	*U.S.A.*	**64**	G1
Minnesota R.	*Minnesota*	**64**	G2
Minorca, I.	*Balearic Is.*	**36**	F2
Minot	*N. Dakota*	**64**	F1
Min Shan, mts.	*China*	**48**	C3
Minsk	*White Russia*	**46**	C3
Minto	*Yukon*	**62**	G5
Minto L.	*Quebec*	**63**	U6
Minusinsk	*U.S.S.R.*	**47**	K3
Minya, El	*Egypt*	**58**	C2
Minya Konka, mt.	*China*	**48**	C4
Miqdādiyah, Al	*Iraq*	**55**	H3
Miquelon I.	*Atlantic Oc.*	**63**	X8
Mirecourt	*France*	**33**	E2
Mirjawa	*Iran*	**52**	H5
Mirzapur	*India*	**53**	M6
Mishan	*China*	**51**	N2
Miskolc	*Hungary*	**35**	F4
Mississippi, state	*U.S.A.*	**65**	H4
Mississippi, R.	*U.S.A.*	**65**	H3
Missoula	*Montana*	**64**	D1
Missouri, state	*U.S.A.*	**65**	H3
Missouri R.	*U.S.A.*	**64**	F1
Mistassini, L.	*Quebec*	**63**	U7
Misurata	*Libya*	**57**	D1
Mitchell	*Queensland*	**77**	H4
Mitchell	*S. Dakota*	**64**	G2
Mitchell, Mt.	*N. Carolina*	**65**	K3
Mitchell R.	*Queensland*	**77**	G2
Mitchell River	*Queensland*	**77**	G2
Mitchelstown	*Eire*	**17**	A5
Mitilini	*Greece*	**39**	G5
Mito	*Japan*	**51**	P4
Mitre Pk.	*New Zealand*	**79**	A6
Mitu	*Colombia*	**72**	C3
Mitumba Mts.	*Congo*	**58**	B5
Miyazaki	*Japan*	**51**	N5
Mizque	*Bolivia*	**72**	D7
Mjosa, L.	*Norway*	**42**	B3
Mlanje, mt.	*Malawi*	**59**	D2
Mława	*Poland*	**35**	F2
Mo	*Norway*	**42**	C2
Moate	*Eire*	**31**	D4
Mobay	*Cent. Afr. Rep.*	**58**	B4
Moberly	*Missouri*	**65**	H3
Mobile	*Alabama*	**65**	J4
Mobile B.	*Alabama*	**69**	F4
Mobridge	*S. Dakota*	**68**	C1
Moçâmedes	*Angola*	**59**	B2
Mocha	*Yemen*	**52**	D8
Mochudi	*Bechuanaland*	**59**	C3
Mocimboa da Praia	*Mozambique*	**59**	E2
Mocorito	*Mexico*	**70**	C2
Moctézuma	*Mexico*	**70**	B2
Mocuba	*Mozambique*	**59**	D2
Modane	*France*	**33**	E4
Modena	*Italy*	**38**	B2
Modica	*Sicily*	**38**	C6
Modling	*Austria*	**34**	E4
Moengo	*Surinam*	**72**	G2
Moffat	*Scotland*	**17**	D4
Mogadishu	*Somalia*	**58**	D4
Mogador	*Morocco*	**57**	B1
Mogaung	*Burma*	**53**	P5
Mogilev	*White Russia*	**43**	C2
Mogilev Podolskiy	*Ukraine*	**43**	C3
Mohembo	*Bechuanaland*	**59**	C2
Mohill	*Eire*	**30**	D4
Moho	*China*	**51**	L1
Mohomeru, mt.	*Java*	**48**	D7
Mointy	*Kazakh.*	**46**	H4
Moissac	*France*	**33**	C4
Mojave Des.	*California*	**64**	C4
Mokai	*New Zealand*	**79**	E3
Mokau R.	*New Zealand*	**79**	E3
Mokpo	*Korea*	**48**	E3
Mold	*Wales*	**26**	D1
Moldavia	*U.S.S.R.*	**46**	C4
Molde & Fd.	*Norway*	**42**	A3
Mole, R.	*England*	**27**	G3
Molepolole	*Bechuanaland*	**59**	C3
Molfetta	*Italy*	**38**	D4
Moline	*Illinois*	**68**	E2
Mollendo	*Peru*	**72**	C7
Molopo, R.	*Cape of Good Hope*	**59**	C3
Molucca Sea	*Indonesia*	**48**	E7
Moluccas, Is.	*Indonesia*	**48**	E7
Mombasa	*Kenya*	**58**	C5
Mona Pas.	*Dominican Rep.*	**71**	L4
Monach Is.	*Scotland*	**28**	A3
Monaco	*S. Europe*	**33**	E5
Monadhliath Mts.	*Scotland*	**28**	D3
Monaghan	*Eire*	**17**	B4
Monasterevan	*Eire*	**31**	D4
Monclova	*Mexico*	**70**	D2
Moncton	*New Brunswick*	**63**	V8
Mondragone	*Italy*	**38**	C4
Monessen	*Pennsylvania*	**66**	B3
Monfalcone	*Italy*	**38**	C2
Monger, L.	*W. Australia*	**76**	B4
Monghyr	*India*	**53**	N5
Mongolia	*E. Asia*	**48**	B2
Mongu	*Zambia*	**59**	C2
Mönhö Hän	*Mongolia*	**51**	J2
Moniaive	*Scotland*	**29**	E5
Monifieth	*Scotland*	**29**	F4
Monivea	*Eire*	**31**	C4
Monkira	*Queensland*	**77**	G3
Monmouth	*Wales*	**17**	D6
Monópoli	*Italy*	**38**	D4
Monroe	*Louisiana*	**65**	H4
Monroeville	*Alabama*	**65**	J4
Monrovia	*Sierra Leone*	**57**	A4
Mons	*Belgium*	**32**	B4
Montana, state	*U.S.A.*	**64**	D1
Montana, La, mts.	*Peru*	**72**	C6
Montargis	*France*	**33**	C3
Montauban	*France*	**33**	C4
Montbard	*France*	**33**	D3
Montbeliard	*France*	**33**	E3
Mont Blanc	*France-Italy*	**33**	E4
Mont Cenis Pass	*France*	**40**	E2
Mont de Marsan	*France*	**33**	B5
Monte Bello Is.	*W. Australia*	**76**	B3
Monte Carlo	*Monaco*	**33**	E5
Montecristo	*Dominican Rep.*	**71**	K4
Montecristo, I.	*Italy*	**38**	B3
Montego Bay	*Jamaica*	**71**	J4
Montélimar	*France*	**33**	D4
Montello	*Nevada*	**64**	D2
Montemorelos	*Mexico*	**70**	E2
Montenegro	*Yugoslavia*	**38**	E3
Montepulciano	*Italy*	**38**	B3
Monterey	*California*	**67**	B4
Monte Rosa, mt.	*Switzerland*	**37**	B2
Monterrey	*Mexico*	**70**	D2
Montes Claros	*Brazil*	**72**	J7
Montevideo	*Uruguay*	**73**	F10
Montgomery	*Alabama*	**65**	J4
Montgomery	*Wales*	**17**	D5
Monthey	*Switzerland*	**37**	B1
Monticello	*Utah*	**67**	E4
Montluçon	*France*	**33**	C3
Montmedy	*France*	**33**	D2
Montmorillon	*France*	**33**	C3
Montpelier	*Idaho*	**67**	D3
Montpelier	*Vermont*	**65**	M2
Montpellier	*France*	**33**	D5
Montreal	*Quebec*	**63**	U8
Montreuil	*France*	**33**	C1
Montreux	*Switzerland*	**37**	B1
Montrose	*Colorado*	**64**	E3
Montrose	*Scotland*	**16**	D3
Montserrat, I.	*West Indies*	**71**	M4
Monywa	*Burma*	**50**	E7
Monza	*Italy*	**38**	B2
Moonie	*Queensland*	**78**	H3
Moonie R.	*Queensland*	**78**	G2
Moora	*W. Australia*	**76**	B5
Moore L.	*W. Australia*	**76**	B4
Moorfoot Hills	*Scotland*	**29**	E5
Moorhead	*Minnesota*	**64**	G1
Moose L.	*Manitoba*	**63**	P7
Moose Jaw	*Saskatchewan*	**62**	N7
Moosomin	*Saskatchewan*	**62**	O7
Moosonee	*Ontario*	**63**	S7
Mopti	*Mali*	**57**	B3
Mora	*Sweden*	**42**	C3
Moradabad	*India*	**53**	L5
Morar, L.	*Scotland*	**16**	C3
Morava, R.	*Czechoslovakia*	**34**	E4
Morava R.	*Yugoslavia*	**39**	F2
Moravia	*Czechoslovakia*	**34**	E4
Moravian Gate	*Czechoslovakia*	**41**	H1
Moray, co.	*Scotland*	**16**	D3
Moray Firth	*Scotland*	**16**	D3
Morden	*Manitoba*	**63**	P7
Mordov A.S.S.R.	*U.S.S.R.*	**43**	F2
Morea	*Greece*	**39**	F6
Morecambe	*England*	**25**	C2
Morecambe B.	*England*	**17**	D5
Moree	*New South Wales*	**77**	H5
Morelia	*Mexico*	**70**	D4
Morena, Sierra, mts.	*Spain*	**36**	C3
Morenci	*Arizona*	**67**	E5
Moresby I.	*Br. Columbia*	**62**	H7
Moreton	*England*	**27**	F3
Moreton B.	*Queensland*	**77**	J4
Moreton Hampstead	*England*	**26**	D4
Morgan	*S. Australia*	**77**	F5
Morgan City	*Louisiana*	**65**	H5
Morgantown	*W. Virginia*	**66**	B4
Morioka	*Japan*	**51**	P4
Morlaix	*France*	**33**	A2
Mornington I.	*Queensland*	**77**	F2
Morocco	*N.W. Africa*	**57**	B1
Morogoro	*Tanzania*	**58**	C5
Moron	*Cuba*	**71**	J3
Morona, R.	*Braz.-Ecuad.*	**72**	B4
Morondava	*Malagasy Rep.*	**59**	E3
Morpeth	*England*	**17**	E4
Morrinsville	*New Zealand*	**79**	E2
Morriston	*Wales*	**26**	D3
Mortagne	*France*	**33**	C2
Mortain	*France*	**33**	B2
Morte Pt.	*England*	**26**	C3
Morven	*Queensland*	**77**	H4
Morven	*Scotland*	**29**	C4
Moscow	*Idaho*	**67**	C2
Moscow	*U.S.S.R.*	**46**	D3
Moselle, R.	*France-Ger.*	**34**	B3
Mosgiel	*New Zealand*	**79**	C6
Moshi	*Tanzania*	**58**	C5
Mosjöen	*Norway*	**42**	C2
Moskva R.	*U.S.S.R.*	**43**	E1
Moss	*Norway*	**42**	B4
Mossbank	*Scotland*	**28**	A1
Mossel Bay	*C. of Good Hope*	**59**	C4
Most	*Czechoslovakia*	**34**	D3
Mostaganem	*Algeria*	**57**	C1
Mostar	*Yugoslavia*	**38**	D3
Mosul	*Iraq*	**52**	D3
Motala	*Sweden*	**42**	C4
Motherwell	*Scotland*	**16**	D4
Motihari	*India*	**53**	M5
Motueka	*New Zealand*	**79**	D4
Moudon	*Switzerland*	**37**	B1
Mould Bay	*N.-W. Terr., Can.*	**62**	L2
Moulins	*France*	**33**	D3
Moulmein	*Burma*	**53**	P7
Moundou	*Chad*	**57**	D4
Mountain Ash	*Wales*	**26**	D3
Mount Bellew	*Eire*	**31**	C4
Mount Dutton	*S. Australia*	**77**	F4
Mount Gambier	*S. Australia*	**77**	G6
Mount Isa	*Queensland*	**77**	F3
Mt. Lofty Ra.	*S. Australia*	**77**	F5
Mount Magnet	*W. Australia*	**76**	B4
Mount Maunganui	*N. Z.*	**79**	F2
Mountmellick	*Eire*	**31**	D4
Mount Morgan	*Queensland*	**77**	J3
Mount Pleasant	*New York*	**66**	E2
Mountrath	*Eire*	**31**	D4
Mounts B.	*England*	**26**	B4
Mount Somers	*New Zealand*	**79**	C5
Mount Vernon	*W. Australia*	**76**	B3
Moura	*Portugal*	**36**	B3
Mourne Mts.	*N. Ireland*	**17**	B4
Moussoro	*Chad*	**57**	D3
Moutiers	*France*	**33**	E4
Moville	*Eire*	**17**	B4
Moy, R.	*Eire*	**17**	A5
Moyale	*Kenya*	**58**	C4
Mozambique	*E. Africa*	**59**	D3
Mozambique	*Mozambique*	**59**	E2
Mozambique Chan.	*E. Africa*	**59**	D3
Mozyr	*White Russia*	**43**	C2
Mpanda	*Tanzania*	**58**	C5
Mpika	*Zambia*	**59**	D2
Mtwara	*Tanzania*	**59**	E2
Muang Phitsanulok	*Thailand*	**53**	Q7
Muang Ubun	*Thailand*	**53**	Q7
Muchalls	*Scotland*	**28**	F3
Muchinga Mts.	*Zambia*	**59**	D2
Muck, I.	*Scotland*	**29**	B4
Muckle Flugga	*Scotland*	**28**	B1
Much Wenlock	*England*	**26**	E2
Mudgee	*New South Wales*	**77**	H5
Mugford, C.	*Labrador*	**63**	W6
Muglad, El	*Sudan*	**58**	B3
Muharran	*Bahrain*	**52**	F5
Mühldorf	*Germany, W.*	**34**	D4
Mühlhausen	*Germany, E.*	**34**	C3
Muine Bheag	*Eire*	**17**	B5
Muirkirk	*Scotland*	**29**	D5
Mukalla	*E. Aden*	**52**	E8
Mulege	*Mexico*	**70**	B2
Mulhacen, mt.	*Spain*	**36**	C4
Mülheim	*Germany, W.*	**34**	B3
Mulhouse	*France*	**33**	E3
Mull, I.	*Scotland*	**16**	C3
Mullewa	*W. Australia*	**76**	B4
Mullingar	*Eire*	**17**	B5
Multan	*W. Pakistan*	**53**	K4
Mumbles	*Wales*	**26**	C3
München Gladbach	*Germany, W.*	**34**	B3
Muncie	*Indiana*	**65**	J2
Münden	*Germany, W.*	**34**	C3
Mundesley	*England*	**27**	J2
Mundiwindi	*W. Australia*	**76**	C3
Mundrabilla	*W. Australia*	**76**	D5
Munich	*Germany, W.*	**34**	C4
Munku Sardyk, mt.	*U.S.S.R.-Mongolia*	**47**	K3
Munster	*Eire*	**31**	B5
Münster	*Germany, W.*	**34**	B3
Muonio & R.	*Finland*	**42**	E2

Ningwu	*China*	**51**	J4
Niobrara R.	*Nebraska*	**64**	F2
Nioro	*Mali*	**57**	B3
Niort	*France*	**33**	B3
Nipigon, L.	*Ontario*	**63**	R8
Nipissing, L.	*Ontario*	**63**	S8
Niriz	*Iran*	**52**	F5
Niš	*Yugoslavia*	**39**	F3
Nitchequon	*Quebec*	**63**	U7
Niterói	*Brazil*	**73**	J8
Nith, R.	*Scotland*	**17**	D4
Nithsdale, valley	*Scotland*	**29**	E5
Nitra	*Czechoslovakia*	**35**	F4
Nivelles	*Belgium*	**32**	C4
Niya	*Sinkiang*	**50**	C4
Nizamabad	*India*	**53**	L7
Nizhne Kamchatsk	*U.S.S.R.*	**47**	R3
Nizhneudinsk	*U.S.S.R.*	**47**	K3
Nizhniye Kolymsk	*U.S.S.R.*	**47**	R2
N'Kongsamba	*Cameroun*	**57**	D4
Noatak R.	*Alaska*	**62**	B4
Nobber	*Eire*	**17**	B5
Nogales	*Arizona*	**64**	D4
Nogent-le-Rotrou	*France*	**33**	C2
Nogent-sur-Seine	*France*	**33**	D2
Noirmoutier I.	*France*	**33**	B3
Nome	*Alaska*	**62**	A5
Nonacho L.	*N.-W. Terr., Can.*	**62**	N5
Nong Khai	*Thailand*	**53**	Q7
Noonkanbah	*W. Australia*	**76**	C2
Noord Brabant	*Netherlands*	**32**	C3
Noorvik	*Alaska*	**62**	B4
Nord Fd.	*Norway*	**42**	A3
Nordenskiold Arch.	*U.S.S.R.*	**47**	K1
Nordhausen	*Germany, E.*	**34**	C3
Nordkyn	*Norway*	**42**	F1
Nordvik	*U.S.S.R.*	**47**	M1
Nore, R.	*Eire*	**17**	B5
Norfolk, co.	*England*	**17**	F5
Norfolk	*Nebraska*	**64**	G2
Norfolk	*Virginia*	**65**	L3
Norfolk Broads	*England*	**27**	J2
Norfolk I.	*Pacific Oc.*	**10**	D6
Norfolk Res.	*Arkansas*	**65**	H3
Norfolk Edge	*England*	**27**	H2
Norg	*Netherlands*	**32**	E1
Norman	*Oklahoma*	**68**	D3
Normandy	*France*	**33**	B2
Normanton	*Queensland*	**77**	G2
Norman Wells	*N.-W. Terr., Can.*	**62**	J4
Nornalup	*W. Australia*	**76**	B6
Norris L.	*Tennessee*	**69**	G3
Norristown	*Pennsylvania*	**66**	D3
Norrköping	*Sweden*	**42**	D4
Norseman	*W. Australia*	**76**	C5
Norsk	*U.S.S.R.*	**47**	O3
North C.	*New Zealand*	**79**	D1
North C.	*Norway*	**42**	F1
North, C.	*Nova Scotia*	**63**	W8
North Chan.	*Ontario*	**63**	S8
North Chan.	*Scot.-N. Ire.*	**17**	B4
North Sea	*N.W. Europe*	**46**	A3
North Adams	*Massachusetts*	**66**	E2
Northallerton	*England*	**17**	E4
Northam	*W. Australia*	**76**	B5
Northampton	*England*	**17**	E5
Northampton	*Massachusetts*	**66**	E2
Northampton	*W. Australia*	**76**	A4
North Battleford	*Saskatchewan*	**62**	N7
North Bay	*Ontario*	**63**	T8
North Bend	*Oregon*	**67**	B3
North Berwick	*Scotland*	**29**	F4
North Borneo, *see* Sabah			
North Carolina, state	*U.S.A.*	**65**	K3
North Dakota, state	*U.S.A.*	**64**	F1
North Downs	*England*	**17**	F6
North Dvina R.	*U.S.S.R.*	**46**	E2
Northern Circars	*India*	**53**	M7
Northern Ireland	*British Isles*	**17**	B4
Northern Sporades, Is.	*Greece*	**39**	G5
Northern Territory	*Australia*	**76**	E2
North Foreland	*England*	**27**	J3
North Frisian Is.	*Germany, W.*	**34**	B1
North Holland	*Netherlands*	**32**	C2
Northiam	*England*	**27**	H4
North Island	*New Zealand*	**79**	D2
Northland	*New Zealand*	**79**	D1
Northleach	*England*	**27**	F3
North Magnetic Pole	*N.-W. Terr., Can.*	**62**	O3
North Minch	*Scotland*	**16**	B2
North Platte	*Nebraska*	**64**	F2
North Platte R.	*Nebraska-Wyoming*	**64**	F2
North Rhine-Westphalia	*Germany, W.*	**34**	B3
North Rona, I.	*Scotland*	**16**	C2
North Ronaldsay I.	*Scotland*	**28**	F1
North Saskatchewan R.	*Alberta-Sask.*	**62**	M7
North Shields	*England*	**25**	D1
North Somercotes	*England*	**25**	F3
North Taranaki Bight	*New Zealand*	**79**	D3
North Tonawanda	*New York*	**66**	B2
North Uist, I.	*Scotland*	**16**	B3
Northumberland, co.	*England*	**17**	D4
Northumberland Is.	*Queensland*	**77**	H3
Northumberland Str.	*Pr. Edward I., etc.*	**63**	W8
North Walsham	*England*	**27**	J2
North West, C.	*N.-W. Terr., Can.*	**63**	P1
North West C.	*W. Australia*	**76**	A3
Northwest Territories	*Canada*	**62**	K5
Northwich	*England*	**25**	C3
Northwold	*England*	**27**	H2
Norton	*Kansas*	**68**	D3
Norton B.	*Alaska*	**62**	B5
Norton Sd.	*Alaska*	**62**	B5
Norwalk	*Connecticut*	**66**	E3
Norway	*N.W. Europe*	**42**	B3
Norwegian Sea	*N.W. Europe*	**11**	L1
Norwich	*Connecticut*	**66**	E3
Norwich	*England*	**17**	F5
Norwich	*New York*	**66**	D2
Norwick	*Scotland*	**28**	B1
Noshiro	*Japan*	**51**	O3
Noss, I. of	*Scotland*	**28**	B1
Nossi Bé, I.	*Malagasy Rep.*	**59**	E2
Notre Dame B.	*Newfoundland*	**63**	X8
Notre Dame Mts.	*Quebec*	**63**	U8
Nottingham	*England*	**17**	E5
Nouakchott	*Mauritania*	**57**	A3
Noumea	*New Caledonia*	**10**	D6
Nova Lisboa	*Angola*	**59**	B2
Novara	*Italy*	**38**	A2
Nova Scotia, prov.	*Canada*	**63**	V9
Nova Sofala	*Mozambique*	**59**	D3
Novaya Zemlya, I.	*U.S.S.R.*	**46**	F1
Nové Zamky	*Czechoslovakia*	**35**	F4
Novgorod	*U.S.S.R.*	**43**	D1
Novi Ligure	*Italy*	**38**	A2
Novi Pazar	*Yugoslavia*	**39**	E3
Novi Sad	*Yugoslavia*	**39**	E2
Novocherkassk	*U.S.S.R.*	**43**	E3
Novo Gaia	*Angola*	**59**	B1
Novokuznetsk	*U.S.S.R.*	**47**	J3
Novo Redondo	*Angola*	**59**	B2
Novorossiysk	*U.S.S.R.*	**43**	E4
Novosibirsk	*U.S.S.R.*	**46**	J3
Novo Sibirskiye Os., Is.	*U.S.S.R.*	**47**	P1
Nový Jicin	*Czechoslovakia*	**35**	F4
Nowra	*New South Wales*	**77**	J5
Nowy Sacz	*Poland*	**35**	F4
Nowy Targ	*Poland*	**35**	F4
Noyon	*France*	**33**	C2
Nubian Des.	*Sudan*	**58**	C2
Nueces, R.	*Texas*	**68**	D5
Nueltin L.	*N.-W. Terr., Can.*	**63**	P5
Nueva Rosita	*Mexico*	**70**	D2
Nuevitas	*Cuba*	**71**	J3
Nuevo Laredo	*Mexico*	**70**	D2
Nugsuak Pen.	*Greenland*	**63**	Y3
Nukus	*Uzbek.*	**46**	F4
Nulato	*Alaska*	**62**	C5
Nullagine	*W. Australia*	**76**	B3
Nullarbor	*S. Australia*	**76**	E5
Nullarbor Plain	*S. & W. Australia*	**76**	D5
Nuneaton	*England*	**27**	F2
Nunivak I.	*Alaska*	**62**	A5
Nunkiang	*China*	**51**	M2
Nuoro	*Sardinia*	**38**	B4
Nurmes	*Finland*	**42**	G3
Nürnberg	*Germany, W.*	**34**	C4
Nushagak	*Alaska*	**62**	C6
Nushki	*W. Pakistan*	**52**	J5
Nutak	*Labrador*	**63**	W6
Nutarawit L.	*N.-W. Terr., Can.*	**63**	P5
Nutts Corner	*N. Ireland*	**30**	E3
Nyala	*Sudan*	**58**	B3
Nyasa, L.	*Malawi, etc.*	**59**	D2
Nyda	*U.S.S.R.*	**46**	H2
Nyenchentanglha Ra.	*Tibet*	**50**	D5
Nyíregyháza	*Hungary*	**35**	G5
Nykarleby	*Finland*	**42**	E3
Nykøbing	*Denmark*	**42**	C5
Nykoping	*Sweden*	**42**	D4
Nymagee	*New South Wales*	**77**	H5
Nymme	*Estonia*	**42**	F4
Nyngan	*New South Wales*	**77**	H5
Nyon	*Switzerland*	**37**	B1
Nyons	*France*	**33**	D4
Nysa	*Poland*	**35**	E3
Nyurba	*U.S.S.R.*	**47**	M2
N'Zérékoré	*Guinea*	**57**	B4
Oahe Res.	*N. Dakota-S. Dakota*	**64**	F1
Oakengates	*England*	**26**	E2
Oakham	*England*	**17**	E5
Oakland	*California*	**64**	B3
Oak Ridge	*Tennessee*	**65**	K3
Oamaru	*New Zealand*	**79**	C6
Oates Land	*Antarctica*	**80**	M7
Oatlands	*Tasmania*	**78**	L12
Oaxaca de Juarez	*Mexico*	**70**	E4
Ob, G. of	*U.S.S.R.*	**46**	H1
Ob, R.	*U.S.S.R.*	**46**	G2
Oban	*New Zealand*	**79**	B7
Oban	*Scotland*	**16**	C3
Obbia	*Somalia*	**58**	D4
Obeid, El	*Sudan*	**58**	B3
Oberammergau	*Germany, W.*	**34**	C5
Oberhausen	*Germany, W.*	**34**	B3
Oberland	*Switzerland*	**37**	B1
Obidos	*Brazil*	**72**	F4
Obuasi	*Ghana*	**57**	B4
Ocala	*Florida*	**65**	K5
Occidental, Cord., mts.	*Peru*	**72**	B6
Ocean I.	*Pacific Oc.*	**10**	D5
Ocean Falls	*Br. Columbia*	**62**	J7
Ochil Hills	*Scotland*	**29**	E4
Ochiltree	*Scotland*	**29**	D5
Ocotepeque	*Honduras*	**70**	G5
October Revolution I.	*U.S.S.R.*	**47**	K1
Oda, Jebel, mt.	*Sudan*	**58**	C2
Odadhahraun, lava-field	*Iceland*	**42**	K6
Odda	*Norway*	**42**	A4
Odense	*Denmark*	**42**	B5
Odenwald, mts.	*Germany, W.*	**34**	B4
Oder, R.	*Germany, etc.*	**34**	D2
Odessa	*Texas*	**68**	C4
Odessa	*Ukraine*	**46**	D4
Odienné	*Ivory Coast*	**57**	B4
Offaly, co.	*Eire*	**17**	B5
Offenbach	*Germany, W.*	**34**	B3
Offenburg	*Germany, W.*	**34**	B4
Ogaden	*Ethiopia*	**58**	D4
Ogbomosho	*Nigeria*	**57**	C4
Ogden	*Utah*	**64**	D2
Ogdensburg	*New York*	**66**	D1
Ogooué R.	*Gabon*	**57**	D4
Ogulin	*Yugoslavia*	**38**	D2
Ohai	*New Zealand*	**79**	A6
Ohakune	*New Zealand*	**79**	E3
Ohata	*Japan*	**49**	E3
Ohau L.	*New Zealand*	**79**	B6
Ohio, state	*U.S.A.*	**65**	K2
Ohio R.	*U.S.A.*	**65**	J3
Ohre, R.	*Czechoslovakia*	**34**	D3
Oich, L.	*Scotland*	**28**	D3
Oil City	*Pennsylvania*	**66**	B3
Oise, R.	*France*	**33**	D2
Ojos del Salado, mt.	*Arg.-Chile*	**73**	D9
Oka, R.	*U.S.S.R.*	**46**	D3
Oka R.	*U.S.S.R.*	**47**	L3
Okahandja	*S.W. Africa*	**59**	B3
Okaihau	*New Zealand*	**79**	D1
Okavango Swamp	*Bechuanaland*	**59**	C2
Okayama	*Japan*	**49**	C5
Okeechobee, L.	*Florida*	**65**	K5
Okehampton	*England*	**26**	C4
Okhotsk & Sea of	*U.S.S.R.*	**47**	P3
Okinawa Gunto, I.	*Japan*	**48**	E4
Oklahoma, state	*U.S.A.*	**64**	G3
Oklahoma City	*Oklahoma*	**64**	G3
Okmulgee	*Oklahoma*	**68**	D3
Okuru	*New Zealand*	**79**	B5
Öland, I.	*Sweden*	**42**	D4
Olavarria	*Argentina*	**73**	E11
Olbia	*Sardinia*	**38**	B4
Old Castile	*Spain*	**36**	C2
Oldcastle	*Eire*	**17**	B5
Old Crow	*Yukon*	**62**	G4
Oldenburg	*Germany, W.*	**34**	B2
Oldenburg	*Germany, W.*	**34**	C1
Oldham	*England*	**17**	D5
Old Meldrum	*Scotland*	**28**	F3
Old Providence I.	*W. Indies*	**71**	H5
Olekma R.	*U.S.S.R.*	**47**	N3
Olekminsk	*U.S.S.R.*	**47**	N2
Olenek R.	*U.S.S.R.*	**47**	M2
Oléron I.	*France*	**33**	B4
Olga	*U.S.S.R.*	**47**	O4
Olifants, R.	*Transvaal, etc.*	**59**	D3
Ollerton	*England*	**27**	F1
Olney	*England*	**27**	G2
Olney	*Illinois*	**65**	J3
Olomouc	*Czechoslovakia*	**34**	E4
Oloron	*France*	**33**	B5
Olsztyn	*Poland*	**35**	F2
Olten	*Switzerland*	**37**	B1
Olteniţa	*Rumania*	**39**	G2
Olympia	*Washington*	**64**	B1
Olympus, Mt.	*Greece*	**39**	F4
Olympus, Mt.	*Washington*	**67**	B2
Olyutorskiy	*U.S.S.R.*	**47**	R2
Omagh	*N. Ireland*	**17**	B4
Omaha	*Nebraska*	**64**	G2
Oman, G. of	*Arabia-Iran*	**52**	G6
Omaruru	*S.W. Africa*	**59**	B3
Omdurman	*Sudan*	**58**	C3
Ominato	*Japan*	**51**	P3
Omo R.	*Ethiopia*	**58**	C4
Omoloi R.	*U.S.S.R.*	**47**	O2
Omolon, R.	*U.S.S.R.*	**47**	R2
Omsk	*U.S.S.R.*	**46**	H3
Ondör Hän	*Mongolia*	**51**	J2
Onega & L.	*U.S.S.R.*	**46**	D2
Onehunga	*New Zealand*	**79**	E2
O'Neill	*Nebraska*	**68**	D2
Ongar	*England*	**27**	H3
Onich	*Scotland*	**29**	C4
Onitsha	*Nigeria*	**57**	C4
Onjül	*Mongolia*	**50**	H2
Onon, R.	*U.S.S.R.*	**47**	M3
Onslow	*W. Australia*	**76**	B3
Onslow B.	*N. Carolina*	**65**	L4
Ontario, prov.	*Canada*	**63**	R8
Ontario, L.	*New York-Ontario*	**63**	T9
Oodnadatta	*S. Australia*	**77**	F4
Ooldea	*S. Australia*	**76**	E5
Opatów	*Poland*	**35**	G3
Opava	*Czechoslovakia*	**35**	E4
Opelousas	*Louisiana*	**68**	E4
Opinaca R.	*Quebec*	**63**	T7
Opole	*Poland*	**35**	E3
Oporto	*Portugal*	**36**	B2
Opotiki	*New Zealand*	**79**	F2
Oradea	*Rumania*	**35**	G5
Öræfa-Jökull, mt.	*Iceland*	**42**	K6
Oran	*Algeria*	**57**	B1
Orange	*France*	**33**	D4
Orange	*New South Wales*	**77**	H5
Orange	*Texas*	**65**	H4
Orange, R.	*S. Africa*	**59**	B3
Orangeburg	*S. Carolina*	**65**	K4
Orange Free State, prov.	*S. Africa*	**59**	C3
Oranienburg	*Germany, E.*	**34**	D2
Oranmore	*Eire*	**31**	C4
Orawia	*New Zealand*	**79**	A7
Orbetello	*Italy*	**38**	B3
Orbost	*Victoria*	**77**	H6
Orchila, I.	*West Indies*	**71**	L5
Ord, Mt. & R.	*W. Australia*	**76**	D2
Ordos Plat.	*China*	**48**	C3
Ord River	*W. Australia*	**76**	D2
Ordzhonikidze	*U.S.S.R.*	**46**	E4
Orebro	*Sweden*	**42**	C4
Oregon, state	*U.S.A.*	**64**	B2
Oregon City	*Oregon*	**67**	B2
Orekhovo-Zuyevo	*U.S.S.R.*	**43**	E1
Orel	*U.S.S.R.*	**46**	D3
Orenburg	*U.S.S.R.*	**46**	F3
Orense	*Spain*	**36**	B1
Orford	*England*	**27**	J2
Orihuela	*Spain*	**36**	D3
Orinoco R.	*Venezuela*	**72**	D2
Orissa, state	*India*	**53**	M7
Oristano	*Sardinia*	**38**	A5
Orivesi, L.	*Finland*	**42**	G3
Orizaba	*Mexico*	**70**	E4
Orkney Is.	*Scotland*	**16**	D2
Orlando	*Florida*	**65**	K5
Orléans	*France*	**33**	C3
Orlov	*U.S.S.R.*	**43**	E2
Ormskirk	*England*	**25**	C3
Orne, R.	*France*	**33**	B2
Örnsköldsvik	*Sweden*	**42**	D3
Oronsay, I.	*Scotland*	**29**	B4
Orontes R.	*Syria, etc.*	**52**	C3
Orsa	*Sweden*	**42**	C3
Orsha	*White Russia*	**46**	D3
Orsk	*U.S.S.R.*	**46**	F3

Orşova	*Rumania*	**39**	F2
Orthez	*France*	**33**	B5
Ortles, mt.	*Italy*	**38**	B1
Ortona	*Italy*	**38**	C3
Orulgan Mts.	*U.S.S.R.*	**47**	N1
Oruro	*Bolivia*	**72**	D7
Orvietto	*Italy*	**38**	C3
Osage R.	*Missouri, etc.*	**65**	H3
Osaka	*Japan*	**48**	F3
Oshawa	*Ontario*	**63**	T9
Oshkosh	*Wisconsin*	**65**	J2
Oshnoviyeh	*Iran*	**55**	H1
Oshogbo	*Nigeria*	**57**	C4
Osijek	*Yugoslavia*	**38**	E2
Oskarshamn	*Sweden*	**42**	D4
Oslo	*Norway*	**42**	B3
Oslo Fd.	*Norway*	**42**	B4
Osnabrück	*Germany, W.*	**34**	B2
Osorno	*Chile*	**73**	C12
Ossa, mt.	*Greece*	**39**	F5
Ossa, Mt.	*Tasmania*	**77**	H7
Ossining	*New York*	**66**	E3
Ostend	*Belgium*	**32**	A3
Osterdal, valley	*Norway*	**42**	B3
Oster Dal, R.	*Sweden*	**42**	C3
Osterö, I.	*Faeroes*	**42**	N8
Ostersund	*Sweden*	**42**	C3
Osthammar	*Sweden*	**42**	D3
Ostrava	*Czechoslovakia*	**35**	F4
Ostróda	*Poland*	**35**	F2
Ostrołeka	*Poland*	**35**	G2
Ostrov	*U.S.S.R.*	**43**	C1
Ostrovnoe	*U.S.S.R.*	**47**	R2
Ostrów	*Poland*	**35**	E3
Ostrowiec	*Poland*	**35**	G3
Ostrów Mazowiecka	*Poland*	**35**	G2
Ostuni	*Italy*	**38**	D4
Osumi Arch.	*Japan*	**49**	C5
Oswego	*Kansas*	**64**	G3
Oswego	*New York*	**65**	L2
Oswestry	*England*	**17**	D5
Otago	*New Zealand*	**79**	A6
Otago Harb. & Pen.	*New Zealand*	**79**	C6
Otahuhu	*New Zealand*	**79**	E2
Otaki	*New Zealand*	**79**	E4
Otaru	*Japan*	**51**	P3
Otavalo	*Ecuador*	**72**	B3
Otavi	*S.W. Africa*	**59**	B2
Otematata	*New Zealand*	**79**	C6
Othrys Mts.	*Greece*	**39**	F5
Otira	*New Zealand*	**79**	C5
Otjiwarongo	*S.W. Africa*	**59**	B3
Otley	*England*	**25**	D3
Otranto	*Italy*	**38**	E4
Otranto, Str. of	*Italy-Albania*	**38**	E4
Ottawa	*Kansas*	**68**	D3
Ottawa	*Ontario*	**63**	T8
Ottawa R.	*Ont.-Que.*	**63**	T8
Otterburn	*England*	**25**	C1
Otterswick	*Scotland*	**28**	A1
Ottery, R.	*England*	**26**	C4
Ottery St. Mary	*England*	**26**	D4
Ottumwa	*Iowa*	**65**	H2
Otway, C.	*Victoria*	**77**	G6
Otztal Alps	*Austria-Italy*	**38**	B1
Ouachita Mts.	*Ark.-Okla.*	**68**	D4
Ouachita, R.	*Arkansas*	**68**	E4
Ouagadougou	*Up. Volta*	**57**	B3
Ouahigouya	*Up. Volta*	**57**	B3
Ouanda-Djalle	*Cent. Afr. Rep.*	**58**	B4
Ouargla	*Algeria*	**57**	C1
Oudtshoorn	*Cape of Good Hope*	**59**	C4
Oued, El	*Algeria*	**57**	C1
Ouesso	*Congo Rep.*	**57**	D4
Oughterard	*Eire*	**31**	B4
Ouham, R.	*Chad, etc.*	**57**	D4
Oulu & L. & R.	*Finland*	**42**	F2
Ounas, R.	*Finland*	**42**	F2
Oundle	*England*	**27**	G2
Ouse, R.	*Norfolk, etc., Eng.*	**17**	F5
Ouse, R.	*Yorks, Eng.*	**25**	D3
Outjo	*S.W. Africa*	**59**	B2
Ouyen	*Victoria*	**77**	G6
Ovalle	*Chile*	**73**	C10
Over Flakkee, I.	*Netherlands*	**32**	C3
Overijssel	*Netherlands*	**32**	E2
Overton	*Wales*	**26**	E2
Oviedo	*Spain*	**36**	C1
Owensboro	*Kentucky*	**65**	J3
Owen Sound	*Ontario*	**63**	S9
Owyhee R.	*Oregon, etc.*	**64**	C2
Ox Mts.	*Eire*	**17**	A4
Oxford	*England*	**17**	E6
Oxley's Pk.	*New South Wales*	**77**	H5
Oxus R.	*Turkmen., etc.*	**52**	H2
Oykell, R.	*Scotland*	**28**	D3
Oyo	*Nigeria*	**57**	C4
Oyster B.	*Tasmania*	**77**	H7
Ozark Mts.	*Missouri, etc.*	**65**	H4
Ozarks, L. of the	*Missouri*	**65**	H3
Paan	*China*	**48**	B3
Paarl	*Cape of Good Hope*	**59**	B4
Pabbay, I.	*Scotland*	**28**	A3
Pabjanice	*Poland*	**35**	F3
Pacasmay	*Peru*	**72**	B5
Pachuca	*Mexico*	**70**	E3
Pacific Ocean	—	**10**	D4
Padang	*Sumatra*	**48**	C7
Paderborn	*Germany, W.*	**34**	B3
Padlei	*N.-W. Terr., Can.*	**63**	P5
Padloping Island	*N.-W. Terr., Can.*	**63**	W4
Padre I.	*Texas*	**64**	G5
Padstow	*England*	**17**	C6
Padua	*Italy*	**38**	B2
Paducah	*Kentucky*	**65**	J3
Paeroa	*New Zealand*	**79**	E2
Pago Mission	*W. Australia*	**76**	D1
Pahiatua	*New Zealand*	**79**	E4
Pahlavi	*Iran*	**52**	E3
Paicheng	*China*	**51**	L2
Paicheng	*Sinkiang*	**50**	C3
Paide	*Estonia*	**42**	F4
Paignton	*England*	**26**	D4
Paijanne, L.	*Finland*	**42**	F3
Pailingmiao	*China*	**51**	J3
Painted Des.	*Arizona*	**67**	D4
Paisley	*Scotland*	**16**	C4
Paita	*Peru*	**72**	A5
Pakhoi	*China*	**50**	H7
Pakistan	*S. Asia*	**52-53**	—
Pakokku	*Burma*	**53**	O6
Palana	*U.S.S.R.*	**47**	R3
Palapye Road	*Bechuanaland*	**59**	C3
Palatinate	*Germany, W.*	**34**	B4
Palau Is.	*Pacific Oc.*	**48**	F6
Palawan, I.	*Philippines*	**48**	D6
Paldiski	*Estonia*	**42**	E4
Palembang	*Sumatra*	**48**	C7
Palencia	*Spain*	**36**	C1
Palermo	*Sicily*	**38**	C5
Palestine, reg.	*Israel-Jordan*	**54**	C4
Palestine	*Texas*	**68**	D4
Palk Str.	*Ceylon-India*	**53**	L9
Palliser B. & C.	*New Zealand*	**79**	E4
Palm Is.	*Queensland*	**77**	H2
Palma	*Balearic Is.*	**36**	E3
Palmas, C.	*Liberia*	**57**	B4
Palmerston	*New Zealand*	**79**	C6
Palmerston North	*New Zealand*	**79**	E4
Palmi	*Italy*	**38**	D5
Palm Springs	*California*	**67**	C5
Palmyra	*Syria*	**52**	C4
Palmyra I.	*Pacific Oc.*	**10**	E4
Palopo	*Celebes*	**48**	E7
Pamiers	*France*	**33**	C5
Pamirs, mts.	*Tadzhik.*	**53**	K3
Pamlico Sd.	*N. Carolina*	**65**	L3
Pampa	*Texas*	**68**	C3
Pampas, plains	*Argentina*	**73**	E11
Pamplona	*Spain*	**36**	D1
Panama	*Cent. America*	**71**	H6
Panama	*Panama*	**71**	J6
Panama Can. & G.	*Panama*	**71**	J6
Panama City	*Florida*	**69**	F4
Pänay, I.	*Philippines*	**48**	E5
Pancevo	*Yugoslavia*	**39**	E2
Panevezys	*Lithuania*	**42**	F5
Pangbourne	*England*	**27**	F3
Pangkalpinang	*Indonesia*	**48**	C7
Pangkiang	*China*	**51**	J3
Pangnirtung	*N.-W. Terr., Can.*	**63**	V4
Panja	*Sinkiang*	**50**	E4
Panjim	*India*	**53**	K7
Panovo	*U.S.S.R.*	**47**	L3
Paoki	*China*	**50**	H5
Paola	*Italy*	**38**	D5
Paoshan	*China*	**50**	F6
Paoting	*China*	**51**	K4
Paotow	*China*	**48**	C2
Papakura	*New Zealand*	**79**	E2
Papa Stour, I.	*Scotland*	**28**	A1
Papa Westray, I.	*Scotland*	**28**	F1
Papua, *see* New Guinea			
Para	*Brazil*	**72**	H4
Paragould	*Arkansas*	**68**	E3
Paraguay & R.	*S. America*	**73**	F8
Parakou	*Dahomey*	**57**	C4
Paramaribo	*Surinam*	**72**	F2
Paramonga	*Peru*	**72**	B6
Paramushir, I.	*Kuril Is.*	**47**	Q3
Paraná	*Argentina*	**73**	E10
Paraná Plat.	*Brazil*	**73**	G8
Paraná R.	*Argentina, etc.*	**85**	F9
Paranaguá	*Brazil*	**73**	H9
Parchim	*Germany, E.*	**34**	C2
Pardubice	*Czechoslovakia*	**34**	E3
Parecis, Sa. dos, mts.	*Brazil*	**72**	E6
Paricutin, mt.	*Mexico*	**70**	D4
Parika	*Br. Guiana*	**72**	F2
Paris	*France*	**33**	C2
Paris	*Tennessee*	**65**	J3
Paris	*Texas*	**64**	G4
Park Ra.	*Colorado*	**67**	E3
Parkersburg	*W. Virginia*	**65**	K3
Parkes	*New South Wales*	**77**	H5
Parma	*Italy*	**38**	B2
Parnaiba	*Brazil*	**72**	J4
Parnaiba R.	*Brazil*	**72**	H5
Pärnu	*Estonia*	**42**	F4
Paroo R.	*N.S.W.-Qnsld.*	**77**	G4
Páros, I.	*Greece*	**39**	G6
Parracombe	*England*	**26**	D3
Parramatta	*New South Wales*	**77**	J5
Parras	*Mexico*	**70**	D2
Parrett, R.	*England*	**26**	E3
Parry Is.	*N.-W. Terr., Can.*	**62**	M2
Parry Sound	*Ontario*	**63**	T8
Parsons	*Kansas*	**68**	D3
Parthenay	*France*	**33**	B3
Partry Mts.	*Eire*	**30**	B4
Pas, The	*Manitoba*	**62**	O7
Pasadena	*California*	**64**	C4
Pasadena	*Texas*	**68**	D5
Paşcani	*Rumania*	**35**	H5
Paso Robles	*California*	**64**	B3
Passau	*Germany, W.*	**34**	D4
Passo Fundo	*Brazil*	**73**	G9
Pasto	*Colombia*	**72**	B3
Patagonia	*Argentina*	**73**	C13
Patea	*New Zealand*	**79**	E3
Pateley Bridge	*England*	**25**	D2
Paterson	*New Jersey*	**65**	M2
Paterson Inlet	*New Zealand*	**79**	B7
Pathfinder Res.	*Wyoming*	**67**	E3
Patkai Ra.	*Burma-India*	**53**	P5
Patmos, I.	*Greece*	**39**	G6
Patna	*India*	**53**	N5
Patos, L.	*Brazil*	**73**	G10
Patras	*Greece*	**39**	F5
Patrington	*England*	**25**	E3
Pau	*France*	**33**	B5
Paulatuk	*N.-W. Terr., Can.*	**62**	K4
Paulis	*Congo*	**58**	B4
Paulistana	*Brazil*	**72**	J5
Paulo Alfonso Falls	*Brazil*	**72**	K5
Pavia	*Italy*	**38**	B2
Pavlodar	*Kazakh.*	**46**	H3
Pawtucket	*Rhode I.*	**66**	F3
Payerne	*Switzerland*	**37**	B1
Payette	*Idaho*	**67**	C3
Payne Bay	*Quebec*	**63**	U5
Payne's Find	*W. Australia*	**76**	B4
Paysandu	*Uruguay*	**73**	F10
Pazardzhik	*Bulgaria*	**39**	G3
Peace R.	*Alberta-B.C.*	**62**	K6
Peace River	*Alberta*	**62**	L6
Peak, The, mt.	*England*	**17**	E5
Peak Hill	*W. Australia*	**76**	B4
Pearl, R.	*Mississippi*	**68**	F4
Pearl Harbor	*Hawaii*	**10**	E3
Peary Chan.	*N.-W. Terr., Can.*	**62**	O2
Peć	*Yugoslavia*	**39**	E3
Pechenga	*U.S.S.R.*	**46**	D2
Pechora R.	*U.S.S.R.*	**46**	F2
Pecos	*Texas*	**64**	F4
Pecos, R.	*New Mexico, etc.*	**64**	F4
Pécs	*Hungary*	**35**	F5
Pedreiras	*Brazil*	**72**	J4
Peebles	*Scotland*	**16**	D4
Peekskill	*New York*	**66**	E3
Peel	*Isle of Man*	**17**	C4
Peel Fell, mt.	*England*	**17**	D4
Peel R.	*N.-W. Terr.-Yukon*	**62**	H4
Peera Peera Poolanna L.	*S. Australia*	**77**	F4
Pegasus B.	*New Zealand*	**79**	D5
Pegu	*Burma*	**53**	P7
Pegu Yoma, mts.	*Burma*	**53**	P6
Pehan	*China*	**51**	M2
Peipus, L.	*Estonia-U.S.S.R.*	**42**	F4
Pekela	*Netherlands*	**32**	F1
Peking	*China*	**48**	D2
Pelly L.	*N.-W. Terr., Can.*	**62**	O4
Pelly Pt.	*N.-W. Terr., Can.*	**62**	O3
Pelly R.	*Yukon*	**62**	H5
Pelly Bay	*N.-W. Terr., Can.*	**63**	R4
Pelly Crossing	*Yukon*	**62**	G5
Peloponnesus	*Greece*	**39**	F6
Pelotas	*Brazil*	**73**	G10
Pelvoux, Mt.	*France*	**33**	E4
Pemba I.	*E. Africa*	**58**	C5
Pembridge	*England*	**26**	E2
Pembroke	*Ontario*	**63**	T8
Pembroke	*Wales*	**17**	C6
Pembroke Dock	*Wales*	**26**	C3
Penang, I.	*Malaya*	**48**	B6
Penarth	*Wales*	**26**	D3
Penas, G. of	*Chile*	**73**	B13
Pencader	*Wales*	**26**	C3
Pendleton	*Oregon*	**67**	C2
Pend Oreille L.	*Idaho*	**64**	C1
Pengpu	*China*	**51**	K5
Peniche	*Portugal*	**36**	A3
Penicuik	*Scotland*	**16**	D4
Peñiscola	*Spain*	**36**	E2
Penistone	*England*	**25**	D3
Penki	*China*	**51**	L3
Penkilan Hd.	*Wales*	**26**	C2
Penkridge	*England*	**27**	E2
Pennine Alps	*Switz.-Italy*	**37**	B1
Pennine Chain	*England*	**17**	D4
Pennsylvania, state	*U.S.A.*	**65**	L2
Penny Highland, mt.	*N.-W. Terr., Can.*	**63**	V4
Penong	*S. Australia*	**76**	E5
Penrith	*England*	**17**	D4
Penryn	*England*	**26**	B4
Pensacola	*Florida*	**65**	J4
Pentland Firth	*Scotland*	**16**	D2
Pentland Hills	*Scotland*	**29**	E5
Pentland Skerries	*Scotland*	**28**	F2
Penyghent, mt.	*England*	**17**	D4
Penza	*U.S.S.R.*	**46**	E3
Penzance	*England*	**17**	C6
Penzhina	*U.S.S.R.*	**47**	R2
Peoria	*Illinois*	**65**	J2
Perdido, Mt.	*Spain*	**36**	E1
Pergamino	*Argentina*	**73**	E10
Perigord, reg.	*France*	**33**	C4
Périgueux	*France*	**33**	C4
Perim I.	*Red Sea*	**52**	D8
Perm	*U.S.S.R.*	**46**	F3
Pernambuco	*Brazil*	**72**	K5
Péronne	*France*	**33**	C2
Perpignan	*France*	**33**	C5
Perranporth	*England*	**26**	B4
Perry River	*N.-W. Terr., Can.*	**62**	O4
Persepolis	*Iran*	**52**	F5
Pershore	*England*	**27**	E2
Persia (Iran)	*S.W. Asia*	**52**	F4
Persian Gulf	*S.W. Asia*	**52**	E5
Perth	*Scotland*	**16**	D3
Perth	*W. Australia*	**76**	B5
Peru	*S. America*	**72**	B6
Perugia	*Italy*	**38**	C3
Pesaro	*Italy*	**38**	C3
Pescara	*Italy*	**38**	C3
Peshawar	*W. Pakistan*	**53**	K4
Petah Tiqva	*Israel*	**54**	C4
Petauke	*Zambia*	**59**	D2
Peterborough	*England*	**17**	E5
Peterborough	*Ontario*	**63**	T9
Peterborough	*S. Australia*	**77**	F5
Peterculter	*Scotland*	**28**	F3
Peter I I.	*Antarctica*	**80**	R8
Peterhead	*Scotland*	**16**	E3
Peterlee	*England*	**17**	E4
Petermann Pk.	*Greenland*	**63**	Z3
Petermann Ra.	*W. Aust.-N. Terr.*	**76**	D3
Peter Pond L.	*Saskatchewan*	**62**	N6
Petersburg	*Alaska*	**62**	H6
Petersburg	*Virginia*	**65**	L3
Petersfield	*England*	**27**	G3
Peterstow	*England*	**26**	E3
Peter the Gt. B.	*U.S.S.R.*	**47**	O4
Petitsikapau L.	*Labrador*	**63**	V7
Petone	*New Zealand*	**79**	E4
Petra	*Jordan*	**54**	C4
Petropavlovsk Kamchatskiy	*U.S.S.R.*	**47**	Q3
Petropolis	*Brazil*	**73**	J8
Petroseni	*Rumania*	**39**	F2
Petrovavlovsk	*Kazakh.*	**46**	G3
Petrozavodsk	*U.S.S.R.*	**46**	D2
Pettigo	*Eire*	**30**	D3
Petworth	*England*	**27**	G4
Pewsey & Vale of	*England*	**27**	F3
Pforzheim	*Germany, W.*	**34**	B4
Phan Rang	*Vietnam*	**48**	C5
Phenix City	*Alabama*	**69**	F4
Philadelphia	*Pennsylvania*	**65**	L3
Philippeville	*Algeria*	**57**	C1

Puerto Natales *Chile* **73** C14
Puerto Plata *Dominican Rep.* **71** K4
Puerto Rico, I. *West Indies* **71** L4
Puerto Suarez *Bolivia* **72** F7
Puget Sd. *Washington* **64** B1
Puget Theniers *France* **33** E5
Pukaki, L. *New Zealand* **79** C6
Pukekohe *New Zealand* **79** E2
Pula *Yugoslavia* **38** C2
Pullman *Washington* **67** C2
Pulog, Mt. *Philippines* **48** E5
Puluntohai *Sinkiang* **50** D2
Pumpsaint *Wales* **26** D2
Punakha *Bhutan* **53** N5
Punjab *India-W. Pakistan* **53** K4
Puno *Peru* **72** C7
Punta Arenas *Chile* **73** C14
Puntarenas *Costa Rica* **71** H6
Pur, R. *U.S.S.R.* **46** H2
Purbeck Downs *England* **26** E4
Puri *India* **53** N7
Purley *England* **27** G3
Purmerend *Netherlands* **32** C2
Purnea *India* **50** D6
Purus, R. *Brazil* **72** E5
Pusan *Korea* **48** E3
Pusha *Sinkiang* **50** B4
Pushkin *U.S.S.R.* **43** C1
Putao *Burma* **53** P5
Putaruru *New Zealand* **79** E3
Putien *China* **48** D4
Putorana Mts. *U.S.S.R.* **47** K2
Putumayo R. *Brazil, etc.* **72** C4
Puulavesi, L. *Finland* **42** F3
Puy, le *France* **33** D4
Pweto *Congo* **59** C1
Pwllheli *Wales* **26** C2
Pyasina, R. *U.S.S.R.* **47** J1
Pyatigorsk *U.S.S.R.* **43** F4
Pylus *Greece* **41** J4
Pyongyang *Korea* **48** E3
Pyramid L. *Nevada* **64** C2
Pyrénees, mts. *France-Spain* **33** B5

Qairwan *Tunisia* **57** D1
Qatar *Arabia* **52** F5
Qatrun, El *Libya* **57** D2
Qattara Depression *Egypt* **58** B2
Qena *Egypt* **58** C2
Qishn *E. Aden* **52** F6
Qizan *Saudi Arabia* **52** D7
Quantock Hills *England* **26** D3
Quebec *Quebec* **63** U8
Quebec, prov. *Canada* **63** U7
Queen Adelaide Arch. *Chile* **73** C14
Queen Alexandra Ra. *Antarctica* **80** L6
Queen Charlotte Is. & Sd. *Br. Columbia* **62** H7
Queen Charlotte Str. *Br. Columbia* **42** J7
Queen Elizabeth Is. *N.-W. Terr., Can.* **62** L1
Queen Louise Ld. *Greenland* **11** K1
Queen Mary Land *Antarctica* **80** H7
Queen Maud G. *N.-W. Terr., Can.* **62** O4
Queen Maud Land *Antarctica* **80** C7
Queen Maud Ra. *Antarctica* **80** P6
Queen's Chan. *N. Terr., Aust.* **76** D1
Queensland, state *Australia* **77** G3
Queenstown *Cape of Good Hope* **59** C4
Queenstown *New Zealand* **79** B6
Queenstown *Tasmania* **77** H7
Quelimane *Mozambique* **59** D2
Quelpart I. *Korea* **48** E3
Que Que *Rhodesia* **59** C2
Queretaro *Mexico* **70** D3
Quesnel & L. *Br. Columbia* **62** K7
Quetta *W. Pakistan* **52** J4
Quezaltenango *Guatemala* **70** F5
Quezon City *Philippines* **48** E5
Quiberon *France* **33** A3
Quiche *Guatemala* **70** F4
Quillan *France* **33** C5
Quilpie *Queensland* **77** G4
Quimper *France* **33** A2
Quincy *Illinois* **65** H3
Quincy *Massachusetts* **66** F2
Quirang, mt. *Scotland* **28** B3
Quito *Ecuador* **72** B4
Quorn *S. Australia* **77** F5
Qur ayyat al Milh *Saudi Arabia* **54** D4

Raahe *Finland* **42** E2
Raasay I. & Sd. *Scotland* **28** B3
Rabat *Morocco* **57** B1
Rabaul *New Britain* **10** D5
Race, C. *Newfoundland* **63** Y8
Racibórz *Poland* **35** F3
Racine *Wisconsin* **65** J2
Rădăuţi *Rumania* **35** H4
Radnor, co. *Wales* **17** D5
Radnor Forest *Wales* **26** D2
Radom *Poland* **35** G3
Radomsko *Poland* **35** F3
Radstadt *Austria* **34** D5
Radstock *England* **26** E3
Rae *N.-W. Terr., Can.* **62** L5
Rae Isthmus *N.-W. Terr., Can.* **63** R4
Rae Bareli *India* **53** M5
Raetihi *New Zealand* **79** E3
Rafsinjan *Iran* **52** G4
Raga *Sudan* **58** B4
Raga *Tibet* **50** D6
Ragusa *Sicily* **38** C6
Raigarh *India* **53** M6
Rainier, Mt. *Washington* **64** B1
Rainy R. *Minn.-Ont.* **63** Q8
Raipur *India* **53** M6
Raja, mt. *Borneo* **48** D7
Rajasthan, state *India* **53** K5
Rakahanga I. *Pacific Oc.* **10** E5
Rakaia, R. *New Zealand* **79** C5
Rakvere *Estonia* **42** F4
Raleigh *N. Carolina* **65** L3
Raleigh B. *N. Carolina* **65** L4
Ramadi *Iraq* **52** D4
Ramah *Labrador* **63** W6
Ramelton *Eire* **30** D2
Ramorantin *France* **33** C3
Ramsbottom *England* **25** C3
Ramsey *England* **27** G2
Ramsey *Isle of Man* **17** C4
Ramsey I. *Wales* **26** B3
Ramsgate *England* **17** F6
Rancagua *Chile* **73** C10
Ranchi *India* **50** C7
Randalstown *N. Ireland* **30** E3
Randers *Denmark* **42** B4
Randolph *Vermont* **66** E2
Ranfurly *New Zealand* **79** C6
Rangaunu B. *New Zealand* **79** D1
Rangiora *New Zealand* **79** D5
Rangitaiki, R. *New Zealand* **79** F3
Rangitata, R. *New Zealand* **79** C5
Rangoon *Burma* **53** P7
Rankin Inlet *N.-W. Terr., Can.* **63** Q5
Rann, The *India* **53** K6
Rannoch, L. *Scotland* **16** C3
Rannoch Moor *Scotland* **29** D4
Rantekombola, mt. *Celebes* **48** D7
Rapallo *Italy* **38** B2
Raphoe *Eire* **30** D3
Rapid City *S. Dakota* **64** F2
Raqqa *Syria* **54** E2
Ras Dashan, mt. *Ethiopia* **58** C3
Rashad *Sudan* **58** C3
Rasht *Iran* **52** E3
Rathdrum *Eire* **17** B5
Rathkeale *Eire* **17** A5
Rathlin I. *N. Ireland* **17** B4
Rathnew *Eire* **31** E5
Raton *New Mexico* **67** F4
Rattray Hd. *Scotland* **16** E3
Raukumara Ra *New Zealand* **79** F3
Rauma *Finland* **42** E3
Ravenglass *England* **17** D4
Ravenna *Italy* **38** C2
Ravensburg *Germany, W.* **34** C5
Rawalpindi *W. Pakistan* **53** K4
Rawandiz *Iraq* **55** H1
Rawene *New Zealand* **79** D1
Rawlinna *W. Australia* **76** D5
Rawlins *Wyoming* **64** E2
Rawson *Argentina* **73** E12
Rayleigh *England* **27** H3
Raymond *Alberta* **62** M8
Ré I. *France* **33** B3
Reading *England* **17** E6
Reading *Pennsylvania* **65** L2
Read Island *N.-W. Terr., Can.* **62** M4
Reawick *Scotland* **28** A1
Recanati *Italy* **38** C3
Recherche Arch. *W. Australia* **76** C5
Rechitsa *White Russia* **43** C2
Recife *Brazil* **72** K5
Red Basin *China* **48** C3
Red L. *Minnesota* **65** H1
Red R. *Louisiana, etc.* **65** H4
Red R. *Manitoba, etc.* **63** P7
Red R. *Vietnam, etc.* **53** Q6
Red Sea *Africa-Asia* **52** C6
Red Bluff *California* **67** B3
Redcar *England* **25** D2
Red Cedar R. *Iowa, etc.* **65** H2
Red Deer & R. *Alberta* **62** M7
Redditch *England* **17** E5
Redfield *S. Dakota* **64** G2
Redhill *England* **27** G3
Red Lodge *Montana* **67** E2
Redmond *Oregon* **67** B3
Redon *France* **33** B3
Redruth *England* **26** B4
Redwater *Alberta* **62** M7
Redwood City *California* **67** B4
Ree, L. *Eire* **17** B5
Reedham *England* **27** J2
Reefton *New Zealand* **79** C5
Reeth *England* **25** D2
Regensburg *Germany, W.* **34** D4
Reggan *Algeria* **57** B2
Reggio-di-Calabria *Italy* **38** D5
Reggio-nell-Emilia *Italy* **38** B2
Regina *Saskatchewan* **62** O7
Rehoboth *S.W. Africa* **59** B3
Reigate *England* **17** E6
Reims *France* **33** D2
Reindeer L. *Saskatchewan* **62** O6
Reindeer Depot *N.-W. Terr., Can.* **62** G4
Remiremont *France* **33** E2
Renaix *Belgium* **32** B4
Rendsburg *Germany, W.* **34** C1
Renfrew *Scotland* **29** D5
Renfrew, co. *Scotland* **16** C4
Renmark *S. Australia* **77** G5
Rennes *France* **33** B2
Reno *Nevada* **64** C3
Reno, R. *Italy* **38** B2
Rensselaer *New York* **66** E2
Republican R. *Nebraska* **64** F2
Repulse B. *Queensland* **77** H3
Repulse Bay *N.-W. Terr., Can.* **63** R4
Rerwick *Scotland* **28** A2
Resistencia *Argentina* **73** F9
Resolution I. *New Zealand* **79** A6
Resolution Island *N.-W. Terr., Can.* **63** W5
Rethel *France* **33** D2
Réunion, I. *Indian Oc.* **11** M6
Reus *Spain* **36** E2
Reuss, R. *Switzerland* **37** C1
Reutlingen *Germany, W.* **34** C4
Revelstoke *Br. Columbia* **62** L7
Revilla Gigedo Is. *Mexico* **70** B4
Rexburg *Idaho* **67** D3
Reykjanes *Iceland* **42** J7
Reykjavik *Iceland* **42** J6
Rezaiyeh *Iran* **52** D3
Rezekne *Latvia* **42** F4
Rhaetian Alps *Switzerland* **37** C1
Rhayader *Wales* **26** D2
Rheine *Germany, W.* **34** B2
Rheydt *Germany, W.* **34** B3
Rhine, R. *W. Europe* **34** B3
Rhinebeck *New York* **66** E3
Rhineland *Germany, W.* **34** B3
Rhinelander *Wisconsin* **69** F1
Rhode Island, state *U.S.A.* **65** M2
Rhodes & I. *Greece* **41** M4
Rhodesia *Cent. Africa* **59** C2
Rhodope Mts. *Bulgaria-Greece* **41** K3
Rhondda *Wales* **17** D6
Rhône, R. *France* **33** D4
Rhon Gebirge, mts. *Germany* **34** C3
Rhosllanerchrugog *Wales* **26** D1
Rhyl *Wales* **17** D5
Rhynie *Scotland* **28** F3
Ribble, R. *England* **17** D5
Ribeirão Prêto *Brazil* **73** H8
Ribérac *France* **33** C4
Riberalta *Bolivia* **72** D6
Riccall *England* **25** D3
Riccarton Junct. *Scotland* **29** F5
Richborough *England* **27** J3
Richfield *Utah* **67** D4
Richland *Washington* **64** C1
Richmond *Surrey, Eng.* **17** E6
Richmond *Yorks, England* **17** E4
Richmond *Kentucky* **69** G3
Richmond *New Zealand* **79** D4
Richmond *Queensland* **77** G3
Richmond *Virginia* **65** L3
Rickmansworth *England* **27** G3
Ridgewell *England* **27** H2
Ridgway *Pennsylvania* **66** B3
Riesa *Germany, E.* **34** D3
Rieti *Italy* **38** C3
Rif, Er *Morocco* **40** B5
Rifstangi, pt. *Iceland* **42** L6
Riga *Latvia* **46** C3
Riga, G. of *Latvia* **42** E4
Rigi, mt. *Switzerland* **37** C1
Rigny, mt. *Greenland* **63** Z4
Rigolet *Labrador* **63** X7
Riihimaki *Finland* **42** F3
Rijeka *Yugoslavia* **38** C2
Rimini *Italy* **38** C2
Rimnicu Sarat *Rumania* **39** G2
Rimouski *Quebec* **63** V8
Rinchin Lümbe *Mongolia* **50** F1
Rineanna *Eire* **31** C5
Ringmer *England* **27** H4
Ringvassöy, I. *Norway* **42** D1
Ringwood *England* **27** F4
Riobamba *Ecuador* **72** B4
Rio Branco *Brazil* **72** D5
Rio Bravo del Norte, R. *Mexico* **70** D2
Rio de Janeiro *Brazil* **73** J8
Rio Gallegos *Argentina* **73** D14
Rio Grande *Brazil* **73** G10
Rio Grande, R. *Texas, etc.* **64** F5
Rio Muni *W. Africa* **57** C4
Rio Negro Res. *Uruguay* **73** F10
Rionero *Italy* **38** D4
Rio Turbio *Argentina* **73** C14
Rio Verde *Mexico* **70** E3
Ripley *Derby, Eng.* **27** F1
Ripley *Yorks, Eng.* **25** D2
Ripon *England* **17** E4
Risca *Wales* **26** D3
Riva *Italy* **38** B2
Rivas *Nicaragua* **71** G5
Rivera *Uruguay* **73** F10
Riverina *New South Wales* **77** G6
Riverside *California* **67** C5
Riverton *New Zealand* **79** B7
Riverton *Wyoming* **67** E3
Rivière du Loup *Quebec* **63** V8
Rivoche *Tibet* **50** D6
Riyadh *Saudi Arabia* **52** E6
Roade *England* **27** G2
Roanne *France* **33** D3
Roanoke *Virginia* **65** L3
Roanoke R. *N. Carolina, etc.* **65** L3
Robertsport *Liberia* **57** A4
Robertstown *Eire* **31** E4
Robin Hood's Bay *England* **25** E2
Robinson Ras. *W. Australia* **76** B4
Robinson's *Newfoundland* **63** X8
Robson, Mt. *B.C.-Alberta* **62** L7
Rocha *Uruguay* **73** G10
Rochdale *England* **25** C3
Rochefort *France* **33** B4
Rochelle, la *France* **33** B3
Rocher River *N.-W. Terr., Can.* **62** M5
Rochester *England* **17** F6
Rochester *Minnesota* **65** H2
Rochester *New York* **65** L2
Roche-sur-Yon, la *France* **33** B3
Rochford *England* **27** H3
Rockford *Illinois* **65** J2
Rockhampton *Queensland* **77** J3
Rockingham *England* **27** G2
Rock Island *Illinois* **65** H2
Rockport *Texas* **64** G5
Rock Springs *Wyoming* **64** E2
Rocky Mts. *Can.-U.S.A.* **64** D1
Rocky Mount *N. Carolina* **69** H3
Rodel *Scotland* **28** B3
Roden *Netherlands* **32** E1
Rödbyhavn *Denmark* **34** C1
Rodez *France* **33** C4
Rodriguez, I. *Indian Oc.* **11** N5
Roebourne *W. Australia* **76** B3
Roes Welcome Sd. *N.-W. Terr., Can.* **63** R5
Rolla *Missouri* **65** H3
Roma *Queensland* **77** H4
Romain, C. *S. Carolina* **69** H4
Romaine R. *Quebec* **63** W7
Roman *Rumania* **35** H5

Romans *France* **33** D4
Romanzof, C. *Alaska* **62** A5
Rome *Georgia* **65** J4
Rome *Italy* **38** C4
Rome *New York* **66** D2
Romford *England* **27** H3
Romney Marsh *England* **27** H3
Romsdal, valley *Norway* **42** A3
Romsey *England* **27** F4
Roncador, Sa. do, mts. *Brazil* **72** G6
Roncesvalles *Spain* **36** D1
Ronda *Spain* **36** C4
Ronge, L. la *Saskatchewan* **62** O6
Ronne B. *Antarctica* **80** S7
Roosendaal *Netherlands* **32** C3
Roosevelt I. *Antarctica* **80** N7
Roosevelt L. *Arizona* **67** D5
Roosky *Eire* **30** D4
Roper R. *N. Terr., Aust.* **77** E1
Roraima, mt. *Br. Guiana-Venez.* **72** E2
Röros *Norway* **42** B3
Rorschach *Switzerland* **37** C1
Rosario *Argentina* **73** E10
Rosario *Mexico* **70** A2
Rosario *Mexico* **70** C3
Roscommon *Eire* **17** A5
Roscrea *Eire* **17** B5
Roseau *West Indies* **71** M4
Roseburg *Oregon* **64** B2
Rosehearty *Scotland* **28** F3
Roseires, Er *Sudan* **58** C3
Rosemarkie *Scotland* **28** D3
Rosenheim *Germany, W.* **34** D5
Rosetta *Egypt* **58** C1
Roseville *California* **67** B4
Roslavl *U.S.S.R.* **43** D2
Ross *England* **26** E3
Ross *New Zealand* **79** C5
Ross Dependency *Antarctica* **80** N7
Ross I. *Antarctica* **80** M7
Ross Sea *Antarctica* **80** N7
Ross & Cromarty, co. *Scotland* **16** C3
Rossano *Italy* **38** D5
Rosscarbery *Eire* **31** B6
Rossland *Br. Columbia* **62** L8
Rosslare Harb. *Eire* **17** B5
Rosslea *N. Ireland* **30** D3
Rosso *Mauritania* **57** A3
Ross River *Yukon* **62** H5
Rosthern *Saskatchewan* **62** N7
Rostock *Germany, E.* **34** D1
Rostov *U.S.S.R.* **46** D4
Roswell *New Mexico* **64** F4
Rosyth *Scotland* **29** E4
Rothbury *England* **25** D1
Rothenburg *Germany, W.* **34** C4
Rother, R. *England* **27** H3
Rotherham *England* **17** E5
Rothes *Scotland* **28** E3
Rothesay *Scotland* **16** C4
Rotorua & L. *New Zealand* **79** F3
Rotterdam *Netherlands* **32** C3
Rottumeroog, I. *Netherlands* **32** E1
Rotuma *Pacific Oc.* **10** D5
Roubaix *France* **33** D1
Rouen *France* **33** C2
Roulers *Belgium* **32** B4
Round mt. *New South Wales* **77** J5
Roundup *Montana* **67** E2
Rousay, I. *Scotland* **16** D2
Rouyn *Quebec* **63** T8
Rovaniemi *Finland* **42** F2
Rovereto *Italy* **38** B2
Rovigo *Italy* **38** B2
Rovno *Ukraine* **43** C2
Rowley Shoals *Indian Oc.* **76** B2
Roxburgh *New Zealand* **79** B6
Roxburgh, co. *Scotland* **17** D4
Royal Can. *Eire* **31** E4
Royale, Isle *Michigan* **65** J1
Royan *France* **33** B4
Royston *England* **27** G2
Rtishchevo *U.S.S.R.* **43** F2
Ruabon *Wales* **26** D2
Ruahine Ra. *New Zealand* **79** E4
Ruapehu, mt. *New Zealand* **79** E3
Ruapuke I. *New Zealand* **79** B7
Rub al Khali, des *Arabia* **52** E6
Rubinéia *Brazil* **72** G7
Rubtsovsk *U.S.S.R.* **46** J3
Ruby *Alaska* **62** D5
Ruddington *England* **27** F2
Rudolf, L. *Ethiopia-Kenya* **58** C4
Rudolstadt *Germany, E.* **34** C3
Rudyard Res. *England* **27** E1
Rufiji R. *Tanzania* **58** C5
Rugby *England* **17** E5
Rugby *N. Dakota* **68** D1
Rugeley *England* **27** F2
Rügen, I. *Germany, E.* **34** D1
Ruhr, R. *Germany, W.* **34** B3
Rukwa, L. *Tanzania* **58** C5
Rum, I. *Scotland* **16** B3
Rumania *S.E. Europe* **41** J2
Rum Cay *Bahamas* **71** J3
Rum Jungle *N. Terr., Aust.* **76** E1
Rumoi *Japan* **51** P3
Runanga *New Zealand* **79** C5
Runaway, C. *New Zealand* **79** F2
Runcorn *England* **25** C3
Runswick *England* **25** E2
Rupert R. *Quebec* **63** T7
Rupert House *Quebec* **63** T7
Ruse *Bulgaria* **39** G3
Rushden *England* **27** G2
Russell *New Zealand* **79** E1
Russia, *see* U.S.S.R.
Russko Ust'inskoye *U.S.S.R.* **47** P1
Rutba *Iraq* **52** D4
Rutherglen *Scotland* **29** D5
Ruthin *Wales* **26** D1
Rutland *Vermont* **65** M2
Rutland, co. *England* **17** E5
Ruvuma, R. *Tanzania* **59** D2
Ruwenzori Ra. *Congo-Uganda* **58** B4
Ruzomberok *Czechoslovakia* **35** F4
Rwanda *Cent. Africa* **58** B5
Ryan, L. *Scotland* **17** C4
Ryazan *U.S.S.R.* **46** E3
Ryazhsk *U.S.S.R.* **43** F2
Rybachye *Kirgiz.* **53** L2
Rybinsk & Res. *U.S.S.R.* **46** D3
Rybnoye *U.S.S.R.* **47** L1
Ryde *England* **27** F4
Rye *England* **27** H4
Ryukyu Arch. *Japan* **48** E4
Rzeszów *Poland* **35** G3
Rzhev *U.S.S.R.* **43** D1
Saale, R. *Germany* **34** C3
Saanen *Switzerland* **37** B1
Saarbrücken *Germany, W.* **34** B4
Saaremaa, I. *Estonia* **42** E4
Saarland *Germany, W.* **34** B4
Sabadell *Spain* **36** E2
Sabah (North Borneo) *Malaysia* **48** D6
Sabàudia *Italy* **38** C4
Sabine R. *Texas* **65** H4
Sablé *France* **33** B3
Sable, C. *Florida* **65** K5
Sable, C. *Nova Scotia* **63** V9
Sable I. *Atlantic Oc.* **63** X9
Sabzawar *Iran* **52** G3
Sachs Harbour *N.-W. Terr., Can.* **62** K3
Sacramento *California* **64** B3
Sacramento Mts. *New Mexico* **67** E5
Sacramento R. *California* **64** B2
Sá da Bandeira *Angola* **59** B2
Sadiya *India* **53** P5
Sado, I. *Japan* **51** O4
Safad *Israel* **54** C3
Saffron Walden *England* **27** H2
Safi *Morocco* **57** B1
Safranbolu *Turkey* **52** B2
Sagaing *Burma* **53** P6
Saginaw *Michigan* **65** K2
Sagiz *Kazakh.* **52** F1
Sagua la Grande *Cuba* **71** H3
Saguenay, R. *Quebec* **63** U8
Sahagun *Spain* **36** C1
Sahara *Algeria* **57** B2
Sahara, des *N. Africa* **57** B2
Saharan Atlas, mts. *Algeria* **57** C1
Saharanpur *India* **53** L5
Sahuaripa *Mexico* **70** C2
Saigon *Vietnam* **48** C5
Saimaa, L. *Finland* **42** F3
St. Abb's Hd. *Scotland* **29** F5
St. Agnes *England* **26** B4
St. Agnes *Scilly Is.* **26** A5
St. Albans *England* **17** E6
St. Albans Hd. *England* **17** E6
St. Andrews *Scotland* **16** D3
St. Andrews I. *West Indies* **71** H5
St. Asaph *Wales* **26** D1
St. Augustine *Florida* **65** K5
St. Austell & B. *England* **26** C4
St. Bees *England* **25** B2
St. Bees Hd. *England* **17** D4
St. Blazey *England* **26** C4
St. Boniface *Manitoba* **63** P7
St. Bride's B. *Wales* **17** C6
St. Calais *France* **33** C3
St. Catherines Pt. *England* **27** F4
St. Charles, C. *Labrador* **63** X7
St. Chaumond *France* **33** D4
St. Clair, L. *Ont.-Mich.* **69** G2
St. Claude *France* **33** D3
St. Clears *Wales* **26** C3
St. Cloud *Minnesota* **65** H1
St. Columb *England* **26** C4
St. Croix, I. *West Indies* **71** M4
St. Davids *Wales* **26** B3
St. David's Hd. *Wales* **17** C6
St. Day *England* **26** B4
St. Denis *France* **33** C2
St. Dié *France* **33** E2
St. Dizier *France* **33** D2
St. Dogmells *Wales* **26** C2
St. Elias, Mt. *Alaska-Yukon* **62** F5
St. Elias Mts. *Alaska-B.C.* **62** F5
Saintes *France* **33** B4
St. Etienne *France* **33** D4
Saintfield *N. Ireland* **30** F3
St. Fillans *Scotland* **29** D4
St. Flour *France* **33** D4
St. Francis, C. *Cape of Good Hope* **59** C4
St. Gallen *Switzerland* **37** C1
St. Gaudens *France* **33** C5
St. George *Queensland* **77** H4
St. George *Utah* **64** D3
St. George's *West Indies* **71** M5
St. George's B. *Newfoundland* **63** X8
St. George's Chan. *Wales-Eire* **17** B6
St. Germain *France* **33** C2
St. Germans *England* **26** C4
St. Girons *France* **33** C5
St. Gotthard Pass *Switzerland* **37** C1
St. Gowans Hd. *Wales* **26** C3
St. Helena, I. *Atlantic Oc.* **11** K5
St. Helens *England* **25** C3
St. Helier *Channel Is.* **33** B2
St. Hyacinthe *Quebec* **63** U8
St. Ives *Cornwall, England* **17** C6
St. Ives *Hunts, England* **27** G2
St. Ives B. *England* **26** B4
St. Jacobiparochie *Netherlands* **32** D1
St. Jean *France* **33** E4
Saint John *New Brunswick* **63** V8
St. John, C. *Newfoundland* **63** X7
St. John, L. *Quebec* **63** U8
Saint John R. *Maine-N.B.* **63** V8
St. John's *Newfoundland* **63** Y8
St. John's Chapel *England* **25** C2
St. Joseph *Missouri* **65** H3
St. Joseph *Quebec* **63** U8
St. Joseph I. *Ontario* **63** S8
St. Joseph, L. *Ontario* **63** Q7
St. Julien *France* **33** E3
St. Just *England* **26** B4
St. Kilda, I. *Scotland* **16** A3
St. Kitts, I. *West Indies* **71** M4
St. Lawrence *Queensland* **77** H3
St. Lawrence, G. of *Canada* **63** W8
St. Lawrence I. *Bering Sea* **62** A5
St. Lawrence R. *Can.-U.S.A.* **63** V8
St. Lawrence Seaway *Quebec-New York* **66** D1
St. Leonards *England* **27** H4
St. Lô *France* **33** B2
St. Louis *Mauritania* **57** A3
St. Louis *Missouri* **65** H3
St. Lucia, I. *West Indies* **71** M5
St. Luis de Nord *Haiti* **71** K4
St. Magnus B. *Scotland* **16** E1
St. Malo & G. of *France* **33** B2
St. Margaret's Hope *Scotland* **28** F2
Ste. Marie, C. *Malagasy Rep.* **59** E3
St. Martin *West Indies* **71** M4
St. Martins *Scilly Is.* **26** A5
St. Mary B. *Newfoundland* **63** Y8
St. Mary Pk. *S. Australia* **77** F5
St. Marys *Scilly Is.* **26** A5
St. Marys *Tasmania* **77** H7
St. Marys *Scotland* **28** F2
St. Mary's L. *Scotland* **29** E5
St. Matthew I. *Bering Sea* **47** T2
St. Maurice, R. *Quebec* **63** U8
St. Michael *Alaska* **62** B5
St. Mihiel *France* **33** D2
St. Moritz *Switzerland* **37** C1
St. Nazaire *France* **33** B3
St. Neots *England* **27** G2
St. Nicolas *Belgium* **32** C3
St. Omer *France* **33** C1
St. Paul *Minnesota* **65** H1
St. Paul I. *Indian Oc.* **11** N6
St. Peter Port *Channel Is.* **33** B2
St. Petersburg *Florida* **65** K5
St. Pierre *West Indies* **71** M5
St. Pölten *Austria* **34** E4
St. Quentin *France* **33** D2
St. Stephen *New Brunswick* **63** V8
St. Stephens *Alabama* **65** J4
St. Teath *England* **26** C4
St. Trond *Belgium* **32** D4
St. Valery *France* **33** C1
St. Valery *France* **33** C2
St. Veit *Austria* **34** D5
St. Vincent G. *S. Australia* **77** F6
St. Vincent, I. *West Indies* **71** M5
St. Yrieix *France* **33** C4
Saipan I. *Pacific Oc.* **10** C4
Sajama, mt. *Bolivia* **72** D7
Sakai *Japan* **51** O5
Sakakak *Saudi Arabia* **55** F5
Sakania *Congo* **59** C2
Sakarya R. *Turkey* **52** B2
Sakhalin, I. *U.S.S.R.* **47** P3
Sakishima Gunto, I. *Japan* **48** E4
Salado, R. *Argentina* **73** E9
Salala *Muscat & Oman* **52** F7
Salama *Guatemala* **70** F4
Salamanca *Spain* **36** C2
Salamat, R. *Chad* **58** B3
Salamis *Greece* **39** F6
Sala y Gomez, I. *S. Pacific Oc.* **10** G6
Salcombe *England* **26** D4
Sale *England* **25** C3
Sale *Victoria* **77** H6
Salekhard *U.S.S.R.* **46** G2
Salem *India* **53** L8
Salem *Massachusetts* **66** F2
Salem *Oregon* **64** B2
Salen *Scotland* **29** C4
Salerno & G. of *Italy* **38** C4
Salford *England* **17** D5
Salgueiro *Brazil* **72** K5
Salima *Malawi* **59** D2
Salina *Kansas* **64** G3
Salina Cruz *Mexico* **70** E4
Salinas *California* **67** B4
Salisbury *England* **17** E6
Salisbury *Rhodesia* **59** D2
Salisbury I. *N.-W. Terr., Can.* **63** T5
Salisbury Plain *England* **17** D6
Salmon *Idaho* **64** D1
Salmon R. *Idaho* **64** C1
Salmon Gums *W. Australia* **76** C5
Salmon River Mts. *Idaho* **67** C3
Salo *Finland* **42** E3
Salonica *Greece* **39** F4
Salt *Jordan* **54** C3
Salt Des. *Iran* **52** F4
Salta *Argentina* **73** D8
Saltash *England* **26** C4
Saltburn *England* **25** E2
Saltcoats *Scotland* **29** D5
Saltdal *Norway* **42** C2
Saltfleet *England* **25** F3
Saltillo *Mexico* **70** D2
Salt Lake City *Utah* **64** D2
Salto *Argentina* **73** F10
Salton *California* **64** C4
Salton Sea *California* **64** C4
Saluzzo *Italy* **38** A2
Salvador *Cent. America* **70** G5
Salvador *Brazil* **72** K6
Salween R. *S.E. Asia* **53** P7
Salzburg *Austria* **34** D5
Salzgitter *Germany, W.* **34** C2
Salzwedel *Germany, E.* **34** C2
Samani *Japan* **49** E3
Samar, I. *Philippines* **48** E5
Samarai *Papua* **77** J1
Samarinda *Borneo* **48** D7
Samarkand *Uzbek.* **46** G5
Sāmarrā' *Iraq* **55** G2
Samawah, As *Iraq* **55** H4
Sambalpur *India* **50** C7
Samnan *Iran* **52** F3
Samoan Is. *Pacific Oc.* **10** E5
Samos, I. *Greece* **39** G6
Samothrace, I. *Greece* **39** G4
Samsu *Korea* **51** M3
Samsun *Turkey* **52** C2
Samut Prakan *Thailand* **53** Q8
San *Mali* **57** B3
San'a *Yemen* **52** D7
Sanaga, R. *Cameroun* **57** D4

San Ambrosio, I. *Pacific Oc.* **11** H6
Sanandaj *Iran* **52** E3
San Andreas Tuxtla *Mexico* **70** E4
San Andres Mts. *New Mexico* **67** E5
San Angelo *Texas* **64** F4
San Antonio *Texas* **64** G5
San Antonio, C. *Argentina* **73** F11
San Benedetto del Tronto *Italy* **38** C3
San Benito *Texas* **68** D5
San Bernardino *California* **64** C4
San Bernardino Pass *Switzerland* **37** C1
San Blas *Mexico* **70** C3
San Carlos L. *Arizona* **64** D4
San Carlos de Bariloche *Argentina* **73** C12
San Cristobal *Venezuela* **72** C2
San Cristobal, I. *Galapagos Is.* **73** O17
Sancti Spiritus *Cuba* **71** J3
Sandakan *Sabah* **48** D6
Sanday, I. *Scotland* **16** D2
Sandbach *England* **26** E1
Sandefjord B. *Antarctica* **80** G8
Sandgate *England* **27** J3
Sandgate *Queensland* **77** J4
San Diego *California* **64** C4
Sandnes *Norway* **42** A4
Sandness *Scotland* **28** A1
Sandö, I. *Faeroes* **42** N9
Sandoa *Congo* **59** C1
Sandown *England* **27** F4
Sandringham *England* **27** H2
Sandstone *W. Australia* **76** B4
Sandusky *Ohio* **65** K2
Sandwich *England* **27** J3
Sandwick *Scotland* **28** A2
Sandy *England* **27** G2
Sandy C. *Queensland* **77** J3
Sandy L. *Ontario* **63** Q7
San Felix *Venezuela* **72** E2
San Felix I. *Pacific Oc.* **73** B9
San Fernando *Chile* **73** C10
San Fernando *Philippines* **48** E5
San Fernando *Spain* **36** B4
San Fernando de Atabapo *Venezuela* **72** D3
Sanford *Florida* **69** G5
Sanford *Maine* **66** F2
Sanford, Mt. *Alaska* **62** F5
San Francisco *California* **64** B3
San Francisco, Mt. *Arizona* **64** D3
Sangay, mt. *Ecuador* **72** B4
Sangihe Is. *Indonesia* **48** E6
Sangre do Cristo Mts. *Colorado-New Mex.* **64** E3
Sanguesa *Spain* **36** D1
San Joaquin R. *California* **64** B3
San Jorge, G. of *Argentina* **73** D13
San Jose *Bolivia* **72** E7
San Jose *California* **64** B3
San José *Costa Rica* **71** H6
San José *Guatemala* **70** F5
San Juan *Peru* **72** B7
San Juan *Puerto Rico* **71** L4
San Juan Mts. *Colorado, etc.* **64** E3
San Juan, R. *Costa Rica* **71** H5
San Juan R. *Utah, etc.* **64** E3
San Juan de Guadalupe *Mexico* **70** D3
San Juan del Norte *Nicaragua* **71** H5
San Juan del Sur *Nicaragua* **71** G5
Sankuru, R. *Congo* **59** C1
San Lorenzo *Ecuador* **72** B3
San Lucas, C. *Mexico* **70** B3
San Luis *Argentina* **73** D10
San Luis *Mexico* **70** C2
San Luis Obispo *California* **64** B3
San Luis Potosi *Mexico* **70** D3
San Marino *Italy* **38** C3
San Mateo *California* **67** B4
San Matias, G. of *Argentina* **73** E12
San Miguel *Salvador* **70** G5
San Miguel de Tucumán *Argentina* **73** E9
San Pedro Sula *Honduras* **70** G4
Sanquhar *Scotland* **17** D4
San Quintin *Mexico* **70** A1
San Rafael *Argentina* **73** D10
San Remo *Italy* **38** A3
San Salvador *Salvador* **70** G5
San Salvador I. *Bahamas* **71** K3
San Salvador de Jujuy *Argentina* **73** D8
Sansanne Mango *Togo* **57** C3
San Sebastian *Spain* **36** D1
Sansepolcro *Italy* **38** C3
San Severo *Italy* **38** D4
Santa Ana *Bolivia* **72** D6
Santa Ana *California* **67** C5
Santa Ana *Salvador* **70** G5
Santa Barbara *California* **64** C4
Santa Barbara *Honduras* **70** G4
Santa Barbara *Mexico* **70** C2
Santa Barbara Chan. *California* **64** B4
Santa Catalina, I. *California* **64** C4
Santa Catalina, mt. *Mexico* **70** A1
Santa Clara *Cuba* **71** J3
Santa Clemente, I. *California* **64** C4
Santa Cruz *Argentina* **73** D14
Santa Cruz *Bolivia* **72** E7
Santa Cruz *California* **64** B3
Santa Cruz *Canary Is.* **57** A2
Santa Cruz, I. *California* **64** C4
Santa Cruz, I. *Galapagos Is.* **73** N17
Santa Cruz, I. *Pacific Oc.* **10** D5
Santa Cruz del Sur *Cuba* **71** J3
Santa Fé *Argentina* **73** E10
Santa Fé *New Mexico* **64** E3
Santai *China* **50** H5
Santa Ines I. *Chile* **73** C14
Santa Isabel *Fernando Póo* **57** C4
Santa Maria *Brazil* **73** G9
Santa Maria *California* **67** B5
Santa Maria del Rio *Mexico* **70** D3
Santa Marta *Colombia* **72** C1
Santander *Spain* **36** C1
Santarem *Brazil* **72** G4
Santa Rosa *Argentina* **73** E11
Santa Rosa *California* **64** B3
Santa Rosa *New Mexico* **67** F5
Santa Rosa, I. *California* **64** B4
Santa Rosalia *Mexico* **70** B2
Santee, R. *S. Carolina* **69** H4
Santhia *Italy* **38** A2
Santiago *Chile* **73** C10
Santiago de Compostela *Spain* **36** B1
Santiago de Cuba *Cuba* **71** J4
Santiago del Estero *Argentina* **73** E9
Santo Antonio do Zaire *Angola* **59** B1
Santo Domingo *Dominican Rep.* **71** L4
Santos *Brazil* **73** H8
San Valentin, mt. *Chile* **73** C13
São Francisco R. *Brazil* **72** J6
São Leopoldo *Brazil* **73** G9
São Luis *Brazil* **72** J4
São Manuel R. *Brazil* **72** E6
Saône, R. *France* **33** D3
São Paulo *Brazil* **73** H8
São Roque, C. de *Brazil* **72** K5
São Tomé, I. *G. of Guinea* **57** C4
Sapporo *Japan* **48** G2
Sapulpa *Oklahoma* **68** D3
Saqqez *Iran* **55** J1
Saragossa *Spain* **36** D2
Sarajevo *Yugoslavia* **38** E3
Sarakhs *Iran* **46** G5
Saransk *U.S.S.R.* **43** G2
Sarapul *U.S.S.R.* **43** H1
Saratoga Springs *New York* **66** E2
Saratov *U.S.S.R.* **46** E3
Sarawak *Malaysia* **48** D6
Saray *Turkey* **39** H4
Sardinia, I. *Italy* **38** B5
Sareks Nat. Pk. *Sweden* **42** D2
Sarektjakko, mt. *Sweden* **42** D2
Sargans *Switzerland* **37** C1
Sarina *Queensland* **77** H3
Sari Su, R. *Kazakh.* **46** G4
Sark, I. *Channel Is.* **33** B2
Sarlat *France* **33** C4
Sarnau *Wales* **26** C2
Sarnen *Switzerland* **37** C1
Sarnia *Ontario* **63** S9
Saronic G. *Greece* **39** F6
Sarpsborg *Norway* **42** B4
Sarrebourg *France* **33** E2
Sarreguemines *France* **33** E2
Sarthe, R. *France* **33** B3
Sasaram *India* **50** C7
Sasebo *Japan* **51** M5
Saskatchewan, prov. *Canada* **62** N7
Saskatchewan R. *Man.-Sask.* **62** O7
Saskatoon *Saskatchewan* **62** N7
Sassandra & R. *Ivory Coast* **57** B4
Sassari *Sardinia* **38** A4
Sassnitz *Germany, E.* **34** D1
Sassyk Kol, L. *Kazakh.* **46** J4
Satpura Ra. *India* **53** L6
Satu Mare *Rumania* **35** G5
Saudi Arabia *S.W. Asia* **52** D5
Sault St. Marie *Ont.-Mich.* **63** S8
Saumur *France* **33** B3
Saunders, C. *New Zealand* **79** C6
Saundersfoot *Wales* **26** C3
Sauquira B. *Muscat & Oman* **52** G7
Saurashtra *India* **53** K6
Sava R. *Yugoslavia* **39** E2
Savannah & R. *Georgia* **65** K4
Savanna la Mar *Jamaica* **71** J4
Save, R. *Mozambique* **59** D3
Saverne *France* **33** E2
Savona *Italy* **38** A2
Savonlinna *Finland* **42** G3
Savukoski *Finland* **42** G2
Savu Sea *Indonesia* **48** E7
Sawston *England* **27** H2
Saxmundham *England* **27** J2
Sayan Mts. *U.S.S.R.* **47** K3
Sayhan *Mongolia* **50** G2
Sayula *Mexico* **70** D4
Sca Fell Pike *England* **25** B2
Scalby *England* **25** E2
Scalloway *Scotland* **16** E1
Scapa Flow *Scotland* **16** D2
Scarborough *England* **17** E4
Scavaig, L. *Scotland* **16** B3
Schaffhausen *Switzerland* **34** B5
Schagen *Netherlands* **32** C2
Schärding *Austria* **34** D4
Schefferville *Quebec* **63** V6
Scheibbs *Austria* **34** E4
Schelde, R. *Belgium* **34** A3
Schelde, E. & W., Rs. *Netherlands* **32** B3
Schenectady *New York* **65** M2
Scheveningen *Netherlands* **32** C2
Schiedam *Netherlands* **32** C3
Schiehallion, mt. *Scotland* **16** C3
Schiermonnikoog, I. *Netherlands* **32** E1
Schio *Italy* **38** B2
Schleswig *Germany, W.* **34** C1
Schleswig Holstein *Germany, W.* **34** C1
Schouwen, I. *Netherlands* **32** B3
Schull *Eire* **31** B6
Schwaner Mts. *Borneo* **48** D7
Schweinfurt *Germany, W.* **34** C3
Schwerin *Germany, E.* **34** C2
Schwyz *Switzerland* **37** C1
Scilly, Is. of *England* **17** B6
Scole *England* **27** J2
Scone *Scotland* **29** E4
Scoresby Ld. *Greenland* **11** K1
Scoresbysund *Greenland* **11** K1
Scotia Sea *Antarctica* **80** A9
Scotland *British Isles* **16** C3
Scott I. *Antarctica* **80** N8
Scott Reef *Timor Sea* **76** C1
Scott City *Kansas* **68** C3
Scottsbluff *Nebraska* **68** C2
Scottsdale *Tasmania* **77** H7
Scourie *Scotland* **28** C2
Scrabster *Scotland* **28** E2
Scranton *Pennsylvania* **65** L2
Scunthorpe *England* **17** E5
Scutari *Albania* **39** E3
Scutari *Turkey* **41** L3
Scutari, L. *Yugoslavia* **38** E3
Seaford *England* **27** H4
Seaham *England* **25** D2
Seal L., Upr. & Lr. *Quebec* **63** U6
Searcy *Arkansas* **68** E3
Seaton *England* **26** D4
Seattle *Washington* **64** B1
Sebha *Libya* **57** D2
Sechura Des. *Peru* **72** A5
Secretary I. *New Zealand* **79** A6
Secunderabad *India* **53** L7
Sedalia *Missouri* **65** H3
Sedan *France* **33** D2
Sedbergh *England* **25** C2
Seddonville *New Zealand* **79** C4
Sedgefield *England* **25** D2
Ségou *Mali* **57** B3
Segovia *Spain* **36** C2
Séguéla *Ivory Coast* **57** B4
Seinäjoki *Finland* **42** E3
Seine, R. *France* **33** C2
Seistan, reg. *Afghan.-Iran* **52** H4
Sekondi-Takoradi *Ghana* **57** B4
Selby *England* **25** D3
Selenga, R. *Mongolia-U.S.S.R.* **48** C2
Selenginsk *U.S.S.R.* **47** L3
Selestat *France* **33** E2
Selfoss *Iceland* **42** J7
Selima Oasis *Sudan* **58** B2
Selkirk *Manitoba* **63** P7
Selkirk *Scotland* **16** D4
Selkirk Ra. *Br. Columbia, etc.* **62** L7
Selma *Alabama* **65** J4
Selsey Bill *England* **17** E6
Selsöyvik *Norway* **42** C2
Selvas *Brazil* **72** D5
Selwyn *Queensland* **77** G3
Selwyn Mts. *Yukon* **62** H5
Selwyn Ra. *Queensland* **77** F3
Semara *Sp. Sahara* **57** A2
Semarang *Java* **48** D7
Semidi Is. *Alaska* **62** C6
Semipalatinsk *Kazakh.* **46** J3
Semmering Pass *Austria* **41** G2
Semojovel de Allende *Mexico* **70** F4
Sena *Mozambique* **59** D2
Sendai *Japan* **48** G3
Senegal *W. Africa* **57** A3
Sénégal, R. *Mauritania-Senegal* **57** A3
Senhor do Bonfim *Brazil* **72** J6
Senigallia *Italy* **38** C3
Senj *Yugoslavia* **38** C2
Senja, I. *Norway* **42** D1
Senlis *France* **33** C2
Sennar *Sudan* **52** B8
Sennar Dam *Sudan* **58** C3
Sennen *England* **26** B4
Senta *Yugoslavia* **39** E2
Seoul *Korea* **48** E3
Sept Iles *Quebec* **63** V7
Seraing *Belgium* **32** D4
Seram I. & Sea *Indonesia* **48** E7
Serbia *Yugoslavia* **39** F3
Serowe *Bechuanaland* **59** C3
Serpa Pinto *Angola* **59** B2
Serpukhov *U.S.S.R.* **43** E1
Serrai *Greece* **39** F4
Sesfontein *S.W. Africa* **59** B2
Setana *Japan* **49** D3
Sète *France* **33** D5
Settle *England* **25** C2
Setubal *Portugal* **36** B3
Seul, L. *Ontario* **63** Q7
Sevastopol *Ukraine* **46** D4
Sevenoaks *England* **27** H3
Severn, R. *Eng.-Wales* **17** D6
Severn R. *Ontario* **63** R7
Severnaya Zemlya, Is. *U.S.S.R.* **47** K1
Sevier L. *Utah* **64** D3
Seville *Spain* **36** C4
Seward Pen. *Alaska* **62** A4
Seychelles, Is. *Indian Oc.* **11** M5
Seydhisfjördhur *Iceland* **42** L6
Seymchan *U.S.S.R.* **47** Q2
Sézanne *France* **33** D2
Sezze *Italy* **38** C4
Sfax *Tunisia* **57** D1
Sgurr Mor, mt. *Scotland* **28** C3
Shabani *Rhodesia* **59** D3
Shackleton Ice Shelf *Antarctica* **80** H8
Shaftesbury *England* **27** E3
Shāhābād *Iran* **55** J2
Shāhīn Dezh *Iran* **55** J1
Shahjahanpur *India* **53** M5
Shahreza *Iran* **52** F4
Shahrud *Iran* **52** G3
Shahsien *China* **51** K6
Sham, Jebel, mts. *Muscat & Oman* **52** G6
Shāmīyah, des. *Iraq-Syria* **54** E2
Shamva *Rhodesia* **59** D2
Shangchih *China* **51** M2
Shanghai *China* **48** E3
Shanklin *England* **27** F4
Shannon *Eire* **17** A5
Shannon, R. *Eire* **17** A5
Shantung Pen. *China* **48** E3
Shap *England* **25** C2
Shapinsay, I. *Scotland* **28** F1
Shaqra *Saudi Arabia* **52** E5
Sharangad *Mongolia* **50** H2
Sharasume *Sinkiang* **53** N1
Shark B. *W. Australia* **76** A4
Sharya *U.S.S.R.* **43** G1
Shasta, Mt. *California* **64** B2
Shat al Arab, R. *Iraq* **52** E5
Shawnee *Oklahoma* **64** G3

Sheboygan	*Wisconsin*	**65**	J2
Sheenjek R.	*Alaska*	**62**	F4
Sheep Haven	*Eire*	**17**	B4
Sheerness	*England*	**17**	F6
Sheffield	*England*	**17**	E5
Shefford	*England*	**27**	G2
Sheklung	*China*	**51**	J7
Shelby	*Montana*	**64**	D1
Shelekhova, G. of	*U.S.S.R.*	**47**	Q3
Shelford	*England*	**27**	H2
Shelikof Str.	*Alaska*	**62**	C6
Shenyang	*China*	**48**	E2
Shepparton	*Victoria*	**77**	H6
Sheppey, I. of	*England*	**17**	F6
Shepton Mallet	*England*	**26**	E3
Sherborne	*England*	**26**	E4
Sherbrooke	*Quebec*	**63**	U8
Sheridan	*Wyoming*	**64**	E2
Sheringham	*England*	**27**	J2
Sherman	*Texas*	**68**	D4
Sherwood	*Texas*	**64**	F4
Shiant Is.	*Scotland*	**28**	B3
Shibeli R.	*Ethiopia-Somalia*	**58**	D4
Shibetsu	*Japan*	**49**	E3
Shickshock Mts.	*Quebec*	**63**	V8
Shiel, L.	*Scotland*	**16**	C3
Shieldaig	*Scotland*	**28**	C3
Shifnal	*England*	**26**	E2
Shigatse	*Tibet*	**50**	D6
Shihkiachwang	*China*	**51**	J4
Shihr	*E. Aden*	**52**	E8
Shihwei	*China*	**51**	L1
Shikarpur	*W. Pakistan*	**52**	J5
Shikoku, I.	*Japan*	**48**	F3
Shilka R.	*U.S.S.R.*	**47**	M3
Shillelagh	*Eire*	**17**	B5
Shillong	*India*	**53**	O5
Shimonoseki	*Japan*	**48**	E3
Shimo Yubetsu	*Japan*	**49**	E3
Shin, L.	*Scotland*	**16**	C2
Shinyanga	*Tanzania*	**58**	C5
Shipdham	*England*	**27**	H2
Shipka Pass	*Bulgaria*	**39**	G3
Shipki Pass	*Tibet*	**53**	L4
Shipley	*England*	**25**	D3
Shipston	*England*	**27**	F2
Shiraz	*Iran*	**52**	F5
Shire, R.	*Malawi*	**59**	D2
Shiukwan	*China*	**48**	D4
Shoeburyness	*England*	**27**	H3
Sholapur	*India*	**53**	L7
Shoreham-by-Sea	*England*	**27**	G4
Shoshone	*Idaho*	**64**	D2
Shoshone Mts.	*Nevada*	**67**	C4
Shota Kuduk	*Sinkiang*	**50**	B3
Shotley	*England*	**27**	J3
Shreveport	*Louisiana*	**65**	H4
Shrewsbury	*England*	**17**	D5
Shropshire, co.	*England*	**17**	D5
Shu'aiba,	*Iraq*	**55**	J4
Shuangtzeno	*China*	**51**	M2
Shuqra	*S. Arabia*	**52**	E8
Shushtar	*Iran*	**52**	E4
Shuswap, L.	*Br. Columbia*	**62**	L7
Shwangliao	*China*	**51**	L3
Shwebo	*Burma*	**53**	P6
Siakwan	*China*	**50**	G6
Sialkot	*W. Pakistan*	**53**	L4
Siam (Thailand)	*S.E. Asia*	**53**	Q7
Siam, G. of	*S.E. Asia*	**53**	Q8
Sian	*China*	**48**	C3
Siangfan	*China*	**51**	J5
Siangtan	*China*	**48**	D4
Siangyang	*China*	**51**	J5
Šiauliai	*Lithuania*	**42**	E5
Sibenik	*Yugoslavia*	**38**	D3
Siberia	*U.S.S.R.*	**46**	H2
Sibiu	*Rumania*	**39**	G2
Sibolga	*Sumatra*	**48**	B6
Sichang	*China*	**50**	G6
Sicilian Chan.	*S. Europe*	**38**	C6
Sicily, I.	*Italy*	**38**	C6
Siderno	*Italy*	**38**	D5
Sidi Ifni	*Ifni*	**57**	A2
Sidlaw Hills	*Scotland*	**29**	E4
Sidmouth	*England*	**26**	D4
Sidney	*Nebraska*	**64**	F2
Sidon	*Lebanon*	**54**	C3
Sidra, G. of	*Libya*	**58**	A1
Siedlce	*Poland*	**35**	G2
Siem Reap	*Cambodia*	**53**	Q8
Siena	*Italy*	**38**	B3
Sieradz	*Poland*	**35**	F3
Sierra Leone	*W. Africa*	**57**	A4
Sierra Madre Plat.	*New Mexico*	**64**	E4
Sierra Mojada	*Mexico*	**70**	D2
Sierra Morena, mts.	*Spain*	**36**	C3
Sierra Nevada, mts.	*Spain*	**36**	C4
Sierra Nevada, mts.	*U.S.A.*	**64**	B2
Sighet	*Rumania*	**35**	G5
Sighisoara	*Rumania*	**35**	H5
Siglufjördhur	*Iceland*	**42**	K6
Sikasso	*Mali*	**57**	B3
Sikhote Alin, mts.	*U.S.S.R.*	**47**	O4
Si Kiang, R.	*China*	**48**	D4
Sikkim	*S. Asia*	**53**	N5
Siktyakh	*U.S.S.R.*	**47**	N2
Silchar	*India*	**53**	O6
Silinhot	*China*	**51**	K3
Silistra	*Bulgaria*	**39**	H2
Silloth	*England*	**17**	D4
Silva Porto	*Angola*	**59**	B2
Silver City	*New Mexico*	**67**	E5
Silverton	*Colorado*	**64**	E3
Silverton	*New South Wales*	**78**	C5
Simcoe, L.	*Ontario*	**63**	T9
Simferopol	*Ukraine*	**46**	D4
Simla	*India*	**53**	L4
Simleu Silvaniei	*Rumania*	**35**	G5
Simplon Pass	*Switzerland*	**37**	B1
Simpson Des.	*N. Terr., Aust., etc.*	**77**	F4
Simushir, I.	*Kuril Is.*	**47**	Q4
Sinai, Mt.	*Egypt*	**52**	B5
Sinai Pen.	*Egypt*	**54**	B5
Sinaloa	*Mexico*	**70**	C2
Sinclair's B.	*Scotland*	**16**	D2
Sind	*W. Pakistan*	**52**	J5
Singa	*Sudan*	**58**	C3
Singapore	*Malaysia*	**48**	C6
Singsingsia	*Sinkiang*	**50**	F3
Singtai	*China*	**51**	J4
Sinhsien	*China*	**51**	J4
Sinhwa	*China*	**51**	J6
Sining	*China*	**50**	G4
Sinkiang	*China*	**53**	M2
Sinop	*Turkey*	**52**	C2
Sinsiang	*China*	**51**	J4
Sinuiji	*Korea*	**51**	L3
Sinyang	*China*	**51**	J5
Sion	*Switzerland*	**37**	B1
Sioux City	*Iowa*	**64**	G2
Sioux Falls	*S. Dakota*	**64**	G2
Sioux Lookout	*Ontario*	**63**	Q7
Siple, Mt.	*Antarctica*	**80**	Q7
Sir Darya, R.	*Kazakh., etc.*	**46**	G4
Sir Edward Pellew Group, Is.	*N. Terr., Aust.*	**77**	F2
Siret R.	*Rumania, etc.*	**35**	J5
Sirḫān, Wādī as	*Saudi Arabia*	**54**	E4
Sirjan	*Iran*	**52**	G5
Siros & I.	*Greece*	**39**	G6
Sirte	*Libya*	**57**	D1
Sishen	*Cape of Good Hope*	**59**	C3
Sisteron	*France*	**33**	D4
Sitka	*Alaska*	**62**	G6
Sittingbourne	*England*	**27**	H3
Sivas	*Turkey*	**52**	C3
Siwa	*Egypt*	**58**	B2
Siwalik Ra.	*India*	**53**	L4
Siwuchu	*China*	**51**	K3
Sixmilebridge	*Eire*	**31**	C5
Skagerrak, chan.	*Den.-Norway*	**42**	A4
Skagway	*Alaska*	**62**	G6
Skaw, The, pt.	*Denmark*	**42**	B4
Skeena R.	*Br. Columbia*	**62**	J7
Skegness	*England*	**17**	F5
Skelleftea	*Sweden*	**42**	E2
Skerries	*Eire*	**30**	E4
Skerryvore, I.	*Scotland*	**16**	B3
Skibbereen	*Eire*	**17**	A6
Skiddaw, mt.	*England*	**17**	D4
Skien	*Norway*	**42**	B4
Skipsea	*England*	**25**	E3
Skipton	*England*	**17**	D5
Skiros, I.	*Greece*	**39**	G5
Skomer I.	*Wales*	**26**	B3
Skopje	*Yugoslavia*	**39**	F3
Skövde	*Sweden*	**42**	C4
Skovorodino	*U.S.S.R.*	**47**	N3
Skye, I.	*Scotland*	**16**	B3
Slagelse	*Denmark*	**42**	B5
Slaithwaite	*England*	**25**	D3
Slane	*Eire*	**30**	E4
Slaney, R.	*Eire*	**31**	E5
Slave R.	*Alberta-N.-W. Terr.*	**62**	M5
Slavgorod	*U.S.S.R.*	**46**	H3
Slavonia	*Yugoslavia*	**38**	D2
Slavyansk	*Ukraine*	**43**	E3
Sleaford	*England*	**17**	E5
Sleat, Sd. of	*Scotland*	**16**	C3
Sleeper Is.	*N.-W. Terr., Can.*	**63**	S6
Slieve Aughty Mts.	*Eire*	**17**	A5
Slieve Bernagh, mts.	*Eire*	**31**	C5
Slieve Bloom Mts.	*Eire*	**31**	D4
Slieve Donard, mt.	*N. Ireland*	**30**	F3
Sligachan	*Scotland*	**28**	B3
Sligo & B.	*Eire*	**17**	A4
Slioch, mt.	*Scotland*	**28**	C3
Sliven	*Bulgaria*	**39**	G3
Slough	*England*	**27**	G3
Slovakia	*Czechoslovakia*	**35**	F4
Slovenia	*Yugoslavia*	**38**	C2
Słupsk	*Poland*	**35**	E1
Sma' Glen	*Scotland*	**29**	E4
Smethwick	*England*	**27**	E2
Smith Sd.	*N.-W. Terr., Can.*	**63**	T2
Smith River	*Br. Columbia*	**62**	J6
Smithton	*Tasmania*	**77**	G7
Smoky Hill R.	*Kansas*	**64**	F3
Smolensk	*U.S.S.R.*	**46**	D3
Smyrna	*Turkey*	**39**	H5
Snæfell, mt.	*Iceland*	**42**	L6
Snæfell, mt.	*Isle of Man*	**17**	C4
Snæfells-Jökull, mt.	*Iceland*	**42**	J6
Snaith	*England*	**25**	D3
Snake R.	*Idaho-Wash.*	**64**	D2
Sneek	*Netherlands*	**32**	D1
Sneem	*Eire*	**31**	B6
Snizort, L.	*Scotland*	**16**	B3
Snöhetta, mt.	*Norway*	**42**	B3
Snowdon, mt.	*Wales*	**17**	C5
Snowdrift	*N.-W. Terr., Can.*	**62**	M5
Snowy Mts.	*New South Wales*	**77**	H6
Snyder	*Texas*	**68**	C4
Soalala	*Malagasy Rep.*	**59**	E2
Soay, I.	*Scotland*	**28**	B3
Sobat R.	*Sudan*	**58**	C4
Society Is.	*Pacific Oc.*	**10**	E5
Socorro	*New Mexico*	**64**	E4
Socorro, I.	*Mexico*	**70**	B4
Socotra I.	*Arabian Sea*	**52**	F8
Sodankyla	*Finland*	**42**	F2
Soddu	*Ethiopia*	**58**	C4
Söderhamn	*Sweden*	**42**	D3
Södertälje	*Sweden*	**42**	D4
Sofia	*Bulgaria*	**39**	F3
Sogne Fd.	*Norway*	**42**	A3
Soham	*England*	**27**	H2
Soho-ri	*Korea*	**51**	M3
Soissons	*France*	**33**	D2
Sokode	*Togo*	**57**	C4
Sokolka	*Poland*	**35**	G2
Sokota	*Ethiopia*	**58**	C3
Sokoto	*Nigeria*	**57**	C3
Solent, str.	*England*	**17**	E6
Solihull	*England*	**27**	F2
Solimões (Amazon) R.	*Brazil*	**72**	E4
Solleftea	*Sweden*	**42**	D3
Solomon Is.	*Pacific Oc.*	**10**	D5
Solothurn	*Switzerland*	**37**	B1
Soltau	*Germany, W.*	**34**	C2
Solund	*Norway*	**42**	A3
Solway Firth	*Scot.-Eng.*	**17**	D4
Solwezi	*Zambia*	**59**	C2
Somalia	*E. Africa*	**58**	D4
Sombor	*Yugoslavia*	**38**	E2
Sombrerete	*Mexico*	**70**	D3
Somerset, co.	*England*	**17**	D6
Somerset I.	*N.-W. Terr., Can.*	**63**	P3
Somerton	*England*	**26**	E3
Somme, R.	*France*	**33**	C2
Sondre Strömfjord	*Greenland*	**63**	Y4
Sondrio	*Italy*	**38**	B1
Songea	*Tanzania*	**59**	D2
Songkhla	*Thailand*	**53**	Q9
Songkoi R.	*China-Vietnam*	**53**	Q6
Sonora, R.	*Mexico*	**70**	B2
Sonsonate	*Salvador*	**70**	G5
Soo Canals	*Canada-U.S.A.*	**65**	K1
Soochow	*China*	**48**	E3
Sopley	*England*	**27**	F4
Sopron	*Hungary*	**34**	E5
Sorel	*Quebec*	**63**	U8
Sorell	*Tasmania*	**77**	H7
Soria	*Spain*	**36**	D2
Sorocaba	*Brazil*	**73**	H8
Soroti	*Uganda*	**58**	C4
Söröya, I.	*Norway*	**42**	E1
Sorsele	*Sweden*	**42**	D2
Sosnowiec	*Poland*	**35**	F3
Soudan	*N. Terr., Aust.*	**77**	F3
Souris	*Manitoba*	**62**	O8
Souris R.	*Sask.-N. Dakota*	**64**	F1
Sourton	*England*	**26**	C4
Sousa	*Brazil*	**72**	K5
South Africa, Rep. of	*Africa*	**59**	B4
Southam	*England*	**27**	F2
Southampton	*England*	**17**	E6
Southampton, C.	*N.-W. Terr., Can.*	**63**	S5
Southampton I.	*N.-W. Terr., Can.*	**63**	R5
South Arabia, Fed. of	*S.W. Asia*	**52**	E8
South Auckland	*New Zealand*	**79**	E2
South Australia, state	*Australia*	**76**	E5
South Bend	*Indiana*	**65**	J2
Southborough	*England*	**27**	H3
Southbridge	*New Zealand*	**79**	D5
South Carolina, state	*U.S.A.*	**65**	K4
South Cave	*England*	**25**	E3
South China Highlands	*China*	**48**	D4
South China Sea	*S.E. Asia*	**48**	D5
South Dakota, state	*U.S.A.*	**64**	F2
South Downs, hills	*England*	**17**	E6
Southend	*England*	**17**	F6
Southern Alps, mts.	*New Zealand*	**79**	B6
Southern Cross	*W. Australia*	**76**	B5
Southern Uplands	*Scotland*	**29**	D5
South Foreland	*England*	**27**	J3
South Georgia, I.	*S. Atlantic Oc.*	**73**	K14
South Holland	*Netherlands*	**32**	C2
South Indian L.	*Manitoba*	**63**	P6
South Island	*New Zealand*	**79**	B5
Southland	*New Zealand*	**79**	A6
Southminster	*England*	**27**	H3
South Molton	*England*	**26**	D3
South Orkneys, Is.	*Antarctica*	**80**	A9
South Otterington	*England*	**25**	D2
South Platte R.	*Colorado*	**64**	F2
Southport	*England*	**17**	D5
Southport	*Queensland*	**77**	J4
South Ronaldsay, I.	*Scotland*	**16**	D2
South Sandwich Is.	*S. Atlantic Oc.*	**11**	K7
South Saskatchewan R.	*Alberta-Sask.*	**62**	M7
South Shetlands, Is.	*Antarctica*	**80**	A9
South Shields	*England*	**17**	E4
South Taranaki Bight	*New Zealand*	**79**	D3
South Uist, I.	*Scotland*	**16**	B3
Southwell	*England*	**27**	G1
South West C.	*New Zealand*	**79**	A7
South West Africa	*Africa*	**59**	B3
South Willingham	*England*	**25**	E3
Southwold	*England*	**27**	J2
Sovetsk	*U.S.S.R.*	**42**	E5
Sovetskaya Gavan	*U.S.S.R.*	**47**	O4
Spa	*Belgium*	**32**	D4
Spain	*S.W. Europe*	**36**	C2
Spalding	*England*	**17**	E5
Spandau	*Germany*	**34**	D2
Spanish Sahara	*N.W. Africa*	**57**	A2
Spanish Town	*Jamaica*	**71**	J4
Sparks	*Nevada*	**67**	C4
Sparta	*Greece*	**41**	J4
Spartanburg	*S. Carolina*	**69**	G4
Spean Bridge	*Scotland*	**29**	D4
Spence Bay	*N.-W. Terr., Canada*	**63**	Q4
Spencer	*Iowa*	**68**	D2
Spencer G.	*S. Australia*	**77**	F5
Spennymoor	*England*	**25**	D2
Sperrin Mts.	*N. Ireland*	**17**	B4
Spey, R.	*Scotland*	**16**	D3
Speyer	*Germany, W.*	**34**	B4
Spezia	*Italy*	**38**	B2
Spilsby	*England*	**27**	H1
Spinazzolala	*Italy*	**38**	D4
Spithead	*England*	**27**	F4
Spitsbergen, I.	*Arctic Oc.*	**46**	B1
Spittal	*Austria*	**34**	D5
Spittal	*England*	**25**	D1
Split	*Yugoslavia*	**38**	D3
Splugen & Pass	*Switzerland*	**37**	C1
Spokane	*Washington*	**64**	C1
Spoleto	*Italy*	**38**	C3
Sporades, Is.	*Greece*	**39**	G6
Spree, R.	*Germany, E.*	**34**	D2
Springbok	*Cape of Good Hope*	**59**	B3
Springer	*New Mexico*	**67**	F4
Springfield	*Illinois*	**65**	J3
Springfield	*Massachusetts*	**66**	E2
Springfield	*Missouri*	**65**	H3
Springfield	*Ohio*	**65**	K3
Springfield	*Oregon*	**67**	B3
Springfield	*Vermont*	**66**	E2
Springsure	*Queensland*	**77**	H3

Springville	*Utah*	**67**	D3
Spurn Hd.	*England*	**17**	F5
Sredne Kolymsk	*U.S.S.R.*	**47**	Q2
Sretensk	*U.S.S.R.*	**47**	M3
Srinagar	*Kashmir*	**53**	L4
Stack Skerry, I.	*Scotland*	**16**	C2
Stadskanaal	*Netherlands*	**32**	E1
Staffa, I.	*Scotland*	**16**	B3
Stafford	*England*	**17**	D5
Staines	*England*	**27**	G3
Stainmore Gap	*England*	**25**	C2
Stalbridge	*England*	**26**	E4
Stalham	*England*	**27**	J2
Stamford	*Connecticut*	**66**	E3
Stamford	*England*	**27**	G2
Stanger	*Natal*	**59**	D3
Stanke Dimitrov	*Bulgaria*	**39**	F3
Stanley	*Falkland Is.*	**73**	F14
Stanley Falls	*Congo*	**58**	B4
Stanley Pool	*Congo*	**59**	B1
Stanleyville	*Congo*	**58**	B4
Stanovoy Mts.	*U.S.S.R.*	**47**	N3
Stans	*Switzerland*	**37**	C1
Stansmore Ra.	*W. Australia*	**76**	D3
Stanthorpe	*Queensland*	**77**	J4
Stanton	*N.-W. Terr., Can.*	**62**	J4
Staraya Russa	*U.S.S.R.*	**43**	D1
Stara Zagora	*Bulgaria*	**39**	G3
Starbuck I.	*Pacific Oc.*	**10**	E5
Stargard	*Poland*	**34**	E2
Starobelsk	*Ukraine*	**43**	E3
Start B.	*England*	**26**	D4
Start Pt.	*England*	**17**	D6
Stassfurt	*Germany, E.*	**34**	C3
Staten I.	*New York*	**66**	D3
Staunton	*Virginia*	**65**	L3
Stavanger	*Norway*	**42**	A4
Staveley	*England*	**27**	F1
Staveren	*Netherlands*	**32**	D2
Stavropol	*U.S.S.R.*	**46**	E4
Stawell	*Victoria*	**78**	D8
Steamboat Springs	*Colorado*	**67**	E3
Steelton	*Pennsylvania*	**66**	C3
Steinkjer	*Norway*	**42**	B2
Stellenbosch	*C. of Good Hope*	**59**	B4
Stendal	*Germany, E.*	**34**	C2
Stenness, L. of	*Scotland*	**28**	E1
Stensele	*Sweden*	**42**	D2
Stephenville	*Newfoundland*	**63**	X8
Sterea	*Greece*	**39**	F5
Sterling	*Colorado*	**67**	F3
Steubenville	*Ohio*	**69**	G2
Stevenage	*England*	**17**	E6
Stewart	*Br. Columbia*	**62**	J6
Stewart I.	*New Zealand*	**79**	A7
Stewarton	*Scotland*	**29**	D5
Stewart River	*Yukon*	**62**	G5
Steyning	*England*	**27**	G4
Steyr	*Austria*	**34**	D4
Stikine R.	*Alaska-B.C.*	**62**	H6
Stillwater	*Oklahoma*	**68**	D3
Stirling	*Scotland*	**16**	D3
Stirling Ra.	*Western Australia*	**76**	B5
Stockbridge	*England*	**27**	F3
Stockholm	*Sweden*	**42**	D4
Stockport	*England*	**17**	D5
Stockton	*California*	**64**	B3
Stockton	*England*	**17**	E4
Stoke Ferry	*England*	**27**	H2
Stoke-on-Trent	*England*	**17**	D5
Stokesley	*England*	**25**	D2
Stone	*England*	**27**	E2
Stonehaven	*Scotland*	**16**	D3
Stonehenge	*England*	**27**	F3
Stoneykirk	*Scotland*	**29**	D6
Stony Rapids	*Saskatchewan*	**62**	N6
Stony Stratford	*England*	**27**	G2
Stora Lulevatten, L.	*Sweden*	**42**	D2
Stora Sjöfallets Nat. Pk.	*Sweden*	**42**	D2
Stornoway	*Scotland*	**16**	B2
Storr, The, hill	*Scotland*	**28**	B3
Storsjön, L.	*Sweden*	**42**	C3
Storuman, L.	*Sweden*	**42**	D2
Stour, R.	*Dorset, England*	**17**	D6
Stour, R.	*Kent, England*	**17**	F6
Stourbridge	*England*	**27**	E2
Stourport	*England*	**27**	E2
Stow	*Scotland*	**29**	F5
Stowmarket	*England*	**27**	J2
Stow-on-the-Wold	*England*	**27**	F3
Strabane	*N. Ireland*	**17**	B4
Stradbally	*Eire*	**31**	D4
Stradbroke	*England*	**27**	J2
Strahan	*Tasmania*	**77**	H7
Straiton	*Scotland*	**29**	D5
Stralsund	*Germany, E.*	**34**	D1
Strangford	*N. Ireland*	**30**	F3
Strangford L.	*N. Ireland*	**17**	C4
Strangways Springs	*S. Aust.*	**77**	F4
Stranorlar	*Eire*	**30**	D3
Stranraer	*Scotland*	**17**	C4
Strasbourg	*France*	**33**	E2
Stratford	*New Zealand*	**79**	E3
Stratford on Avon	*England*	**17**	E5
Strathaven	*Scotland*	**29**	D5
Strath Carron, valley	*Scotland*	**28**	D3
Strathmore, valley	*Scotland*	**29**	E4
Strathpeffer	*Scotland*	**28**	D3
Strath Spey, valley	*Scotland*	**28**	E3
Strathyre	*Scotland*	**29**	D4
Stratton	*England*	**26**	C4
Straubing	*Germany, W.*	**34**	D4
Streaky Bay	*S. Australia*	**77**	E5
Street	*England*	**26**	E3
Strensall	*England*	**25**	D2
Strichen	*Scotland*	**28**	F3
Strokestown	*Eire*	**30**	C4
Stroma, I.	*Scotland*	**28**	E2
Stromboli, I.	*Lipari Is.*	**38**	D5
Stromeferry	*Scotland*	**28**	C3
Stromness	*Scotland*	**16**	D2
Strömö, I.	*Faeroes*	**42**	M8
Stromsund	*Sweden*	**42**	C3
Stronsay, I.	*Scotland*	**16**	D2
Stroud	*England*	**27**	E3
Struan	*Scotland*	**29**	E4
Struma, R.	*Bulgaria-Greece*	**39**	F4
Strumble Hd.	*Wales*	**17**	C5
Strzyzów	*Poland*	**35**	G4
Stuart Highway	*N. Terr., Aust.*	**77**	E2
Stuart L.	*Br. Columbia*	**62**	K7
Stuart Ra.	*S. Australia*	**77**	E4
Sturminster Newton	*England*	**26**	E4
Sturt Cr.	*W. Australia*	**76**	D2
Sturt Des.	*Qnsld.-S. Aust.*	**77**	G4
Stuttgart	*Germany, W.*	**34**	C4
Stykkishólmur	*Iceland*	**42**	J6
Suakin	*Sudan*	**58**	C3
Suanhwa	*China*	**51**	K3
Subotica	*Yugoslavia*	**39**	E1
Suceava	*Rumania*	**35**	H5
Suck, R.	*Eire*	**17**	A5
Sucre	*Bolivia*	**72**	D7
Sudan	*N.E. Africa*	**58**	B3
Sudbury	*England*	**27**	H2
Sudbury	*Ontario*	**63**	S8
Sudd, reg.	*Sudan*	**58**	B4
Sudety, mts.	*Poland, etc.*	**34**	D3
Suez	*Egypt*	**58**	C1
Suez Can.	*Egypt*	**58**	C1
Suez, G. of	*Egypt*	**54**	B5
Suffolk, co.	*England*	**17**	F5
Sugluk	*Quebec*	**63**	T5
Sugsundong Gompa	*Tibet*	**50**	E5
Suhl	*Germany, E.*	**34**	C3
Suihwa	*China*	**51**	M2
Suilven, mt.	*Scotland*	**28**	C2
Suir, R.	*Eire*	**17**	B5
Suiteh	*China*	**50**	H4
Sukarnapura	*W. Irian*	**48**	G7
Sukarno, Pk.	*W. Irian*	**48**	F7
Sukhona, R.	*U.S.S.R.*	**46**	E2
Sukhumi	*Georgia*	**46**	E4
Sukkertoppen	*Greenland*	**63**	Y4
Sula Is.	*Indonesia*	**48**	E7
Sulaiman Mts.	*W. Pakistan*	**53**	J4
Sulaimiya	*Saudi Arabia*	**52**	E6
Sula Sgeir, I.	*Scotland*	**28**	B1
Sulaymāniyah	*Iraq*	**55**	H2
Sule Skerry, I.	*Scotland*	**16**	C2
Sulina	*Rumania*	**39**	H2
Sulisker, I.	*Scotland*	**16**	B2
Sulitjelma, mt.	*Sweden*	**42**	D2
Sullivan, L.	*Alberta*	**62**	M7
Sulu Arch.	*Philippines*	**48**	E6
Sulu Sea	*Philippines*	**48**	D6
Sulzberger B.	*Antarctica*	**80**	O7
Sumatra, I.	*Indonesia*	**48**	B6
Sumba, I.	*Indonesia*	**48**	D7
Sumbawa, I.	*Indonesia*	**48**	D7
Sümber	*Mongolia*	**50**	H2
Sumburgh Hd.	*Scotland*	**16**	E2
Summer Is.	*Scotland*	**28**	C2
Sumter	*S. Carolina*	**69**	G4
Sumy	*Ukraine*	**43**	D2
Sunart, L.	*Scotland*	**29**	C4
Sunda Str.	*Indonesia*	**48**	C7
Sundance	*Wyoming*	**64**	F2
Sundarbans	*India-E. Pakistan*	**53**	N6
Sunderland	*England*	**17**	E4
Sundsvall	*Sweden*	**42**	D3
Sungari, R.	*China*	**48**	E2
Superior	*Wisconsin*	**65**	H1
Superior, L.	*U.S.A.-Canada*	**65**	J1
Sur	*Muscat & Oman*	**52**	G6
Surabaja	*Java*	**48**	D7
Surat	*India*	**53**	K6
Surat Thani	*Thailand*	**53**	P9
Surgut	*U.S.S.R.*	**46**	H2
Suri	*India*	**50**	D7
Surinam (Neth. Guiana)	*S. America*	**72**	F3
Surrey, co.	*England*	**17**	E6
Sursee	*Switzerland*	**37**	C1
Susa	*Italy*	**38**	A2
Susa	*Tunisia*	**57**	D1
Sušak	*Yugoslavia*	**38**	C2
Susitna R.	*Alaska*	**62**	D5
Sussex, co.	*England*	**17**	E6
Sussex, Vale of	*England*	**27**	H4
Sutherland, co.	*Scotland*	**16**	C2
Sutherland Falls	*New Zealand*	**79**	B6
Sutlej R.	*India-Pakistan*	**53**	K5
Sutton	*Cambridge, Eng.*	**27**	H2
Sutton	*Surrey, Eng.*	**27**	G3
Sutton	*Yorks, Eng.*	**25**	E3
Sutton Coldfield	*England*	**27**	F2
Sutton-on-Sea	*England*	**25**	F3
Suva	*Fiji Is.*	**10**	D5
Suvorov I.	*Pacific Oc.*	**10**	E5
Suwałki	*Poland*	**35**	G1
Suweidiya, Es	*Syria*	**52**	C4
Svalbard, Is.	*Arctic Oc.*	**46**	C1
Svartenhuk Pen.	*Greenland*	**63**	X3
Sveg	*Sweden*	**42**	C3
Sverdlovsk	*U.S.S.R.*	**46**	G3
Sverdrup Is.	*N.-W. Terr., Can.*	**63**	P2
Svishtov	*Bulgaria*	**39**	G3
Svitavy	*Czechoslovakia*	**34**	E4
Svolvær	*Norway*	**42**	C1
Swadlincote	*England*	**27**	F2
Swakopmund	*S.W. Africa*	**59**	B3
Swale, R.	*England*	**17**	E4
Swaledale	*England*	**25**	C2
Swan R.	*W. Australia*	**76**	B5
Swanage	*England*	**27**	F4
Swan Hill	*Victoria*	**77**	G6
Swansea	*Tasmania*	**77**	H7
Swansea & B.	*Wales*	**17**	D6
Swanton	*Vermont*	**66**	E1
Swatow	*China*	**48**	D4
Swaziland	*S. Africa*	**59**	D3
Sweden	*N.W. Europe*	**42**	C4
Sweetwater	*Texas*	**68**	C4
Swift Current	*Saskatchewan*	**62**	N7
Swilly, L.	*Eire*	**17**	B4
Swindon	*England*	**17**	E6
Swineshead	*England*	**27**	G2
Swinford	*Eire*	**30**	C4
Swinoujście	*Poland*	**34**	D2
Switzerland	*Europe*	**37**	B1
Swords	*Eire*	**31**	E4
Syasstroy	*U.S.S.R.*	**43**	D1
Syderö, I.	*Faeroes*	**42**	M9
Sydney	*New South Wales*	**77**	J5
Sydney	*Nova Scotia*	**63**	W8
Sydproven	*Greenland*	**63**	Z5
Syktyvkar	*U.S.S.R.*	**46**	F2
Sylhet	*E. Pakistan*	**53**	O6
Sylt	*Germany, W.*	**34**	B1
Symington	*Scotland*	**29**	E5
Syracuse	*New York*	**65**	L2
Syracuse	*Sicily*	**38**	D6
Syria	*S.W. Asia*	**52**	C4
Syrian Des.	*Saudi Arabia, etc.*	**52**	C4
Syston	*England*	**27**	F2
Syzran	*U.S.S.R.*	**43**	G2
Szczecin	*Poland*	**34**	D2
Szczecinek	*Poland*	**34**	E2
Szechwan	*China*	**53**	Q4
Szeged	*Hungary*	**35**	F5
Szemao	*China*	**50**	G7
Szentes	*Hungary*	**35**	F5
Szeping	*China*	**51**	L3
Szolnok	*Hungary*	**35**	F5
Szombathely	*Hungary*	**34**	E5
Tabora	*Tanzania*	**58**	C5
Tabou	*Ivory Coast*	**57**	B4
Tabriz	*Iran*	**52**	E3
Tacna	*Peru*	**72**	C7
Tacoma	*Washington*	**64**	B1
Tadcaster	*England*	**25**	D3
Tademait Plat.	*Algeria*	**57**	C2
Tadzhikistan (Tadzhik S.S.R.)	*U.S.S.R.*	**46**	H5
Taegu	*Korea*	**51**	M4
Taf, R.	*Wales*	**26**	C3
Taff, R.	*Wales*	**17**	D6
Taganrog	*U.S.S.R.*	**43**	E3
Tagus, R.	*Spain-Portugal*	**36**	B3
Tahakopa	*New Zealand*	**79**	B7
Tahat, mt.	*Algeria*	**57**	C2
Tahcheng	*Sinkiang*	**50**	C2
Tahiti, I.	*Pacific Oc.*	**10**	F5
Tahlequah	*Oklahoma*	**64**	G3
Tahoe L.	*California*	**64**	B3
Tahoua	*Niger*	**57**	C3
Taichung	*Taiwan*	**51**	L7
Taif	*Saudi Arabia*	**52**	D6
Taihape	*New Zealand*	**79**	E3
Tain	*Scotland*	**16**	C3
Tainan	*Taiwan*	**51**	L7
Taipei	*Taiwan*	**48**	E4
Taiping	*Malaya*	**53**	Q10
Taipingchwan	*China*	**51**	L3
Taishun	*China*	**51**	K6
Taital	*Chile*	**73**	C9
Taito Pen.	*Chile*	**73**	B13
Taitung	*Taiwan*	**51**	L7
Taivalkoski	*Finland*	**42**	G2
Taiwan (Formosa), I.	*E. Asia*	**48**	E4
Taiwan Str.	*China, etc.*	**48**	D4
Taiyuan	*China*	**51**	J4
Ta'izz	*Yemen*	**52**	D8
Takapuna	*New Zealand*	**79**	E2
Takla L.	*Br. Columbia*	**62**	J6
Takla Makan, des.	*Sinkiang*	**50**	B4
Talar Ra.	*W. Pakistan*	**52**	J5
Talara	*Peru*	**72**	A4
Talaud Is.	*Indonesia*	**48**	E6
Talavera de la Reina	*Spain*	**36**	C3
Talca	*Chile*	**73**	C11
Talcahuano	*Chile*	**73**	C11
Taldy Kurgan	*Kazakh.*	**46**	H4
Talgarth	*Wales*	**26**	D2
Tali	*China*	**50**	F6
Tali	*China*	**50**	H5
Tallahassee	*Florida*	**65**	K4
Tallangatta	*Victoria*	**78**	F8
Tallinn	*Estonia*	**46**	C3
Tallow	*Eire*	**31**	D5
Talybont	*Wales*	**26**	D2
Tamale	*Ghana*	**57**	B4
Tamanrasset	*Algeria*	**57**	C2
Tamar, R.	*England*	**17**	C6
Tamatave	*Malagasy Rep.*	**59**	E2
Tamazula	*Mexico*	**70**	C2
Tamazunchale	*Mexico*	**70**	E3
Tambacounda	*Senegal*	**57**	A3
Tambo	*Queensland*	**77**	H3
Tambov	*U.S.S.R.*	**46**	E3
Tammisaari	*Finland*	**42**	E3
Tampa & B.	*Florida*	**65**	K5
Tampere	*Finland*	**42**	E3
Tampico	*Mexico*	**70**	E3
Tamsag Bulag	*Mongolia*	**51**	K2
Tamsweg	*Austria*	**34**	D5
Tamworth	*England*	**27**	F2
Tamworth	*New South Wales*	**77**	J5
Tana Fd.	*Norway*	**42**	G1
Tana, L.	*Ethiopia*	**58**	C3
Tana, R.	*Kenya*	**58**	D5
Tana, R.	*Norway*	**42**	F1
Tanacross	*Alaska*	**62**	F5
Tanami	*N. Terr., Aust.*	**76**	D2
Tanana	*Alaska*	**62**	D4
Tanana R.	*Alaska*	**62**	E5
Tananarive	*Malagasy Rep.*	**59**	E2
Tandil	*Argentina*	**73**	F11
Tandjungselor	*Borneo*	**48**	D6
Tandragee	*N. Ireland*	**30**	E3
Taneatua	*New Zealand*	**79**	F3
Tanezrouft, reg.	*Algeria*	**57**	B2
Tanga	*Tanzania*	**58**	C5
Tanganyika, L.	*E. Africa*	**58**	B5
Tangier	*Morocco*	**57**	B1
Tangku	*China*	**51**	K4
Tanglha Ra.	*Tibet*	**50**	D5
Tangshan	*China*	**51**	K4
Tanimbar, I.	*Indonesia*	**48**	F7
Tannu-ola, mts.	*U.S.S.R.*	**47**	K3
Tanout	*Niger*	**57**	C3
Tanta	*Egypt*	**58**	C1
Tanzania	*E. Africa*	**59**	D1
Taodeni	*Mali*	**57**	B2
Taofu	*China*	**50**	G5
Taonan	*China*	**51**	L2
Tapachula	*Mexico*	**70**	F5
Tapajos R.	*Brazil*	**72**	F5
Tapanui	*New Zealand*	**79**	B6
Tapti, R.	*India*	**53**	K6
Tapuaenuku, mt.	*New Zealand*	**79**	D5
Tara	*Eire*	**17**	B5
Tara	*U.S.S.R.*	**46**	H3
Taradale	*New Zealand*	**79**	F3
Tarahumare, Sa., mts.	*Mexico*	**70**	C2

Taranaki	*New Zealand*	**79**	E3
Tarancon	*Spain*	**36**	D3
Taranto & G. of	*Italy*	**38**	D4
Tarascon	*France*	**33**	D5
Tarbert	*Argyll, Scotland*	**29**	C5
Tarbert	*Harris, Scotland*	**28**	B3
Tarbes	*France*	**33**	C5
Tarim, R.	*Sinkiang*	**50**	C3
Tarland	*Scotland*	**28**	F3
Tarleton	*England*	**25**	C3
Tarn, R.	*France*	**33**	C5
Tarnów	*Poland*	**35**	G3
Tarporley	*England*	**26**	E1
Tarragona	*Spain*	**36**	E2
Tarsus	*Turkey*	**52**	B3
Tartu	*Estonia*	**42**	F4
Tashkent	*Uzbek.*	**46**	G4
Tasman, Mt.	*New Zealand*	**79**	C5
Tasman Mts. & B.	*New Zealand*	**79**	D4
Tasman Sea	*Aust.-N.Z.*	**10**	D6
Tasmania, state & I.	*Australia*	**77**	H7
Tatar A.S.S.R.	*U.S.S.R.*	**43**	H1
Tatra, mts.	*Poland-Czech.*	**41**	H1
Tattershall	*England*	**27**	G1
Tatvan	*Turkey*	**52**	D3
Taunton	*England*	**17**	D6
Taunton	*Massachusetts*	**66**	F3
Taunus, mts.	*Germany, W.*	**34**	B3
Taupo, L.	*New Zealand*	**79**	E3
Taurage	*Lithuania*	**42**	E5
Tauranga	*New Zealand*	**79**	F2
Taurus Mts.	*Turkey*	**41**	L4
Tavistock	*England*	**17**	C6
Taw, R.	*England*	**26**	D4
Tawe, R.	*Wales*	**26**	D3
Tay, Firth of	*Scotland*	**16**	D3
Tay, L.	*Scotland*	**16**	C3
Tay, R.	*Scotland*	**16**	D3
Taylor, Mt.	*New Mexico*	**64**	E3
Taymyr L. & Pen.	*U.S.S.R.*	**47**	L1
Tayport	*Scotland*	**29**	F4
Tbilisi	*Georgia, U.S.S.R.*	**46**	E4
Team Valley	*England*	**17**	E4
Te Anau, L.	*New Zealand*	**79**	A6
Teapa	*Mexico*	**70**	F4
Tea Tree	*N. Terr., Aust.*	**77**	E3
Tebay	*England*	**25**	C2
Tees, R.	*England*	**17**	D4
Teesdale	*England*	**25**	C2
Tegucigalpa	*Honduras*	**70**	G5
Tehchow	*China*	**51**	K4
Tehran	*Iran*	**52**	F3
Tehuacan	*Mexico*	**70**	E4
Tehuantepec & G. & Isth. of	*Mexico*	**70**	E4
Teifi, R.	*Wales*	**26**	C2
Teign, R.	*England*	**26**	D4
Teignmouth	*England*	**17**	D6
Teith, R.	*Scotland*	**29**	D4
Teixeira de Sousa	*Angola*	**59**	C2
Tekirdag	*Turkey*	**39**	H4
Tel Aviv	*Israel*	**54**	C3
Tell, reg.	*Algeria*	**40**	D4
Tell Atlas, mts.	*Algeria*	**57**	C1
Tell el Amarna	*Egypt*	**54**	A6
Telukbetung	*Sumatra*	**48**	C7
Tema	*Ghana*	**57**	B4
Teme, R.	*England*	**26**	E2
Temirlik	*Sinkiang*	**50**	E4
Temple	*Texas*	**64**	G4
Templemore	*Eire*	**31**	D5
Temuco	*Chile*	**73**	C11
Tenasserim Yoma, mts.	*Burma*	**53**	P7
Tenbury	*England*	**26**	E2
Tenby	*Wales*	**26**	C3
Tenerife, I.	*Canary Is.*	**57**	A2
Tennant Creek	*N. Terr., Aust.*	**77**	E2
Tennessee, state	*U.S.A.*	**65**	J3
Tennessee R.	*U.S.A*	**65**	J4
Tenterden	*England*	**27**	H3
Tenterfield	*New South Wales*	**77**	J4
Ten Thousand Is.	*Florida*	**65**	K5
Tepic	*Mexico*	**70**	D3
Teresina	*Brazil*	**72**	J5
Terezinha	*Brazil*	**72**	G3
Termez	*Uzbek.*	**46**	G5
Termoli	*Italy*	**38**	C3
Termonde	*Belgium*	**32**	C3
Ternate	*Indonesia*	**48**	E6
Terni	*Italy*	**38**	C3
Terpeniya B. & C.	*U.S.S.R.*	**47**	P4
Terre Haute	*Indiana*	**65**	J3
Terror, Mt.	*Antarctica*	**80**	M7
Terschelling, I.	*Netherlands*	**32**	D1
Teruel	*Spain*	**36**	D2
Teslin & L.	*Yukon*	**62**	H5
Test, R.	*England*	**27**	F3
Tetbury	*England*	**27**	E3
Tete	*Mozambique*	**59**	D2
Tetuan	*Morocco*	**57**	B1
Teutoburger Wald	*Germany, W.*	**34**	B2
Teviot R.	*Scotland*	**29**	F5
Teviotdale, valley	*Scotland*	**29**	F5
Tewkesbury	*England*	**27**	E3
Texarkana	*Texas*	**65**	H4
Texas, state	*U.S.A.*	**64**	F4
Texas City	*Texas*	**68**	E5
Texel, I.	*Netherlands*	**32**	C1
Thailand (Siam)	*S. Asia*	**48**	C5
Thame	*England*	**27**	G3
Thames, R.	*England*	**17**	F6
Thames R.	*New Zealand*	**79**	E2
Thameshaven	*England*	**27**	H3
Thar Des.	*India*	**53**	K5
Thasos, I.	*Greece*	**39**	G4
Thaxted	*England*	**27**	H3
Thebes	*Egypt*	**52**	B5
Theodore	*Queensland*	**77**	J4
Thermai, G. of	*Greece*	**39**	F4
Thermopolis	*Wyoming*	**67**	E3
Thermopylae	*Greece*	**39**	F5
Thessaly	*Greece*	**39**	F5
Thetford	*England*	**17**	F5
Thief River Falls	*Minnesota*	**68**	D1
Thimphu	*Bhutan*	**53**	N5
Thingvellir	*Iceland*	**42**	J6
Thionville	*France*	**33**	E2
Thirsk	*England*	**25**	D2
Thisted	*Denmark*	**42**	B4
Tholen I.	*Netherlands*	**32**	C3
Thomastown	*Eire*	**31**	D5
Thomasville	*Georgia*	**65**	K4
Thom Bay	*N.-W. Terr., Can.*	**63**	Q3
Thompson	*Manitoba*	**63**	P6
Thonon	*France*	**33**	E3
Thornbury	*England*	**26**	E3
Thorne	*England*	**25**	E3
Thornhill	*Scotland*	**29**	E5
Thorshavn	*Færoes*	**42**	N9
Thouars	*France*	**33**	B3
Thourout	*Belgium*	**32**	B3
Thrace	*Greece*	**39**	G4
Thrapston	*England*	**27**	G2
Threshfield	*England*	**25**	C2
Thuin	*Belgium*	**32**	C4
Thule	*Greenland*	**63**	V2
Thun & L. of	*Switzerland*	**37**	B1
Thüringer Wald, mts.	*Germany*	**34**	C3
Thurles	*Eire*	**17**	B5
Thurso	*Scotland*	**16**	D2
Thurston Pen.	*Antarctica*	**80**	R8
Tiber, R.	*Italy*	**38**	C3
Tiberias & L. of	*Israel*	**54**	C3
Tibesti, mts.	*Chad*	**57**	D2
Tibet	*China*	**53**	M4
Tickhill	*England*	**25**	D3
Tidworth	*England*	**27**	F3
Tielt	*Belgium*	**32**	B3
Tien Shan, mts.	*Sinkiang, etc.*	**50**	B3
Tientsin	*China*	**48**	D3
Tierra del Fuego, I.	*Arg.-Chile*	**73**	D14
Tighnabruaich	*Scotland*	**29**	C5
Tigris R.	*Iraq-Turkey*	**52**	E4
Tijoca	*Brazil*	**72**	H4
Tijuana	*Mexico*	**70**	A1
Tilburg	*Netherlands*	**32**	D3
Tilbury	*England*	**27**	H3
Till, R.	*England*	**25**	C1
Timaru	*New Zealand*	**79**	C6
Timbuktu	*Mali*	**57**	B3
Timiskaming, L.	*Ont.-Que.*	**63**	T8
Timisoara	*Rumania*	**39**	F2
Timmins	*Ontario*	**63**	S8
Timor, I.	*Indonesia*	**48**	E7
Timor Sea	*Aust.-Indon.*	**76**	C1
Tinahely	*Eire*	**31**	E5
Tinogasta	*Argentina*	**73**	D9
Tinos, I.	*Greece*	**39**	G6
Tintagel Hd.	*England*	**17**	C6
Tintern	*Wales*	**26**	E3
Tinto, hill	*Scotland*	**16**	D4
Tipperary	*Eire*	**17**	A5
Tipton	*England*	**17**	D5
Tirana	*Albania*	**39**	E4
Tiraspol	*Moldavia*	**43**	C3
Tiree, I.	*Scotland*	**16**	B3
Tirgu Mureș	*Rumania*	**35**	H5
Tirlemont	*Belgium*	**32**	C4
Tiruchchirappalli	*India*	**53**	L8
Tisza, R.	*Hungary*	**35**	F5
Titicaca, L.	*Bolivia-Peru*	**72**	D7
Titograd	*Yugoslavia*	**39**	E3
Titusville	*Pennsylvania*	**66**	B3
Tiverton	*England*	**17**	D6
Tivoli	*Italy*	**38**	C3
Tlacotalpan	*Mexico*	**70**	E4
Tlemcen	*Algeria*	**57**	B1
Tobago, I.	*Trinidad & Tobago*	**71**	M5
Tobermory	*Scotland*	**16**	B3
Tobol, R.	*U.S.S.R.*	**46**	G3
Tobolsk	*U.S.S.R.*	**46**	G3
Tobruk	*Libya*	**58**	B1
Tocantins, R.	*Brazil*	**72**	H4
Tocopilla	*Chile*	**73**	C8
Todmorden	*England*	**25**	C3
Togo	*W. Africa*	**57**	C4
Toijala	*Finland*	**42**	E3
Tokanui	*New Zealand*	**79**	B7
Tokelau Is.	*Pacific Oc.*	**10**	E5
Tokyo	*Japan*	**48**	G3
Tolaga Bay	*New Zealand*	**79**	G3
Tolbukhin	*Bulgaria*	**39**	H3
Toledo	*Ohio*	**65**	K2
Toledo	*Spain*	**36**	C3
Tomaszów Mazowiecka	*Poland*	**35**	F3
Tomatin	*Scotland*	**28**	D3
Tomintoul	*Scotland*	**28**	E3
Tomsk	*U.S.S.R.*	**47**	J3
Tonala	*Mexico*	**70**	F4
Tonbridge	*England*	**27**	H3
Tønder	*Denmark*	**42**	B5
Tone, R.	*England*	**26**	D4
Tonga Is.	*Pacific Oc.*	**10**	E5
Tongareva I.	*Pacific Oc.*	**10**	E5
Tongking, G. of	*Vietnam, etc.*	**48**	C4
Tongres	*Belgium*	**32**	D4
Tongue	*Scotland*	**16**	C2
Tonlé Sap, L.	*Cambodia*	**53**	Q8
Tonopah	*Nevada*	**64**	C3
Tonsberg	*Norway*	**42**	B4
Toowoomba	*Queensland*	**77**	J4
Topeka	*Kansas*	**64**	G3
Topsham	*England*	**26**	D4
Tor B.	*England*	**26**	D4
Torne, R.	*Sweden*	**42**	E2
Tornio	*Finland*	**42**	F2
Toronto	*Ontario*	**63**	T9
Tororo	*Uganda*	**58**	C4
Torphins	*Scotland*	**28**	F3
Torquay	*England*	**17**	D6
Torrelavega	*Spain*	**36**	C1
Torrens, L.	*S. Australia*	**77**	F5
Torréon	*Mexico*	**70**	D2
Torres Str.	*Aust.-New Guinea*	**10**	C5
Torridon, L.	*Scotland*	**28**	C3
Tortosa	*Spain*	**36**	E2
Tortuga I.	*West Indies*	**71**	L5
Toruń	*Poland*	**35**	F2
Totnes	*England*	**26**	D4
Tottori	*Japan*	**51**	N4
Touggourt	*Algeria*	**57**	C1
Toul	*France*	**33**	D2
Toulon	*France*	**33**	D5
Toulouse	*France*	**33**	C5
Touquet, le	*France*	**33**	C1
Tourane	*Vietnam*	**48**	C5
Tourcoing	*France*	**33**	D1
Tournai	*Belgium*	**32**	B4
Tours	*France*	**33**	C3
Towcester	*England*	**17**	E5
Townsend, Mt.	*N.S.W.*	**78**	G8
Townsville	*Queensland*	**77**	H2
Towy, R.	*Wales*	**26**	C3
Towyn	*Wales*	**17**	C5
Toyohashi	*Japan*	**51**	O5
Tozeur	*Tunisia*	**57**	C1
Trabzon	*Turkey*	**52**	C2
Trafalgar, C.	*Spain*	**36**	B4
Tralee	*Eire*	**17**	A5
Tramore	*Eire*	**17**	B5
Transvaal, prov.	*S. Africa*	**59**	C3
Transylvania	*Rumania*	**35**	G5
Transylvanian Alps	*Rumania*	**41**	J2
Trapani	*Sicily*	**38**	C5
Trasimeno, L.	*Italy*	**38**	C3
Tredegar	*Wales*	**26**	D3
Trefnant	*Wales*	**26**	D1
Tregaron	*Wales*	**26**	D2
Tregoney	*England*	**26**	C4
Trelleborg	*Sweden*	**42**	C5
Trent, R.	*England*	**17**	E5
Trentino Alto-Adige	*Italy*	**38**	B1
Trent Junction	*England*	**27**	F2
Trento	*Italy*	**38**	B1
Trenton	*Missouri*	**65**	H2
Trenton	*New Jersey*	**65**	M2
Tréport, le	*France*	**33**	C1
Tresco	*Scilly Is.*	**26**	A5
Treshnish Is.	*Scotland*	**29**	B4
Treviso	*Italy*	**38**	C2
Trichinopoly	*India*	**53**	M8
Trier	*Germany, W.*	**34**	B4
Trieste	*Italy*	**38**	C2
Trikkala	*Greece*	**39**	F5
Trim	*Eire*	**17**	B5
Trincomalee	*Ceylon*	**53**	M9
Trinidad	*Colorado*	**64**	F3
Trinidad, I.	*S. Atlantic Oc.*	**11**	K6
Trinidad, I.	*West Indies*	**71**	M5
Trinidad & Tobago	*West Indies*	**71**	M5
Trinity & B.	*Newfoundland*	**63**	Y8
Trinity R.	*Texas*	**64**	G4
Tripoli	*Lebanon*	**54**	C2
Tripoli	*Libya*	**57**	D1
Tripolis	*Greece*	**39**	F6
Tripura, terr.	*India*	**53**	O6
Tristan da Cunha, I.	*S. Atl. Oc.*	**11**	K6
Trivandrum	*India*	**53**	L9
Trnava	*Czechoslovakia*	**35**	E4
Trois Rivières	*Quebec*	**63**	U8
Trollhattan	*Sweden*	**42**	C4
Tromso	*Norway*	**42**	D1
Trondheim & Fd.	*Norway*	**42**	B3
Trool, L.	*Scotland*	**29**	D5
Troon	*Scotland*	**29**	D5
Trossachs	*Scotland*	**29**	D4
Trout Lake	*Ontario*	**63**	R7
Trouville	*France*	**33**	C2
Trowbridge	*England*	**27**	E3
Troy	*New York*	**65**	M2
Troy	*Turkey*	**39**	G5
Troyes	*France*	**33**	D2
Trucial States	*Arabia*	**52**	F6
Trujillo, mt.	*Dominican Rep.*	**71**	K4
Truk I.	*Pacific Oc.*	**10**	C4
Truro	*England*	**17**	C6
Truro	*Nova Scotia*	**63**	W8
Truro	*S. Australia*	**78**	B7
Truth or Consequences	*New Mexico*	**67**	E5
Tsaidam Swamp	*China*	**53**	O3
Tsangpo, R.	*Tibet, etc.*	**50**	D6
Tsela Dzong	*Tibet*	**50**	E6
Tselinagrad	*Kazakh.*	**46**	H3
Tshela	*Congo*	**59**	B1
Tsimlyansk Res.	*U.S.S.R.*	**46**	E4
Tsinan	*China*	**48**	D3
Tsingtao	*China*	**48**	E3
Tsining	*In. Mongolia*	**51**	J3
Tsitsihar	*China*	**48**	E2
Tsugaru Str.	*Japan*	**48**	F2
Tsumeb	*S.W. Africa*	**59**	B2
Tsunyi	*China*	**50**	H6
Tsushima Str.	*Korea-Japan*	**48**	E3
Tsuyung	*China*	**50**	G6
Tuam	*Eire*	**17**	A5
Tuamotu Arch.	*Pacific Oc.*	**10**	F5
Tuapse	*U.S.S.R.*	**46**	D4
Tubbercurry	*Eire*	**30**	C3
Tubuai Is.	*Pacific Oc.*	**10**	F6
Tucson	*Arizona*	**64**	D4
Tuktoyaktuk	*N.-W. Terr., Can.*	**62**	H4
Tula	*U.S.S.R.*	**46**	D3
Tulare	*California*	**67**	C4
Tulcea	*Rumania*	**39**	H2
Tulla	*Eire*	**31**	C5
Tullamore	*Eire*	**17**	B5
Tullow	*Eire*	**31**	E5
Tulsa	*Oklahoma*	**64**	G3
Tulun	*U.S.S.R.*	**47**	L3
Tumaco	*Colombia*	**72**	B3
Tummel, R.	*Scotland*	**29**	D4
Tunbridge Wells	*England*	**17**	F6
Tunghao	*China*	**51**	L3
Tunghwa	*China*	**51**	M3
Tung Ting L.	*China*	**48**	D4
Tunguska R. & Lr.	*U.S.S.R.*	**47**	K2
Tunis	*Tunisia*	**57**	D1
Tunisia	*N.W. Africa*	**57**	C1
Tunja	*Colombia*	**72**	C2
Tunstall	*England*	**27**	E1
Tupelo	*Mississippi*	**69**	F4
Tupiza	*Peru*	**73**	D8
Turbo	*Colombia*	**72**	B2
Turfan & Depression	*Sinkiang*	**50**	D3
Turgutlu	*Turkey*	**39**	H5
Turin	*Italy*	**38**	A2
Turkestan	*Kazakh.*	**46**	G4
Turkey	*W. Asia*	**52**	A3
Turkmenistan (Turkmen S.S.R.)	*U.S.S.R.*	**46**	F5
Turks Is.	*W. Indies*	**71**	K3
Turku	*Finland*	**42**	E3
Turnberry	*Scotland*	**29**	D5
Turnditch	*England*	**27**	F1
Turner Valley	*Alberta*	**62**	M7

Turnhout *Belgium* **32** C3
Turnovo *Bulgaria* **39** G3
Turnu Severin *Rumania* **39** F2
Turriff *Scotland* **28** F3
Tuscaloosa *Alabama* **65** J4
Tuscany *Italy* **38** B3
Tutbury *England* **27** F2
Tutuila I. *Pacific Oc.* **10** E5
Tutuko, Mt. *New Zealand* **79** B6
Tuxford *England* **27** G1
Tuy *Spain* **36** B1
Tūysarkān *Iran* **55** K2
Tuz, L. *Turkey* **52** B3
Tweed, R. *Scotland* **16** D4
Tweedmouth *England* **25** D1
Tweedsmuir Hills *Scotland* **29** E5
Twin Falls *Idaho* **67** D3
Tyler *Texas* **64** G4
Tyndrum *Scotland* **29** D4
Tyne Gap *England* **25** C2
Tyne, R. *England* **17** D4
Tynemouth *England* **17** E4
Tyre *Lebanon* **54** C3
Tyrone, co. *N. Ireland* **17** B4
Tyrrhenian Sea *Mediterranean* **38** B4
Tyumen *U.S.S.R.* **46** G3
Tzeyang *China* **51** K4

Uberaba *Brazil* **72** H7
Uckfield *England* **27** H4
Udaipur *India* **53** K6
Udine *Italy* **38** C1
Udmurt A.S.S.R. *U.S.S.R.* **43** H1
Ufa *U.S.S.R.* **46** F3
Uffculme *England* **26** D4
Uganda *E. Africa* **58** C4
Uig *Scotland* **28** B3
Uinta Mts. *Utah* **67** D3
Uitenhage *Cape of Good Hope* **59** C4
Ujjain *India* **53** L6
Ujpest *Hungary* **35** F5
Ukraine *U.S.S.R.* **46** C4
Ulan Bator *Mongolia* **48** C2
Ulanhot *China* **51** L2
Ulan Ude *U.S.S.R.* **47** L3
Ulceby *England* **25** E3
Ullapool *Scotland* **16** C3
Ullswater *England* **25** C2
Ulm *Germany, W.* **34** C4
Ulster *Eire-N. Ire.* **30** D3
Ulverston *England* **17** D4
Uman *Ukraine* **43** D3
Umbria *Italy* **38** C3
Umea *Sweden* **42** E3
Umtali *Rhodesia* **59** D2
Umtata *Cape of Good Hope* **59** C4
Umvuma *Rhodesia* **59** D2
Ungava B. *Quebec* **63** V6
Union of Soviet Socialist Republics (U.S.S.R.) *Europe-Asia* **46-47**
Uniontown *Pennsylvania* **66** B4
United Arab Rep. (Egypt) *N.E. Africa* **58** B2
United Kingdom of Gt. Britain & N. Ireland (U.K.), *see* Gt. Britain
United States of America (U.S.A.) *N. America* **64-65**
Unst, I. *Scotland* **16** E1
Un Uaimh *Eire* **30** E4
Upernavik *Greenland* **63** X3
Upington *Cape of Good Hope* **59** C3
Upminster *England* **27** H3
Upper Hutt *New Zealand* **79** E4
Upper Volta *W. Africa* **57** B3
Uppingham *England* **27** G2
Uppsala *Sweden* **42** D4
Upton *England* **27** E2
Ur *Iraq* **55** J4
Ural Mts. & R. *U.S.S.R.* **46** F3
Uralsk *Kazakh.* **46** F3
Urandangi *Queensland* **77** F3
Uranium City *Saskatchewan* **62** N6
Urbino *Italy* **38** C3
Ure, R. *England* **17** E4
Ures *Mexico* **70** B2
Urfa *Turkey* **52** C3
Urmia, L. *Iran* **52** E3
Uruapan del Progreso *Mexico* **70** D4
Uruguaiana *Brazil* **73** F9
Uruguay *S. America* **73** F10
Uruguay, R. *S. America* **73** F9
Urumchi *Sinkiang* **50** D3
Ushant I. *France* **33** A2
Ushuaia *Argentina* **73** D14
Usk *Wales* **26** E3
Usk, R. *Wales* **17** D6
Üsküdar *Turkey* **52** A2
Uspallata Pass *Arg.-Chile* **73** C10
Ussel *France* **33** C4
Ussuriysk *U.S.S.R.* **47** O4
Ust Kut *U.S.S.R.* **47** L3
Ust Urt Plat. *U.S.S.R.* **46** F4
Ust Usa *U.S.S.R.* **46** F2
Usumbura *Burundi* **58** B5
Utah, state *U.S.A.* **64** D3
Utah L. *Utah* **64** D2
Utica *New York* **65** L2
Utrecht *Netherlands* **32** D2
Utrera *Spain* **36** C4
Utsunomiya *Japan* **51** O4
Uttar Pradesh, state *India* **53** M5
Uttoxeter *England* **27** F2
Uusikaupunki *Finland* **42** E3
Uxbridge *England* **27** G3
Uzbekistan (Uzbek S.S.R.) *U.S.S.R.* **46** G4

Vaal, R. *Transvaal, etc.* **59** C3
Vaasa *Finland* **42** E3
Vadso *Norway* **42** G1
Valdai Hills *U.S.S.R.* **43** D1
Valdés Pen. *Argentina* **73** E12
Valdivia *Chile* **73** C11
Valdosta *Georgia* **69** G4
Valence *France* **33** D4
Valencia *Spain* **36** D3
Valencia *Venezuela* **72** D1
Valencia, G. of *Spain* **36** E3
Valenciennes *France* **33** D1
Valentia I. *Eire* **17** A6
Valentine *Nebraska* **64** F2
Valga *Estonia* **42** F4
Valladolid *Spain* **36** C2
Valle d'Aosta *Italy* **38** A2
Vallejo *California* **64** B3
Valletta *Malta* **41** G5
Valleyfield *Quebec* **63** U8
Valls *Spain* **36** E2
Valparaiso *Chile* **73** C10
Van, L. *Turkey* **52** D3
Vancouver *Br. Columbia* **62** K8
Vancouver *Washington* **67** B2
Vancouver I. *Br. Columbia* **62** J8
Van Diemen G. *N. Terr., Aust.* **76** E1
Vanern, L. *Sweden* **42** C4
Vannas *Sweden* **42** D3
Vannes *France* **33** B3
Varanasi *India* **53** M5
Varanger Fd. & Pen. *Norway* **42** G1
Varazdin *Yugoslavia* **38** D1
Varberg *Sweden* **42** C4
Vardar, R. *Greece-Yugoslavia* **39** F4
Varese *Italy* **38** A2
Varna *Bulgaria* **39** H3
Vasteras *Sweden* **42** D4
Vastervik *Sweden* **42** D4
Vatican, City of the *Italy* **38** C4
Vatna Jökull, mt. *Iceland* **42** K6
Vattern, L. *Sweden* **42** C4
Veliki Kikinda *Yugoslavia* **39** E2
Velikiye Luki *U.S.S.R.* **43** D1
Velletri *Italy* **38** C4
Venado Tuerto *Argentina* **73** E10
Vendôme *France* **33** C3
Veneto *Italy* **38** B2
Venezuela *S. America* **72** D2
Venezuela, G. of *Venezuela* **72** C1
Venice & G. of *Italy* **38** C2
Vennacher, L. *Scotland* **29** D4
Ventnor *England* **17** E6
Ventspils *Latvia* **42** E4
Veracruz *Mexico* **70** E4
Verde, C. *Senegal* **57** A3
Verdon, le *France* **33** B4
Verdun *France* **33** D2
Vereeniging *Transvaal* **59** C3
Verkhoyansk & Mts. *U.S.S.R.* **47** O2
Vermont, state *U.S.A.* **65** M2
Véroia *Greece* **39** F4
Verona *Italy* **38** B2
Versailles *France* **33** C2
Verviers *Belgium* **32** D4
Vesoul *France* **33** E3
Vest Fd. *Norway* **42** C2
Vesterålen, Is. *Norway* **42** C1
Vestmannæyjar *Iceland* **42** J7
Vesuvius, volcano *Italy* **38** C4
Vetluga & R. *U.S.S.R.* **43** G1
Vézère, R. *France* **33** C4
Viborg *Denmark* **42** B4
Vicenza *Italy* **38** B2
Vichy *France* **33** D3
Vicksburg *Mississippi* **65** H4
Victor Harbour *S. Australia* **77** F6
Victoria, state *Australia* **77** G6
Victoria *Br. Columbia* **62** K8
Victoria *Hong Kong* **48** D4
Victoria Falls *Zambia-Rhodesia* **59** C2
Victoria I. *N.-W. Terr., Can.* **62** M3
Victoria, L. *E. Africa* **58** C5
Victoria Land *Antarctica* **80** L7
Victoria R. *N. Terr., Aust.* **76** E2
Victoria de Durango *Mexico* **70** D3
Victoria River Downs *N. Terr., Aust.* **76** E2
Victoria West *C. of Good Hope* **59** C4
Vidin *Bulgaria* **39** F2
Viedma *Argentina* **73** E12
Vienna *Austria* **34** E4
Vienne *France* **33** D4
Vienne, R. *France* **33** C4
Vientiane *Laos* **53** Q7
Vietnam *S.E. Asia* **48** C5
Vila da Ponte *Angola* **59** B2
Vila Luso *Angola* **59** B2
Vila Manica *Mozambique* **59** D2
Vila Salazar *Angola* **59** B1
Vila Velha *Brazil* **73** J8
Villach *Austria* **34** D5
Villa Cisneros *Sp. Sahara* **57** A2
Villa Maria *Argentina* **73** E10
Villa Montes *Peru* **73** E8
Villarrica *Paraguay* **73** F9
Villa San Giovanni *Italy* **38** D5
Vilnius *Lithuania* **46** C3
Vilyuy R. *U.S.S.R.* **47** L2
Viña del Mar *Chile* **73** C10
Vincennes *Indiana* **65** J3
Vindhya Ra. *India* **53** L6
Vinh *Vietnam* **48** C5
Vinita *Oklahoma* **64** G3
Vinnitsa *Ukraine* **46** C4
Virgin Is. *West Indies* **71** L4
Virginia *Eire* **30** D4
Virginia, state *U.S.A.* **65** L3
Virginia City *Nevada* **64** C3
Virton *Belgium* **32** D5
Visby *Sweden* **42** D4
Viscount Melville Sd. *N.-W. Terr., Can.* **62** N3
Vishakhapatnam *India* **53** M7
Vistula, R. *Poland* **35** F3
Vitebsk *White Russia* **46** C3
Viterbo *Italy* **38** C3
Vitim & Plat. & R. *U.S.S.R.* **47** M3
Vitoria *Brazil* **72** K8
Vitoria *Spain* **36** D1
Vizianagram *India* **50** C8
Vlaardingen *Netherlands* **32** C3
Vladimir *U.S.S.R.* **43** F1
Vladivostok *U.S.S.R.* **47** O4
Vlieland, I. *Netherlands* **32** C1
Vltava, R. *Czechoslovakia* **34** D4
Voe *Scotland* **28** A1
Voi *Kenya* **58** C5
Volga, R. *U.S.S.R.* **46** E3
Volgograd *U.S.S.R.* **46** E4
Volkhov & R. *U.S.S.R.* **43** D1
Volkrust *Transvaal* **59** C3
Vologda *U.S.S.R.* **46** D3
Volos *Greece* **39** F5
Volsk *U.S.S.R.* **43** G2
Volta, R. *Ghana* **57** B4
Volta Redonda *Brazil* **73** J8
Volterra *Italy* **38** B3
Voorne, I. *Netherlands* **32** B3
Voronezh & R. *U.S.S.R.* **43** E2
Vosges, mts. *France* **33** E2
Vratsa *Bulgaria* **39** F3
Vršac *Yugoslavia* **39** F2
Vryburg *Cape of Good Hope* **59** C3
Vryheid *Natal* **59** D3
Vyazma *U.S.S.R.* **43** D1
Vyrnwy, L. *Wales* **26** D2

Waal, R. *Netherlands* **32** D3
Wabash R. *Indiana, etc.* **65** J3
Waco *Texas* **64** G4
Waddenzee *Netherlands* **32** D1
Waddesdon *England* **27** G3
Waddington, Mt. *Br. Columbia* **62** J7
Wadebridge *England* **26** C4
Wadi Halfa *Sudan* **58** C2
Wagga Wagga *N.S.W.* **77** H6
Waiau & R. *New Zealand* **79** D5
Waidhofen *Austria* **34** D5
Waikaia *New Zealand* **79** B6
Waikato R. *New Zealand* **79** E2
Waimate *New Zealand* **79** C6
Wainfleet *England* **27** H1
Waipara *New Zealand* **79** D5
Wairoa *New Zealand* **79** F3
Waitara *New Zealand* **79** E3
Waiuku *New Zealand* **79** E2
Wakayama *Japan* **51** O5
Wake I. *Pacific Oc.* **10** D4
Wakefield *England* **25** D3
Wakkanai *Japan* **48** G2
Walachia *Rumania* **39** G2
Wałbrzych *Poland* **34** E3
Walcheren, I. *Netherlands* **32** B3
Wales *British Isles* **17** C6
Wall *England* **25** C1
Walsall *England* **17** E5
Walsh *Queensland* **77** G2
Walsingham, C. *N.-W. Terr., Can.* **63** W4
Waltham *England* **27** H3
Walton-on-the-Naze *England* **27** J3
Walvis Bay *S.W. Africa* **59** B3
Wallace *Idaho* **64** C1
"Wallace Line" *S.E. Asia* **48** E6
Wallal *W. Australia* **76** C2
Wallaroo *S. Australia* **77** F5
Wallingford *England* **27** F3
Walls *Scotland* **28** A1
Walmer *England* **27** J3
Walney, I. *England* **25** B2
Wanaka & L. *New Zealand* **79** B6
Wanganui & R. *New Zealand* **79** E3
Wangaratta *Victoria* **77** H6
Wankie *Rhodesia* **59** C2
Wansford *England* **27** G2
Wantage *England* **27** F3
Ware *England* **27** G3
Wareham *England* **27** E4
Wark *England* **25** C1
Warminster *England* **27** E3
Warnemünde *Germany, E.* **34** D1
Warragul *Victoria* **77** H6
Warren *Idaho* **64** C2
Warren *Ohio* **66** A3
Warrenpoint *N. Ireland* **30** E3
Warrington *England* **17** D5
Warrnambool *Victoria* **77** G6
Warsaw *Poland* **35** F2
Warta, R. *Poland* **34** E2
Warwick *England* **17** E5
Wasatch Mts. *Utah* **64** D2
Wash, The *England* **17** F5
Washington *D.C.* **65** L3
Washington, state *U.S.A.* **64** B1
Washington I. *Pacific Oc.* **10** E4
Watchet *England* **26** D3
Waterbury *Connecticut* **66** E3
Waterford *Eire* **17** B5
Waterford & Harb. *Eire* **17** B5
Waterloo *Iowa* **65** H2
Watertown *New York* **65** L2
Watertown *S. Dakota* **64** G1
Waterville *Maine* **65** N2
Watford *England* **27** G3
Watling I. *Bahamas* **71** J3
Watlington *England* **27** F3
Watten *Scotland* **28** E2
Watton *England* **27** H2
Wau *Sudan* **58** B4
Waukegan *Illinois* **69** F2
Wausau *Wisconsin* **65** J2
Waveney, R. *England* **17** F5
Wawa *Ontario* **69** G1
Waverly *Pennsylvania* **66** C3
Waycross *Georgia* **65** K4
Wayne *Nebraska* **64** G2
Weald, The *England* **17** E6
Wear, R. *England* **17** D4
Weardale *England* **25** C2
Weaver, R. *England* **26** E1
Weddell Sea *Antarctica* **80** A7
Wednesbury *England* **17** E5
Wei Ho, R. *China* **48** C3
Weimar *Germany, E.* **34** C3
Weipa *Queensland* **77** G1
Weiser *Idaho* **64** C2
Weisshorn, mt. *Switzerland* **37** B1
Welbourn *England* **27** G1
Welkom *Orange Free State* **59** C3
Welland, R. *England* **17** E5
Wellingborough *England* **27** G2
Wellington *New Zealand* **79** E4
Wellington *Shropshire, Eng.* **26** E2
Wellington *Somerset, Eng.* **26** D4
Wells *England* **17** F5
Wels *Austria* **34** D4
Welshpool *Wales* **17** D5
Welwyn Garden City *England* **27** G3